Ethnographically

Speaking

Ethnographic Alternatives Book Series

Series Editor
Carolyn Ellis
Arthur P. Bochner
(both at the University of South Florida)

About the Series:
Ethnographic Alternatives emphasizes experimental forms of qualitative writing that blur the boundaries between social sciences and humanities. The editors encourage submissions that experiment with novel forms of expressing lived experience, including literary, poetic, autobiographical, multivoiced, conversational, critical, visual, performative, and coconstructed representations. Emphasis should be on expressing concrete lived experience through narrative modes of writing.

We are interested in ethnographic alternatives that promote narration of local stories; literary modes of descriptive scene setting, dialogue, and unfolding action; and inclusion of the author's subjective reactions, involvement in the research process, and strategies for practicing reflexive fieldwork.

Please send proposals to:
Carolyn Ellis and Arthur P. Bochner
College of Arts and Sciences
Department of Communication
University of South Florida
4202 East Fowler Avenue, CIS 1040
Tampa, FL 33620-7800
e-mail: cellis@chuma.cas.usf.edu

Books in the Series:
Volume 1, *Composing Ethnography: Alternative Forms of Qualitative Writing,* Carolyn Ellis and Arthur P. Bochner, editors
Volume 2, *Opportunity House: Ethnographic Stories of Mental Retardation,* Michael V. Angrosino
Volume 3, *Kaleidoscope Notes: Writing Women's Music and Organizational Culture,* Stacy Holman Jones
Volume 4, *Fiction and Social Research: By Fire or Ice,* Anna Banks and Stephen P. Banks, editors
Volume 5, *Reading Auschwitz,* Mary Lagerwey
Volume 6, *Life Online: Researching Real Experience in Virtual Space,* Annette N. Markham
Volume 7, *Writing the New Ethnography,* H. L. Goodall Jr.
Volume 8, *Between Gay and Straight: Understanding Friendship Across Sexual Orientation,* Lisa Tillmann-Healy
Volume 9, *Ethnographically Speaking: Autoethnography, Literature, and Aesthetics,* Arthur P. Bochner and Carolyn Ellis, editors
Volume 10, *Karaoke Nights: An Ethnographic Rhapsody,* Rob Drew

Ethnographically Speaking

Autoethnography, Literature, and Aesthetics

EDITED BY

ARTHUR P. BOCHNER

AND

CAROLYN ELLIS

ALTAMIRA
PRESS

A Division of
ROWMAN & LITTLEFIELD PUBLISHERS INC.
Walnut Creek ■ Lanham ■ New York ■ Oxford

AltaMira Press
A Division of Rowman & Littlefield Publishers, Inc.
1630 North Main Street, #367
Walnut Creek, CA 94596
www.altamirapress.com

Rowman & Littlefield Publishers, Inc.
4720 Boston Way
Lanham, MD 20706

12 Hid's Copse Road
Cumnor Hill, Oxford OX2 9JJ, England

Copyright © 2002 by AltaMira Press

British Library Cataloguing in Publication Information Available

Library of Congress Cataloging-in-Publication Data

Bochner, Arthur P.
  Ethnographically speaking : autoethnography, literature, and aesthetics / Arthur P.
  Bochner and Carolyn Ellis.
      p. cm.
  Based on a conference entitled the Couch Stone Symposium, for the year 2000,
  held on St. Petersburg Beach in Florida.
  Includes bibliographical references and index.
  ISBN 0-7591-0128-0 (cloth : alk. paper)—ISBN 0-7591-0129-9 (pbk. : alk. paper)
  1. Ethnology—Authorship—Congresses. 2. Social sciences—Authorship—
  Congresses. 3. Symbolic interactionism—Congresses. 4. Literature and
  anthropology—Congresses. I. Ellis, Carolyn, 1950– II. Title.

  GN307.7 .B63 2002
  025.04—dc21

                                                            2001034314

Printed in the United States of America

♾️™ The paper used in this publication meets the minimum requirements of American National Standard for Information Sciences—Permanence of Paper for Printed Library Materials, ANSI/NISO Z39.48–1992.

For our mothers,
Minnie Bochner
and
Katherine Ellis

Contents

BEFORE

How Does a Conference Begin?
  Arthur P. Bochner and Carolyn Ellis   1

OPENING

Ethnographic Representation As Relationship
  Mary M. Gergen and Kenneth J. Gergen   11

**CULTURE EMBODIED: PERFORMING
AUTOETHNOGRAPHY**

For Father and Son: An Ethnodrama with No Catharsis
  Ronald J. Pelias   35
The Way We Were, Are, and Might Be: Torch Singing
  As Autoethnography
  Stacy Holman Jones   44
Making a Mess and Spreading It Around: Articulation
  of an Approach to Research-Based Theater
  Ross E. Gray, Vrenia Ivonoffski, and Christina Sinding   57

INTERLUDE Breaking Habits and Cultivating Home
  Lesa Lockford   76

WOUNDED STORYTELLERS: VULNERABILITY, IDENTITY, AND NARRATIVE

Stories that Conform/Stories that Transform:
A Conversation in Four Parts
Douglas Flemons and Shelley Green   87

    Part 1 Autoethnographies: Constraints, Openings,
    Ontologies, and Endings   87

My Father's Shoes: The Therapeutic Value of
Narrative Reframing
Christine E. Kiesinger   95

    Part 2 Autoethnography, Therapy, and the
    Telling of Lives   115

Erotic Mentoring: Pygmalion and Galatea at
the University
Janice Hocker Rushing   122
Breathing Life into Work
Arthur P. Bochner and Janice Hocker Rushing   150

    Part 3 Publish *and* Perish   165

Searching for Autoethnographic Credibility:
Reflections from a Mom with a Notepad
Elaine Bass Jenks   170

    Part 4 Healing and Connecting   187

Border Crossings: A Story of Sexual Identity
Transformation
Beverley Dent   191
Rebirthing "Border Cossings"
Carolyn Ellis and Beverley Dent   201

INTERLUDE Autoethnography: Self-Indulgence or
Something More?
Andrew C. Sparkes   209

ETHNOGRAPHIC AESTHETICS: ARTFUL INQUIRY

PRELUDE "Collage" 233

The Hard Road Home: Toward a Polyphonic Narrative
of the Mother–Daughter Relationship
Kathryn Church 234

Living the Hyphenated Edge: Autoethnography,
Hybridity, and Aesthetics
Caroline Joan ("Kay") S. Picart 258

The Visitor: Juggling Life in the Grip of the Text
Karen Scott-Hoy 274

INTERLUDE "If the Color Changes" (1996–1997)
Mel Bochner 295

BETWEEN LITERATURE AND ETHNOGRAPHY

The Griot's Many Burdens—Fiction's Many Truths
Paul Stoller 297

Beirut Letters
Laurel Richardson and Ernest Lockridge 308

Babaji and Me: Reflections on a Fictional Ethnography
Michael V. Angrosino 327

Men Kissing
Lisa M. Tillmann-Healy 336

INTERLUDE High Noon: A 'Fictional' Dialogue
Carolyn Ellis and Douglas Flemons 344

CLOSING

Between the Ride and the Story: Illness and Remoralization
Arthur W. Frank 357

INTERLUDE The Metaphor Is the Message
Laurel Richardson 372

AFTER

Narrative Heat
   H. L. Goodall Jr.   377
When Does a Conference End?
   Carolyn Ellis and Arthur P. Bochner   388

Name Index   *Judy Perry*   393
Subject Index   *Judy Perry*   399
About the Contributors   405

How Does a Conference Begin?

ARTHUR P. BOCHNER AND CAROLYN ELLIS

August 1998

"I WANT US to showcase ethnographic projects that blur the boundaries between social science and literature," Art says definitively, jotting notes on his yellow pad.

"Yes, the conference should be a stage for imagining and enacting different versions of what ethnography can become in the twenty-first century," Carolyn responds, speaking passionately and gesturing wildly with her hands. Both nod, pleased to agree.

We are meeting in our living room to write the "Call for Papers" for the 2000 Couch-Stone Symposium, the millennium meeting of the Society for the Study of Symbolic Interaction, which will be held on St. Petersburg Beach in Florida. After the publication in 1996 of our edited volume, *Composing Ethnography* (AltaMira Press), which featured autoethnographic, poetic, narrative, and performative works, we began discussing the idea of hosting a conference at the turn of the century. The topic we had in mind for the conference was *ethnographic alternatives,* a term we use to represent ethnographic work that links social science to literature. Now the time has come to make our vision for the conference concrete.

"I want the symposium to be as inclusive and inviting as possible," Carolyn suggests, now sitting high on the raised back of the couch.

"Yes," replies Art. "And we need to make it clear that this symposium will emphasize the work of scholars and graduate students in different fields who are breaking new ground."

"And researchers who are experimenting with hybrid forms of ethnographic representation," Carolyn adds. "I'm thinking of all these people we've never met who wrote to us after they found *Composing Ethnography* and told us how much it meant to them." For emphasis, Carolyn picks up a file from the pile on the floor, opens it, and begins flipping through copies of loosely arranged e-mail messages. One catches her attention.

"What are you reading?" Art asks, observing how engrossed Carolyn has become.

"Listen to this," she says, shaking the paper in front of Art, ignoring the dogs that descend on her from their various beds spread around the room. They want in on all the excitement. Sunya, the Australian Shepherd, drops a ball on the couch and waits patiently; Ande, the Jack Russell, drags in a rope toy and wags her tail; Likker and Traf, the father and daughter Rat Terrier pair, bite and chase each other playfully. Carolyn reads:

Hello Carolyn and Art: I am reading your book, *Composing Ethnography.* I am excited and confused. What excites me is that at last I have found "the thing" I have been doing and talking about doing for a long time. I am a Black, forty-year-old woman with a background in the arts and counseling. I have a master's degree in marriage and family counseling and a B.S. in Africana Studies. In 1990 I created and directed a production entitled "We Shall Not Be Moved," a historical and theatrical production of my bittersweet experiences in this country. I am an artist and a storyteller, and I have been dying to research, write, and perform stories that haunt me. I am in a Ph.D. program and I am interested in internalized oppression, expressive arts, and how owning/telling our stories can release the pain of such oppression. I am interested in researching and telling my own stories. I believe this will help others to own their stories. I am not sure where to start. I want to know more about autoethnography. I am taking an ethnography class, but I do not think my professors are giving sufficient attention to autoethnography. I have many questions. Can I research my life? What are the methods of doing so? I want more information about autoethnography and how I can use it. I am grateful for your book and I look forward to hearing from you. Evette Hornsby-Minor

"What a heartfelt letter," Art comments. "I wish she had said more about what confused her."

"She does say she's confused about where to start, for one thing. My guess is the autoethnographic pieces resonated so deeply with how she wants to think about and do research that she found it perplexing that her professor didn't give more attention to autoethnography. She knows in her heart that it's legitimate, but she may not be getting the sort of validation she needs to carry on the work and projects she finds meaningful."

"That sounds right," Art replies in a depressing tone. He thinks about the despair many students and young scholars often have expressed when they face roadblocks in using unconventional research methodologies or writing practices, such as those promoted in *Composing Ethnography*. After a brief pause, Art looks up and continues in an upbeat tone, "I think you've put your finger on the inspiration for this symposium. We want to knock down the barriers to this kind of work, lessen the confusion, and increase the excitement."

"Yes! Yes! The excitement! And we can do that by building a community of interpretive ethnographers who communicate with each other across disciplinary lines." Carolyn talks passionately and more quickly as she expresses the political goals of the symposium. The dogs take this as their cue to chase each other out the doggy door, with Sunya herding the three little ones, all barking loudly. Carolyn speaks over the noise. "We need to encourage participation from a wide range of people in different disciplines who share an interest in work that crosses the boundaries between social science, literature, and the arts. We give a lot of lip service to the goal of interdisciplinary collaboration, but only rarely do we structure conferences in ways that encourage conversation that bridges different disciplines."

"That's a great point," Art responds, the excitement resonating in his voice too. "We've talked a lot about how performance, visual arts, and embodied narration can give ethnography more evocative power and encourage empathy and engagement on the part of its audiences, but we haven't created opportunities to bring together people in different fields who are doing work that purposefully merges the arts, social sciences, and literature. Do you think we would get a good response to such a call?"

"Yes," Carolyn replies without hesitation, "especially among the creative breed of ethnographers, who are breathing new life into their fieldwork by using photography, performance, poetry, painting, and music. I think we're going to find a lot of artists and writers who are using their talents ethnographically and will jump at the opportunity to explore the connections between creative and empirical work."

"Okay, but this means we'll have to choose our keynote speakers carefully. We need to select individuals who have strong credentials as social scientists, but who also have shown a lot of imagination and creativity."

"Yes, let's see, we could ask . . ."

"Wait," Art interrupts. "Let's talk more about our goals first. I'd want individuals who have made a noteworthy contribution to the goal of bridging social sciences and humanities. Ideally I'd like to have keynoters who have taken some risks, for example, someone who has written a personal narrative or performed an evocative text or encouraged an epistemological openness to different ways of knowing and methods of inquiry." Art pauses as he reads from the expression on Carolyn's face that she is turning over possibilities, then queries, "Do you have someone in mind?"

"I thought you'd never ask," Carolyn chuckles. "I have a perfect person who fits all your criteria." She smiles knowingly, but doesn't continue.

"Who?" Art asks impatiently.

"Arthur Frank. He has a passion for illness narratives, and he's one of the few social scientists who have written evocatively about their own illnesses. His book *At the Will of the Body* is an autoethnographic account of his own experience with cancer and heart disease."

Art's dark brown eyes widen, reflecting the enthusiasm in his voice, as he adds, "And he's also published a theoretical book about illness narratives, *The Wounded Storyteller,* which focuses on the storytelling practices of people whose lives are interrupted by illness and on the moral choices they necessarily face."

"I especially like how he is able to integrate ethics, cultural criticism, and personal narrative," Carolyn says.

"And he's a gifted writer," adds Art. "One of the few I know who seems equally able to write academic discourse and personal narrative. Yes, definitely, let's invite him. He's a terrific choice."

"Who comes to your mind?" Carolyn asks, thinking that it would be best if Art got to choose the other speaker.

"Two people, or maybe I should say, a couple. I'm thinking of Mary and Ken Gergen. Recently they've been writing about how social scientists can bring theory to life through the embodiments offered by performance. By animating theory performatively, research becomes more accessible for social action and cultural transformation."

"Performing theory! That's perfect for what we're trying to do at the symposium. Ken has been a risk taker nearly all of his professional life. Since their work focuses on a relational ideology, I really like the idea of a joint keynote that would include both of their voices. You know, I've been a fan of Ken's work since I was in graduate school. And Mary's added an emotional voice that really embellishes Ken's. I hope they'll come," Carolyn says, somewhat anxiously.

"I'm not too worried about that," Art replies. "Ken has been working to transform social psychology into a more value-centered, politically conscious, and methodologically open discipline for more than twenty years. I think he'll see this as a unique opportunity to link his work to a wider audience. Besides, he and Mary are fun-loving people and I bet they'll be attracted to being on the Florida beach in late January. I know I would."

"Okay," Carolyn says, returning to her task-oriented voice. "I'll call Art Frank and the Gergens this week, but let's get back to the issue of the 'Call for Papers.' What do we want to say in the announcement that we're sending out? My suggestion is that we start by inviting concrete forms of experimental, ethnographic representation such as coconstructed narratives, short stories, personal narratives, autoethnographies . . ."

"We'll want some sessions on cultural studies," Art says, interrupting Carolyn's endeavor to make a longer list of specific topics, but then he can't resist providing specifics for his category. "And these should include media studies, popular culture, and critical theory as they apply to ethnography. We should feature the kind of film criticism that Norman Denzin does."

"And let's not forget methodological innovations," Carolyn adds quickly, picking up her yellow tablet and beginning to write down the list.

"What would you ideally include under methodology?" Art asks, as he fumbles for a pen to write some notes of his own.

"Well, keeping in mind the goal of being inclusive, I'm thinking of feminist ethnography, performance as method, interactive modes of interviewing, art as a mode of inquiry, narrative methods, and performative writing," Carolyn suggests, hesitating momentarily, then continuing. "Oh, I also would want to emphasize work that reconfigures ethnography as an embodied, morally engaged subject."

"That would include the notion of ethnographers as storytellers and writing as a mode of inquiry," Art responds.

"As well as strategies for practicing reflexivity."

"And let's not forget ethical dimensions of ethnographic practices," says Art. "Then there's community and activist ethnography."

"And subjectivity in the research process," Carolyn offers, as she and Art both scribble furiously. "And we certainly want to welcome papers emphasizing cultural multiplicity, identity politics, polyvocal representation, and visual arts."

Art puts down his pen, looks down at his pad, and turns over the list in his mind. "Okay, this is a long list, but there's a good deal of overlap too. Here's a quick synthesis. We've got three broad categories: concrete forms of experimental ethnographic representation, methodological papers, and cultural and critical works. What do you think?"

"That works for me as long as we emphasize that we're defining ethnography broadly," Carolyn observes.

"Do you mean there should still be a place for realist ethnography and grounded theory?"

"Yes, that's exactly what I mean," Carolyn asserts. "After all, the title for the symposium is 'Ethnography for the Twenty-First Century: Alternatives and Opportunities.'"

"What's your point?"

"Traditional work is one alternative, of course," Carolyn says, smiling wryly.

September 1999

"Okay, let's get started," Carolyn says, as she, Donileen Loseke, Spencer Cahill, and Art take positions on the floor around the low, rosewood coffee table in the family room. One of the Rat Terriers sits on Art's lap, while the other three dogs assume their usual positions on the couch behind the table. We are meeting to select presentations from among more than 130 papers and a dozen panel proposals that have been submitted. Two large black file boxes and scattered files, arranged loosely in piles, form boundaries around and between us. Doni and Spencer have read most of the papers that foreground social and critical theory as well as those that by title appear to fall within their particular areas of research interest, such as social construction, identity and socialization, children's communication, race and gender, cultural studies, urban spaces, social action, and policy research. Art and Carolyn have read the papers that focus on personal narrative, performance, autoethnography, literature, spirituality, sexuality, and qualitative methods. We have divided the papers difficult to classify.

"There are a lot of good papers here," Art begins, "but we have only so many rooms at the Dolphin Beach Resort."

"And not nearly enough time for all the good papers to be presented," adds Doni, "unless we want more than two sessions running simultaneously."

"No, I'd rather have fewer presentations, higher attendance at the sessions, and more conversation," Carolyn replies emphatically.

"We also want to have a lot of open space and beach time scheduled in," Art advises. "Otherwise we're going to lose people to the beach."

"We may lose them anyway," Spencer replies. "The Canadians, Brits, and northern 'snowbirds' are going to be hungry for the Florida beach and sunshine." We laugh and nod in agreement.

"Anyway, we've been fortunate to get some generous funding from the Society for the Study of Symbolic Interaction Couch and Stone Foundations," Carolyn says in her organizer voice. "This will help us put on a nice banquet and hire a cool band for the dance. And we'll provide coffee breaks and snacks. Maybe even free drinks. And don't forget the audiovisual. I hate to see how much that will cost."

"Do we have funding from any other sources?" Spencer asks.

"Yes, the Colleges of Arts and Sciences and Education at USF and our Institute for Interpretive Human Studies," Carolyn replies.

"And some departments, such as Communication, have kicked in too," Art observes.

"And Sociology and Interdisciplinary Studies," echo Doni and Spencer, proud of their home departments' contributions.

"Enough of this money talk, " Doni admonishes, picking up the first pile of papers. "Let's get to the task at hand. Here's our file containing the papers on race and sexual identity. There's quite a few good papers on this topic. I guess we can have two sessions, one on sexual identity and one on race."

"I suppose that makes sense, though some of the papers may fit in both categories," Carolyn comments, recalling the paper that she read by Myron Beasley about his identity struggles as a gay, Black man.

We shuffled and reshuffled the papers many times that night. The dogs tried to help by occasionally running through the piles we created and grabbing one of the files as if it were a toy. As the discussion continued late into the night, however, the dogs grew increasingly bored and escaped to their beds. Finally we arrived at the first of many versions of the conference program. The next day, our graduate assistant for the conference, Yasmin Forlenza, typed the first draft of the program and returned it to us. Looking it over, we saw a number of glitches that would need to be corrected, but smiled contentedly, realizing that our fantasy conference was beginning to take the shape of something real and tangible.

January 27, 2000

"Welcome," Art says to the yawning but enthusiastic early-morning crowd gathered in the Cypress Room at the Dolphin Beach Resort. He pauses and waits for the conversational noise to quiet, then continues. "Many of you in this room have been to dozens of conferences and conventions over the course of your academic or professional lives. If you're like me, you probably take it for granted when a conference runs smoothly, but when you think about it, you realize that a lot of people have to pull together to make a gathering like this one work. Carolyn and I are grateful for the assistance we've received from many individuals who have given their hard work and time unselfishly to make this event possible. We'd especially like to thank our colleagues, Donileen Loseke and Spencer Cahill, who teamed with us as a selection committee and worked through every detail with us to get ready for today. Spencer is the person you want to see during the next three days if you have any special needs for media support or your equipment breaks down. All of our graduate students in interpretive ethnography at USF helped us enormously. We called repeatedly on Yasmin Forlenza, our assistant at the Institute for Interpretive Human Studies, and now she is the person sitting behind the registration table waiting to assist you if you have any problems or questions throughout the symposium. If she's not there, one of our other students will be. You'll also meet our students in the book exhibit, where coffee and Danish will be served each morning."

Art looks over at Carolyn, smiles, then continues. "To a certain extent every conference takes on a unique psychological climate characterized by the feeling, spirit, and energy flowing through it. In this conference, there is enormous goodwill, a spirit of collaboration, appreciation, and positive energy. More than anyone else, Carolyn Ellis, to whom I now give over this microphone, is the person responsible for creating this atmosphere."

There is loud applause, then Carolyn takes the mike and says, "Thanks Art. Now, I want to keep everything on time so I'll make this short. I thought you might want to know that we have registered 262 persons representing four countries: the United States, Canada, Great Britain, and Australia. My colleagues and I have tried very hard to make this a multidisciplinary meeting and I think we have succeeded. The last time I looked, we had registered scholars and practitioners representing more than thirty different disciplines. Please indulge me as I read these to you: communication, sociology, art education, American studies, anthropology, social science and interdisciplinary studies, religious studies, women's studies, philosophy, humanities, social work, family therapy, applied ethics, bioethics, nursing, medicine, human and social development, child development, childhood education, adult and continuing education, curriculum studies, performance studies, theater, English, psychology, family and consumer services, management, marketing, special education, aging studies, gerontology, justice studies, journalism and mass communications, and marine science. The qualitative inquiry revolution certainly appears to be knocking down some walls.

"I want to call your attention to the first keynote address, or I should say 'academic performance,' which will be presented by Mary and Ken Gergen tonight at eight o'clock in this room. Dessert and coffee will be served across the hall in the Royal Dolphin Room after the keynote. During the conference we will have two featured ethnographic performances. Ross Gray and his associates from the Toronto-Sunnybrook Regional Cancer Centre will perform 'Handle with Care: An Ethnodrama about Living with Metastatic Breast Cancer.' Their performance will involve participation from several cancer survivors whose stories are told on the stage. The audience's reactions will be filmed for broadcast on Canadian Public Television. Also, you won't want to miss 'Dis/Enchanted by Academe,' a performance written and directed by Patricia Geist with the assistance of Linda Welker and several of Patricia's students. All of you disenchanted and alienated professors and graduate students out there should identify with this story. Finally, I encourage you to attend the two multimedia presentations, one by Larry Frey on 'The Fragile Community— Living Together with AIDS'; the other by Mary Finney on 'New Media/Digital Storytelling.' As you can see in your programs, we have included a broad range of programs, including panels on ethnography and spirituality, ethnographies of race, feminist ethnography, wounded storytelling, gay and lesbian identity work, ethnographic aesthetics, urbanism, institutional ethnography, pressure-cooker projects, the interface of therapy and autoethnography, cultural studies, and media ethnography. We have tried to organize the symposium in a fashion that will encourage dialogue and provide an opportunity for many of us to make new friends as we consider ways to bridge art and science, theories and stories, literature and social science. Plus we have given you time to enjoy the beach."

Carolyn smiles contentedly and concludes, "Now let's get started."

Ethnographic Representation As Relationship

MARY M. GERGEN AND KENNETH J. GERGEN

> Words do not signify things but intimate relations.
> —MARTIN BUBER, *I and Thou*

"**ONE BEGINNING** and one ending for a book is a thing I could not agree with . . ." With these words Flann O'Brien (1966) began his lively little book, *At Swim-Two-Birds*. We hold the same opinion as we undertake the present writing. For our narratologist readers we might tell a story—perhaps a personal account of how our own relationship brought us into the space of these ideas. For autoethnographers, we would lace our account with glimpses into our particular motives, desires, and fears. In contrast, for theoretically oriented readers we might begin with a discussion of Althusser's concept of interpellation, or Bakhtin's ventriloquation. At the same time, we might wish to honor our academic mentors, those guardians of intellectual conscience to whose many works we owe considerable debt.

How are we to relate to you, the reader, as we engage in the act of writing? Or, more provocatively, how does our form of inscription shape the trajectory of our relationships together? Like other forms of research, ethnographic inquiry traditionally functions as a means of representation. Ethnographers attempt to represent the lives, practices, beliefs, values and feelings of some person or group. An enormous literature has sprung to life in recent years concerning the validity, rhetoric and politics of representation.[1] This literature suggests that representation does far more than communicate about a subject; it simultaneously creates forms of relationship. It carries the traces of one community into another, and thus stands to dislocate the traditions of both (Rose 1993), opening the possibilities for new forms of relationship. To echo Marshall McLuhan (1967), "The relationship is the message."

In what follows, we focus on the relational consequences of ethnographic representation. We shall first scan a range of representational forms—both traditional and experimental—and inquire into their relational implications. We shall then open the door to new horizons that emerge when we take seriously the theoretical dimension of human inquiry. As we move beyond ethnography as description, to consider its performative potentials, we open a space for conceptual flowering. Here we shall relate some of our own attempts to perform theory.

Writing and Relationship

The process of ethnographic research places the ethnographer into a matrix of significant relationships. When researchers embark on the process of inquiry, for example, they go beyond an array of previous relationships—those with former coauthors, research participants, editors, and others involved in completed projects. At the same time, entering the lives of those who are "under study" initiates new relationships. These relationships are affected by the ways in which researchers reveal the "results of inquiry." Additionally, researchers strike up relationships with those who are exposed to the "findings." The circle of relatedness is ever widening. At least two of these relationships have received considerable attention in recent years. In the wake of the renaissance in qualitative research, many scholars have become attuned to the relationship between the researcher and the researched. We see ways in which the traditional treatment of research "subjects" was inclined to be alienating, demeaning, and exploitative. We challenge the traditional subject/object dichotomy, and the stance of the researcher as a neutral and dispassionate observer of an alterior world (M. Gergen 1988). And we explore new methods that are more humane, collaborative, and participatory. Closely related, the field has given substantial attention to the responsibility of researchers to their research participants in the subsequent characterizations of their lives. We are now highly sensitized to the "politics of representation," the ways in which we as researchers construct—for good or ill—those whose lives we attempt to illuminate. A new array of collaborative, polyvocal, and self-reflexive methodologies has thus been given birth (see, for example, Denzin and Lincoln 2000).

Yet, there is one relational domain that has received little attention to date, that is, the relationship between rhetor and reader, researcher and audience. As deeply engaged social scientists, the way we represent the world to our colleagues and related audiences contributes to our ongoing relationships within these life worlds (see Shotter 1997). Our words constitute forms of action that invite others into certain forms of relationship as opposed to others. Thus our manner of writing and speaking contributes to life forms that may be extended throughout the educational sphere and into public modes of existence. In this light, consider the kinds of relationship invited by the following examples of academic writing:

> This principle states a necessary condition of anything's serving as a criterion of identity. It clearly does not state a sufficient condition; still less does it state a sufficient condition of anything's being, for a given type of thing T, a philosophically satisfactory criterion of identity for T's. In particular (and this was the basis of the later part of my original argument), no principle P will be a philosophically satisfactory criterion of identity for Ts if the only thing that saves P from admitting many-one relations among Ts is a quite arbitrary provision.[2]

> Semantic analysis of natural language terms requires an understanding of complex cognitive processes such as the profiling of a base and the establishment

of the relationship of a trajector to a landmark. Meaning is not reducible to a conjunctive association of features, or some similar logically based formulation. The way in which the word *gone* builds on the structure of *go*, which is built on the structure of increasing "awayness" across time, illustrates a major characteristic of human semantics.[3]

These samples share important relational similarities. Both distance the writer from the reader. In their formality, their cryptic phrasings, and their certitude, they imply an author who is a bounded, autonomous entity—different from and superior to the reader. The writer is the source, the seer, the knower; the audience is positioned by the writing as passive or ignorant. The rhetor does not consider the audience as equally enlightened. This form of social science writing sustains alienated and hierarchical relationships. The listener remains a spectator, dependent upon the Other's actions.

The qualitative methods movement promotes experimental alternatives to traditional writing (see, for example, Angrosino 1997; Davies 2000; Ellis and Bochner, 1996; Taussig 1993; and many contributions to *Qualitative Inquiry*). Alternative ethnographers break away from the conventions of social science inscription to experiment with polyvocality, poetry, pastiche, performance, and more. These experiments open new territories of expression; they also offer new spaces of relationship. They take different stances toward readers, describing them in new ways, calling into being alternative possibilities for going on together. Both to appreciate these potentials, and to consider the ways in which we remain limited, we urge an open, reflexive discussion of alternatives. We offer the following to stimulate dialogue.

Autoethnography represents a significant expansion in both ethnographic form and relational potential. In using oneself as an ethnographic exemplar, the researcher is freed from the traditional conventions of writing. One's unique voicing—complete with colloquialisms, reverberations from multiple relationships, and emotional expressiveness—is honored. In this way the reader gains a sense of the writer as a full human being. Consider Carol Ronai's (1996) account of what it is like to be parented by a mentally retarded mother:

> I resent the imperative to pretend that all is normal with my family, an imperative that is enforced by silence, secrecy, and "you don't talk about this to anyone" rhetoric. Our pretense is designed to make events flow smoothly,

but it doesn't work. Everyone is plastic and fake around my mother, including me. Why? Because no one has told her to her face that she is retarded. We say we don't want to upset her. I don't think we are ready to deal with her reaction to the truth. . . . Because of [my mother] and because of how the family as a unit has chosen to deal with the problem, I have compartmentalized a whole segment of my life into a lie.[4]

Compare your sense of connection to Ronai with your reaction to the earlier samples of traditional academic writing. If you are like us, you feel far more involved, curious, and engaged in the present case. Ronai reduces the distance between writer and reader. Her first person expression of private matters—not even available to her mother—brings us into a space of intimacy. We feel that we are in-dwelling—roaming about the author's mental interior and sharing the contents with her. The hierarchy implicit in traditional writing is removed. By shunning the goal of stylized perfection, Ronai admits to being one of us—neither superior nor inferior. If anything, Ronai holds out a hand for us to grasp in a show of support. Like traditional writers, she offers illumination, but not to an audience of the ignorant; rather she invites others to hear her story through their own frames. This is not to say that such writing represents the new standard to which all should aspire. Like every form of writing, as certain possibilities open, others are closed. Ronai appears in her story as a bounded subjectivity—in possession of an interior self that simultaneously creates the reader as separate. The implicit message is that "these are *my* experiences," and "I *chose* to share them with you." Further, this interior region is a coherent one; there is little here in the way of fragmentation or inconsistency. The reader is thus invited into a space where coherence counts, a space that can sometimes be threatening or repressive. Nor can we be certain of the intimacy that is implied. After all, this piece is written for everyone, and if we are everyone are we then anyone in particular?

For another writing that maintains connection but challenges consistency, let us turn to an engaging autoethnographic account. Here sociologist Karen Fox (1996) fashions two, first-person narratives derived from interviews with a convicted child sexual abuser (Ben) and his victimized stepdaughter (Sherry). The author, herself a victim of childhood sexual abuse, simultaneously adds her own voice to the mix. In the published account, the individual voices are displayed as three columns of consecutive expression—as in the following:

Ben-Sex Offender

I love her, you know. You see
we really have a good relationship.
She loves me, she told me that.

Karen-Researcher

I want to believe Ben. I guess.
I've always hoped that I meant
something to my abuser.
That he really did love me;
that he really did feel I was
special

Sherry-Victim

I never felt romantic love for
him. That area disgusts me. . . . I've had
feelings of love for him, like for a
father.[5]

Fox's triadic form of writing allows her to include her "personal voice" within the account, but in her inclusion of the additional voices she creates a certain diffusion of her identity. In carefully selecting and refashioning the narratives of Ben and Sherry, she also colors these voices with her own. They appear as separate individual voices, and yet fragments of her own being are included. Subtly the writing begins to reduce the boundary between Karen and others. In a broader sense, each voice contains the traces of other voices in the conversation, just as readers we now ingest the voices of the writer. The unified and coherent personality coveted by the modernist tradition gives way to a fragmentation. We are thus enabled, as readers, to lose our defenses against our own multiplicities. And yet, at the same time the sense of artifice within the text remains. Are these "authentic" voices, we wish to know? Perhaps the question is born of another historical era. And yet, the question remains.

This revelation of self-incoherence is more fully accentuated in the following excerpt from the work of feminist scholar Laurel Richardson (1997), who reflects on daily life during the time she is focused on writing a book.

While I Was Writing a Book

my son, the elder, went crazy
my son, the younger, went sad
nixon resigned
the saudis embargoed
rhodesia somethinged
and my dishwasher failed

my sister, the elder, hemorrhaged
my brother didn't speak to me
my ex gurued and overdosed
hemlines fell and rose
texans defeated the e.r.a.
and my oil gaskets leaked

my friend, the newest, grew tumors
my neighbor to the right was shot
cincinnati censured sin
and my dracena plant rotted

I was busy.[6]

The irony of this piece invites us to abandon the posture of defensive coherence often provoked by traditional writing. It also calls us to reflect critically on the entire realm of professional writing of which we are a part. We at once can appreciate the academic value of our pursuits, but as well realize the extent to which they numb us to the immediate world about us; in our professional concentrations, we are rendered irresponsible in our relationships with others. Moreover, this work is self-consciously aware of itself as artifice. Traditional writing in the social sciences inherits realist forms of expression. That is, the writing manifests itself as a reflection of the real—for example, the reality of the cultural life under study, or the *actual* thoughts and feelings of another person (or indeed, oneself as ethnographer).

What concerns us here is the relational implications of a realist posture. In our view, a major limitation of realist writing lies in the restrictions it sets on dialogue. Discourse that asserts something to be the case informs the reader that if he or she is to remain a conversational ally this premise is beyond question. If a person announces, "I feel very happy about this," to remain in fruitful coordination one must grant the reality of the state of happiness. To question it—for example, as a construction of the self—would alienate one from the conversation. Here artifice becomes important. When Richardson uses poetry as her vehicle of expression, she moves us out of the register of "real-world talk." She does not suggest a reality about which we become suspicious. Rather, we are directly informed that the expression is guided by an aesthetic—or, "one way of putting things." We are thus liberated, as an audience, to consider this as a possible standpoint—not the only one we can take. We may offer alternatives with little likelihood of animosity on the author's part. Thus, we are invited into dialogue with her point of view from the perspective of our own.

Toward the Performative

> The concrete language of the theater can fascinate and ensnare the organs.
> . . . It liberates a new lyricism of gesture which . . . ends by surpassing the
> lyricism of words. It ultimately breaks away from the intellectual subjugation of language.
>
> —ANTON ARTUAD, *Theater of the Absurd*

We admire, enjoy, and are inspired by the new range of writing now flourishing within the ethnographic literature. These attempts represent a substantial enrichment in the range and quality of relationships that we now seek with our readers. However, as we become increasingly conscious of representation as relationship, it also becomes apparent to us that writing is but one medium among many. Of course, we have long been aware of the representational potentials of photography and film. But given the twin assumptions that scholarship is inherently the work of the rationally engaged mind, and that words are the finest expression of rational deliberation, the visual media are typically treated as secondary to the more important craft of writing. It is high time to challenge the prevailing logocentrism of this tradition, not only with visual media but also with the entire range of communicative expressions at our disposal. There is little reason that ethnographic representation should not become as rich in its forms of expression as the arts, with painting, music, dance, poetry, multimedia, and performance all serving as potential sources of communication. And with each alternative we are opened to different avenues of relationship.

In this vein the two of us have been increasingly attracted to dramatic performance. Performance shares much with the poetic form discussed earlier. It reveals itself as artifice, and thus fails to declare a sacred territory of the undiscussable. Or to put it another way, it declares a reality but simultaneously reveals it as make-believe. Further, when one enters the realm of performance there are no limits on the genres of verbal expression available. One can employ the formalisms of traditional literature, but as well the poetic, the profane, the ironic, the emotionally explosive, and so on. As we expand our modes of expression so do we expand the number of people with whom we can join in the dance of understanding. Performance can also express a panoply of voices, thus opening the audience to multiple voice/communities within themselves. And of special importance, performance is embodied in a way that writing is not. Here we break with the logocentric tradition, enabling the message to be carried by a fully expressive body in motion. Scholarship is not chained by the imperative of cerebral order, but is given full latitude of revelation in action. In our view, dramatic performance invites a more fully engaged relationship with the audience as well. If the performance is effective, the audience participates in an embodied fashion.

Our treatment of performance draws sustenance from a substantial corpus of significant writing. The work of Victor Turner (1982), for example, was groundbreaking. He argued not only for the dramaturgical character of cultural life, but as well for the desirability of participating in performed replicas of this life in order to fully understand its character. Ethnography was not, then, about the textual representation of others' lives, so much as offering opportunities for people to participate in alterior patterns of performance. The work of Richard Schechner (1985) explores the relationship between theater and the social sciences, preparing the way for a blending of performance art and social critique, a matrix that is being fruitfully explored by activist scholars searching for means of disrupting the oppression of the ordinary (see Case, Brett, and Foster 1995; Conquergood 1985). When performance art seeds cultural reflection the science/art binary is destroyed (see Goldberg 1979). These confluences, along with Augusto Boal's (1979) use of theater to unseat forces of cultural domination, have kindled our interest in the power of performance—over and above the abstract argument—to create reflection and resistance. Richard Bauman's work (1977) is also important in accentuating the character of performance as a medium of relationship. And the writing of Fred Newman (1996) and the work of the Performance of a Lifetime group in New York, draw our attention to the vital function of performance in expanding our capacities for creative human relationship.

To introduce our experiments in performance, we offer Mary Gergen's account of the life of the American woman passing through middle age. She has performed this work, which is partially autoethnographic, in a variety of settings, including International Communication Association meetings in Monterey, California, and a conference on the Postmodern Self in Berlin, both in 1999. The title of the work is "Woman As Spectacle," and the full text is published in *Feminist Reconstructions in Psychology: Narrative, Gender, and Performance* (2001). While providing access to a certain vision of this period of life, the work is also critical of psychological theorizing. It functions, then, not only to express a widely shared construction of womanhood, but also to subvert and ultimately replace it. After sharing a portion of the work, we will consider further its relational potentials.

[*The performer enters wearing a highly colorful, even garish costume, including a shimmering fuchsia cape, long gloves, a gold lamé bag, a purple scarf, a pink boa, and gold high heels. Underneath she wears a low-cut, orange, full-length sheath, with side slits, over a sheer black top. She is also wearing a large, curly blond wig. As her monologue unfolds, she begins taking off pieces of clothing— subtly evoking the image of a strip-show—lights up a cigar, and occasionally takes a drink of brandy from a hip flask. The following excerpt occurs midway through the performance.*]

At my age (chronological that is), I am meant to disappear. I should have been gone long ago. In the dance of the life cycle, I am being propelled against the wall. [*moving backward as though being pushed from the front, arms extended, curled in the middle*] Centrifugal forces spin me to the chairs, from which I rose so long ago . . . arms that circled me, and kept me on the floor. Oh, how I could dance. [*does a bit of a cha cha cha . . . takes up a sheer purple scarf that is tucked into the purse*] Now they've let me go. My dance card is empty. [*places the large scarf over her head, covering her face*] Now, I'm melding with the walls . . . pressing into paper . . . melting with the glue. . . . Stuck, not pinned and wriggling like Eliot's Prufrock, but misting into mottled lavender, without a muscle's twitch. [*standing with arms out, covered by the veil of purple*] This is the fate of a woman of a mature age.

[*removes scarf, keeps it in hand*] She is somewhere over forty, and, according to some, about as useful as a fruit fly (at least *they* have the courtesy to die swiftly when their breeding days are done). If she cannot procreate she is lifeless you see, but not dead. She never should attract attention. She learns to be the antispectacle. Yet she is the object of our gaze.

[*short pause*]

Such hatred we sometimes feel for her. [*wringing scarf as though it were a neck*] That shameful blot on the image of our youth. Couldn't we just wring her neck? Be done with her. No one needs her . . . hoarder of Medicare . . . Social Security sad sack . . . our tax dollars feeding a body no one wants to see. But lest we discard her so quickly she is also me, and perhaps you. She is our destiny, those of the female persuasion. Ugghhh, should we call for our pills, ply ourselves with hormones? Slather on our creams? Invite the knife to cut into our own throats, and pay for that pleasure? [*making slitting gestures*] Or shall we tipple into our drugs of sweet forgetting? [*takes another sip from flask*]

Is there anyone to call? Will 911 give us any help?

With this critical and ironic image further extended, the performance takes a turn toward a creative activism. Women are challenged to refuse and disrupt the dominant discourse, and to replace it with an alternative form of life. The following excerpt illustrates the move.

We need to draw dirty pictures . . . do unruly things . . . un-ruly . . . against the rulers, against the rules.

Making it up as we go along.

Woman under construction. Or on Top of?

Topsy-turvy, turning the world upside down . . . or perhaps more potently, sidling up . . . saddling up.

Women on Top . . . Controlling the pace . . . taking in as much as she wants. Finding a hip bone for her lip bone.

A missionary in her position, evading the law.

A butterfly wing stroking in sweet rebellion. Stirring up the airwaves in spunky surrender.

The image of the disorderly woman stirring the cauldron, . . . widen options for women . . . a temporary release, there's no grand solution anymore.

but Lady Godiva rides, and politics are rampant.

. . . Let's make some "gender trouble" as Judith Butler says:

Myths of gender, however alluring, are the bane of women's lives.

Weapon one in our wayward wars of transgression: Fool with Mother Nature: Rub on the line that divides the sexes. (MMMMmm that always feels good to rub on that line.)

Cross over the line, erase the line, blur the line? Is there a politics of lines? Watch out for the dangerous curves.

. . . We may be trapped in social orderings, tattooed within our proper place, but in outlandish moments we are freed to create the possibility of cultural change. Let us go on from here:

To revel in our specialness. To blush only when it suits us. To hold our heads up and be proud, no matter where and how we are.

To celebrate the lifted yoke of fertility and rejoice in our wholeness again. Like girls, to prance in moonlight and in sun.

To remember that the calendar is only one—bureaucratic—measurement of time. It cannot tell the age of spirit, heart, and mind.

Our spectacles are opportunities to glamour into being other forms of life. As we soar over the edge of respectability . . . let us make a joyful noise and be glad of our excesses. Let us find a way to celebrate. Let us dare to strut our stuff and when we die, die laughing.

Of course, it is difficult for these words to bring readers into the same relationship of the full performance to an audience. However, when performed effectively, we find that this material creates a strong bond between the performer and the audience. They have participated in the pathos, the anger, the joys of resistance, and the optimism of alternatives. Symbolically they have walked in the shoes of the performer, and seem to appreciate and be expanded by the opportunity.

Yet, there are also relational shortcomings in the work as well. The performance fundamentally is a monologue. The performer is in full control of the materials, which will change but little from one audience to the next. In effect, the audience may join in vicariously, but not as an active participant "in the conversation." There is a "watch me–appreciate me" characteristic of the performance that is not reciprocated. In its demonstration of itself as play, the piece does invite the audience to entertain alternatives they may bring to the event. However, there is no space made available in which to voice these alternatives.

Performing Relational Theory

To find the right formulation and tone: more than the art of writing, the art of living and dying.

—EDMOND JABES, *The Book of Dialogue*

At this point the path of our argument makes another turn. Specifically we want to share with you some of our attempts to bring theory to life through performance. There are at least two ways in which this turn is of special relevance to ethnography. One of the chief criticisms of much ethnographic inquiry—both traditional and experimental—is its lack of theoretical content. In earlier times the critique was voiced in terms of the hypothetico-deductive cast of science: much ethnographic work didn't derive from theory, and therefore was dubiously related to the truth or falsity of any particular theory of human behavior. The postpositivist dialogues of the past several decades have largely put this form of critique to rest. However, there is an analogue in these postmodern times, to whit, the meaning of ethnographic work is too often exhausted in the subject matter itself. The reader is invited to comprehend/appreciate/experience the actions and subjectivities of this or that minority, marginalized group, or particular individual—full stop. One is immersed in the life of the other, but as in the case of a fine meal or a fascinating jazz riff, there is no obvious place to go with it. And by "place to go," the critic typically means that the ethnography fails to inform or have implications for any extant dialogue or set of conceptual issues of intellectual or societal importance. There is no future that is implied by the presentation beyond that directly given.

There is more to the problem: As currently conducted, ethnographic inquiry does little to generate new conceptual resources. It may attempt to make intelligible otherwise alien discourses, but the outcome is seldom an increment in our vocabularies of social action. In a sense, the importance of theorists such as Freud, Marx, or Skinner is that—for good or ill—they generated vocabularies out of which new forms of societal practice could be forged. They did not so much "reflect the nature of the real" as transform it through new forms of discourse. And their theoretical languages were appropriated and applied to alter the course of cultural life. The capacity for creating generative theory, however, often seems lacking in ethnographic accounts. At the same time, the skills in alternative modes of expression now emerging in "new ethnographies" are wonderfully suited for the creation of new realities. As the domain of expression is enriched, so is the capacity to realize new worlds—expanding then on the possibility of relationship.

Deliberations such as these have fed much of our experimental work in recent years. We have asked how we can animate theory so that its vocabularies become available for action. By sampling some of these attempts, we try to gain further insight into the relational potentials of performance. First, consider an attempt by one of us (Mary Gergen) to use performance to speak to issues in postmodern theory. The piece was stimulated by a talk Stephen Tyler gave to an audience of anthropologists in Amsterdam in 1989. Tyler is well known for his experiments in postmodern writing, especially in *The Unspeakable* (1987). While admirable in certain respects, however, elements of an androcentric tradition seemed to persist. The performance piece was thus created both as a feminist critique and a loving embrace of the postmodern moves in theory. The piece was originally performed at a psychology and postmodernism conference in Aarhus, Denmark; the full text can be found in Steinar Kvale's edited work, *Psychology and Postmodernism* (1992). We join the party as First Woman responds to Postmodern Man's joyous remonstrances over his capacities for deconstruction:

First Woman: Who are they trying to scare off? Full of Power and Manipulative Control, Abundant Resources, Speed, Complete management. The New Army, complete with portable Zenises. Pulling the rug out from under the OLD GUARD. (Didn't we all want to run out of the stands and CHEER!!!?) Down with the OLD ORDER . . . Foundations of Modernity, split into Gravity's Rainbow/Rules shredded ribbons adorning the May POLE, wavering in the Breeze of breathtaking words/ABSOLUTE-ly nothinged by the shock-ing PM tropes/smashing icons with iron(ic)s/Wreaking CON-SENSE with NON-SENSE/
PARODYING
PARADING
PANDERING
PARADOXING
PLAYING
POUNDING
PRIMPING
PUMPING
What fun! [*singing*] . . . "London Bridges Falling Down. [*then shouting*] (DE-CONSTRUCT-ED) [*resumes singing*] MY FAIR LADY."

Where can WE jump in? Shall we twirl your batons? Can we all form a circle? Dance around the fire? the Pole? the falling bridges? Give us a hand. Give us a hand? Give us a hand . . .

PM Man: All they ever want are hand-outs. . . . Give 'em an inch they'll take a mile. How many inches do they think we've got? [*a brief pause, then, addressing Women*] Besides can't you see we've got play to do? It's not easy just going off to play each day. It takes practice . . . dedication . . . grace. It's not something you can just join in like that. We've got our formation. Can't you see you'll just muck it up? We're in the wrecking business. What business is that of yours? "You make, we break": We can write it on the truck. Next thing you'll want us to settle down and play house. We've got to be movin' on. It's part of the code. Girls can't be in combat. Besides John Wayne doesn't talk to them, so adios. Don't call us, we'll call you.

First Woman: That call has a familiar ring to it. The call of the WILD.

PM Man: We aren't animals; and don't call us an army! Better a merry dis-band-ment of (dis) Con-victors;

  (dis) Con-artists;   (dis)co-dandies;
              (dis)iden-ticals;
  (dis)-sent-uals;   (dis)-coursers;
  (dis)i-paters;   (dis)contents . . .

The women continue to grill PM Man, making the androcentric implications of postmodern critique increasingly clear. Perhaps the climax is reached in the following exchange:

PM Man: . . . That's another thing. We don't make promises. Just another word for COMMITMENT (the really big C-word, the one that gets you behind bars, and I don't mean mixing martinis). A rolling stone gathers no moss and no mille-deux.

First Woman: Mick Jagger has children.

PM Man: Babies are phallic. If you need one, get one.

First Woman: But your phallus doesn't need bread.

PM Man: "Let them eat cake," as good ol' Marie put it. She had a feel for our rap.

First Woman: That doesn't solve the problem.

PM Man: It's not my problem. Postmodern life is, as Deleuze sez, nomadic. And S.T. added, "We are all homeless wanderers on the featureless, postindustrial steppe, tentless nomads, home packed up." And as a NATO tank commander once said, "You can't have an army when you gotta bring along the outhouse for the dames."

First Woman: Looks like it's going to be a short revolution—about one generation.

PM Man: Au contraire, Baby, we've just begun. I mean the trashing is in dis-progress. Disciplines to dismantle/Methods to maul/Truth to trash

First Woman: Who's on the cleanup committee?

PM Man: You sound like somebody's mother. Whose side are you on anyway? Few minutes ago you wanted to dance in the streets. Down with the old, up with the new. (Never satisfied; always want something ya can't get . . . Bitch, bitch, bitch.)

First Woman: You sound de-fence-ive. Have I got your goat?

PM Man: Now you're getting down to something. Thanks, but no thanks. I get off graphically. Who needs flesh. And I can logoff any time . . . any time . . . any time . . . Let's leave it at that. Stephen Tyler has said: "Postmodernism accepts the paradoxical CONsequences of . . . irreconcilable ambiguity without attempting to end the CONflict by imposing CLOSURE . . .

We're a-dispersing . . . "dis-pursing" . . . we are getting further and further away. Space is beautiful.

First Woman: It's gonna be mighty COLD out there . . .

PM Man: Earthling, do you read me? . . . do you read my books?? . . . do you . . . reeeeead . . . ??? (*voice fading*)

First Woman: You're fading Major Tom.

The signal is getting weaker and weaker. It is running out in space. It is running out of space. Soon there is nothing but
　　　　SILENCE

When performed effectively, this piece is intellectually engaging—even provocative—while simultaneously evoking laughter and resonating misgivings about unbridled deconstruction. It also functions as an alternative to traditional intellectual writing, and thus opens paths to expanding the domain of scholarly expression. Yet, as a means of relating to an audience it does have its limitations. Although polyvocal in format, the performance is a self-contained monologue. The audience remains distanced. More importantly, the action within the performance is carried almost altogether through wordplay. There are protagonists, but they do little more than move through registers of rhetoric. Certainly there is a place for such linguistic pyrotechnics (Tom Stoppard is perhaps the consummate craftsman), but there are significant limits to the action-potential of the language; one can scarcely transport this performance form into relationships outside the scholarly/linguistic. How, then, can we develop expressions of theory, without resorting so fully to a strictly theoretical argot? How can we create, through performance, a "lived experience" of theory?

Our answer to these questions can best be understood in terms of our present theoretical investments, which focus on the character of relationships. This concern grows from our social constructionist moorings, in which relationships are viewed as the fundamental matrix from which human meaning is born. This orientation stands in strong contrast to the modernist tradition, in which the individual mind is held to be the basic atom of cultural life. While there is an enormous accumulation of discourse creating the reality of individual minds, accounts of relationship are relatively meager. Traditionally we hold individuals to be the units out of which relationships are constructed, thus rendering relationships secondary and synthetic. Our theoretical work attempts to reverse this sequence, holding relationship as the necessary prior to individual being (K. Gergen 1994, 2000; M. Gergen 2000).

With these issues foregrounded, we attempt to generate performances that are relationally focused. We move away from the monologue to dialogic performance in which at least two actors are involved. Our major means of avoiding reliance on abstract, didactic discourse is to limit the performances to exemplifications—not theory in itself, but theory by implication. To secure the link, we typically contextualize each relational vignette in broader theoretical terms.

To illustrate, one of our major attempts is to reconstruct the language of individual minds in relational terms. That is, rather than abandoning individualist discourse the attempt is to demonstrate how our referents for this discourse do not lie in the private region of individual minds, but rather, in the relational realm—"the domain of the between." Consider emotions, for example. Traditionally emotions are viewed as the sine qua non of individual mental life. Psychologists tell us that our emotions are essentially private events. Further, philosophers, psychologists, and biologists have argued for their universality. In effect, we are positioned by our cultural conventions to view ourselves as biologically prepared to experience and express the basic set of universal human emotions. In relational vignettes we attempt to subvert these assumptions. In the following script, for example, we demonstrate the cultural nonsense that would ensue if emotions were indeed biological.

Doris: Do you love me, Alan?

Alan: Well, this is a little difficult to say . . . I only have access to my pulse rate just now, and you know how variable that can be. And besides it's a little elevated in any case because I just finished dinner. But look, I have a doctor's appointment tomorrow, and I think I'm having an EKG; I'll bring home the results tomorrow, and we can look over the patterns.

Doris: I really don't trust the EKG for this one; too much is at stake . . . I mean our whole future, our marriage, the kids, and everything. I think we really have to be absolutely certain about this. Why don't we take a little from our savings and get an MRI and a CAT scan too?

Alan: Great idea. And I don't think we should just trust our own doctor for this one; we should have a second or third opinion. You can't be too careful about these things.

Doris: And then, if we find out that you do love me . . . and I so hope the results come out this way . . . then I will have to go and have a checkup myself. I mean, it just would be lopsided if we found you loved me but I didn't love you. I couldn't live in a marriage like that.

Alan: Great, Doris . . . but let me ask . . . umm, if we both come out okay in these exams, do you think . . . well, umm, do you think it's possible we could have sex again?

Once several critical vignettes are in place, we shift toward the relational alternative. Our concern here is to demonstrate that emotions themselves are cultural performances. They only make sense within the constructed world of a given culture at a particular point in history. Like theatrical performances, emotions can be portrayed poorly or well. To do them poorly is to fail to make sense within the culture, as the following vignette illustrates.

The scene takes place within the office of an assertiveness trainer; she is speaking with a client, Arnold, who is having difficulties in expressing anger.

Trainer: So you want to be more assertive. You've got to learn to express your emotions. You mentioned problems in expressing anger. Show me how you express you feelings when you are angry . . . let's say when your teenage son comes in and tells you he ran into a wall with your car.

Arnold: I'm very angry. (*said quietly and meekly*)

Trainer: No, no, that's all wrong. Try to put a bit more force into your voice.

Arnold: I'm very angry (*said in a loud, high-pitched voice*)

Trainer: Oh, you can't do that, it sounds like the castrati. Try again in a lower tone.

Arnold: I'm very angry. (*said in a low, strong tone, but without any facial expression*)

Trainer: Oh come on, let's see some facial expression . . .

Arnold: I'm very angry. (*repeats but this time smiling*)

Trainer: No! Stop smiling . . . look stern, show your teeth . . .

Arnold: I'm very angry. (*obeys the command, but his body is inert*)

Trainer: Now you are getting somewhere, but look, Arnold, I want to see your whole body involved, not just your voice.

Arnold: I'm very angry. (*waving his hands in the air like a bird*)

Trainer: No, no, no . . . you have to make fists and bend forward . . .

Arnold: I'm very angry. (*perfectly executing the trainer's commands*)

Trainer: Oh, Arnold, that is wonderful . . . you expressed yourself so powerfully. I am so pleased.

Arnold: I'm very happy. (*performed in the loud, seething style of the preceding expression of anger*)

We follow this vignette with several others designed to demonstrate that emotional performances make cultural sense only when placed in an interdependent relationship with the actions of others. Thus, one's expression of anger (love, fear, sadness, and so on) are not the possession of the individual actor, but more properly of the relational dance of which this action is a part. In the same way, one might say, while the individual player may serve a tennis ball, the player is essentially performing a meaningful action within the game. He or she does not so much possess the act as play the appropriate part within the form of life.

But, we must ask, how do these particular performance pieces function in terms of our relationship with the audience? They do carry with them the advantages of embodiment, polyvocality, and the suppression of the authoritative (truth-proclaiming) voice. Because they are relevant to broad conceptual issues, they also invite conversational rejoinders. The attempt to use relationships to create the reality of relational process also implies an interdependent relationship of performer to audience. At the same time, we have been concerned with the limits of these vignettes in terms of inviting the audience into a dialogic relationship. We search for ways to include audience members within the performance itself. We do find ourselves restrained here by certain structural and intellectual impediments. For instance, we do not want to embarrass audience members.

Perhaps our most successful way of avoiding some of these problems and incorporating the audience into our play is by asking audience members—at critical times within a scenario—to generate dialogue for us. In the case of emotional performances, for example, we try to show that certain relational scenarios are deeply problematic within Western culture. Especially dangerous is the mutual exchange of anger—a scenario that traditionally invites escalation. With escalation comes alienation and sometimes violence. The challenge, then, is to come up with alternative moves that are intelligible within the existing scenario, but subvert the pattern. Can we locate or create lines, we ask, that would allow us to create new forms of life? To illustrate, we confront the audience with this task in the following exchange between husband and wife:

Flo: The American Express bill came today. You charged over $400 for that dinner you had with your old buddy from school. What kind of restaurant was that? The Pink Pussycat? Is that one of those "gentleman's clubs"? I don't work hard everyday so you can go spend it like that with your friends.

Mac: Come on, Flo . . . get off my back . . . we've got money in the bank . . . it's no big deal . . . just lay off!

Flo: Oh yeah . . . easy come, easy go huh . . . I can't stand that attitude . . . that you would just waste money like that, throwing it away . . . burning it up, like there's no end to it.

Mac: Little Miss Righteousness . . . look at you . . . you spend twice that much for a dress . . . and what about all that makeup, and god, when I think of what you put into shoes . . . hell, I'll go out and drink with my buddies whenever and wherever I want . . .

Flo: Look, Mr. Big Spender, I work hard . . . I need everything I buy . . . it's my money . . . so get off this macho shtick . . . (*voice rising*)

Mac: You make shit . . . that's what it is . . . shit . . . I'm the one who brings in the real bucks. (*each voice continues to rise as the remainder of the dialogue ensues*)

Flo: Yeah, yeah, yeah . . . you make some money . . . but where did you get that job . . . from my father. Without my family you would be a slug . . . stuck somewhere down in a gutter.

Mac: Your family, I've had that bunch of fascists up to here . . . and you're just like 'em . . .

Flo: You bastard . . . (*shouting*)

Mac: (*raises his fist and starts to strike*)

At this point we stop the action and ask the audience for Mac's next line, and especially a line that will terminate this downward spiraling exchange. We have found most audiences wonderfully resourceful in their suggestions. To recall some of them:

- Apologize to her, and tell her how wrong you have been.
- Suggest you both take a walk and cool off a bit.
- Ask her what she would want you to do now.
- Tell her how much you were trying to please your old friend, to whom you owe a great deal.
- Suggest that this is about abandonment and loss of love, and not about the money.
- Ask "Why are we doing this to each other?" and suggest we start over.

As they are offered, we demonstrate them by repeating critical moments in the scenario. Do they function as hoped? Are there variants that might be more successful? These are discussions in which all opinions are valid. The event becomes a communal sharing of knowledge.

Conclusion

Finally we return to the relational implications of the present offering. Here we suspect that we come full circle: we might end as we began, with multiple closings matching the fragmentation of our opening desires. We have employed many voices in this writing, and each may strike a different relation with any given reader. As authors we are scarcely in control of our destiny; it is out of our relationship as writer and reader that our futures will be molded. There is no "one best way" in the matter of representation; relationships can be many and varied and to apply a single criterion to the matrix is to constrain our potential. At the same time, in the present offering we have shamelessly advocated forms of representation that reduce alienating distance, hierarchy, and single-mindedness; we find ourselves deeply drawn to relationships that favor an infinite merging and recombining of meanings. This view has informed our ideals of ethnographic and scholarly representation. We take this stand not from a transcendental high ground but as a result of our own immersion in action-with-others. Yet, in the same way that flexibility and continuous innovation are requirements for living in the complexities and rapid transformations of modern life, so too should we savor variety in our forms of representation. There is much to be said for discarding our style manuals at this point, along with the strangulating writing requirements of our major academic journals. As we enrich the range of representation so do we soften the rules of tradition and enrich the possibilities of relationship.

Notes

1. For a review of this work see Gergen and Gergen 2000.
2. B. Williams (1973), *Problems of the Self.* Cambridge: Cambridge University Press.
3. R. D'Andrade (1990), "Some Propositions about the Relations between Culture and Human Cognition." In *Cultural Psychology,* ed. J. W. Stigler, R. A. Shweder, and G. Gerdt (pp. 65–129). New York: Cambridge University Press.
4. Carol Ronai (1996), "My Mother Is Mentally Retarded," 115.
5. Karen V. Fox (1996), "Silent Voices," 336–39.
6. Laurel Richardson (1997), *Fields of Play,* 203–4.

References

Angrosino, Michael V. 1997. *Opportunity House: Ethnographic Stories of Mental Retardation.* Walnut Creek, Calif.: AltaMira.
Bauman, Richard. 1977. *Verbal Art As Performance.* Rowley, Mass.: Newbury House.
Boal, Augusto. 1979. *Theater of the Oppressed.* New York: Urizen.
Buber, Martin. 1970. *I and Thou,* trans. W. Kaufmann. New York: Scribner's Sons.
Case, Sue-Ellen, Philip Brett, and Susan L. Foster, eds. 1995. *Cruising the Performative.* Bloomington: University of Indiana Press.
Ceglowski, Deborah. 2000. "Research As Relationship." *Qualitative Inquiry* 6: 88–103.
Conquergood, Dwight. 1985. "Performing As a Moral Act: Ethical Dimensions of the Ethnography of Performance." *Literature in Performance* 5: 332–73.
Davies, Brownwyn. 2000. *(In)scribing Body/Landscape Relations.* Walnut Creek, Calif.: AltaMira.
Denzin, Norman K., and Yvonna S. Lincoln, eds. 2000. *Handbook of Qualitative Research,* 2nd ed. Thousands Oaks, Calif.: Sage.
Ellis, Carolyn, and Arthur P. Bochner, eds. 1996. *Composing Ethnography.* Walnut Creek, Calif.: AltaMira.
Fox, Karen V. 1996. "Silent Voices, a Subversive Reading of Child Sexual Abuse." In *Composing Ethnography,* ed. Carolyn Ellis and Arthur P. Bochner (pp. 330–56). Walnut Creek, Calif.: AltaMira.
Gergen, Kenneth J. 1994. *Realities and Relationships.* Cambridge, Mass.: Harvard University Press.
———. 2000. *Invitations to Social Construction.* Thousand Oaks, Calif.: Sage.
Gergen, Mary. 1988. "Towards a Feminist Metatheory and Methodology in the Social Sciences." In *Feminist Thought and the Structure of Knowledge,* ed. Mary Gergen (pp. 87–104). New York: New York University Press.

———. 2001. *Feminist Reconstructions in Psychology: Narrative, Gender, and Performance.* Thousand Oaks, Calif.: Sage.

Gergen, Mary, and Kenneth J. Gergen. 2000. "Qualitative Inquiry: Tensions and Transformations." In *Handbook of Qualitative Research,* 2nd ed., ed. Norman Denzin and Yvonna S. Lincoln (pp. 1025–46). Thousand Oaks, Calif.: Sage.

Goldberg, RoseLee. 1979. *Performance Art: From Futurism to the Present.* London: Thames and Hudson.

Jabes, Edmond. 1987. *The Book of Dialogue.* Middletown, Conn.: Wesleyan University Press.

Kvale, Steinar, ed. 1992. *Psychology and Postmodernism.* London: Sage.

McLuhan, Marshall. 1967. *The Medium Is the Message.* New York: Bantam Books.

Newman, Fred. 1996. *Performance of a Lifetime.* New York: Castillo.

O'Brien, Flann. 1966. *At Swim-Two-Birds.* New York: New American Library.

Richardson, Laurel. 1997. *Fields of Play.* New Brunswick, N.J.: Rutgers University Press.

Ronai, Carol. 1996. "My Mother Is Mentally Retarded." In *Composing Ethnography,* ed. Carolyn Ellis and Arthur P. Bochner (pp. 109–31). Walnut Creek, Calif.: AltaMira.

Rose, Dan. 1993. "Ethnograpy As a Form of Life: The Written Word and the Work of the World." In *Anthropology and Literature,* ed. P. Benson (pp. 192–224). Urbana: University of Illinois Press.

Schechner, Richard. 1985. *Between Theater and Anthropology.* Philadelphia: University of Pennsylvania Press.

Shotter, John. 1997. "Textual Violence in Academe: On Writing with Respect for One's Others." In *Transgressing Discourses: Communication and the Voice of the Other,* ed. M. Huspek and G. P. Radford (pp. 17–46). Albany: SUNY Press.

Taussig, Michael. 1993. *Mimesis and Alterity.* New York: Routledge.

Turner, Victor. 1982. *From Ritual to Theatre.* New York: Performing Arts Journal Publications.

Tyler, Stephen. 1987. *The Unspeakable.* Madison: University of Wisconsin Press.

CULTURE EMBODIED: PERFORMING AUTOETHNOGRAPHY

For Father and Son: An Ethnodrama with No Catharsis

RONALD J. PELIAS

Genre

It's a mystery. What happened? How did we get here? What will happen next? Is there some character who will come on stage and explain it all? What details are needed to make everything clear? What loose ends need to be tied up? Whom should we fear? Whom should we not trust? Who will surprise us in the end? Is it explainable? Is there an author?

It's a futurist one act. The curtain opens. A phone sits on a table. A man looks at the phone. It does not ring. Curtain.

It's a farce, performed by characters cast in different plays. The scenes repeat themselves. No character enters when another is on stage, no character talks with another, no character speaks the truth. All characters are ridiculous.

It's a melodrama in which I am the villain twirling my son's mustache.

It's a tragedy that is based on a simple tragic flaw. There is no Oedipal drive, no Promethean heroism, no Narcissian vanity. It is a simple case of avoidance. Out of mind, there is no problem. Out of mind, there is no need for contact. Out of mind, there are no promises.

It's a comedy of manners where I, the fumbler, never quite know what is right.

It's an absurdist drama. The curtain opens. Two phones sit on a table. A man looks at the phones. A phone rings. He picks up the receiver of the one not ringing. "Hello. Hello?" he calls out. He hangs up and cries out, "There must be more phones." He leaves the stage only to return with another phone. The pattern repeats itself until the stage is filled with phones. He never selects the phone that rings. His final words are, "Hello. I said, 'hello.' Can't you hear me? Is anyone there? Hello? Hello?" Curtain.

It's a comedy of errors, but no one is laughing.

Plot

It tells how a father could let his son become involved with the wrong crowd, become involved with drugs, become someone else.

It tells how a son never listened to anyone, except those he shouldn't.

It tells how a father's guilt can lead in the opposite direction to his desire.

It tells how the space between the reader and writer is the page and how the space between father and son is the heart.

It tells how families are formed and forgotten.

It tells how inaction becomes an action.

It tells how a son resents his father for never being there, for never being what a father should be, for rejecting him, and how he still seeks his father's approval.

It tells how a father cannot bring himself to give his son the approval he desires.

It tells how heredity can leave no mark, no claims, no love.

It tells how stepfathers can triumph over fathers, how allegiance can trump blood, how ties can untwist.

It tells how time figures and fixes fate.

It tells how sadness becomes set, etched in memory, settled as a scar.

It tells how silence is a strategy, an ongoing conversation between two listeners.

Characters

Father: middle-age man who wants to say, "Son, come here."
Son: mid-twenties man who wants to say, "Father, why?"
Wives, stepfathers, daughters, grandparents, friends: various ages, who constantly
   say, "I don't know what to say."

Thought

You want, as a father, to be the father that your father was. You want to be present. You want to say what is possible and pertinent. You want to show what can be. You want to believe in your father's words. You want them to hold steady.

You want, as a son, your father to be the father you never had. You understand absence. You cannot speak. You do not know what you represent. You listen for your father's words but you hear no sounds. Nothing is secure. You have nothing to repeat.

Scenes

Scene 1: Divorced Parents Discuss Their Child

Mother: I won't have it. I won't. I'll not have him living in my house any
   longer.
Father: I can understand that. You have every right to feel that way. I wouldn't
   want him and his friends in my house doing drugs either.
Mother: Well, what are you going to do?
Father: I don't know what I can do. I'll talk to him if you like.
Mother: Don't you think I've tried that?
Father: I'm sure you have.
Mother: I can't live like this any longer.
Father: Tell him to move.
Mother: I've told him I want him to but he won't get out. He says he doesn't
   have enough money to get a decent place.
Father: If we give him any money, he'll just blow it on drugs.
Mother: I was thinking that if we got him an apartment and if we paid the
   rent, then he couldn't blow it on drugs. And he would be away from here.
   I have to get him out of my house.

Father: Should we be paying his rent? Isn't it time he took on some responsibility?
Mother: All I know is that I want him out of my house.

Scene 2: A Conversation between Father and Son

Father: I'm not going to give you ten thousand dollars for another car. I'm sorry. That's just too much.
Son: Well, I guess I'll have to ask my grandmother again. I just don't think I should always be asking her to bail me out.
Father: Right. I don't think you should either.
Son: Well, I got to have a car.
Father: Yeah, but you do not need a ten-thousand-dollar T-Bird.
Son: You just want me to buy a piece of shit.
Father: No. I want you to buy something reasonable, something that will be reliable, something that will get you to work every day.
Son: That T-Bird is a reliable car. It's in great shape.
Father: The last thing you need is another car that calls attention to itself.
Son: That car is like a family car.
Father: Yeah, right.
Son: How much are you willing to put in?
Father: Depends on what car you're talking about.
Son: So, you won't even pitch in a few thousand dollars? I mean, if you put a few thousand, then I think Grandma would go the rest.
Father: You're missing the point.
Son: No, you are. I've gotta have a car.

Scene 3: A Husband and Wife Plan for His Arrival

Wife: I wish he wasn't coming.
Husband: I can't tell my son he can't come to the house on Christmas.
Wife: I know, but he'll just ruin the day. I hate how he always gets to you.
Husband: Maybe he won't stay long.
Wife: Is he expecting to have Christmas dinner with us?
Husband: I don't know. I didn't say anything to him about it.
Wife: When is he coming?
Husband: I told him to come around two o'clock.
Wife: Is he planning to spend the night?

Husband: I don't know. We didn't discuss it.

Wife: I would just like to know what to prepare for.

Scene 4: Another Conversation between Father and Son

Father: How long have you been working as a roofer now?

Son: Eight years.

Father: Wow. I didn't realize it was for so long. Are you getting any benefits?

Son: No.

Father: No? What would happen if you fell?

Son: I know how to move up there. You just go, go, go. You don't think about it.

Father: Anyone could fall.

Son: I've fallen a couple of times. Never really got hurt though.

Father: You're lucky.

Son: I guess, but I can't imagine myself doing this work when I'm thirty-five. My legs are already giving out. When I'm carrying a load of shingles up a ladder, my legs just shake.

Father: That should tell you something.

Son: I can't do anything else and make enough money. I'm not a brain surgeon.

Father: You were a smart kid.

Son: That was long ago.

Father: Before you fucked yourself up on drugs.

Son: Don't start.

Father: I'm not. I'm just saying that you were smart.

Son: I'm not fucking with that shit anymore.

Father: Good.

Son: I can't. If I just go near it, I'm fucked.

Father: Well, stay away. (*pause*) So, you gave Jenny a ring?

Son: Yeah.

Father: And what does that mean to you?

Son: I don't know.

Father: Are you planning to get married?

Son: Not now. We can't afford a wedding.

Father: It only takes a few bucks to go to the justice of the peace.

Son: Yeah, I guess. But things are going along fine now. We don't want to mess anything up.

Father: Is Jenny still stripping?

Son: Yeah.

Father: Are you okay with that?

Son: I don't get jealous, if that's what you mean. Sometimes I go watch her. I'll say to some guy sitting next to me at the bar, "See that girl. I'm going home with her tonight." He'll say, "No way," and before you know it, I've made a twenty.

Father: Does Jenny get any benefits?

Son: No.

Father: What would you do if either of you got sick? Or if Jessica got sick?

Son: We survive. We get along. Just last week we went up to Chicago to hear Nine Inch Nails. We took off from work around two o'clock and hauled ass. They were awesome. We didn't get back home until around five-thirty the next morning.

Father: Sounds like fun. Do you have your license again?

Son: It cost me a fortune. I had to pay this lawyer a ton of money.

Father: For what?

Son: I kept getting pulled over while I was under suspension. I had to get to work.

Father: How many tickets did you get?

Son: A whole shitload.

Father: What is your insurance costing you now?

Son: Nothing.

Father: What do you mean?

Son: I don't have any insurance. I couldn't afford it. I got this guy I know to fix the records so that it showed that I had insurance so I could get my license. I had to get my license back.

Father: You could take public transportation or you could let Jenny drive.

Son: Jenny doesn't have her license. She never bothered to get one in Missouri after her Illinois one expired.

Father: So neither of you has a valid license?

Son: I have a valid license, just no insurance, and Jenny has insurance but no valid license.

Father: I see. That sounds like a problem to me.

Son: Well, we do what we gotta do.

Father: There are other options.

Son: Only for people like you, man. I don't have options. I do what I gotta do.

Father: Well, you "gotta do" some things for Jessica. You have some responsibility for her, even if she is Jenny's child.

Son: I'm responsible. That child listens. She knows that she better not give us any shit.

Father: She's a sweet kid.

Son: Yeah, but she's fucking up in school.

Father: What's the problem?

Son: It just takes her forever to learn anything. She's got this friend that she plays with—you tell her something and she's got it like that (*snaps his fingers*). Jessica, you tell over and over, and she still doesn't get it.

Father: Maybe she has some kind of learning disability. Has she been tested at school?

Son: She's had some tests, but they didn't find anything.

Father: You'll just have to work with her. That's all you can do with your kid.

Son: Did you work with me?

Father: The best I knew how.

Son: Well, you fucked up, didn't you?

Scene 5: A Monologue: A Father Speaks about His Other Child

Father: "Doug called. He wants you to call him back," my thirteen-year-old daughter reports on her half brother. Her words break a silence from him of nine months, nine months without contact, without any connection with my son. "Are you going to call him back?" she asks. "Yes," I answer but I delay doing so. My mind races to the impact of his presence on my wife who doesn't want him in the house, on my daughter who wants some relationship with this man, and on me who believes in the obligation of blood, of family, of father to son but who, like his wife, doesn't want him in the house.

"Call him back," she orders and I, still delaying, say with impatience, "I will." A day passes, and then another. "Have you called Doug yet?" she wants to know, wondering how a parent could turn on a child.

Diction

Shall I claim the word "father," claim it as if I earned the right to stake such a claim? Who should I say I am? Who should I say he is? Dare I use the word "son"? He was my "dependent" who learned not to depend on me. We live a legacy of wasted words, inherit our empty intentions, and procreate the unspoken. I, who did not take on the name of father, breed a child who did not take on the name of son.

Where are the words? How can I arrange them in the right order? How can I place them in the right rhythm? How can I put them in harmony? Why won't they settle into easy iambs? Where is the rhyme and reason of it all? My words are nothing more than crusted platitudes, predictable as poison, pounding the blood from our hearts. There is nothing here but what is left unsaid.

Spectacle

Drop the fliers. Roll in the set. Start the music. Turn the lights up full. Put us on the revolving stage. Spin it faster and faster. Make it so we can hardly stand. It is a sight to see. Pull the curtain as we become a spectacle.

Waiting for Catharsis

This is a play, coauthored, that I cannot forget. I remember him at two. The night the marriage ended, I stood at the door and saw his soft smile, knowing he did not understand and knowing he never would.

I remember him at five. He called himself Dougie-the-Cowboy and thumped through the house on his stick horse. When I phoned, he would cry. "Be a big cowboy, stop crying. Daddy will see you soon."

"When is soon?" he asks.

"Maybe a few weeks, buddy."

"That's not soon. Come tonight."

"I can't, but it won't be long before I get to see my boy. Let me talk to your mother." Bang Bang. You're dead.

"He waits by the phone every week," she says.

"When can I see him?"

"Soon," she replies.

I remember him at thirteen. Dirty from a day at school, he comes to visit. We speak rehearsed lines like tired actors from a long run. He knows he lives in a world beyond my shelves of books. "Well," I say, "how's it feel to be a teenager?" A shrug and I want to shout: Don't you realize that your years define me as much as you, that distance kept you from being my son, that time is running out, that I am not your father. Instead, we talk of weekend plans and I, like a camp counselor with a whistle around my neck, chatter on about our scheduled hours: movies, cake, and this and that until each minute is arranged to blur all contact. When our allotted time ends, we leave each other relieved, safe, ready to return to our world, having fulfilled our responsibility and feeling the lie we decided to keep.

I remember him at eighteen, graduation night. Sitting next to his mother, I watch him cross the stage. "It wasn't easy," she says under her breath. I know she is right. And as he drives away for his night of celebration, he waves good-bye to us and I think, "It's never going to be this easy again."

I remember him now, his tough, hard body beginning to crack from the years of roofing and from the years of postponed intentions. He wears his clothes as if they were oddly creased. Denying his curls, he combs his hair back, slick, as if he understood style. He walks, head turning from side to side, as if he were being watched. When he counts his money, he does so with either too much flourish or too much privacy. He fell from the middle class with a thud. He fell as I watched from my suburban home. Now, he falls on my couch, large, laden, lost. I offer him a Coke.

This is a play to remember. But there is no catharsis, no purging of emotions, emotions that sit inside us like jagged rocks. There is no release, no act of purification. This play ends in silence. There is no applause, no final bow. The curtain cannot close.

The Way We Were, Are, and Might Be: Torch Singing As Autoethnography

STACY HOLMAN JONES

A Beginning, Tentative

**T**wo ideas:

1. Torch singing—performing songs of unrequited love—is, for audiences and singers, a type of autoethnographic performance. Torch singing is how the body *does* and *undoes* the experience of unrequited love (adapted from Jones 1996: 132).[1]

2. Torch singing is, for me, an autoethnographic performance, a doing and undoing of my own love in the act of research.

These are ideas about subjectivity, and because of this, they conjure stories of my own desires and disappointments. I'd like to tell a few of those stories. Then I'll return to the idea that torch singing is an autoethnographic performance—a performance that invites us to experience the longing and participate in the revolution of unrequited love.

An Ending, Repeated

Katie rushes to cross a busy New York City street. She is late for her shift to collect signatures and distribute leaflets urging her government to "Ban the Bomb." She is in charge, informed, and loud. She is Jewish, political, and proud.

Katie looks up from her work—her cause, her passion—and sees Hubbell (once her work, her cause, and her passion) emerge from a car across the street. He is beautiful, intractable, All-American.

Hubbell waves. Katie rushes to cross the busy New York City street. They kiss, then embrace. A beautiful, perhaps intractable, and certainly All-American woman moves into the scene. She is Hubbell's fiancée. Katie, Hubbell, and the fiancée make small talk and empty promises to meet for drinks, then say good-bye. Katie returns to her work to Ban the Bomb.

But this isn't the end. Now Hubbell crosses the busy New York City street. He tells Katie that she never gives up (he means her work). She says that she only gives up when she is absolutely forced to (she means her work, too, including Hubbell). They kiss, embrace, and say good-bye.

Hubbell returns to his fiancée. Katie returns, once again, to her work. Barbra sings, "Memories . . ."

A Performance, Hidden

I am crying. I cry each time I see the final scene between Katie and Hubbell in *The Way We Were*. I have to see only that last scene, hear only those last sounds. "Memories . . ."

I cry for Katie and Hubbell, for the way they tried, but just couldn't make their relationship work. I cry for Katie's refusal to give up on her causes or her passions. I cry for how she feels forced to choose between her work and her love. Most of all, I cry for how much I feel like Katie during the last moments of the film, listening to that song.

Today, as I watch the final moments of *The Way We Were*, my husband comes into the room. As Katie rushes to cross the busy New York City street, I feel my husband's eyes on me. He knows I will cry at the end, and he watches me, waiting. When Hubbell returns to his fiancée and Katie to her work, I get up from the couch and rush into my office. I sit at my desk and cry, not wanting my husband to see me. I don't want him to see me weep for my own longings, refusals, and choices. I want to be alone with Katie and Hubbell and that song of unrequited love. I lay my head on the desk and sing "The Way We Were." I play the final scene over in my head, only this time I am Katie and you are Hubbell.

The scene ends the same, with you returning to your fiancée and me to my work. And I cry again, only this time I don't feel the stab of unrequited desire and the ache of lost opportunities. No, I feel strangely . . . curious. I am curious about whether this story has another sort of ending. I am curious about whether I can play Katie with all of her caring and conviction.

A Reader, Imagined

Our meeting does not happen by chance. I don't catch a glimpse of you across some downtown street. No, when I visit my parents and our hometown, I call you. I give my name to the receptionist and wait for you to come on the line. My heart is pounding. I fight the urge to hang up. You are surprised to hear from me, and at first the conversation is awkward and hesitant. We ask each other about families and jobs, about spouses and children. After a while, we settle into a comfortable rhythm and move on to questions of happiness and ambitions. As the conversation winds down, I (trying to be casual) say we should get together for a drink the next time I'm in town. You suggest we have lunch the next day.

I don't sleep at all that night.

I wait for you in the front of a small Thai restaurant. I sit on a hard chair next to the door. Each time it swings open, I hold my breath. I try standing, but imagine I look too expectant. I sit again, then pick up a day-old newspaper and pretend to read. The door opens and you explode into the tiny space (or so it seems to me). When I stand to meet your embrace, I can't feel my legs beneath me.

We're seated at a table next to the window. I order a large glass of water, which I drink greedily when it arrives at the table. I don't remember being this nervous about speaking to anyone—ever. The first moments pass in a haze. We discuss Thai food and order something from the menu. We return to questions of families and careers. And then something odd happens.

You say you know about the book I wrote, an ethnography on women's music. I don't believe this, but I am flattered that you mention it. You say you haven't seen it, but you know it's a *feminist* book, which doesn't surprise you. You say you are proud of me, that you knew I would become an author. I think about how many times I have imagined you reading my words. I think about my story about you and me and Billie Holiday and feminism and I wonder if I was wrong.

A Memory, Inscribed

The story about you and me and Billie Holiday and feminism? Oh yes, well, you wouldn't have seen that. I wrote that story when I first began researching torch singing—songs about unrequited love typically sung by women. Mind if I indulge in a bit of background here? I'll try to keep it brief.

The torch song is quite an old form, descending from the French *chanson*, or song-poem, which dates to the eleventh century. Torch songs tell stories of desire, seduction, and heartbreak. They are designed to arouse "intense emotion in both singer and audience" (Clements 1998: 32). A great *chanson* evokes a "powerful melancholy that can make listeners experience longing and consolation, often simultaneously" (Clements: 32). However, the torch singer does not leave her audiences despairing or languishing in the afterglow of catharsis. No, she uses her story to understand the past and to "nurture the future" (Moore 1989: 45, 53).

Yes, the afterglow of catharsis! Okay, well maybe I got a bit carried away there . . . . I'm getting to the story about you. . . .When I began my research on torch singing, I started with Billie Holiday, one of my favorites. I tried to remember the first time I heard Holiday's voice. I tried to remember what her words and her songs of unrequited love *meant* to me then. I sat down at my desk, and I wrote. . . .

Some days I wonder if, after all the hours I've spent in seminar rooms and alone in front of my computer writing, I have been reduced to making lists of words, to scripting fragments. Unable to express in finely wrought sentences the injustice of oppression or the beauty of a solution, I make lists that signify worlds, words that set off explosions of thought and feeling.

A recent list:

shared experience of oppression
the abyss of representation
demanding voice and redress
a red dress
a smoky voice
Billie Holiday

This list makes me think of you. Why you? Why now? I think of the cassette tapes you made for me—tapes that now reside, sticky with age, in a blue shoebox. A blue shoebox buried deep in an ocean of report cards, prom photos, pages filled with the rush and slope of your words. I add

homemade tapes

to the list, and then something clicks and tilts and I'm in Ames, Iowa, in our steamy, windowless downtown apartment. I see your guitar-calloused fingertips pressing the eject button, offering me Laurie Anderson and The Specials and this or that Beatle and R.E.M. Your recorded undergraduate music education course packed in tight against my own cassette rebellion—Prince and Sting and Billie. Torchers every one.

I find Billie in the bargain bin at your favorite music store. You detest the tinny piano and her pleading voice. Your guitar-calloused fingertips press the eject button.

You use those fingertips to educate me in the finer-points of a scornful, noisy, jealous love.

I hear this music in and around your smile and biting remarks, in and around the fury of your anger. And over what? That I wanted to go to graduate school. That I wanted more for myself than you.

After it was over, you said you were sorry it happened the way it did. You said you treated me like an animal.

And I said yes, but only because you couldn't coax and tame me into your note-filled consciousness without a fight.

You said you were sorry. Don't be. I still have them. I still hear their voices. Laurie and Sting and Billie. Every one.

The cursor blinks, waiting for an explanation. I delete homemade tapes from the list. I add

feminist theory

because that is what remains. You gave me music, but I gave myself Billie Holiday.

A Curiosity, Confessed

I think about this story of you and me and Billie Holiday and feminism and know I was wrong. Looking at you now, in the Thai restaurant, I decide not to tell you the story I've been telling myself all these years. I rewrite it then and there. Instead of pitting your wants and desires for marriage and family against my own for a career and an intellectual life, I say that you taught me to write my book.

You look confused. I say it was your curiosity—about music and about life—that inspired *me* to be intellectually and emotionally curious. You still look confused. I say that your desire to learn everything you could about the music you loved—songs and performers and recordings and performances and playing—

inspired me to listen more closely, to really feel and think about music. But more than that—more than music—you taught me how to ask questions and piece together answers. You taught me how to be a thinker. You made me want to be a writer. It took me a long time to understand that. I say these words to you and I mean them. You don't look confused anymore. Instead, you look away.

An Author, Blinking

A few weeks before our lunch, I found a poem lurking in a file titled "Music and Literature." I didn't remember writing this poem or placing it among the ideas I've collected about music and literature. It begins with these words, written by Peggy Phelan (1993: 16): "All seeing is hooded with loss. . . . In looking at the other . . . the subject seeks to see" herself. Then, my words about you . . .

> I feel the slipping away, welcome it.
> Turn over the memory of a long, lost
> other. Blurring vision and breath coming fast,
> swallowing so hard the longing catches in my throat.
>
> Your eyes, green like mine, on me. Steadily
> watching myself reflected in your gaze. Look
> at you seeing *me,* better one, now two, three, now four,
> recognizable at last, this image in green, is mine.
>
> I blink, dismantle the sudden need. Strip motives bare.
> Symptom of too much criticism, discourse, disguise.
> Fashioning shards of regret into bone—no children, two
> mortgages, no investments, save your own mind.
>
> I want to live the torch song I think, write, dream about.
> Waking surfaces the absurdity of this dim remembrance.
> I get back to work on the novel, the essay, the poem, the book.
> I do.

Here, now, I watch you looking out the window of the Thai restaurant. I think of the poem filed under "Music and Literature," and wonder if I will revise it as well. Then I suddenly remember a scene in Milan Kundera's (1991) novel *Immortality*. In the scene, Paul, a character in the novel, speaks to Kundera, a character in the novel and also the author of the novel. I can hear their exchange:

"My wife adores Mahler," [Paul] continued. "She told me that two weeks before the premiere of his Seventh Symphony he locked himself up in a noisy hotel room and spent the whole night rewriting the orchestration."

"Yes," I agreed, "it was in Prague, in 1906. The name of the hotel was the Blue Star."

"I visualize him sitting in the hotel room, surrounded by manuscript paper," Paul continued, refusing to let himself be interrupted. "He was convinced that his whole work would be ruined if the melody were played by a clarinet instead of an oboe during the second movement."

"That is precisely so," I said, thinking of my novel. (Kundera 1991: 335)

"That is precisely so," I say, thinking of my poem and my work and my curiosity. You look at me, finally, with eyes green like mine. You say that no one knows you better than I do. That no one knows me better than you.

I blink. I am sitting here with you, thinking of a hundred things, and all I can do is blink.

A Blue Star, Whispered

You suggest that we leave the restaurant, that we get some air. We walk into a brilliant daylight and stand facing each other in the parking lot. You ask to kiss me. I hear you say that no one knows you better than I do. That no one knows me better than you. I close my eyes. I feel your lips on mine and I fall back into some other place, some other romance. Your urgent, familiar kiss returns to me. I hear you whisper something about a hotel.

I am awake now, eyes open, standing in the parking lot and looking into green eyes unfamiliar to me. I think about Mahler and music and memory. I see Katie in an earlier scene, before she and Hubbell parted. She is crying, oh, I want, I *want* . . .

Kundera (1991: 314) says, "memory does not make films, it makes photographs." Obviously he has not seen *The Way We Were* or the noon movie of you and me in the parking lot of a Thai Restaurant, with a hotel between us, waiting for an answer.

I ask if you mean the Blue Star. I am nervous, and I laugh. You don't blink; you smile. I ask you *how*? How can we live two lives? How can we be purposefully duplicitous and ever be sure or right or true again?

You say we all live two lives. You say it's like that book, *The Unbearable Lightness of Being*. You say our mistake would be to burden others with the duplicity of our true selves, the facts of our being.

Kundera interrupts. He says he was wrong about the unbearable lightness of being. He says, "What is unbearable in life is not being but being one's self" (1991: 258).

I hear Kundera. I look at you, smiling. I'm not sure.

A Torch Song

We make empty promises to phone each other. I look at you, then walk away.

I stop and turn around and ask if you were wrong. I ask if we were wrong. I ask you and Kundera and Katie and myself.

You say that I never give up.

I say that I give up only when I am absolutely forced to, and I mean both you and my work. Then I say that I can listen to both Billie Holiday *and* "The Way We Were." That I can be Katie *and* myself. That I can have love *and* feminism. You look confused. I say that you taught me to write this book, and now I'm going to write it.

I get in my car and start the engine. Barbra's voice begins low as I put the car in gear. She sings "Memories." I cry, just hearing that song. I sing along. I drive away from you and back to somewhere else, someone else.

Two Ideas, Revisited

I began this essay by proposing two ideas. First, that torch singing is a kind of autoethnographic performance. To borrow a phrase about ethnography from Joni Jones, torch singing is how the body does and undoes the experience of unrequited love (1996: 132). Second, torch singing is, for me, an autoethnographic performance. A "doing" and "undoing" of my own love in the act of research. I also said that these ideas were about subjectivity. Let's return to that.

Autoethnography and torch singing are storytelling activities (Van Maanen 1995: 3; Hamm 1979: 292). Autoethnography and torch singing both enact a life story within larger cultural and social contexts and histories (Reed-Danahay 1997: 9; Moore 1989: 43). Further, these stories are often deeply nostalgic; they are often lamentations (Clements 1998: 32; Ellis and Flaherty 1992: 35). Why do we tell such tales? To inscribe our own melancholy, mourning, and release, and to evoke these same emotions in our readers and our audiences. More than this, though, we seek to create a live, charged *exchange* with an audience (Dolan 1993: 151).

Within this exchange, performers and audiences inhabit and move outside the "subject" of the text. As an ethnographer, I am not the people I work with

and write about, even when I am writing about myself. Nor is the actor the character she performs. Nor is the torch singer the woman she sings about. And the
woman (or man) in the audience? She is not the woman in the song or the character on stage or the "subject" of the ethnography. Why? Because the stories of torch
and autoethnography are incomplete. They are partial, fragmented performances
of subjectivity (Abu-Lughod 1993: 9). And yet because these stories move from and
in and through *real* bodies, their performance can move us in *our* bodies, hearts,
and minds (Pobryn 1993: 71). That is why we can *feel* Billie Holiday's pain and
defiance when she sings "My Man": "It cost me a lot, but there's one thing that I've
got, it's my man, it's my man. . . ." (quoted in White 1987: 117). And that is why,
when we hear Fanny Brice or Barbra Streisand sing "My Man," we feel a *different*
sort of pain and defiance. Torch singing and autoethnography allow us to "try on"
the subjectivity of another—to gauge how the "glove" fits and doesn't fit and to
show the "seams" of our acts to an audience (Anna Deavere Smith, quoted in Capo
and Langellier 1994: 72). In performing "others," we discover how the body, heart,
and mind does and undoes unrequited love or the experience of immigration or the
dilemmas of doing fieldwork and writing ethnographic accounts (see, for example,
Holiday 1992; Conquergood 1985; Jones 1996; Behar 1996).

The example of torch singing points up an interesting question about the
force and effect of subjectivity in performances and in texts. Does torch performance afford performers and audiences access to the longing and consolation of
another and nothing more? Does the torch singer enable an audience to confirm
(and perhaps become complicit with) the experience of victimization or, worse,
to dismiss the performance as unproductive for women's lives? (See, for example,
Moore 1989; Paglia 1996.) These are also valid questions for the autoethnographer. And if I wish to answer "no" to both sets of questions, I must examine how
the performance of torch songs and autoethographic texts moves audiences both
within themselves and within the world.

Here is my answer. First, the torch song and the autoethnography are both
acts of love (see Tedlock 1991: 69; Anna Deavere Smith quoted in Crawford
1996: 167). Their performance (in writing or on stage) is a conscious act of being
in love with another and staying true to that love in our representations. The
torch singer and the autoethnographer invite audiences into this love. As performers, we ask our listeners to live in our—and their own—desire for the other,
even when this desire may seem destructive and painful and politically impotent.

However, being in love is not always (or only) easy or natural or cathartic.
Being in love can also be startling and alienating and instructive. For the torch

singer, this means infusing the lyrics with not only the pain and longing, but also the irony and wisdom of unrequited love. How does the torch singer perform both "sides" of being in love? In "Lover, Come Back to Me," Billie Holiday sings the rote, lyrical meaning of the song (lover, come back), adding a contrapuntal discourse just beneath and behind the beat—a discourse that says, "Lover, please stay away—I am immensely enjoying this state of freedom" (Davis 1998: 175). The torch singer encourages audiences to say, in Bertolt Brecht's terms, "Yes, I have felt like that too—Just like me—It's only natural—It'll never change," *as well as*, "I'd never have thought it—That's not the way—That's extraordinary, hardly believable—It's got to stop" (1964: 71).

How does Holiday inspire her audiences to engage this "doubled" meaning of her lyrics? She invites us to participate in the performance, to meet her halfway in creating a heightened emotional atmosphere and embarking on the passionate journey wrought in her material (Clements 1998: 32). She works on our inner thoughts and feelings as well as our presence in the world around us. She engages us as individuals and as social beings (Moore 1989: 45). Music scholar Will Friedwald notes, "Billie Holiday's art is the kind that takes you deeper inside yourself and ultimately out again" (1990: 126). Angela Davis adds, "in her phrasing, her timing, the timbre of her voice, the social roots of pain and despair in women's emotional lives are given a lyrical legibility" (1998: 177). It is this inward, then outward, journey that makes torch performances profoundly moving in ways that are, at times, difficult to express.

Autoethnographies also move from the inside of the author to outward expression while working to take readers inside themselves and ultimately out again (Denzin 1997: 208). Readers and audiences are invited to share in the emotional experience of an author. The test of such texts and performances comes down to whether they evoke in readers a "feeling that the experience described is authentic, that it is believable and possible" (Ellis 1995: 318–19). In telling their stories, autoethnographers ask readers to embark on a collaborative journey that tacks between individual experience and social roles, relationships, and structures (Jackson 1989: 18). As Michael Jackson notes, the stories of autoethnography begin "with the experience of one person, but others make it over to themselves and give it new uses and interpretations" (1989: 18).

This is what thinking about torch singing as autoethnography (and autoethnography as torch singing) teaches me: Create a highly charged atmosphere and heightened emotional state with and for my audience. Then use this energy to understand and critique my own relationships, as well as the place of

STACY HOLMAN JONES

these relationships in larger social structures and histories (Moore 1989: 45). Within the intimate, sensual contact among readers and texts, torch singing and autoethnography create a space of "critical vigilance" in which "communities of resistance are forged to sustain us"; a place where we come to know that "we are not alone" (adapted from hooks 1995: 220–21).[2] In these spaces and places, torch singing and autoethnography become memory and performance, passion and cause, unbearable and light, a torch song and a political protest. They become the way we were, the way we are, and the way we might be.

I type these last words and save the file. I have been and remain done and undone by my subjectivity and the ways my subjectivity touches and blurs with and hinges on the subjectivities of others. I leave my office and return to the living room. I watch the last scene of the film again. I see Katie spy Hubbell across a busy New York street. I watch Hubbell return to his fiancée and Katie return to her work. I hear Barbra sing. I let my husband see me cry.

Notes

1. Joni Jones writes that performance ethnography "honors the embodied acts of interaction and dialogue. Indeed, performance ethnography is how the body does culture" (1996: 132).
2. Hooks writes these words about African American performance artists. She views African American performance as a place where identities, subjugated knowledges, and historical memories must be reclaimed (1995: 220). These goals can also be said to motivate and sustain feminist performance practices, including torch singing and, in many cases, autoethnography.

References

Abu-Lughod, Lila. 1993. *Writing Women's Worlds: Bedouin Stories*. Berkeley: University of California Press.

Behar, Ruth. 1996. *The Vulnerable Observer: Anthropology That Breaks Your Heart*. Boston: Beacon Press.

Brecht, Bertolt. 1964. *Brecht on Theater: The Development of an Aesthetic,* ed. and trans. John. Willet. 1957. Reprint, New York: Hill and Wang.

Capo, Kay Ellen, and Kristin M. Langellier. 1994. "Anna Deavere Smith on 'Fires in the Mirror,'" *Text and Performance Quarterly* 14(1): 62–75.

Clements, Marcelle. 1998. "Sighing, a French Sound Endures." *New York Times* (October 18), AR1, 32–35.

Conquergood, Dwight. 1985. *Between Two Worlds: The Hmong Shaman in America* (documentary film). Chicago: Siegel Productions.

Crawford, Lyall. 1996. "Personal Ethnography." *Communication Monographs* 63: 158–70.

Davis, Angela Y. 1998. *Blues Legacies and Black Feminism: Gertrude "Ma" Rainey, Bessie Smith, and Billie Holiday.* New York: Pantheon.

Denzin, Norman K. 1997. *Interpretive Ethnography: Ethnographic Practices for the 21st Century.* Thousand Oaks, Calif.: Sage.

Dolan, Jill. 1993. *Presence and Desire: Essays on Gender, Sexuality, Performance.* Ann Arbor: University of Michigan Press.

Ellis, Carolyn. 1995. *Final Negotiations: A Story of Love, Loss and Chronic Illness.* Philadelphia: Temple University Press.

Ellis, Carolyn, and Michael G. Flaherty. 1992. "An Agenda for the Interpretation of Lived Experience." In *Investigating Subjectivity: Research on Lived Experience,* ed. Carolyn Ellis and Michael G. Flaherty (pp. 1–13). Newbury Park, Calif.: Sage.

Friedwald, Will. 1990. *Jazz Singing: America's Great Voices from Bessie Smith to Bebop and Beyond.* New York: Scribner's Sons.

Hamm, Charles. 1979. *Yesterdays: Popular Song in America.* New York: W. W. Norton.

Holiday, Billie. 1992. *Lady Sings the Blues,* written with William Dufty. 1956. Reprint, New York: Penguin.

hooks, bell. 1995. "Performance Practice As a Site of Opposition." In *Let's Get It On: The Politics of Black Performance,* ed. Catherine Ugwu (pp. 210–32). Seattle, Wash.: Bay Press.

Jackson, Michael. 1989. *Paths Toward a Clearing: Radical Empiricism and Ethnographic Inquiry.* Bloomington: Indiana University Press.

Jones, Joni L. 1996. "The Self As Other: Creating the Role of Joni the Ethnographer for 'Broken Circles.'" *Text and Performance Quarterly* 16(2): 131–45.

Kundera, Milan. 1991. *Immortality,* trans. Peter Kusi. New York: Perennial Classics.

———. 1985. *The Unbearable Lightness of Being,* trans. Michael Henry Heim. New York: Harper & Row.

Moore, John. 1989. "'The Hieroglyphics of Love': The Torch Singers and Interpretation." *Popular Music* 8(1): 31–58.

Paglia, Camille. 1996. "The Way She Was." In *Diva: Barbra Streisand and the Making of a Superstar,* ed. Ethlie Ann Vare (pp. 221–26). New York: Boulevard Books.

Phelan, Peggy. 1993. *Unmarked: The Politics of Performance*. New York: Routledge.

Pobryn, Elspeth. 1993. "Moving Selves and Stationary Others: Ethnography's Ontological Dilemma." In *Sexing the Self: Gendered Positions in Cultural Studies*, ed. Elspeth Pobryn (pp. 58–81). New York: Routledge.

Reed-Danahay, Deborah E. 1997. "Introduction." In *Autoethnography: Rewriting the Self and the Social*, ed. Deborah E. Reed-Danahay (pp. 1–17). Oxford: Berg.

Sayre, Henry M. 1989. *The Object of Performance: The American Avant-Garde since 1970*. Chicago: University of Chicago Press.

Stark, Ray, producer, and Sidney Pollack, director. 1973. *The Way We Were* (film). Raystar Productions, Burbank, California.

Streisand, Barbra. 1974. "The Way We Were." On *The Way We Were* (recording). Burbank, Calif.: Columbia.

Tedlock, Barbara. 1991. "From Participant Observation to the Observation of Participation: The Emergence of Narrative Ethnography." *Journal of Anthropological Research* 47: 69–94.

Van Maanen, John. 1995. "An End to Innocence: The Ethnography of Ethnography." In *Representation in Ethnography*, ed. John Van Maanen (pp. 1–35). Thousand Oaks, Calif.: Sage.

White, John. 1987. *Billie Holiday*. New York: Universe.

Making a Mess and Spreading It Around: Articulation of an Approach to Research-Based Theater

Ross E. Gray, Vrenia Ivonoffski, and Christina Sinding

Since 1998 we have been engaged in the heady, dangerous work of linking social science research to drama. Similar to others in this fledgling field, we are interested in the complicated process of producing "messy texts" that expand the relevance of qualitative research (for example, Conquergood 1991; Denzin 1997; Ellis and Bochner 1992; Jackson 1989; Marcus 1994; McCall 2000; Mienczakowski 1996; Pelias 1999; Trinh 1991; Walstrom 1996). We agree with Denzin that performance texts have the potential to be "the single most powerful way for ethnography to recover yet interrogate the meanings of lived experience" (1997: 94). Research presented in dramatic form communicates findings viscerally, beyond or below the usual cognitive filtering mechanisms familiar to academic discourse. In this chapter, we will discuss our experiences in trying to achieve the potential of research-based drama. We offer this description of our approach not as the right way to do things, but as one possibility among many. We offer it to move forward the discussion of how research-based drama gets done. With notable exceptions (Mienczakowski

1999; Mienczakowski and Morgan 1998; Pelias 1999; Saldana 1998), we have found little of such detailed discussion among the writings of those experimenting with performance texts. Perhaps future social scientists will be spared the extremities of terror we faced in trying to figure things out from scratch. Perhaps we can spare them nothing, and terror is just part of the experience.

Recent experimentations with performance texts have taken various forms, organized conceptually by Denzin into categories (dramatic texts, natural texts, performance science texts, ethnodramas). Our work best fits within the most complicated of these genres—"ethnodramas that merge natural script dialogues with dramatized scenes and the use of composite characters" (1997: 99). We have produced two forty-minute dramas, described briefly below.

Handle with Care? arose out of two qualitative research studies. In the first study, focus groups were held in Ontario with women with metastatic breast cancer. Our purpose was to investigate their information needs and the life issues they were facing. Then we interviewed oncologists, asking them about the issues that women in the focus group study had identified as important. Our research team did a thematic analysis of interview transcripts, wrote it up, and got it published in a cancer journal (Gray et al. 1998). But on an impulse, born of years of festering dissatisfaction with the academic publishing game, of creative juices too long left unattended, and of making too little of a difference in the world, Ross decided to write a proposal to "translate" the research findings into a drama. A partnership was achieved with Act II Studio, a theater program for older adults at Ryerson Polytechnic University in Toronto. As artistic director of Act II Studio, Vrenia agreed to bring her skills to the development of the drama. Chris signed on to document the entire process. Although initially reluctant, both Ross and Chris ended up extending their usual researcher roles by becoming actors in the production. And Vrenia extended her usual directorial role by engaging with the conventions of social science research.

There are two versions of *Handle with Care?*—one for health professionals working in oncology and one for community audiences. The performance consists of a series of interconnecting vignettes that reveal the dilemmas faced by ill women and those who care for them. The production has been very well received (Gray, Sinding, et al. 2000). By the time *Handle with Care?* ended in June 2000, we had done close to 200 performances across North America, mostly in Canada. Media coverage was extensive, with countless local and regional television and newspaper reports. A documentary radio show was broadcast nationally, and a film documentary is in process.

Our more recent research-based dramatic production (opened in February 2000), *No Big Deal?*, documents the issues facing men with prostate cancer and their spouses. Gendered responses to health and illness are performed and problematized. Once again, the starting point was funded and research undertaken by Ross and a team at the Toronto-Sunnybrook Regional Cancer Centre (Gray, Fitch, et al. 2000). Men and their spouses had been interviewed (separately) three times: before surgery to remove the men's prostates, two months after surgery, and a year later.

Although we have done only six performances at the time of this writing, there has already been an enthusiastic response to *No Big Deal?* An Ontario-wide tour is scheduled. We have also been invited to present at conferences, including a plenary performance at the annual conference for Canadian family physicians. And the media is primed to follow up on the success of *Handle with Care?* Joe Fiorito (2000), a columnist for the *National Post,* one of Canada's national newspapers, attended an early rehearsal for *No Big Deal?* and described it as "smart, sharp and oddly compelling." He also wrote, "*No Big Deal?* is a pastiche, a series of quick sketches, some of which are funny and some of which are bare-bones tragic, performed with few props and a full dose of sports and war metaphors."

In what follows we trace the major features of our work with research-based theater. We describe the original research aspect, move on to the script development (and continued research) process, discuss principles of performance and the role of audiences, and end with reflections on dissemination and fund-raising.

It's important, before diving into the specific components of our approach, to first say a bit about the overall decision-making process. One of the elements of Denzin's (1997) characterization of performance texts as "messy" is that many perspectives/experiences are potentially brought to bear in creating a production. We join him in celebrating such multiple influences. In the process of developing two dramatic productions, we deliberately created spaces for inputs from a variety of stakeholders. Thus, the final productions were the result of intense and prolonged negotiations across perspectives and across individuals. This was not a value-free process, and perspectives did not have equal weight in influencing what would eventually be included in the dramas. Script content was mostly derived from the recorded voices of women with breast cancer and men with prostate cancer (and their spouses) discussing their experiences. This decision to focus primarily on patient experiences (instead of, for example, researchers' theoretical interpretations or the artistic director's aesthetic sensibilities) is in keeping with the postmodernist concern of encouraging voices often silenced by dominant discourses, including that of biomedicine (Frank 1995). When it's agreed that no perspective holds ultimate authority, a privileging of the perspective of those most directly affected (by, for example, prostate cancer) is a position of basic respect (Richter 1994). Of course, the decision to put the perspectives of ill people at the forefront of our script development still left many decisions to be negotiated, such as which voices to include from among the many women and men with cancer.

In constructing our dramas, we did not feel compelled to stick to realistic, "in life" scenes, such as were actually described by research participants. We gave ourselves permission to go beyond issues of accurate representation, to dramatically evoke the essential aspects of ill peoples' experiences. For example, during *Handle with Care?* a magician appears and casts a spell on the audience. She warns them that when she says the magic words "I have metastatic breast cancer," that they will no longer see her. In her place they will now see an invalid or a victim or a warrior hero. *No Big Deal?* includes a series of battle scenes, where men and women duck and bob to avoid bombs and machine-gun fire. The maps they have been provided, to show them how to proceed in the campaign, are useless. The losses they experience are greater than they had expected. With these and other scenes we move away from concern with verisimilitude in the traditional sense, invoking a more evocative epistemology (Denzin 1997).

By the time we arrived at negotiated outcomes we were ready to treat our dramatic productions, complete with evocative and symbolic scenes, *as if* they were "truth." This was not the revealed truth of a realist tale (Van Maanen 1988), but rather an agreed upon construction that had been forged through enormous effort and lengthy conversation, privileging the experiences of people with cancer (as defined by them). Those of us involved with the projects were clear that no individual associated with the productions had the right to mess with these multiple-influenced constructions without reengaging in broader consultation. So while we continued to make changes over time, these were not undertaken lightly. We agreed to respect the work that had already gone into creating the productions.

The Original Research Phase

Some participatory researchers interested in drama do not engage in a formal study preceding script development (for example, Community Education Team 1999). They involve members of the community of interest directly in the creative process, so that the research process overlaps entirely with script development. While this approach has indisputable merit, especially for mobilizing community participation, we have chosen an approach that includes the experiences of a broader spectrum of the community (not just those willing to participate in theater), and that is temporally separated from script development. We think this has the benefit of broadening the conversation about the topic under consideration, giving us more to work with in the later script development phase. It also provides a kind of touchstone outside the script development group—to check that we have not strayed too far from the perspectives of those most directly affected by illness. Our inclusion of a formal and recognizable research phase has a political (as well as, possibly, a methodological) benefit in that it provides a level of credibility that can appeal to scholars and health professionals (that is, future audience members) who might otherwise be skeptical about arts-related approaches.

What are the requirements for studies that inform drama? We think that virtually any qualitatively oriented study that focuses on participants' own telling of their life situations can provide a foundation for later dramatic work—although the parameters of the study may put limits on what the drama can subsequently address. In both of our projects, we found it necessary to supplement originally gathered information with interviews with other groups (for example, physicians) in order to provide a richer perspective on the issues facing study participants.

In undertaking a formal research phase, we think it's important to involve members of the group under study in roles as investigators or consultants as well as in roles as research participants, so that their perspectives shape projects from the beginning. For example, a woman with breast cancer led the focus group discussions that informed *Handle with Care?* Just as with the later script development phase, we felt that the constitution of our research group needed to include multiple perspectives, so that our investigations did not inadvertently become too narrowly focused and come to serve the interests (material or academic) of a single dominant group (for example, health educators or oncologists). The interpretation of the focus group results and the writing of conclusions for publication in a journal involved a negotiation among team members, including patients/survivors, social scientists, and medical staff. These qualitative studies that informed our dramas, as with (we would argue) all qualitative studies, were thus deserving of the label "messy."

The Script Development Phase

In both of our projects we formed script development groups, which played a major part in the construction of the eventual performances. We will first describe the participants in these groups and then discuss the process we underwent.

Participants

Script development groups consisted of members of the research team, people with cancer (and spouses of patients, in the case of *No Big Deal?*), volunteer actors, and community activists.

The major collaboration across our two projects has been between Ross, as social scientist, and Vrenia, as artist/director. The two of us have learned much from each other about our respective worlds of expertise. But our reading of other performance texts leads us to believe that such collaboration is rarely sought, and where it exists it is usually less extensive. More typically, a social scientist writes a script based on his or her research and then either performs it him/herself or looks for other people to perform it. Sometimes a director is consulted about staging considerations. While the model of a single researcher/writer/director may be warranted for that rare individual who is multitalented (for example, Mienczakowski 1992–1994; Mienczakowski and Morgan 1993; Pelias 1999), in other cases it likely leads to bad theater. And by bad theater we mean representations that fail to deliver the promise of an engaging and visceral connection to the research material. Most social scientists would be well advised to seek collaboration with an expert in the expressive arts. In addition to increasing the likelihood of effective drama, collaboration also shows acknowledgment of and respect for the artistic skills that others have spent years crafting.

The presence of members of the research team seems to us important for the script development phase—as they provide a link to the original work and to the voices/experiences of the many people interviewed as part of that work. For our breast cancer project, Ross and Chris and another research team member participated actively in the script development process. In contrast, Ross was the only research team member present during group meetings to discuss the script for *No Big Deal?*—which at times made for a weak link to the voices of men interviewed as part of the original study. For example, he found himself defending some men in the initial study who stated that they were not deeply affected by their postsurgical impotence. While others (including two men with prostate cancer) in the script development group could be skeptical about such apparent "denial," Ross vividly recalled being convinced by a man he interviewed in his office. Yes, he and his wife had enjoyed a good sex life, but now he was surprised that the loss of sex was much less painful than he had feared. This story exemplifies the value of having researchers present and vocal during script development. The difficult trick is for them to engage in this process while also avoiding the claim of too much authority.

While the researcher plays one key role in script development, the artistic director is also critically important. It would have been inconceivable to undertake our two projects without the benefit of Vrenia's expertise. Drawing on her training in Paris with Jacques Lecoq, she influenced Ross and Chris about the value of a prolonged period of uncertainty in developing scripts. Vrenia is wary of charted paths, thrives on the creative energy of chaos, and is determined to let the form emerge from the work. While Ross and Chris were experienced in the necessary chaos of qualitative research, the shift to the unfamiliar context of theater seemed to require new capacities for tolerating uncertainty. Sometimes, during our first project, Vrenia had to provide reassurance that a production would indeed, eventually, emerge from the messy process of script development.

We have found it critically important to have members of the community of interest participate directly in script development. Although their perspectives were present through interview transcripts from the original research phase, it was extremely helpful to have ongoing direct interaction with women with metastatic breast cancer and men with prostate cancer about the issues in their lives—especially as these related to potential scenes being constructed for the respective dramas. While it would have been ideal to have participants in the original studies also participate in the script development groups, this was difficult to achieve for practical reasons. In each project, we had one person with cancer who participated both in the initial research and the script development phases.

One benefit of having people with cancer participate in script development related to the immediacy of feedback available about relevance of scenes to patients' experiences. Another benefit had to do with confronting the writers and acting group with illness-related issues in a direct, personal manner. When two of the men with prostate cancer were no longer able to regularly attend discussions and improvisations for the *No Big Deal?* production, our script development process temporarily floundered.

The participation of individuals relatively naive to the area under study has also proven useful to our creative process. For example, volunteer actors resisted acknowledging the medical seriousness of metastatic breast cancer in the early *Handle with Care?* meetings (lack of clear communication from the research team may have played a role here). We had to grapple with that resistance, learn to acknowledge the grim prognosis associated with metastatic disease, and eventually move on to focus on "living with" serious illness. These experiences helped us to better recognize the ways in which women with metastatic disease are rendered largely invisible in our society. It also highlighted the dominance of death-denying and positive-thinking discourses operating on a broad social level (Gray, Sinding, and Fitch, 2001), and to ensure their representation and problematizing in the eventual production.

Process

The process of working on script development involved two aspects, each interacting with the other. One was the attempt to present the findings from the original research studies in dramatic form. The other was to continue the knowledge development process beyond the original research, exploring additional dimensions of illness experience (listening to the stories of people with cancer, responding to those stories, and emotionally and bodily connecting to illness realities). This latter aspect of the script development could be considered a second research process (Sinding and Gray, unpublished), in which members of the group both engaged in secondary analysis of our studies with men with prostate cancer and women with metastatic breast cancer and were at the same time immersed in participatory research inquiry into those same topics.

In both our projects, the script development process began with a series of meetings to inform the newly constructed group about general information relevant to metastatic breast cancer or prostate cancer, and to discuss and review material from the original research studies. As we proceeded beyond the early informational phase, the women with metastatic breast cancer and men with prostate cancer participating in the script development groups told stories about their experiences. Other group members raised impressions, fears, and concerns in response to these stories. This mode of working reflected the assumption that interpersonal interaction can produce understandings that are difficult or impossible to achieve through more unidirectional information giving (Ellis and Berger, 2002). The interactive process also involved engaging the emotional experiences of group members to create deeper, sometimes new, understandings about illness experience. At times this occurred deliberately, as when a woman with metastatic disease in the *Handle with Care?* group insisted on informing others through acting out the agony of her diagnosis with metastatic disease. The result: Other group members came to better sense what it must be like to receive such a diagnosis. This intervention was in keeping with the writing of feminist theorists who have argued that emotions are central to knowledge construction processes (Jaggar 1989; Ellis 1991; Stanley and Wise 1993). Other interventions in the script development group were less deliberate but had a similar effect in shaping and defining understanding. A man with prostate cancer spoke poignantly to the *No Big Deal?* script development group about his ongoing struggles with postsurgical impotence. A new and deeper level of sympathy for men's experience was suddenly present in the room, especially among the women who had previously tended to downplay the importance of sexual intercourse (as opposed to other expressions of physical intimacy) for a couple's satisfaction with marital relationship and with life in general.

The script development process shifted, and took on greater intensity, when Vrenia insisted we get on our feet and bodily improvise scenes related to the themes identified in the original research and through group discussions. While some improvisations were language-based, others were entirely silent, involving the digestion of verbal/emotional material into visual images. Improvisation of scenes went on for a long time in both projects, and we collectively came to "know" the issues of metastatic breast cancer and prostate cancer in new ways— through our bodies. Each of us played patients, doctors, and family members, and felt the varying positions of helplessness, awkwardness, or competence as we shifted and changed according to circumstances.

The use of improvisation exercises is consistent with a growing recognition of the place of the body in constructing knowledge (Conquergood 1991). For example, Jackson has written about the importance for ethnographers to reestablish "the intimate connection between our bodily experience in the everyday world and our conceptual life" (1989: 18). An embodied research process is thus one that features deliberate inclusion of a full range of sensory experience for intensifying cultural understanding.

While the exploration process involved in script development work felt confusing some of the time, it allowed material to experientially coalesce for group participants. Vrenia encouraged participants to immerse themselves in the worlds of, for example, women with breast cancer or oncologists. This joining process was key not only for informing script development, but also because many of the group participants would eventually act out their understandings on stage.

The eventual result of the various script development processes was a menu of images, scenes, and quotes, drawn from the improvisation exercises, from the stories of those participating in the script development groups and from the interview transcripts from the original research. Deciding what to include in the script from the menu was arrived at in large part through group discussion, but also involved a sorting process undertaken by the scriptwriter(s), as well as feedback about drafts of the script from group members. For *Handle with Care?* Vrenia wrote most of the script, with others contributing selected pieces. For *No Big Deal?* Vrenia and Ross cowrote the script in roughly equal measures. Both processes had their advantages. Because the group contribution was less extensive and rich for *No Big Deal?* than it had been for *Handle with Care?*, it was problematic to determine scene content and tone, leaving more for the scriptwriters to work out on their own. Intense discussion, argument, and improvisation between Vrenia and Ross thus became essential for finalizing a script. Because of considerable tension about representations of gender in the *No Big Deal?* project, it was critical to have both a male and a female perspective represented in the writing process.

As we proceeded with script development, we deliberately sought feedback from sources outside the group. For example, Vrenia's partner, John Pike, read the *No Big Deal?* script and complained that men too often were being portrayed as inept at coping. His input contributed to an ongoing negotiation between Ross and Vrenia about this very issue, and eventually led to a decision to make script changes. Then there were readings and trial performances to groups, including members of the original research team, health professionals, people with cancer (including, where possible, participants in the original studies), and individuals with theater training. Input was recorded, reviewed, and debated. Many, but not all, suggested changes were made. Each new rewrite had to be considered in light of the original research, the accumulated learning of the script development group, as well as the feedback from readers and audience members. While a decision to rewrite had to be approved by both Vrenia and Ross, they typically consulted with all or at least part of the script development group.

Changes to the script continue to be made over time, as reactions from audiences help to clarify points of unintended ambiguity, problems in tone, or neglected features of illness experience. For example, we added some material to help reflect single women's experiences with cancer after it was pointed out to us that many scenes and lines were family related. But we also have had to decide that we could not be all things to all people, and have sometimes not added suggested scenes about legitimate aspects of cancer patients' experiences. For example, several people have wondered about the experiences of aboriginal women with metastatic disease (or of women from other nondominant ethnic groups). Our lack of relevant research material has kept us from trying to dramatically formulate a response to the question. Similarly, our study with men with prostate cancer focused only on men who chose prostatectomy as their treatment, leaving us largely silent about the comparative experiences of, for example, men who chose treatment with radiation seed implants.

Staging the Performance

Both *Handle with Care?* and *No Big Deal?* are tightly scripted. Actors are expected (although they/we do not always succeed in efforts) to speak the exact words in their scripts, using tones and bodily gestures and postures that have been carefully chosen and practiced. Many hours and days of rehearsal are required. Before each new performance we go over it all again, reminding ourselves, reminding our bodies, of our commitment to getting it "right." This is not to suggest that we think we have found, or are presenting through our drama, the ultimate truths about cancer, and that no other representations would have value. We are just concerned about being as faithful as possible to our own negotiated version of truth, with its privileging of the voices of ill people in our studies. When it comes to performance, then, we abandon our previous commitment to messiness. We seek a performance that is, as much as possible, deliberately fixed in a shape that we have predetermined.

Our approach stands in contrast to improvisational theater. While we see the potential value for more improvisational types of research-based drama, especially in academic settings where the usual forms of knowledge representation are ripe for maximal disruption, this is not our way. Improvisation, except when used within carefully circumscribed parameters, substitutes the value of individual expression for that of negotiated collective understanding. An improvisational approach may also make it less likely that groups under study will recognize themselves on stage, which is one possible criterion by which to judge an ethnographic or performance text (Ellis and Flaherty 1992). When an actor in the *Handle with Care?* project balked at using the terminology that came from an interview transcript with an oncologist, we explained to him that this is how oncologists talked when we interviewed them, this is one way they will know that they have been understood, and this is what will keep them from walking out in the middle of our presentation at hospital Grand Rounds.

We have included postmodern sensibilities in our productions by representing many different voices and perspectives. For example, some men speak on stage about being devastated by erectile dysfunction, some say it's been rough but they have learned to cope, some say it's no big deal. Individual actors also take on different roles—women with metastatic disease become doctors and Ross, the obvious choice as doctor, becomes an angry adolescent, then an insensitive husband.

Who should do the acting in research-based drama productions? Two of the actors in *Handle with Care?* are women with metastatic disease. When they are on stage it adds an extra dimension of poignancy to the performance. Their presence also opens unique possibilities for ill women in the audience, as they explore life options for themselves through identification with the actors with metastatic disease. But when actors without cancer have immersed themselves in the issues of illness, and are willing to follow the artistic director's detailed instructions for representing ill persons (or doctors or nurses), there is plenty of poignancy, and the impact can still be huge. Actors who represent the community under study are thus an added benefit, not a necessity.

Audience

Audiences at our two productions play very much the role that most audiences do when they attend formal theater productions. They sit and watch, sometimes laugh, sometimes cry. Afterward, we have a discussion period. During this time, audience members give their responses to what they have seen, share their own illness or health care system experiences, and ask questions about the project. When the formal discussion ends, people approach individual cast members to ask other questions, share other details. We can see other possibilities for audience involvement. For example, postperformance small group discussions might work well for groups of patients in a workshop context.

Given the type of material we present, we would not deliberately seek audience participation during the performance itself. We would avoid the type of scenario described by Denzin, in which "the author can even bring the audience into the performance, do a sing-along, hand out a script, give audience members speaking parts, or make a communal performance out of a scholarly text" (1997: 123).

Why do we take this restrained approach to audience participation? To be honest, personal preference is involved. The three of us would avoid going to a production that we knew employed high levels of audience participation. We suspect our retrogressive attitudes are representative of a majority of the public. This suggests a reduced dissemination potential for productions featuring active audience participation.

Especially in the early performances of *Handle with Care?* we often had small audiences. Women with metastatic breast cancer were afraid to attend in case their hope would be undermined, causing them to leave in despair. They already were vulnerable and often chose not to risk any engagement that might increase their vulnerability. Often, the day after a performance we would be invited to come back to the same city and perform again. Those who saw the production now were able to reassure others that it was funny and helpful and, though difficult in moments, essentially safe. A much larger audience would be ensured for the next performance. In the prostate cancer production, the audience goes entirely quiet during several monologues in which issues about sexuality and incontinence are aired. This is unspeakable stuff, hard for many men to sit through. In these contexts of danger, it would be unconscionable, we believe, to introduce additional risk.

The same principle applies for health professionals. When interviewed about their response to *Handle with Care?*, many noted that seeing the drama on stage gave them the possibility of distance that they were denied in their everyday working lives. At work they would be seated across the desk from the crying woman who has just found out she has metastatic disease. But as audience members, they could sit back and watch, for once freed of the need to figure things out, to act in the moment. And with that freedom, they reported being able to see more clearly their own impact on patients, feel more directly the pain of the patients they worked with, and of their own situations. These health professionals needed distance in order to reflect on their lives. We wouldn't want to mess with that.

We don't wish to give the impression that our audiences do or should take a purely passive stance in relation to the dramas we perform. In contrast, we create the possibility for audience members to actively enter, through imagination, the world of an ill person (and an oncologist and a family member). We challenge audiences to use the material in the plays to interpret and construct their own understandings about the social terrain of health and illness, about the possibilities of suffering and alleviating suffering. Audience members thus become coproducers of the drama, not through action, but through the meanings they bring to the performance and the meanings they construct from the performance.

Dissemination

Although most social scientists give lip service to the importance of dissemination of research findings, it is rare for scholars to seriously attempt to reach beyond academic circles. Laurel Richardson (2000) describes usual dissemination practices as consisting of publishing articles in obscure academic journals and writing books that sit unread in university libraries. She pulls no punches in pointing at the implications of such practices. "It seems foolish at best, and narcissistic and wholly self-absorbed at worst, to spend months or years doing research that ends up not being read and not making a difference to anything but the author's career" (2000: 924).

Part of the appeal of drama is its potential for creating broader access to social science research, making it more likely that researchers can make a difference in the world. But the creation of a drama in no ways ensures such an impact. Indeed, if a research-based theater production is performed solely for small audiences of like-minded academics, as just the newest fashion in representation, one can question whether there is any increased value. A critical point of research-based drama, as we see it, is to move the influence of research outward from universities and other academic settings, to include communities that were originally studied and the general public.

Our dissemination strategy with *Handle with Care?* was aided by history and location. Ross has worked within the cancer care system for more than a decade and is a familiar face in research circles. He also has developed contacts with many cancer patient/survivor groups. The year before we took *Handle with Care?* on the road, he had presented the results of studies with cancer self-help groups (outlining their merits for patients and for the broader health care system) for Grand Rounds at the regional cancer centers around Ontario. We decided to use the same dissemination strategy for our new drama venture. No one blinked twice when Ross booked himself into Grand Rounds in Kingston, and listed the topic of his talk as "Women Living with Metastatic Breast Cancer." Afraid that oncologists would break their habitual attendance at rounds if they found out they would not be getting their usual toneless monologue, complete with slides and pointers, he neglected to mention that a drama would take place. He needn't have been so paranoid. The response from health professionals was so enthusiastic that we quickly came out of the closet. As time progressed, and we encountered physicians in charge of organizing rounds who would become anxious about the possibility of drama being performed on hallowed ground, we would suggest they talk to some of their respected colleagues.

When we went to a city to present at a cancer center, we also held a community performance for the public. As an organizer of the provincewide network of breast cancer self-help groups, Chris was able to find members of local groups that would host the event. Sometimes a local unit of the Canadian Cancer Society would take the lead. We encouraged hosts to involve as many local groups as possible, thereby increasing the likelihood of a sizeable audience, while also fostering community collaboration. Often information tables would be set up, and sometimes there would be receptions after the performance.

People who had seen the production told others about it. We started to get invitations, lots of them. Some were for conference presentations, where we were able to access ready-made audiences without having to do any of the organizing.

We have pushed dissemination along by shamelessly seeking media coverage. For example, we organized a press conference, performing part of the production for Toronto media. We sent out press releases prior to our travel to each new city. We pursued newspaper and magazine reporters and broadcasters. Ross's persistent encouragement of a producer for the Canadian Broadcasting Corporation resulted in her creating the documentary that was aired on radio nationwide. Out-of-province invitations started to arrive. And so it has continued.

The promotional work is a little easier with the new production, as it's become more straightforward to get the attention of the media. Sometimes they come looking for us now, instead of the other way around. Our sponsors have also become more proactive in ensuring that the word gets out. For example, our major sponsor, the Canadian Cancer Society, is organizing a press conference for the beginning of Prostate Cancer Awareness Week, at which *No Big Deal?* will be performed. Learning from past experiences, the preparations for forthcoming performances around Ontario are more extensive, involving host organizations more fully—all in the service of drawing larger audiences. Instead of worrying that no one will be interested, now we worry about our ability to meet requests.

Funding

Money is a problem for those of us interested in research-based theater. Indeed, it makes no sense to discuss the merits of this approach to disseminating social science research without acknowledging the formidable financial barriers. Funding for the original studies on which our dramas were based came from major research funding agencies. But we do not think that these same agencies are ready to approve funding to mount and send on its way a theater production as part of research grants. To be honest, fearing rejection and the interminable waits for said rejection, we have not pursued this path. Instead we have turned to cancer organizations and corporations.

In the beginning, we were fortunate enough to receive an education grant from the Canadian Breast Cancer Foundation, which provided some of the initial money needed to mount the *Handle with Care?* production. But we had to proceed on faith, hoping other funds would be forthcoming. Eventually, after we were already performing for several months and fearing we would not have the money to meet our accumulating commitments, more funding was provided.

We would not have been able to get the production on its feet without additional support from corporate sponsors. Ross had a very steep learning curve as he began to wheel and deal in unfamiliar terrain (Gray, 2000). He quickly learned that sponsorship (for corporations and cancer organizations alike) is only partially related to the quality of a "product." It is also related to what can be provided to sponsors—acknowledgment, profile, access to potential purchasers and clients. We had to strike deals. We could have taken the moral high ground and decided not to accept money from pharmaceutical companies. But then we wouldn't have had a production. And both they and we agreed that they would make no demands about the content of the production.

When the time came to try to raise money for *No Big Deal?*, we ran into trouble. Even given our proven track record, and despite many submissions to foundations and corporations, we could not secure enough to pay Vrenia for her time in writing and directing. A potential major sponsor said they could not commit until they saw the finished production. Another sponsor would commit only after we had raised $50,000. So we had to barge ahead, hoping that success would bring the money. We planned a special preview performance, to which we would invite potential sponsors, and began daily prayers.

In addition to having money to pay Vrenia for her work, we have now raised sufficient funds for a tour of Ontario and to film a video of the *No Big Deal?* production (that will be sold at cost). Additional performances beyond the organized tour will be on a cost-recovery basis. And with all of this we have to pay close attention, balancing the need to treat the volunteer (that is, the unpaid) actors well with the need to keep travel costs down. We are fortunate to have the finance department of the Toronto-Sunnybrook Regional Cancer Centre to manage check requisitions and so on, but we have also found that the requirements of a traveling theater troupe are outside of the usual parameters of hospital business. When Ross and the rest of the troupe returned from a performance in Florida, yet another for which he had to front the expenses through his credit card, he was shocked to discover that he was now waiting to be reimbursed for $8,000 worth of project costs.

Realizing the Potential

Our continuing experience is helping us to better understand how to achieve the enormous potential of research-based theater. To recap, we have found a formal study to be a helpful precursor to the script development phase. During script development, we seek many participants, including an artistic director, researchers, members of the group under study, and nonaffected actors/volunteers. We also seek multiple strategies for exploring the topic, including review of research materials, telling of personal stories, evocation of relevant emotions, group discussion, and improvisation exercises. We value, and allow for, a prolonged period of uncertainty and messiness in developing the script. When it comes to performance, we do our best to achieve a careful, practiced production. Audiences are involved in our performances through engagement in meaning making and through postperformance discussion. Yet we do not ask for active physical/verbal participation in the drama itself. We use established structures and networks within the health care system to ensure that we can reach our target audiences. We relentlessly self-promote and use the media for our own purposes. And we continue to explore new possibilities for funding these projects that straddle the boundary between social science and theater.

Another aspect of realizing the potential of research-based theater, we believe, has to do with the tension between "representing" the worlds of those under study and "interrogating" those same worlds (Denzin 1997). Too much representing can lead to a feel-good formula in which everyone gets their say, but no one is held accountable. Too much interrogating can lead to a strong critique, but may too easily be rejected by those involved. We have struggled to find a balance in which, for example, men with prostate cancer and urologists can recognize themselves (and appreciate that representation), yet are still challenged to look at their own ways of being and coping. The advantages for men of stoicism and silence are shown on stage, but limitations of these approaches also are revealed, including how these ways of dealing with things can negatively affect people who care about them. Similarly, urologists are able to recognize themselves on stage as overworked and struggling to be helpful to men, yet they also are exposed to their own (usually) unwitting neglect of, and insensitivity to, patients.

As a final comment, we have struggled in this chapter about how much to reveal about and expound on the challenges we have encountered in taking research onto the stage. It's been messy work, and although we are mostly ecstatic about how things have gone, not all of the specific messes are so easily celebrated. But we feel it is critical to have open discussions of the complexities inherent in this work. While there's great potential to be realized with research-based drama, there are also endless dilemmas. Let's learn what we can from each other's efforts.

References

Community Education Team. 1999. "Fostering Relationality When Implementing and Evaluating a Collective-Drama Approach to Preventing Violence against Women." *Psychology of Women Quarterly* 23: 95–109.

Conquergood, Dwight. 1991. "Rethinking Ethnography: Towards a Critical Cultural Politics." *Communication Monographs* 58: 179–94.

Denzin, Norman K. 1997. *Interpretive Ethnography: Ethnographic Practices for the 21st Century.* Thousand Oaks, Calif.: Sage.

Ellis, Carolyn. 1991. "Emotional Sociology." *Studies in Symbolic Interaction* 12: 123–45.

Ellis, Carolyn, and Leigh Berger. 2002. "Their Story/My Story/Our Story: Including the Researcher's Experience in Interview Research." In *Handbook of Interview*

Research, ed. Jaber Gubrium and James Holstein (pp. 849–75). Thousand Oaks, Calif.: Sage.

Ellis, Carolyn, and Arthur P. Bochner. 1992. "Telling and Performing Personal Stories: The Constraints of Choice in Abortion." In *Investigating Subjectivity: Research on Lived Experience,* ed. Carolyn Ellis and Michael Flaherty (pp. 79–101). Newbury Park, Calif.: Sage.

Ellis, Carolyn, and Michael Flaherty. 1992. *Investigating Subjectivity: Research on Lived Experience.* Newbury Park, Calif.: Sage.

Fiorito, Joe. 2000. "A Play about What Men Don't Talk About." *The National Post* (January 18): B5.

Frank, Arthur W. 1995. *The Wounded Storyteller: Body, Illness, and Ethics.* Chicago: University of Chicago Press.

Gray, Ross. 2000. "Graduate School Never Prepared Me for This: Reflections on the Challenges of Research-Based Theatre." *Reflective Practice* 1: 337–90.

Gray, Ross, Margaret Fitch, Catherine Phillips, Manon Labrecque, and Karen Fergus. 2000. "Managing the Impact of Illness: The Experiences of Men with Prostate Cancer and their Spouses." *Journal of Health Psychology* 5: 525–42.

Gray, Ross, Marlene Greenberg, Margaret Fitch, Carol Sawka, Ann Hampson, and Manon Labrecque. 1998. "Information Needs of Women with Metastatic Breast Cancer." *Cancer Prevention and Control* 2: 57–62.

Gray, Ross, Christina Sinding, and Margaret Fitch. 2001. "Navigating the Social Context of Metastatic Breast Cancer: Reflections on a Project Linking Research to Drama." *Health* 5: 233–48.

Gray, Ross, Christina Sinding, Vrenia Ivonoffski, Margaret Fitch, Ann Hampson, and Marlene Greenberg. 2000. "The Use of Research-Based Theatre in a Project Related to Metastatic Breast Cancer." *Health Expectations* 3: 137–44.

Jackson, Michael. 1989. *Paths Toward a Clearing: Radical Empiricism and Ethnographic Inquiry.* Bloomington: Indiana University Press.

Jaggar, Alison. 1989. "Love and Knowledge: Emotion in Feminist Epistemology." *Inquiry* 32: 151–76.

Marcus, G. E. 1994. "What Comes (Just) After 'Post'? The Case of Ethnography." In *The Handbook of Qualitative Research,* ed. Norman K. Denzin and Yvonna Lincoln (pp. 563–74). Thousand Oaks, Calif.: Sage.

McCall, Michal M. 2000. "Performance Ethnography: A Brief History and Some Advice." In *The Handbook of Qualitative Research,* 2nd ed., ed. Norman K. Denzin and Yvonna Lincoln (pp. 421–34). Thousand Oaks, Calif.: Sage.

Mienczakowski, Jim. 1992/1994. *Syncing Out Loud: A Journey into Illness.* Brisbane: Griffith University Reprographics.

———. 1996. "On the Road to Catharsis: A Theoretical Framework for Change." *Qualitative Inquiry* 2: 439–62.

———. 1997. "Theatre of Change." *Research in Drama Education* 2: 159–72.

———. 1999. "Ethnography in the Hands of Participants: Tools of Dramatic Discovery." In *Studies in Educational Ethnography, Volume 2: Explorations in Methodology,* ed. Geoffrey Walford and Alex Massey (pp. 1–13). Oxford: JAI Press.

Mienczakowski, Jim, and Steve Morgan. 1993. *Busting: The Challenge of the Drought Spirit.* Brisbane: Griffith University Reprographics.

———. 1998. "Finding Closure and Moving On: An Examination of Challenges Presented to the Constructors of Research Performances." *Drama* 5: 22–29.

Pelias, Ronald J. 1999. *Writing Performance: Poeticizing the Researcher's Body.* Carbondale: Southern Illinois University Press.

Richardson, Laurel. 2000. "Writing: A Method of Inquiry." In *Handbook of Qualitative Methods,* 2nd ed., ed. K. Denzin and Yvonna Lincoln (pp. 923–48). Thousand Oaks, Calif.: Sage.

Richter, D. 1994. "Existentialism and Postmodernism: Continuities, Breaks, and Some Consequences for Medical Theory." *Theoretical Medicine* 15: 253–65.

Saldana, Johnny. 1998. "Ethical Issues in an Ethnographic Performance Text: The Dramatic Impact of Juicy Stuff." *Research in Drama Education* 3: 181–96.

Sinding, Christina, and Ross Gray. Unpublished. "Coming to Knowledge about Metastatic Breast Cancer: A Case Study of Epistemic Practice."

Stanley, Liz, and Sue Wise. 1993. *Breaking Out Again: Feminist Ontology and Epistemology.* London: Routledge.

Trinh, T. M-ha. 1991. *When the Moon Waxes Red: Representation, Gender and Cultural Politics.* New York: Routledge.

Van Maanen, John. 1988. *Tales of the Field: On Writing Ethnography.* Chicago: University of Chicago Press.

Walstrom, M. 1996. "'Mystory' of Anorexia Nervosa: New Discourses for Change and Recovery." *Cultural Studies: A Research Annual* 1: 67–99.

INTERLUDE

Breaking Habits and Cultivating Home

LESA LOCKFORD

N orman Denzin argues that "a text must do more than awaken moral sensibilities. It must move the other and the self to action" (1997: xxi). In general, I agree with Denzin. Yet, as I contemplate the chapters brought together here under the rubric of autoethnographic performance, and as I consider how to respond, what sets in, at least initially, is an inability to be moved to action. I do not mean to say that I experience paralysis, for paralysis connotes not only an inability to move but also an absence of sensation as well. In *Composing Ethnography*, Art Bochner and Carolyn Ellis noted that what they call "ethnographic alternatives" is scholarship that should make us not only think but also feel (1996: 18). The chapters within this section make it nearly impossible for me to come away without an abundance of feeling, without having been moved—not to action—but to stillness, moved to stillness by the power and the pathos of the stories these authors tell. When I say they are stories that move me to stillness, I mean that they call me to take pause, to reflect, to feel. And then, once having taken that time, perhaps I can take up the mantle of Denzin's call to action.

I had the good fortune not only to be present for the performance of these works at the conference, but also now to have gained access to them in textual form so that I could take that pause for reflection before bringing my own voice into the conversation. I am grateful for the opportunity to add my voice to these writings, even while I am mindful that given their diverse range and the space limitations necessarily accorded me here, my contribution can only sound a tiny accompaniment to the amplitude and resonant depth of the chorus I join. As I contemplate these writings that thematically link ethnography, culture, and performance, I consider how their authors each address these three things, and in doing so I reflect how easy and how mistaken it would be for me to treat those things *as* things, as nouns, as stable artifacts subject to evaluation by uncontested criteria and immutable categories. As the scope and diversity of these essays suggest, ethnography, culture, and performance should be thought of as processes, as events, in short, as acts rather than artifacts.

Ethnography, then, is not to be regarded as a type of scholarship so much as a mode of inquiry, a way of access if you will. *Culture,* then, is not to be regarded as something we have or something we go to, but rather as the event or events that we cultivate; that is to say, culture is collectively constituted through the construction, the deconstruction, and the reconstruction of the edifices in which we physically, as well as spiritually, imaginatively, and psychologically, dwell. *Performance,* then, is a process in which through the doing we come to be and, concomitantly, we come to know—to know ourselves, our culture, our world.

Mary Francis Hopkins argues that performance should be viewed as the negotiation of agency within a site of resistance (1995: 233). Similarly, Dwight Conquergood observes that performance, which "flourishes within a zone of contest and struggle," is by virtue of its kinetic momentum capable of "unleash[ing] centrifugal forces that keep culture in motion, ideas in play, [and] hierarchies unsettled," and is thereby both a "culture-creating" and "creative and contentious space" (1995: 137–39). Performance puts the focus once more on situated action, on the act of knowing, and on the struggle that is being-in-the-world. Thus, ethnography is the process that gives us a way in to explore how we, as actors—whether in a theatrical frame or on the cultural "stage"—performatively constitute ourselves and our knowledge through the building, destroying, and rebuilding of that in which we dwell.

Martin Heidegger notes that the words "culture" and "cultivation" derive from the same root word traceable to the origins of the verb "to be" (1977: 349). Thus Heidegger's point is to argue that culture and being share a kind of linguistic bridge, an etymological heritage that suggests that the event of being is to cultivate, that the event of being is to construct culture. Each of these chapters asks us to consider how the actors construct, deconstruct, and/or rebuild their respective cultures; each of these essays also asks us to consider how the scholars who constructed them construct, deconstruct, or reconstruct culture through the performance of these forms of scholarship. Individually and collectively, these essays challenge us to consider how they function as scholarship. Thus as I locate my voice within this conversation, I have two goals. First, following Heidegger, I consider how the actors described within the stories dwell within their respective cultures. I do so in order to suggest how meaning is thereby disclosed. Second, I consider how these writings, which I read as a play script, an autoethnographic memoir, and a staged group performance, function as forms of scholarship in the wider academic community.

The chapters by Pelias and Jones ask us to consider how it is that we come to inhabit roles that we should perhaps find uninhabitable. The authors ask us to consider how it is that we resist abandoning those roles, even when the ground of our dwelling may be infertile and inhospitable. Moreover, they ask how it is that we can continue our habitation there when we may cultivate only divisiveness, destruction, unrequited desire, or despair. Pelias presents a tragic interpersonal script through which we witness the edifice of his relationship being built piece by impenetrable piece, where we witness each actor being rehearsed into roles that continue to maintain and reinforce that deadly structure, and where whatever possibility there may be of altering that structure or changing that script or those accustomed roles repeatedly gets rehearsed as impossible. The roles are habituated to the point where they in-habit the actors themselves. Like all habits, these become, if not comfortable, at least familiar ways of being. Even with the hostility of the terrain, these habits appear to become places within which each actor may retreat in order to psychologically and performatively dwell. Bonds are formed through a tacit agreement that each will play his or her role as rehearsed. With time, the actors become accustomed enough, habituated enough, to live within their roles and to play that script on demand, playing it even when that drama has no catharsis, where the only comfort is the familiarity of habit and where real comfort is perpetually absent. This is a drama where the dramatic conflict *is* the struggle to dismantle the roles in-habited by the actors but that remains a struggle impossible to move beyond, resulting in a perpetual return for all involved to the contained yet restless and habituated space of the status quo. There the actors abide in agitated and helpless inactivity and stumbling inarticulateness. There they constitute a world where what isn't said is more telling than what is, and where they remain incapable of finding the right thing to do, the right thing to say that will cultivate more productive or fulfilling relationships.

Alternatively, Jones inhabits a culture personified by motion and flux. From the here and now to the there and then, from the reel to the real, from the personal to the professional, she spirals along multiple interweaving trajectories, "doing" and "undoing" old habits and new. Even while she lingers lovingly in lamentation, the momentum of her prose gently breathes the promise of resolution, of catharsis. For it is through the lamentation—revisiting then halting the attempt to reassemble the ruins of what was and then refashioning her understanding of what was then and constituting afresh herself in the now—that we witness her "making, breaking, and remaking" (Conquergood 1995: 138) the cultural space of her personal and professional home(s). Reclaiming the old soil, then cultivating the new, she marks, re-marks, and re-marks again the territories of her being. In this autoethnographic lament, Jones is shimmeringly articulate about the ineffable, about those moments where the decision of what act to perform or what line to speak is preceded by the inarticulate gasp of indecision in the face of impending and inevitable consequences, no matter which decision she may ultimately enact. As we encounter and momentarily live in her desire, and our own, we vicariously experience her well-rehearsed and habituated somatic resonances and newfound longings made rich in the moment of recollection. Jones reminds us that a recursive process of searching, with all its stumbling and discomfort, with all its "melancholy, mourning, and release," is the foundation upon which re-search is built.

In Gray, Ivonoffski, and Sinding's chapter, the recursive process of research, and the very messiness that recursivity entails, is the point of entry into inquiry. The performances described reverberate with the messy cacophony that a diagnosis of cancer usually brings to people's lives. *Handle with Care?*, the performance about women living with metastatic disease, was presented at the conference on which this book is based. The stories, deftly orchestrated for performance, tell of fractured worlds, of the collision of cultures among doctor and patient, of the ill and the well; they tell of the collapse of custom and comfort as what was "home," with all the assumptions of stable relationships and role expectations, is made precarious and no longer habitable. The women try to cultivate a hospitable terrain for being within the all-too-present and fearful possibility of imminent nonbeing. Within the inescapable experience of pain visited on them by both the disease and the long arms of medical science, they struggle with the unknown and uncomfortable. The disease afflicts not only the women but also those around them. All must alter their lives to accommodate the new way of being presaged by the onset of breast cancer. Guilt, fear, self-hatred, silence, denial, and the absence of empathy block the road the women negotiate in their quest to reach a stable ground of being. Resentments proliferate: Children squirm in their recognition that their mothers cannot be relied on to do what they used to do; neighbors close their doors and erect walls of frozen, fearful, and fear-inducing silence; clarity and coherence are blocked by medical professionals with their impenetrable barrage of specialized jargon. Clinging to the world in which they once lived but that is no longer available to them in the same familiar ways, these women struggle to discover a path to clarity, communication, and psychological if not physical well-being.

Gray, Ivonoffski, and Sinding take the individual lives made messy by disease and bring to them composure through composition. The resultant arrangement allows isolated individuals to find strength in community wherein their voices may sound together, wherein they may harmonize in discord, and where their experiences resonate palpably beyond the parameter of the stage to those others in the audience who have fallen mute or who cry out unheard under the devastation wreaked upon their lives by cancer. As this community of actors on the stage discover and disclose ways to be and become, they develop an energizing awareness that they need not abide in enervating isolation and they cultivate instead new possibilities.

In all three of these chapters and performances, we see not only how the actors perform their roles but also how their performances are played out within the stultifying shadow of social expectations. The performative social expectations for the roles of "son," "father," "former lover," "academic," "mother," "wife," and "perfect patient" stand as edifices against which the actors' performances are measured. These authors raise the question of what responsibility we have for playing our given roles according to the confines of their socially prescribed definitions. Pelias asks how can the son be the "son" his father expects; how can the father be the "father" his son expects? Jones asks if the role of "academic" can accommodate and legitimate the scholarly performance of desire and torch. Gray, Ivonoffski, and Sinding, and the collective voices of the participants in their study, ask how women living with the life-altering physical and emotional pain of metastatic disease can perform the roles of "good mother," "good daughter," and "good patient" when the social expectations for those roles produce a culture of fumbling inarticulateness or stupefying silence for all involved. Also, we are urged to ask whether abandoning the constraints within those overdetermined roles would free the actors to build better relationships among a father and a son, among a woman, her work and her desire, among patient and doctor, mother and child, wives and husbands. Here is where we move closer to achieving Denzin's call to action. For in answering that question, previously dormant moral sensibilities arise in recognition of our responsibility to our authentic selves. By being present and engaged and offering compassionate voices and deeds to those who require our care, we can doff the apparently cozier habits of negligent inarticulateness.

The three chapters also reveal that as awkward and frustrating as this habituated negligence may be, continuing to cultivate those habits is somehow more comfortable than accepting the challenge to take the risk of changing direction and venturing into new domains. This challenge is evidently felt not only by the actors but also by the audience with whom they must negotiate the meanings. As works that transgress traditional borders of scholarship, they implicitly ask us to consider how we, as audience to these tales, dwell or resist dwelling within them. If we dismiss the actors' contingent choices, remaining outside and removed from the situations they describe, we miss the power and complexity of the performances. Contrarily, Pelias invites us to situate ourselves within his performance at the testy borders between circumstance and communicative choice. There we cannot help but reflect on how those borders are policed and create impenetrable frameworks of being, even in spite of the best intentions of all concerned. Jones invites us to linger in the slips between the indicative, the imperative, and the subjunctive moods constituted by loss and desire, and the expression of those absences. And from that place her song of experience is passionately sung through the antiphony of what has been and what might have been. As she stands in public solitude singing her song, we are invited to chime in as we recognize that the riches we have accumulated by our choices may have come at the expense of what might have blossomed along the road not taken. With Gray, Ivonoffski, and Sinding, we are repeatedly asked to stand at the intractable intersections between competing discourses in the social construction of the meaning of disease. In these junctures and gaps the discourses fail to adequately describe or address the concrete experience with which they purport to be concerned. Gray, Ivonoffski, and Sinding make it clear that it is experience, effect, and the choice to act that makes a difference to the ongoing cultivation of being.

And so it is that in order to dwell within these writings we must be invited in. As I consider the diverse ways these three chapters function as scholarly representation, I am reminded of the caveat Pelias notes in his book, *Writing Performance: Poeticizing the Researcher's Body* (1999), that in order for writing that takes the self as its subject to not be merely some vain, narcissistic act it must have two characteristics: First, "the story told [should] point beyond the self" and, second, it should "remind you that consequences happen on an individual level . . . [that] politics only matter as they unravel in individual lives, and individual lives only matter when they can make a political difference" (1999: 165). After being moved to stillness by these essays, I *am* thus, indeed, called into action. Pelias' chapter demands that I question instances of my own poor communicative choices and the absence of wisdom I have used in constructing whatever poorly built relationships I may have. Moreover, I am led to see more clearly the situational contingencies that structure and influence my flawed and sometimes pathetic ways of being. Pelias' text makes me unavoidably confront his humanity, his tragic human flaws and those of his painfully exposed family. As I do so, I am confronted with his unabashed vulnerability, with the risk he takes with this raw self-portrait. Ultimately, I am confronted on the level of somatic and affective engagement with the persuasive power of personal perspective. I see and feel the drama that is his relationship as an ultimately immutable script in search of an appropriate or perhaps a forgiving genre, none of which appears capable of capturing it or setting it right. By loosely organizing his story under the canopy of "ethnodrama," he continually reminds me that I am a player and at minimum a cowriter of the scripts I perform. My accountabilities are inescapably my own.

Unlike Pelias's chapter, where the resonance beyond the story he tells occurs through metonymy—that is, in order to evoke a meaning beyond his, I substitute my own experience in place of Pelias'—Jones invites me to understand her experience of longing and expression as synecdoche. While it is her lost love, her longing, her desires we are given on the page, it is nonetheless, as she says, a "collaborative journey." With the recurrent inscriptions of remembered beginnings and endings, in the whispered confessions and hidden performances of our own lives, we have come to know the refrain; we have sung it a million times in the privacy of our cars and showers and in the silent darkness of our longings. We are not so much invited to travel to her experience as to travel *with* her, carried on this journey by the wings of desire we all share.

Gray, Ivonoffski, and Sinding orchestrate a polyphonous group performance, enjoining us to access their work via a venerable tradition: chamber theater. This genre is aptly suitable for their staging of these nonliterary, nontraditional texts. Elements of harmony and counterpoint are skillfully interwoven between and among the voices we are privileged to hear. As Kleinau and McHughes (1980: 55) note:

[T]he chief value to be gained through orchestration is the ability to reinforce elements of the text in varying ways. An idea, an emotion, a character presence, or an image structure may be augmented through the use of multiple voices, may be elaborated and thereby extended in time, or may be repeated in various places as an accompanying substructure of sound.

In *Handle with Care?*, phrases are repeated, momentum is built, halted, and shifted; humor is contrapuntally counterpoised with tragedy, a multiplicity of experience resounds, meaning is reinforced, and feeling evoked. One of the chief functions of this layering of voices is that, as Michael Bowman acknowledges, "the spectator is invited to play an active role not just in judging the performance, but in examining and criticizing the narrative text's meaning and structure" (1995: 4). By encouraging active engagement by the audience, the text by Gray, Ivonoffski, and Sinding finds its power beyond the individual experiences recounted by the actors. As performance is generated from various methods of research, be they ethnography, focus groups, oral histories, or other methods, the resultant performance consequently garners a psychosocial or sociopolitical power made meaningful by a shift in how audiences process performance, a shift that Langellier (1986) has described as a move from attending to text to attending to social context.

Gray, Ivonoffski, and Sinding have crafted a performance based on their qualitative research that powerfully exemplifies the utility of Bakhtin's concept of "novelization." Despite its name, novelization does not denote generic qualities. Rather, as Bowman (1995) has argued, it is the interweaving of multiple and different types of utterances, as the self-conscious use of time and space, and as containing the carnivalesque.[1] In the performance, as doctors stumble in their communication with their patients, as spouses, children, neighbors censor each other and deny the reality of the women's situations, and as the women struggle to articulate their way out of being cast as "doomed women" and are not heard, such polyvocality ruptures and disturbs easy, dismissible understandings about their lives. Time and space in *Handle with Care?* highlight how the actors perceive their experience and clarify how their agency is enabled and constrained by the historical and personal contingencies of living with the disease. By the use of parody and travesty, these survivors laugh and make others laugh at the tragedy of their situation thereby putting the carnivalesque into play and unsettling the ways in which they are constructed as "other" by doctors, neighbors, and even family members.

Bowman notes that "'novelization' is functionally synonymous with 'carnivalization'" (1995: 13). As the isolated and potentially tragic experience of illness is disrupted in *Handle with Care?* through the carnivalesque, the subversive potential of novelization is made manifest. The polyphony and juxtapositioning emblematic of the carnivalesque creates an ever-shifting terrain that renders whatever potentially comfortable space there may be uninhabitable for anything more than a momentary respite. In the show, one of the women acting as a neighbor speaks the unspoken but doubtlessly wished for desire that her neighbor who has undergone a mastectomy should wear her prosthetic because "your discomfort makes us feel better." Throughout the performance, as the carnivalesque is employed, we in the audience are made to feel discomfort even while we may laugh with the women. However, unlike the woman cited above whose reactionary longing for comfort is purchased at the expense of another's comfort, the actors do not seek to make us uncomfortable in order to assuage their own discomfort. Rather, through our discomfort they seek to awaken our empathy and to clarify how we might help eradicate the culture of silence and shame shrouding their predicament. Thus a cringing awareness may dawn on us as we recall whatever petty tragedies we may have unthinkingly perpetrated on women living with breast cancer whom we have known. The carnivalesque helps to awaken our understanding, revealing a subversive horizon ripe with the possibility for our cultivating more mindful, humane, and ethical relationships with breast cancer survivors.

The process of composition that Gray, Ivonoffski, and Sinding underwent in crafting their performances is, as they note, a process entailing "endless dilemmas." Particularly important is the politics of privilege accorded to the authors as the creators of the texts. It is a messy process. Yet for all its messiness, the authors have quite rightly understood that their task must be to represent the participants' experiences as justly as possible. The question inevitably hovering over their work and similar performances is, How can every participant's concept of a just representation be honored? Mariangela Maguire and Laila Farah Mohtar note this troubling difficulty in detailing their experience of staging a show about and performed with the women who work and live in a domestic violence shelter: "uppermost in our minds was the knowledge that no matter how much we privilege the voices of the Center, our voices asked the questions, our pens cut the transcripts, and our imaginations created the structure for their expression" (1994: 248).

I am also reminded of my own experience. After performing a show based on my ethnography of exotic dancers, one of the dancers I interviewed and performed as a persona in the show, and who saw the show on opening night, queried me about the way I chose to perform her laugh, which I believed was an accurate portrayal and one that got laughs from the rest of the audience. As I noted the slight glint of pain in her eye when she questioned me, I realized that even though I was the performer, she felt she had been the subject of the audience's laughter. From the ink on the page to the articulation of body and voice on the stage, performances that originate in the lives of living people require that we who compose and stage these lives carefully attune to the interpersonal contract we strike when we ask our subjects to reveal their lives to us. Ethnographic research is more than data collection. When we move into the worlds of our subjects, we must empathize with them to the point of somatic understanding. In short we dwell in their world and their kinesthetic experience, within the limitations of our own beings. As Gray, Ivonoffski, and Sinding discovered, in order to help audiences cultivate understanding about the subjects' lives, before we put those lives on the stage, we must first get messy with our research, then re-search again, and repeatedly, albeit messily, query ourselves and our understandings. What results, of course, is the awareness that once that journey into the other's experience has been taken, we cannot return "home." We can only create a new home, one furnished with the understandings of them and of ourselves that we have developed in the course of our research. Research of this type not only changes the audience, moving them from stillness to action, it also alters where we dwell as scholars and as beings-in-the-world.

I want to end by bringing into play several questions about the meaning of "home." These questions may help us to consider how we apprehend scholarship of the type evinced by these three chapters, as well as who we become when we engage in this type of scholarship. Moving into unfamiliar terrain whether as reader, as researcher, or as audience member is bound to entail resistance. When, as readers/researchers/audience members, are we willing to give up the comfort and familiarity of our "home" and permit ourselves to overcome our resistance in order to inhabit the unfamiliar? In what ways do our comfortable habits affect our appreciation of different homes and homelands? Put another way, when we encounter a text or performance where we can easily accept the authors' invitation to dwell there, is that ease an indication that we are simply coming "home"? Or in order to meet an author's invitation, will it entail our needing to leave the safety of the familiar? And if we leave, are we only willing to make it a temporary move or will we need to deconstruct the familiarity and comfort of our home, get rid of some things, and box up others while we move on to a new place? When circumstances require that we move in order to understand an author's view, do we defensively dig in and resist shifting our intellectual ground (ground in which we have perhaps grown too cozy and insular), even if making that move might mean expanding to a new and wider horizon of experience?

For me, engaging these performative essays has been a moving experience. For all the discomfort they may sometimes summon in me, they make me mindfully question the comfortable perimeters of my scholarly habits and habitats. And as those perimeters expand, fresh horizons fertile with possibilities for how I may better cultivate my personal and professional homes are revealed. Thus, am I moved from stillness to action.

Note

1. Bakhtin refers to these elements as polyglossia, heteroglassia, and chronotopes.

References

Bochner, Arthur P., and Carolyn Ellis. 1996. "Talking over Ethnography." In *Composing Ethnography: Alternative Forms of Qualitative Writing*, ed. Carolyn Ellis and Arthur P. Bochner (pp. 13–45). Walnut Creek, Calif.: AltaMira.

Bowman, Michael. 1995. "'Novelizing' the Stage: Chamber Theatre after Breen and Bakhtin." *Text and Performance Quarterly* 15: 1–23.

Conquergood, Dwight. 1995. "Of Caravans and Carnivals: Performance Studies in Motion." *The Drama Review* 39: 137–41.

Denzin, Norman K. 1997. *Interpretive Ethnography: Ethnographic Practices for the 21st Century.* Thousand Oaks, Calif.: Sage.

Heidegger, Martin. 1977. "Building, Dwelling, Thinking." In *Basic Writings: From Being and Time (1927) to the Task of Thinking (1964)*, ed. David Farrell Krell (pp. 347–63). New York: HarperCollins.

Hopkins, Mary Frances. 1995. "The Performance Turn—and Toss." *The Quarterly Journal of Speech* 81: 228–36.

Kleinau, Marion L., and Janet Larsen McHughes. 1980. *Theatres for Literature: A Practical Aesthetics for Group Interpretation.* Sherman Oaks, Calif.: Alfred.

Langellier, Kristin M. 1986. "From Text to Social Context." *Literature in Performance* 6(2): 60–70.

Maguire, Mariangela, and Laila Farah Mohtar. 1994. "Performance and the Celebration of a Subaltern Counterpublic." *Text and Performance Quarterly* 14: 238–52.

Pelias, Ronald J. 1999. *Writing Performance: Poeticizing the Researcher's Body.* Carbondale: Southern Illinois University Press.

WOUNDED STORYTELLERS: VULNERABILITY, IDENTITY, AND NARRATIVE

Stories that Conform/ Stories that Transform: A Conversation in Four Parts

DOUGLAS FLEMONS AND SHELLEY GREEN

Part 1

Autoethnographies: Constraints, Openings, Ontologies, and Endings

This is the first of four conversations derived from a taped panel discussion titled "Autoethnography and Therapy: Stories that Conform, Stories that Transform." The six participants on the panel—Art Bochner, Carolyn Ellis, Douglas Flemons, Jerry Gale, Shelley Green, and Laurel Richardson—came together to talk about the implications of writing autoethnographies, particularly the effects on the researcher's sense of self. Several audience members also participated, deepening and broadening the panel's musings with thoughts, questions, and stories.

Working from a transcript of the session, we went looking for one or more "narrative filaments" or "thematic plots" weaving in, through, and around the interplay of ideas. Starting at the end of the transcript and working backward, we searched for conversational continuities across spans of time and diverse speakers. When we were finished, we'd untangled four narrative threads (the others can be found on pages 115–122, 165–169, and 187–190). For the sake of readability, we haven't textually indicated the sometimes sizable lapses of time between different points raised in the conversation. Instead, we've attempted to convey something of the improvisational vitality of the original event, as well as the coherence of each of the conversational strains.

Art Bochner: One morning about two and a half years ago, I got an e-mail from a Douglas Flemons at Nova Southeastern University. Douglas, whom I had never met, was responding to a paper of mine that he had read, and that was the beginning of, as they say, "a beautiful friendship." We have been corresponding back and forth since that time, sharing ideas and raising questions about all sorts of things, including personal narratives and storytelling.

When Carolyn and I put out the call for papers and panel ideas for this conference, Douglas wrote and suggested having a spontaneous conversation on the interface between therapy and sociology. And I thought it was a great idea, maybe a risky idea for some of us, but we'll see how it goes.

Our idea here is to have a discussion about narrative, about stories, about story writing, about storytelling, and especially to focus on an issue that Douglas raised with me a couple years ago when our book *Composing Ethnography* came out. He had read a piece in the book by Lisa Tillmann-Healy (who is out in the audience), and he asked some interesting questions about when a story may be healing and when it may not, and how to tell the difference.

Douglas Flemons: Art and I have gathered some of our best friends to chew over these questions with us: Carolyn Ellis and Laurel Richardson, both autoethnographers, and Shelley Green and Jerry Gale, both family therapists and qualitative researchers.

When I first read Lisa Tillmann-Healy's autoethnography on bulimia in *Composing Ethnography,* it moved me greatly. My wife, Shelley Green, and I teach a sex therapy course to family therapy graduate students, and I assigned the chapter as part of the readings for the class. It created a wonderful stir among the students, inspiring a great discussion and prompting a few of the students to share their own struggles with food and dieting and bulimia. But Lisa's chapter also troubled me, so I wrote to Art with some of my thoughts. To help explain my concerns, let me tell you a story.

Thirteen years ago, when Jerry Gale and Shelley and I were all studying family therapy in graduate school together, Shelley and I saw a woman who came into our clinic and said, "I think I'm bulimic, can you help me?" I was the primary therapist, and Shelley and another therapist were behind a one-way mirror, observing the session. I asked the client, "Can you tell me what it is that leads you to that concern, that idea?" and she described how she would eat and throw up, eat and throw up, eat and throw up. I followed up with lots of very specific questions about how often she vomited, how long she'd been doing it, what seemed to be triggers for the eating and for the throwing up, and so on. And then I took a consultation break and met with my colleagues behind the mirror.

After we talked for a while, I came back into the therapy room and I said to the woman, "You've come in asking for help in determining whether you're bulimic. We don't know at this point whether you are or not, but we'd like to further investigate it with you, and so we'd like to ask you to closely observe your eating and throwing up for the next week, make some notes, and come back in a week and tell us about it."

So, she came back in a week and she said, "I did as you asked. I made notes. But I think I may have thrown up less this week than I did before." And so we talked about how she made sense of that. Near the end of the session, I consulted again with my colleagues behind the mirror and then went into the therapy room and said, "What we're thinking at this point is that you aren't suffering from bulimia; we think you're suffering from quasi-bulimia." We gave her a new label. "You're suffering from quasi-bulimia, but we can't be certain, so we'd like you to go and gather further data for us. Come back in a week or two with further information, and we'll take it from there."

She came back in another week or two and described what was going on. It turned out that she had been throwing up still less. Such a response to the sort of observation task we had given her is not unusual, so we were more or less expecting this. She and I had our session, I met again with my team, and at the end, I came back in and pronounced, "We believe the difficulty is not quasi-bulimia after all; rather, we believe you are suffering from pseudo-bulimia [audience laughter]. But we're still not certain, so could you please go do some more observing for us." All of this, in her mind, was in the service of our coming up with a proper diagnosis for her. But of course her way of relating to her throwing up had changed, and this was reflected in the changes taking place.

She came back a week or two later and told me that she hadn't thrown up at all since our previous session. Again we met, again I conferred with my team, and when I returned to the therapy room, I announced that we recognized that she wasn't pseudo-bulimic after all. "Rather," I said, "we believe you have an issue with eating. Certainly for such an issue therapy isn't necessary." So she left—not a bulimic, not a quasi-bulimic, not even a pseudo-bulimic: She left as a person who, at times, had an issue with food.

So the difficulty for me in reading Lisa's beautifully, poignantly, personally written account of bulimia was that she was accepting the diagnosis. If I were her therapist, which obviously I wasn't, but if I were, I would see as my job to *question* her assumption, to tickle the assumption—as we did with this other client—that she *was* a bulimic, opening the possibility of looking at herself in a different light.

This got me thinking, "What are the ethics of writing and publishing an autoethnography?" When you write a story of yourself, you accept an assumption about yourself that then determines in part how you understand yourself, and if you publish this account, then you are defining yourself not only personally but also professionally. To what degree will the reputation that gets stirred up with that make it more difficult for your story to transform your understanding of yourself in the future?

This morning, Fred Steier said in his presentation that he thinks research is both invention and *inter*vention. This resonated with me. To what degree when you're writing an autoethnography—maybe it's true of all ethnography, but certainly with autoethnography—should you pose some sort of methodological question having to do with freedom and constraint: "What's the end result that can arise from doing this, and am I going to write a story that can, that will leave me more constrained than I was when I started? Or am I going to write a story that at the end somehow liberates me, at least in terms of meanings and possible future readings?"

So this is what Art and I started talking about a couple of years ago, and this is why we're here, today.

Jerry Gale: Let me begin by talking about the end. What are we talking about, at "the end"? The end at what point? Any story we write is in a cultural climate, so it may mean something different now than when it comes out in press, and it may mean something very different to the audience than to ourselves. And then the meaning may change again in five years.

I recently read an article by Simon Kennedy in *The Australian and New Zealand Journal of Family Therapy* that recounts a story of Simon's friend, Tim Conaguay. Tim died of AIDS, which he wrote about it in his autobiography, *Holding the Man*. Kennedy talks about how personal Tim's book was, revealing all the warts and troubles of his life. And he said that he had thought about what would have happened had he, as a therapist, helped Tim to develop a different story, a different narrative, another telling of his life that centered his choices and actions in a good way. Tim never asked him to do that, but if he had, would that necessarily have been good for Tim? Because maybe Tim needed to tell his own darker version of the story, with the problems, the shame, the hurt, the troubles. Tim told his story while dying of AIDS, and that too had a bearing on how the story was constructed.

As therapists, we have agendas. What are we doing as we help our clients develop new stories, and is that necessarily good? And at what point are we trying to help clients to make a healing story? I think of Bateson: How do you intervene in the system, and how do you know that what you do is going to have a positive effect in that system?

Shelley Green: I think that's really our dilemma as therapists and researchers: how to let the story be for what it is, rather than for our needing to intervene.

Laurel Richardson: Well I'm not sure that there ever is a story that just "is," so I'd want to address this assumption that there can be an "isness" of a story.

Art: The "isness" of a story, what is "is"?

Laurel: What is "is"? Right. What do you mean by "is"? So I'm not sure that there is an end—I would agree with that one. Sometimes I have students in writing classes take different positions in a story—one time themselves, another their mother, or whatever. And this proposes that they take different positions about themselves in that story, that they're not one self but, rather, *multiple* selves—there's subjective selves, there's selves that change, and so on. I would argue very strongly that the self that is writing the story is changed by the process of writing it. If the person truly is writing an "is" story, an "isness" story, the person will be changed by the process of the writing. So the person who perhaps began by saying they were bulimic, by the end of the story may decide that that's not the category or the name by which she or he wishes to be known or held. It has shifted. Which may mean perhaps writing the same story from another perspective. This begins to open up "story," sociologically at least, as a multiple-faceted possibility.

Douglas: Well, I guess I was thinking along very similar lines, that once you do compose a story, would it make any sense, for methodological reasons, to think about writing from multiple perspectives or making sure that there isn't, at the end of the telling, some sense of closure? It's not so much that I would believe that there is an "isness" about the story but whether the story is *presented* as having an "isness." Does it, for the author, have an "isness"?

Laurel: Hmm. Hmm.

Douglas: So is there a way of challenging the assumptions of the author, perhaps also the reader, to not get settled into there being one version or one final interpretation?

Shelley: But isn't that the dilemma of writing down any story? Because then the moment you write it down, it does have an "isness." You experience it in that moment as having an "isness." How disturbing it is to go back and read what I wrote ten years ago. How could I have written that? I have kept from writing things so as not to concretize them and me, so as not to limit.

Carolyn: When you write a story, it will have different meanings for you every time you go back to it because you will be at a different place. You read your work from where you are, recognizing that it has different meanings depending on how you read it.

I don't have answers here at all—we make them up with the questions—but I've been thinking about the goals of writing autoethnography. How do you end an autoethnography? I've played a *lot* with this question. The whole *process* is inquiry. You start from a point and you don't know where you're going. You play with the story, you go with the story to see where you end up.

To make this a little more concrete, let me tell you about a story I wrote once about coping with a minor speech problem. In my first-draft ending, I said that I didn't really suffer the speech problem as a minor bodily stigma. It hadn't really changed its physical presence, but I didn't respond to it anymore. Okay, so that was an ending, but I wasn't really happy with it. I thought, "Well, where do I want to go now?" I started to push further, asking myself, "Am I just so okay with this that it will never bother me again and I never have to think about it?" The answer was no, it's much more complex than that. There will be times when it bothers me again, it's not so set, and now it may bother me because I still have the speech problem but it also may bother me because I made such a big deal about it. What if people now don't think I have a speech problem? Then that will bother me *too*—here I've made this big deal out of something that shouldn't have been a big deal.

By pushing that first-draft ending, I got to what I thought was a much more complex understanding of the process, and I also worked myself out of feeling, "Well if I ever have a problem with it again I will have failed because I thought I fixed it and now it's not fixed." I don't have the ending to that story yet—it's still in process.

Shelley: But partially that's because you made it public, right? If you announce it to other people, it becomes a different kind of story, and then you have to deal with your relationship to it in connection with the audience.

Carolyn: With how they read it.

Shelley: Right. I talked with my students this week in class about how writing autoethnography, or ethnography in general, becomes an outing process— that you out yourself intentionally or unintentionally—and how uncomfortable that might be. You have to decide if you're ready to be outed or to put yourself out in that way. You have to think about what that will do to your professional identity and your personal relationships.

Jerry: I think there's more to it than simply writing a story though. I, too, wrote a piece about a speech impediment that I had as a child, and writing it helped me define my interest in qualitative research. I recognized that as a child, I tended to be an outsider, an observer, and I could see how this led to my interest in qualitative research and therapy. But I never pushed it as you said you did with your own story. So it became a totalizing story, saying, "Okay, here's why I do what I do." It became too much of an "is," too much of an explanation.

Shelley: End of story.

Jerry: Right, so it's more than just telling the story, there needs to be that pushing and or letting go, or creating that space around it so that other stories can still develop.

Carolyn: And other stories develop in response to people who respond to your story. So it is ongoing in conversation.

Douglas: Well, in your pushing, Carolyn, you demonstrated something that certainly inspires me. You didn't simply tell the story, you told the story and then you challenged your assumptions about it, which led you to a different place with it.

Carolyn: And I think what that did—and this is what we want, or at least I want, autoethnographic stories to do—it created a place that we can live in. My alternative ending to that story created a place I could comfortably live in because if I became upset about my minor bodily stigma, again, it fit within this story, within this scheme.

Douglas: Right.

Carolyn: I wouldn't have to go in and tell another story.

Douglas: You could have left the story in two bad places: 1) "Here I am with this problem," which would then require you to confront the problem whenever you met people who had read the piece; or 2), "Here I am and what was a problem is no longer," which would have put you on the spot if you found yourself still sometimes struggling with it.

Carolyn: Right, I left it open.

Douglas: Yeah.

Carolyn: The back and forth. I'm very interested in how we think about ending stories. Given that most of these stories are about things that we are trying to work through, is it necessary to end the story in a hopeful way? And if so, what if where you are in the story doesn't feel that hopeful? It's part of the object of writing autoethnography to get yourself to the place where you can feel hope. I think of our writing ourselves as survivors, so that has an element of hope to it.

My Father's Shoes: The Therapeutic Value of Narrative Reframing

Christine E. Kiesinger

In 1996 a shift occurred in my understanding of childhood pain and its impact on one's life and narrative. This shift was perpetuated by events that drastically altered the nature of my biography. Since that time I have worked on reframing my life story in ways that empower rather than victimize me. This chapter chronicles my shift in consciousness and shows how the reframing of one's life story is a conscious act that requires courage, creativity, and a willingness to abandon a story that no longer serves one well.

Healing, Part One

In my early twenties, I realized that the anger and hatred I felt toward my father was destroying me. This realization led me to enroll in a workshop titled "Healing the Father–Daughter Relationship." During that time, I wrote a narrative titled "Without a Daddy: A Daughter's Loss." In this narrative I constructed a descriptive portrait of my relationship with my father. Later, I performed this poem in the workshop, only to access deeper levels of emotionality upon hearing myself speak the words. After writing and performing "Without a Daddy . . ." I felt I finally had a story that helped make sense of the depression and despair I had experienced for most of my life.

"Without a Daddy: A Daughter's Loss" is featured in the pages that follow. In this narrative, I cast myself as the main character—a helpless victim with little sense of agency or power. My father is cast as the monster—a man who ruthlessly bullies his child-victim, causing her great confusion and emotional harm. Regardless of any negative implications associated with casting myself as the victim, at the time, this particular tale of my experience became the sustaining fiction I clung to and lived by.

Without a Daddy: A Daughter's Loss

Hating

For years, I hated everything about my father. I hated the heavy pounding of his walk. I hated his eyes—a sagging, mean brown. I hated his sour breath, the heat of his hand against my face, the weight of his body against my small form. I hated the ominous tone of his voice.

I hated that I shriveled in confrontation with him. I hated how diminished I felt when I dared to express myself. I hated how his gaze, words, and posture communicated: "Daughter . . . you are nothing, you mean nothing, you will be nothing."

Most of all, I hated hating him.

Bitter Cold

I was born in late February in a small, coal mining town in northeastern Pennsylvania. I've been told that on the day of my birth the air was still and bitter cold. The sky was a stark, steel gray and nothing was green.

In a photograph taken a few days after my birth, my father holds me, looking into the camera without expression. He does not look happy or sad. He does not look confident, or afraid. He appears blank. Dazed. Frozen. Bitter cold.

He is flushed, ruddy-faced, and twenty-two. I arrived to him that day and forever changed his life.

Invisible

I recall little of my infancy. Family members and relatives tell me that I was a shy, cautious baby. My first steps were particularly tentative and hesitant. My mother has told me hundreds of times that I moved slowly and quietly.

"Like a ghost, you floated from room to room," she would say while reminiscing. "At times, you'd appear out of nowhere. But, you were a good baby," she'd say proudly, folding her hands into her lap. "Most times, we didn't even know you were here with us."

Early on, I learned that being "good" meant being benign, invisible, and as quiet as possible.

The Unbucklings

As a toddler I began to know my father as a remarkably angry and terrifying man.

My fourth birthday. Red velvet dress, white, lace trim. Black patent leather shoes—sleek and shiny. They squeak when I walk. On my head, a party hat.

I am tired. A long party in my honor. Lots of gifts, but not the gift I wanted. The doll . . . a certain doll.

After everyone leaves, Father and Mother give me one last gift to open before bed. It is the doll! So touched, the tears well up inside of me. I cry shamelessly.

Red faced and angry, he shouts: "Knock it off or I'll give you something to cry about!"

Holding the doll close to my chest, my body trembles in response to the force of his words. My small mind struggles to understand. What have I done? How have I offended him? I stuff back my tears. I vow not to cry. I vow not to express anything. Perhaps if I am quiet, so very quiet, he'll never need to speak to me in this way. Perhaps if I am quiet, he will come to like me.

*

Father is a strict disciplinarian. The beatings begin with the unbuckling.

How I hate the sound . . . the unbuckling of his belt. He pulls it out of the loops of his pants and then folds it over so that it is taut, tight—so that it stings my bare, young skin.

The beatings are always the same. He holds me by the arm and pulls down my panties. And then the lashing—the harsh pain of cold, black leather against my skin. The beating continues until my flesh is a rosy pink or until mother yells, "Enough! That is enough!"

Afterward, he sends me to bed. Blushed and warm from sobbing, I lie there waiting. I wait for the heavy shuffle of his feet and the gentle opening of my door. I wait because he will sit on the edge of my bed staring at the floor. I wait because he will say, "I'm sorry." I wait because he will say, "I only hit you . . . because I love you."

As I write this, I still struggle to understand. Although apart and away from my father now for many years, I often feel that I am waiting for something—

some word or gesture, something that will grant resolution, completion, or perhaps an answer to all of my questions about his anger toward me.

Years later, I continue to link pain with love—for you see, father taught me this each time he came to my bedside. He hurt me, because he loved me.

Daddy

"Daddy" is what they call their fathers. Daddy is warm, nice. Daddy scoops daughter up in his arms and daughter nuzzles her face into daddy's chest. Daughter feels safe with daddy. Daughter feels proud of daddy. Daughter wants other girls to know her daddy—to know that he is the best.

I wanted desperately to call him "Daddy." But he was not that. He was "Father"—assigned to me, and if I could have, I would have given him back. I tried hard to understand his anger. I began to suspect that his anger had something to do with me. If he became enraged, I concluded it was my fault.

I began to exhibit as much control over myself and my surroundings as possible. I became hypersensitive to his moods and those things that seemed to upset him.

By the time I was seven, I found comfort in isolation. Frightened and ashamed, I hid in my room for hours at a time. I was ashamed of my father.

Ashamed of my family. Ashamed of myself. I never wanted friends to visit because I feared that they would discover my "secret."

I did not have a "daddy" and this was the secret I was hiding.

*

In the evenings, Father hovers over me as I do my homework. Math. I am not good at math. He senses this weakness in me. He makes things more difficult. He pounds his fist into the table as he stands over me, his breath hot on my neck.

I try to get every problem correct—to solve every one neatly, efficiently, correctly—but every hesitancy on my part is met by his pounding, ranting, and rage.

(Still, even today, my hand trembles as I perform simple subtraction while balancing my checkbook.)

My report card arrives. "See the A's!" I want to shout. But he sees only the few B grades. "Pull those B's up!" he shouts, tossing my report card on the table and then walking away.

The A's go unnoticed . . . and so do I.

Looking

Junior high school. Father begins to look at me differently—or should I say, he tries hard not to look.

Something about me has changed. He is uncomfortable. I am uncomfortable. But the discomfort is undefined . . . unspoken. It is felt. I am aware that he is having trouble looking at me and when he does look, he pretends that he has not.

Instinctively, I knew what this was about.

I developed quite early—almost overnight. I went from playing with dolls to having breasts, and not only did my father act differently but other men did as well. Comments were made. Men talked about me—mostly, they spoke about my body.

*

Saturday, midmorning, he picks me up from dance class. I wear shimmering, frosty blue eye shadow and a creamy, pale pink lipstick. From the rear view mirror he notices the makeup. He turns around, grabs my face. He shouts, "Slut!" It won't be the last time.

*

It is 9:35 P.M. He is tying his shoelaces. Red-faced and frantic, he hits the city streets in search of his slut daughter who is five minutes late! He searches for me in alley ways. He searches near the dumpsters behind the skating rink. He searches the woods along the railroad tracks.

Five minutes late and in his eyes I am: untrustworthy, unappreciative, dirty, irresponsible, and most of all, a whore . . .

"Dear Father, if you looked hard enough you would have found me in the woods near the railroad tracks, behind the Acme market, with my pants hanging loose around my knees, shirt off, my white, lace bra tossed to the ground. You would have found me stoned with some boy—any boy. I did not care about what was happening to me."

*

Sex. Alcohol. Drugs. I reveled in my destructive behavior because I knew that my actions, if discovered, would enrage my father and, in turn, he would probably kill me.

At the tender age of thirteen, I did not care whether I lived or died.

Stronger

Throughout my adolescence, his beatings became much stronger. I rose to the challenge of each one—fighting back with all my strength, which only intensified his rage and increased the force of his blows. I became very good at leaving my body during these episodes. I would fight for so long and then just give in, going with the flow as he throttled me from room to room.

I vividly recall the last beating.

I am seventeen. He beats me from one corner of the house to the other. We work our way through every room. Hitting, biting, pinching, punching. He pushes me into a corner under the kitchen counter and I am trapped. I leave my body.

Later . . . I am huddled in the corner of my bedroom sobbing and wondering how I got there—my heavy oak bureau pushed up against the door to keep him away. How did I have the strength to move that piece of furniture? How long have I been crouched in the corner like a frightened, injured animal?

I reach for my teeth to see if they are still there. I am always afraid that he will punch out my teeth. During his rages I pray, "Not my teeth . . . God save my teeth." Teeth intact, huddled in the corner I wonder when this insanity will end!

And then I recall my mother's words: "When I got my last beating, I was nearly twenty years old." She said this to me once, quite casually, while folding clothes. She said this as if to excuse father's behavior—as if to argue that as my father he had the right to hurt me until I was twenty—as if to say, "Expect this to continue."

Bleeding

I learn I am pregnant at the beginning of my first year of college. My high school beau, Stephen, is the father. The night of conception was a special night, a night of tender lovemaking intensified by the fact that Stephen was leaving for college early the next morning. We spent the night at the Skylight Motel, a dingy, shady place off Route 84. Despite protection, I became pregnant.

*

Parked in his father's station wagon at the edge of a wooded area, I decide to break the news. I open my purse and show him the results of a pregnancy test taken earlier that day. The deep pink line, combined with frequent bouts of intense nausea, convince us that, indeed, the results are positive.

I take the test kit out of Stephen's trembling hands. I hurl it out the window and into the brush. Hearing it land, I burst into tears.

"I do not have any choice," I tell him. "I must have an abortion. I don't know where, or how . . . but I must get rid of this baby. My God, Stephen, if I don't, my father will kill me! He can never, ever know about this."

*

Abortion. For me, there was no other way. No other choice.

*

About one month later, on a warm October evening, at approximately 9 P.M., I lay on a cold, steel table, my feet in stirrups. I weep as a cruel, older man places a tube between my legs and shouts, "Stop crying! We haven't even begun! If you think this hurts, go ahead and carry this child full term—then we will talk about pain!"

I swallow my tears.

Stephen waits in the lobby reading the latest issue of Field and Stream.

Seven long minutes pass. I recall the pressure, the squeezing, a gnashing—a deep, deep pull. I recall the loud sucking sound of the vacuum. I recall the cramping, a twisting deep inside. Bitter tasting beads of sweat flow gently from my forehead over my cheeks, onto my lips.

The doctor walks across the room with a glass jar in his hands. Fully exposed, I see its bloody contents. Red—so much red, with splashes of white interspersed.

"This came from inside of you," he says, lifting the jar as if lifting a wine glass to make a toast.

I swallow hard. "All of that," I murmur to myself, "all of that taken from inside of me."

*

I knew in that moment that I had lost something profound that October night. I lost so much more than the contents floating around inside the clear, glass jar.

*

The trauma of this episode is indelibly etched in my mind. My body, mind, and soul screaming . . . and all the while, the sound of my terror heard only by me.

Abortion.

This decision made for my father . . . this decision made to protect him, to protect me, to protect the child I carried within me because I so feared his wrath. I feared my child knowing his anger, meeting his rage, hiding herself and her voice—having to bury her essence forever.

Abortion. An act of survival. Saving my child. Saving myself.

Searching for Daddy

Less than one week after the abortion, I was having lunch in a large hotel in New York city, overlooking Park Avenue. I was with a man thirteen years older. This lunch marked the beginning of one of the most intense love affairs of my life. Looking down into my lap, I was reminded that I was still bleeding inside.

Despite the strong love I would grow to have for this man, the relationship was destructive and something I was not prepared for at eighteen years of age. Our bond was strained by codependency, numerous episodes of infidelity, and an intense attachment on my part—an attachment unmatched by anything I had ever experienced. I held on to him as if I were clinging to a lifeline.

Robert—my sanctuary, my foundation, my oxygen. I needed him to live, to breathe, to feel alive. At night I curled up in his arms, my nose pressed against his chest. I inhaled his scent, took in his heat. I memorized the sound of his heart beating. Robert was that which I had longed for all along. He became the "daddy" I never had.

I found in Robert what I clearly could not get from my father. I had chosen the perfect candidate to "father" me. Robert was older, wiser, warm, responsible, and mature. He clothed me, helped fund me through college, and assisted me in making important decisions regarding my future. But to seek a "daddy" in the context of an intimate bond with Robert was destructive. Eventually, I grew to feel abandoned by him—abused and invalidated, as he could never really be my "daddy." My expecting him to do so was at the heart of our downfall as a couple.

My relationship with Robert hurt me in ways proportionate to the way I felt hurt in relationship to my father. I wish I could say that being with Robert taught me that I would never find a "daddy" in the men I dated and loved. But I did not learn this lesson. When Robert left, it was on to the next man, and then the next. A dangerous pattern ensued and continued. And the questions never stop:

Father, why does your influence linger? Why do I search for you in the men I love? Do you realize how deeply I've longed for you . . . longed to call you daddy?

And you—did you ever long for my small arms to reach out to you fearlessly—for my soft voice to call out for you.

Father, did you ever long to hear me call you "Daddy"?

Reflection

Years later, as I reflect on "Without a Daddy: A Daughter's Loss," I realize that casting myself as a "victim" and my father as "monster" was key in the initial stages of my recovering from childhood physical abuse. However, I also see that this tale hindered my personal growth and affected the quality of my intimate relationships. For example, I distinctly recall Jason, a man with whom I was romantically involved, telling me how frustrating it felt to be in my presence.

"It's hard to be happy around you," he said. "You carry a darkness in you. I see it each time I look into your eyes. It is heavy and crushing. I'm not sure what it is about, but you must let it go."

Additionally, academic peers and mentors often remarked that the metaphors that dominated my writings about my life were metaphors of strife and struggle. I accounted for my life as an arduous journey of sorts, but a journey that granted little in the way of gifts and rewards. A friend once told me that I seemed to be barely "surviving" my life and that surely life could be more than an act of survival.

Eventually, I began to wonder if my story of abuse was an obstacle to my experiencing a healthier existence. Although I felt committed to having a story that gave voice to my experience, I began to feel that the narrative I was telling no longer served me well. There was no room in it for joy, happiness, and most of all, peace.

Healing, Part Two

> What we are forgiving is not the act . . . we are forgiving the actors . . . we are forgiving their suffering . . . their confusion, their unskillfulness, their desperation, and their humanity. . . . As long as we hold onto how this or that person hurt us . . . we are trapped in a dance of suffering with that person forever . . . we are set free from this cycle of suffering when we forgive our parents and we allow them to be who they were, nothing more, nothing less.
>
> —W. MULLER, *Legacy of the Heart*

I distinctly recall the moment I stopped hating my father. The hating stopped when I saw something I had never really noticed before—my father's shoes.

His running shoes sit in the corner of the room against the large brown rocking chair. They are tattered, stained, and faded. The laces are frayed. I get down on the floor and take them into my hands.

The heels and soles are worn thin. The insoles are slightly damp and a faint, sour odor emanates. Tiny specks of dried mud spill into my palms as I lift and turn his shoes over and over again in my hands.

I think about the weight of his body crushing the soles of these shoes. I think about the heavy pounding of his walk. I think about the ground he's covered while wearing them and the way these shoes have supported him in his journey.

WAIT . . . his journey?

I have never thought about my father's path, the places he's been, the places he's going, his sense of meaning and purpose. As I hold his shoes in my hands, these questions come:

Who is my father? What are his dreams? Is he happy? Did he accomplish all that he had hoped to achieve? What does he embrace in his heart? Does he have a heart? Why don't I know the answers to any of these questions? Why have I never asked?

I never will forget the feel of his shoes in my hands and how deeply in this moment I love him. I love him NOT as a daughter loves her father, but the way one human being loves another when she realizes how the other has suffered, persevered, and tried to live a reasonably good life despite deep, inner wounds.

In this moment I begin forgiving my father. I am not sure that I can forget—but in this moment, forgiving becomes a real possibility.

*

As I held my father's shoes in my hands, it occurred to me that the questions I had about his life were questions, that if answered, might allow me to deepen my perception of him. Perhaps answers would add a certain complexity and texture to him as a main character in my story. By learning more about him as a person, perhaps my role in my own story would change. Might I be more than just a helpless victim? Might my father be more than a monstrous man? If so, could I recognize "us" as more? As I set his shoes back down on the floor, a deep level of healing began.

The moment of insight I experienced while holding my father's shoes was framed by an episode that I had, until that moment, forgotten. This episode occurred a year earlier when my father disclosed a story of childhood abuse to my mother and me. I never thought about this chilling story again until I held his shoes in my hands—until I was able to imagine my father as a human being.

The Missing Piece—My Father's Story

It is a warm and balmy afternoon. My parents and I are having lunch on the terrace of our hotel, overlooking the pool. We are talking about my grandmother, his mother. I am happy as I reflect upon her generous spirit. I am troubled when the conversation shifts.

"Sometimes your grandmother's open heart was a curse," my father says harshly. "She has no idea how dangerous her kindness was. My God! Some of the characters she allowed into our home!" He shifts uncomfortably in his chair.

"What are you talking about?" my mother queries.

"For example," he continues, "Tom Connor—what a bastard! She took him into our home repeatedly without question. She is still delusional when it comes to him."

My father's words astonish me. I am not sure I want his story to go any further because I fear that he is about to shatter a powerful family myth.

*

Tommy Connor is a family legend. We held him in the highest regard.

Apparently, Connor was a famous European actor—my grandmother's cousin. Occasionally, he would make trips to the States to visit and would stay in my grand-parents' home. He last visited when my father was about seven. No one ever saw or heard from Connor again after that visit.

When I was a child, my grandmother would gather her grandchildren and flip through old photographs. We most enjoyed photos of Tommy Connor and always expected Grandma to tell us the story of his fame, his visits, and his mysterious disap-pearance. Each time we heard this story, we felt chilled, excited, and frightened. "What happened to Tom Connor?" we wondered. Was he dead? Murdered? Kidnapped? Did he commit some horrible crime and escape to some remote island? The possibilities were as vast as our childhood imaginations. We savored this family mystery.

*

As my father continues his tirade about Tom Connor and my grandmother's kindness, which he now frames as "naive" and "stupid," I am on the verge of insisting that we change the subject.

"Tom Connor sure as hell did not disappear," my father says, "and he wasn't murdered . . . although, had I the chance, I would have killed him myself!"

Again, my father's words startle me. I feel anxious as he seems insistent on continuing his story.

"Whenever Connor traveled to the States, he always brought a young com-panion with him. They were different—but always young men between the ages of fourteen and seventeen."

"Whenever they visited, Grandma let them stay in my bedroom and I was left to sleep on the sofa in the front room of the house. Connor drank a lot. After dinner he and his companion would hit the local bars and stumble back later in the evening. I dreaded their return."

"I'd try to be as still and as quiet as possible, pretending to be asleep. But the scene would always unfold in the same way. Connor would come in, send his companion upstairs to bed, and then the bastard would crawl onto the couch with me, lift the blanket away and . . ."

As my father speaks, I imagine the scene too vividly.

"That asshole!" my father shouts. "I was seven fucking years old, for Christ's sake! I didn't know what was happening. God, I hated it! It made me sick! But who could I tell? I didn't have a name to put to this experience! I thought I was crazy!"

My mother and I sit in shock.

As the waitress approaches to refill our drinks, she notices my father's expression, and turns away.

"I'm not sure why, but I mustered the courage to tell one person—my Uncle Jud. I barely got the words out and Jud was enraged. He just seemed to know. He told me not to worry. He said that I'd never have to deal with Connor again and that I should never speak of what happened. I knew in that moment that Connor had violated me in the most profound way.

"Connor left abruptly. We never saw or heard from him again. Years later, Uncle Jud told me that the reason Connor never returned was because Jud threatened to kill him if he ever made contact with the family again."

My father is trembling.

"Your grandmother sees what she wants to see, hears what she wants to hear! Her hospitality cost me in ways that she'll never know or understand," he shouts.

"Will you ever tell her?" I ask.

"No," he responds. *"Never."* His tone is harsh and final.

My father pushes his salad away. His face is beet red. His temples are pulsing. His eyes are glazed, flaring, and wild.

And I recognize all of this—the ruddy face, the wild eyes, the trembling hands. I recognize this as my father's rage. For most of my life, this rage was directed at me— his first-born child.

In this same moment, I see that behind this rage is a terrified, seven year-old child, pretending to sleep, as a grown man—reeking of smoke and hard liquor—invaded his body and crushed his child-spirit. This child feels confusion and shame.

In this moment I feel a deep connection to my father. Much like in my experience, the monster my father feared as a little boy was, indeed, very real.

Finally, my father's rage had a home—a "story" around it. I come to realize that his rage was never really about me. I now held in my hands a major missing piece of the puzzle. My father, wounded as a child, was a fragile human being.

My father was very much like me.

Discussion: The Therapeutic Value of Narrative Reframing

My therapist, Kate, sits in silence, listening as I read "Without a Daddy: A Daughter's Loss." It is an emotionally charged hour—heightened for me by her tears. Clearly my story has struck a chord in her. Pregnant with her first child, Kate wraps her long, pale arms around her swollen belly as if embracing her soon-to-be-born infant as I read.

A long silence looms when I finish, and we sit, eyes locked for several minutes.

"This is who I am," I say, breaking the silence while setting my manuscript down on the small table beside me.

"Really?" Kate responds. Her tone is doubtful, even suspicious. "I disagree, Christine," she says, firmly. "I think you are better than all of that."

I am speechless.

"Actually, I believe that you are much more than the character that lives in those pages . . . so much more.

"Think about it," she says. "Your hour is up."

*

On that day, the work of therapy really began for me. I offered Kate the story of my life—or what I assumed to be the whole of who I was. On that day, she pushed me to begin challenging the story I was telling, performing, and living. Her words, "Christine, you are more," would haunt me for years as I moved through the slow, complicated, but endlessly inventive journey of reframing my experience in ways that convinced me, that "yes, I *am* more."

*

Constructing meaningful accounts of emotional experience and believing that our accounts are sufficient is psychologically important to tellers (Denzin 1989; Harvey, Weber, and Orbuch 1990; Kiesinger 1995; Parry and Doan 1994). Complex and painful emotional experiences and inexplicable events tend to stimulate one's narrative need (Sacks 1985: 111). The narrative need is motivated each time one strives to make the unintelligible and the painful, comprehensible and meaningful by contextualizing lived experience within one's larger life story (Harvey, Weber, and Orbuch 1990: 8). Personal narratives work, then, to the degree that they assist us to integrate life events into our histories so that our story is experienced as coherent, intelligible, and meaningful (Bochner 1994; Bochner, Ellis, and Tillmann-Healy 1997; Bruner 1990; Mishler 1995).[1]

The therapeutic value of narrative becomes apparent each time we deconstruct debilitating life narratives and reframe them in ways that empower us, thus improving the quality of our lives (Parry and Doan 1994). In this chapter, I have tried to show how the stories we tell about our lives often become the frameworks of meaning out of which we act, think, interpret, and relate. When our stories break down or no longer serve us well, it is imperative that we examine the quality of the stories we are telling and actively reinvent our accounts in ways that permit us to live more fulfilling lives.

Reframing our story in ways that empower rather than victimize does not mean that we deny painful or abusive experiences, nor does it mean that we excuse others for the ways they have hurt or violated us. What it does mean is that we proactively examine and assess the stories we tell about our lives and experiences. We ask questions such as:

- Does this story serve me well?
- As a central character in my own story, how do I depict myself in relation to those with whom I have close relationships? Do I see myself as an active agent in these relationships or a passive victim?
- How can I reframe my story in ways that allow me to see the main characters in my life with empathy—in ways that help me to see them as the complex people they are?
- How might I reinvent the story of my life in ways that give my life new meaning and purpose?

Therapeutically, narrative reframing begins when we externalize our narrative (White 1988–1989). Externalization requires that we step away from our story and hold it before us as a text for study—"objectifying and personifying the problems in our lives that we experience as painful or oppressive" (White 1988–1989: 3). In this process, we look for the ways in which our life problems and dissatisfactions are linked to a story that may not be serving us well. We look analytically at the narratives that shape our lives and ponder their power and value. White asks us to attend to the story's overall foundation and structure (this includes main characters, supporting characters, patterns, themes, metaphors) and also to any gaps or holes in our story. To do this, Parry and Doan (1994: 55) encourage us to go on a spy mission, courageously seeking the stories of those close to us. We actively seek to find the missing pieces of the puzzle and we seek clarification about storylines that seem fuzzy or don't quite make sense. We ask about events and characters that are rarely spoken about. Often, the spy mission means engaging those close to us in honest dialogue, thus not only accessing the stories of those who are main characters in their own narratives, but coming to learn the role we play in their stories as well (Parry 1991: 43).[2]

Narrative reframing also involves contextualizing our stories within the framework of a larger picture. For example, I might frame the story of my childhood abuse within the context of a strong familial pattern in which abuse is multi-generational. In doing so, I am less likely to feel that the abuse I endured was about "me" personally. Instead, the possibility exists for me to understand abuse as a damaging pattern of relating within my family. Thus, change involves disrupting the relational pattern instead of aiming to "fix" or change myself or the others around me. I might conclude that there is nothing inherently wrong with me, but rather something very wrong with the dynamics that dominate the communicative system within my family.

It has been productive for me to investigate abuse patterns in my own family. This investigation began when I engaged my father in a conversation about the abusive disciplinary tactics used by his parents while he was growing up. I came to learn that my mother endured similar modes of harsh discipline when she was a child. Both of my parents define their childhood experiences as moments of "discipline." In contrast, however, I define these experiences as moments of abuse. In terms of one's life story, there are very different implications when those involved define the very same situation so differently.

Narrative reframing additionally requires that we assess the degree to which we live our stories versus the degree to which our stories live us (Parry 1991). To make this assessment, I grappled with the following questions:

- To what degree am I conscious of the story I live?
- What sort of agency do I assume I have when living this story—to what degree do I take authorship of the story of my life?
- If my story no longer works, am I willing to let go of the plot lines, character depictions, and the major themes and metaphors that dominate my story? Am I willing to experiment with new ways to narrate my experience, and new ways to construct alternative characterizations of myself and the things that happened to me?

As this chapter illustrates, I have gone through the process of narrative reframing and continue to do so. For many years, "Without a Daddy: A Daughter's Loss" was the narrative construct that "lived me." I lived as a victim who struggled in her life and relationships without ever considering the degree to which I allowed this characterization to run my life. It was only when I came close to an emotional breakdown that I began to look closely at the narrative I had constructed about my life.

At this time, it is difficult for me to connect with the "monster-father" that rages his way through the pages of "Without a Daddy: A Daughter's Loss." It is equally difficult for me to identify with the victim-child who deeply hates him. I cannot emphasize enough, however, that I do not deny the things I experienced in my childhood; I just understand these events differently now. Currently, I reject the characterization of myself as broken and damaged, and see myself as a woman who was once wounded—and also as a woman who is inherently "wise, strong, and whole within" (Muller 1992: xiv).

I still question the way I was parented. I am clear that I cannot regain what I lost in childhood, nor can I expect to find a "daddy" in others (Miller 1994: 25). Yet, I have forgiven my father. Although my anger, disappointment, and feelings of loss sometimes surface, my past no longer looms so heavily over my present—nor does my past define my present or shape my expectations for my future as it once did. Most importantly, I no longer look to my father to parent me. I have learned that it is my responsibility to "parent" myself.

Conclusion

The story of my relationship with my father continues to evolve in new and unexpected ways. The process and challenge of healing my childhood wounds is ongoing and never quite ends.

*

I gently place the phone back on its receiver, glance at the clock, and I am astounded to realize that my father and I just spoke for over an hour. Just a few years ago I was unwilling to speak to him on the phone because the tension was unbearable.

Tonight, we spent most of our time discussing the latest episode of "Big Brother." Aired nightly on CBS, "Big Brother" is the latest "reality-based" television show to which both my father and I are addicted. Each broadcast of "Big Brother" captures the day's dynamics within a group of people who live together in a carefully constructed house completely cut off from the outside world. Every week each house member secretly nominates two other house members for banishment. Every two weeks one house member is voted out of the house by the viewing public who cast their votes via telephone based on the nominations generated inside the house. Each time a member leaves, viewers watch how the dynamics in the house shift.

In addition to predicting which house member might be banished next, my father and I discussed the shifting roles and dynamics currently at play in the house. I was surprised by my father's insights into the ways that house members collectively operate much like a family. I was particularly impressed that my father seems so aware of the drastic lengths a person will often go to in order to "survive" in a relational system fraught with tension, conflict, and emotional chaos.

In response to my father's ponderings about the "Big Brother" house, I shared key elements of family systems theory with him. I focused mostly on how the behavior of family members is often enacted as a way to "correct" a troubled family system and to restore a sense of harmony and balance.

"To keep a sense of peace in a family . . . we sometimes have to cease being our-selves," my father said in response to my mini-lecture on systems theory. I noted a sense of sadness in his voice, just as there was sadness in my own voice when I responded, "Yeah, I know exactly what you mean."

Although we were focusing on the behavior of the characters in the "Big Brother" house, I cannot help but think that my father and I were talking around deeper, more personal, and salient issues—particularly his history of childhood abuse and my own.

*

"Damn!" I think to myself as I reflect on this conversation with my father. Our conversation may have been a perfect opening for me to talk about our family system and all the times in my life that I silenced myself or ceased being myself so as not to disrupt the system. Ah! The lengths I went to in order to keep the peace!

But I know that I am not ready to have this conversation. I am not emo-tionally prepared to confront him about his behavior and my response to it. I am not ready to share my story of abuse and journey toward healing with him.

"Hypocrite!" I say to myself as I glance at this manuscript, which sits on the coffee table ready for one more edit. How can I share my story with close friends, mentors, students, and even strangers who will see it in its published form, yet not share it with my father? What prevents me from opening up to him now that we have reached a level of comfort in our relationship?

This is a complex dilemma for me. Although I feel that sharing this manu-script will help others understand and reframe their own abusive pasts, I fear that sharing it with my father will damage our current relationship in irreparable ways.

However, in not sharing my story with him, I fear that I am perpetuating a long-standing, generational family pattern—a pattern in which we cease to be ourselves and express ourselves in order to preserve peace. Can I tolerate know-ing that I am actively enabling this destructive pattern? Perhaps sharing this man-uscript with my father will open up a possibility for us to relate more deeply. But what if sharing my story closes down the way we currently communicate and interferes with the relationship we are now building? I am not sure I am willing to risk losing what we now share. I am not sure where to go from here.

*

My sister phones hours after my conversation with my father about "Big Brother."

"What's up with you and Dad?" she asks inquisitively.

"What do you mean?"

"He's been raving about his earlier conversation with you. He gave us a crash course in family communication tonight. He's really jazzed and said this was the best conversation he's ever had with you!"

I chuckle at the strangeness of this situation. I never would have imagined that my father and I would connect so meaningfully about family dynamics in reference to a television program. But I find delight in our recent connection, regardless of the catalyst. It feels wonderful to know that we spoke in ways that allowed me to feel that I taught him something important and that he wanted to share what he learned with other members of our family.

I put my red editing pen down along with my manuscript while my sister continues talking. I take a deep breath and savor a newfound feeling of closeness with my father. However, in this same moment, I tremble inside when I imagine losing this sense of closeness were I to share my depiction of our relationship with him.

My mind then wanders to the possible reactions and responses of other family members who might read this manuscript. Would my siblings support my decision to publish it? Would they recall the same moments I so vividly depict in my narrative? What if they reject my depiction of my relationship with our father? Will they fear that exposing my story might rock the family foundation, thus defeating all we have sacrificed to achieve a sense of familial peace?

What would my mother say? How would she feel were she to read my words? In the past she has reacted defensively in response to my framing my relationship with my father as abusive. I imagine her reading my manuscript and responding with something like: "You ungrateful, brat! No one taught your father and me how to parent! We did the best we could based on our own experiences! How dare you offer the world this portrait of your father!"

Another possible reaction is one in which my mother responds from a state of denial. Years ago when I asked her to read a narrative account of my struggle with bulimia, my mother pushed my manuscript aside, folded her hands in her lap, looked at me intently, and said, "My, my, what an amazing imagination you have." Shocked by her response, I sat next to her speechless. Although I felt hurt, we never spoke about my narrative or bulimia again.

By the time my sister and I end our phone conversation, I decide that I will not share my manuscript with my father or other family members any time soon. "It's not time," I tell myself. "I'm not ready."

*

I don't know what my future holds in reference to my relationship with my father. I do know that I will risk publishing this manuscript. I know I will continue my own therapeutic work and aim to be a better parent to myself. I look forward to a closer relationship with my father and I will continue to search for healthy ways for us to connect. Most of all, I know that the process of healing my wounds and respecting his, dealing with my anger *toward* him, and my love *for* him, is a process that is, perhaps, lifelong.

Notes

1. For evocative exemplars of narrative accounts that give voice and meaning to complex, unintelligible and painful emotional experiences, consider the following sources: Ellis and Bochner's "Telling and Performing Personal Stories: The Constraints of Choice in Abortion" (1992); Ellis's "Maternal Connections" (1996) and "There Are Survivors" (1993); Fox's "Silent Voices: A Subversive Reading of Child Sex Abuse" (1996); Kiesinger's "Liz: Portrait of an Anorexic Life" (1998b) and "From Interview to Story: Writing Abbie's Life" (1998a); Ronai's "My Mother Is Mentally Retarded" (1996) and "Multiple Reflections of Child Sexual Abuse: An Argument for a Layered Account" (1995); and Tillmann-Healy's "A Secret Life in a Culture of Thinness" (1996).

2. For Parry and Doan, the analogy of the spy mission also involves "gathering all possible information on the thoughts, feelings, and contexts that the old story/problem story uses to remain strong—and doing so in an orderly and systematic way. The process is much the same as scouting an opposing sports team with the intent of discovering how it manages to win so often. Instead, the scouting report is on the old story and the strategies and ploys it has used to author the client's life. This information can be used to devise countering strategies that the client can utilize to revision the story" (1994: 55).

References

Bochner, A. P. 1994. "Perspectives on Inquiry II: Theories and Stories." In *Handbook for Interpersonal Communication,* ed. M. L. Knapp and G. R. Miller (pp. 21–41). Thousand Oaks, Calif.: Sage.

Bochner, A. P., Ellis, C., and Tillman-Healy, L. 1997. "Relationships As Stories." In *Handbook of Personal Relationships,* ed. S. Duck (pp. 307–24). Sussex, England: John Wiley & Sons.

Bruner, J. 1990. *Acts of Meaning.* Cambridge, Mass.: Harvard University Press.

Denzin, N. K. 1989. *Interpretive Biography.* Newbury Park, Calif.: Sage.

Ellis, C. 1993. "'There are survivors': Telling a Story of Sudden Death." *The Sociological Quarterly* 34(4), 711–30.

———. 1996. "Maternal Connections." In *Composing Ethnography: Alternative Forms of Qualitative Writing,* ed. C. Ellis and A. P. Bochner (pp. 240–43). Walnut Creek, Calif.: AltaMira Press.

Ellis, C., and A. P. Bochner. 1992. "Telling and Performing Personal Stories: The Constraints of Choice in Abortion." In *Investigating Subjectivity,* ed. C. Ellis and M. G. Flaherty (pp.79–101). Newbury Park, Calif.: Sage.

Fox, K. V. 1996. "Silent Voices: A Subversive Reading of Child Sex Abuse." In *Composing Ethnography: Alternative Forms of Qualitative Writing,* ed. C. Ellis and A. P. Bochner (pp. 330–56). Walnut Creek, Calif.: AltaMira Press.

Harvey, J. H., A. L. Weber, and T. Orbuch. 1990. *Interpersonal Accounts: A Social Psychological Perspective.* Cambridge, Mass.: Basil Blackwell.

Kiesinger, C. E. 1995. "Anorexic and Bulimic Lives: Making Sense of Food and Eating." Unpublished doctoral dissertation, University of South Florida, Tampa.

———. 1998a. "From Interview to Story: Writing Abbie's Life." *Qualitative Inquiry* 4: 71–95.

———. 1998b. "Liz: Portrait of an Anorexic Life." In *Fiction and Social Research: By Ice or Fire,* ed. Anna Banks and Stephen P. Banks (pp. 115–36). Walnut Creek, Calif.: AltaMira Press.

Miller, A. 1994. *The Drama of the Gifted Child.* New York: Basic Books.

Mishler, E. 1995. "Models of Narrative Analysis: A Typology." *Journal of Narrative and Life History* 5: 87–123.

Muller, W. 1992. *Legacy of the Heart.* New York: Simon and Schuster.

Parry, A. 1991. "A Universe of Stories." *Family Process* 30: 37–54.

Parry, A., and R. E. Doan. 1994. *Story Revisions: Narrative Therapy in a Postmodern World.* New York: Guilford Press.

Ronai, C. R. 1995. "Multiple Reflections of Child Sex Abuse: An Argument for a Layered Account." *Journal of Contemporary Ethnography* 23: 395–426.

———. 1996. "My Mother Is Mentally Retarded." In *Composing Ethnography: Alternative Forms of Qualitative Writing,* ed. C. Ellis and A. P. Bochner (pp. 109–31). Walnut Creek, Calif.: AltaMira Press.

Sacks, O. 1985. "A Matter of Identity." In *The Man Who Mistook His Wife for a Hat.* New York: Simon and Schuster.

Tillmann-Healy, L. 1996. "A Secret Life in a Culture of Thinness." In *Composing Ethnography: Alternative Forms of Qualitative Writing,* ed. C. Ellis and A. P. Bochner (pp. 76–108). Walnut Creek, Calif.: AltaMira Press.

White, M. 1988–1989. "The Externalization of the Problem and the Reauthoring of Lives and Relationships." *Dulwich Centre Newsletter* (Summer): 3–20.

Stories that Conform/Stories that Transform: A Conversation in Four Parts

DOUGLAS FLEMONS AND SHELLEY GREEN

Part 2

Autoethnography, Therapy, and the Telling of Lives

Note: This is the second of four conversations derived from a taped panel discussion titled "Autoethnography and Therapy: Stories That Conform, Stories That Transform." See also pages 87–94, 165–169, and 187–190.

Art Bochner: Let's talk about the process of working with students or scholars writing autobiography, memoir, autoethnography. At this point in time, we don't, methodologically speaking, have standard practices, procedurally, for teaching people to work as autoethnographers. How do you work with their stories as they evolve? Is it simply the telling of a story—"This is what happened to me"—or is it a dialogical process, helping to nurture the movement through various subjectivities, various possible accounts, various kinds of stories?

Is it possible to use reflexive family therapy as an analog, methodologically, for working with, say, aspiring autoethnographers? If you think of a therapy client as the teller of a life, and to that extent an autoethnographer as well, then the therapist is in dialogue with that person's telling and thus the therapist is to some extent critiquing the story as it goes along. In dialogue, you're moving toward a reframing or another story. You [Douglas Flemons, Shelley Green, Jerry Gale] are not only family therapists, but also qualitative researchers, working with students who are writing autoethnographies.

Shelley Green: Which brings up the ethical question, "When does the boundary get blurred between therapy and scholarship and mentoring?" As a therapist or as a faculty member, should you be invested in a corrective story or a healing story?

Carolyn Ellis: I want to tell you what I tell my students and see what you think. I teach a course on writing lives, and I tell my students that one of the goals of the course is that they should become their own therapist. That doesn't mean, I say, there won't be times they go *to* a therapist, but writing can help them have insights about themselves, help them work through problems themselves. In the class, we try to work through these problems, not to solve them or even necessarily to heal them, but to open them up to greater understanding or a multitude of understandings. Hopefully something good comes out of that. I wonder, as therapists, how you feel about my taking that stance.

Shelley: I think it's a wonderful stance; I think it's a stance that therapists would be wise to take. We limit ourselves as therapists when we walk into the therapy room saying, "I'm going to heal this couple in six sessions or less," or "I need this particular outcome." Unfortunately, the realities of surviving in the current HMO-dominated climate encourage us to do just that, to say, "I need these particular outcomes in this number of sessions." I like this idea that people become their own therapists. It might put us out of business.

Douglas Flemons: That would be good. As you were talking about your writing process, Carolyn, I was already thinking that in questioning yourself and opening yourself up to multiple understandings, you were basically doing what a therapist would do.

Carolyn: Yes, and then offering these understandings to other people for interpretations that, in turn, get fed back to me.

Art: Didn't Karen Horney say, in her book *Self Analysis*, that there would never be enough therapists to go around? So what we really have to learn and teach is how people can do self-analysis.

Douglas: Being a teacher of people writing autoethnographies does put you in a strange—or complicated—position. Let's say your students are doing an autoethnography and you wonder whether they're questioning themselves or not, or whether they've come to a premature closure that is limiting possibilities for them. Challenging their assumptions puts you in a quasi-therapeutic role, and that certainly creates complexity.

Carolyn: Um hum, and you have to be prepared for that because it will happen.

Jim King: As methodologists and teachers of this method have you not experienced narratives from students or even from ourselves that were *not* particularly convincing, *weren't* particularly compelling, and didn't *take* you anywhere? I have found myself in this uncomfortable position of saying, "You know, that's not a very good narrative." And that's problematic for me, but it happens.

Art: All the time.

Jim: When I project a narrative I've written, I've already foregrounded what the interpretation will be by accessing some kind of structural component that I intend to be transactive. In other words, if I'm going to tell this story—and it's going to be healing and perceived, if healing is the goal, or convincing if convincing is the goal, or cohesive, or whatever—then I've already preselected some structure that I've pulled out. I may not be cognizant of that, but the extent to which somebody else resonates with that narrative and it causes some kind of an identification or a catharsis or whatever, that means the person and I have transacted on that mythic plane. Otherwise, from my experience it's simply—no, it's *complexly*—that the story is just being blathered out. And it is a release for the blatherer, but it goes no further because it doesn't transact. It has to be in some structure.

Audience member: What is the difference between keeping my own personal journal, for example, and using my own story, as you talked about it, Carolyn, using my own story to connect with others in some way? I think there's a vast difference between a narrative that is more like a personal journal and a narrative that says, "I have a story to tell that maybe someone could use."

Arthur Frank: I had exactly the same line of inquiry. As rich as it is to bring together sociology and therapy, and even though I try to do that in my own life and practice, there also are significant differences, and I'd like to hear you address those. Art, I think I heard you describe the autoethnographer as the teller of a life. Are you treating these two as synonyms, or do you recognize differences between them?

As ethnography was practiced traditionally, the ethnographer went out with rather specific skills, knowing how to compile dictionaries, how to chart kinship, how to measure skulls, and so on. The stories the ethnographer told reflected the specificity of those skills. The teller of a life has the life in all of its richness, but he or she doesn't have any particular skill set, any of the preset structures that are going to connect with certain audiences. The two seem to have quite different purposes. So I'm wondering, first, as the term autoethnography passes into a larger currency in sociology, is this just telling a life? What are the boundaries here? And second, what are the differences between the kind of contract that's involved in engaging in social science and the kind of contract that's involved in engaging in a therapeutic endeavor?

Cristina González: Can I say something? I was once asked to write an autoethnography about a particular experience, and I decided not to, in part because to write such a story and make it autoethnographic, I would have had to go back and systematically find the cultural components of my own experience, find the theory, find those aspects, and in doing that I'd be doing a real number on my own self. And that's where I see the linking between therapy and autoethnography. I have to have a lot of awareness of the therapeutic as I engage in autoethnographic work because, without that awareness and without the years that I've spent reading and studying about it, I would be heading off into what I consider to be very volatile, dangerous territory. I don't want to go back to my journals, I don't want to go code what I'd been writing about, I don't want to connect them with those theories that I know could make sense of them. That's not the story I want to tell.

Carolyn: Then you shouldn't write autoethnography in that particular instance.

Caroline Joan S. Picart: I was struck by the implicit assumptions when you were comparing therapy and autoethnography. It seemed as though therapy was still being set up as some sort of definite structure from which autoethnography could take something or could adopt in order to make it much more authorized. But right now the model of interaction between the two domains is not clear and for me that *precisely* is its richness. Perhaps we can overturn the implicit hierarchy and ask whether a therapist can take something from autoethnography.

Janet Yerby: I want to respond to Arthur Frank's question about the differences between therapy and autoethnography. Myself, I want to know what the *similarities* are. I don't see the boundary separating them as all that clear—they seem so similar.

Shelley: Do you see the boundary as really necessary?

Janet: No, I don't and maybe that's the difference.

Shelley: I guess that's what surprised me about Arthur Frank's comments. I don't see the boundaries as particularly necessary: We can learn from each one.

Audience member: Well, that's a different place to be at.

Carolyn: Yeah, and I would imagine that all good therapists have to be good ethnographers, not just autoethnographers, but ethnographers. And maybe the reverse is true too.

Art: To me the most disturbing thing about ethnography itself, as a category, is the idea that it was somehow fixed in time and that there was one notion of ethnography that is the universal class "ethnography." I remember four years ago I was invited to give a talk for an anthropology department at another university, and I began by talking about some of the innovative ideas with respect to autoethnography and interactive ethnography that were being developed in communication, cultural studies, and performance, and immediately, the first response, before I got out the first paragraph of the talk, was, "Wait a second, ethnography belongs to anthropology! You can't possibly take it from us!"

When Douglas and I started our e-mail connection, I don't think we ever, *ever* said to one another, "Well you're a therapist" or "You're in communication," you know? Disturbing the categories is *very,* very important here. If any innovation or anything interesting is going to happen here, then I'm glad if this is disturbing to a lot of people because out of that disturbance and out of these kinds of conversations might come something important. We are tapping, I hope, into something valuable, something for which we don't yet have the answers. And *that* is *not* troubling to me.

Arthur Frank: I want to raise the question of whether autoethnography itself is a misnomer. It sounds from a lot of what we've been hearing that one of the categories that doesn't really hold much water is the difference between first-person and third-person narratives. This means that all first-person narratives are also third-person, just as all third-person are first-person. So when we talk about narratives as being in dialogue with others, but then call it autoethnography, or call it self-therapy, it seems to me not to really do justice to a dialogical view of the way in which writing relationships occur.

Audience member: This is more of a theoretical concern than a practical concern but, as you know, long ago Nietzsche told us that God is dead. And Foucault followed up on that with the notion of the author disappearing. From what you're saying and what I've seen of autoethnography, it appears to embrace both the poststructuralist/postmodern position and the Romantic (with a capital R) position of Keats and Yeats. And to me these two come in analytic tension with each other to a great degree, and I was wondering if you could explain that.

Art: Tension is good.

Carolyn: Good explanation!

Art: Tension is good and the only persons who I've ever seen invoke or introduce the Romanticist notion of the authentic self into an accusation or criticism of autoethnography are the ones who don't like it. I've never seen an autoethnographer who made claims to a Romantic self. Maybe some exist, but that's an issue for another day.

Laurel: Foucault later retracted that dead author business in interviews, saying, "No, that isn't what I meant; you Americans went and did funny things with my French." But it is really interesting and important to point out that the author died exactly when women and minorities came to voice. It was a political move on the part of some American journals. When some of us who had never talked about ourselves came forward, the journals pulled out Foucault and proclaimed, "The author is dead."

Carolyn: We're very much alive. And we're good at speaking out. [laughter]

Douglas: I'd like to go back for a second to the issue of whether we should be distinguishing between autoethnography and therapy. Instead of arguing over whether we should lump them together or keep them separate, we can say, "If we put them together, juxtaposing them, what can we see that we wouldn't otherwise, both in therapy and autoethnograpy?" And then the opposite question can be posed. "By keeping the two separate, what can we see that we couldn't when we were treating them as one?" It's not a question of which position is right or wrong, but rather of what each action brings forth, what it allows you to see or hear.

Carolyn: And, further, "What can we *feel* that we might not otherwise by putting them together or pulling them apart?" One thing that just occurred to me is that with autoethnography, it is like the patient is speaking back to the therapist: "This is my life, this is my experience of it. This is the way I construct it when I'm doing therapy on my own life, here, have this too, look at this too, have this be a piece."

Arthur Frank: Carolyn, it seems to me that the way that you just described autoethnography is at odds as I hear it from the description that Cristina gave us. She laid out what it would involve to tell a story as an autoethnography and it seems to me that that's something a bit different. What I just heard you saying, Carolyn, is closer to what I would call telling a life, and I think that it is valuable, just as Douglas has said, to see how that differs from autoethnography.

Carolyn: Well, I was talking about what therapy and autoethnography could offer each other. You're now wanting to pull them apart again, which was your question before, as well: "How are these different?"

Arthur Frank: The reason that I'm pulling them apart is that I'm hearing two very different things. Cristina spoke of really quite a methodological, methodical process of coding documents, of relating to theories—of employing *method* in a traditional way. As I listen to you talk, I'm hearing a very different kind of activity, and I can appreciate the value of both; I wouldn't want to do away with either one. But I *am* interested in trying to tease out how this is being used.

Stacy Holman Jones: I think this is a really important point. I'm very interested in the telling of a life in something as simple as a song. It is interesting that the word "just" is so often put in front of "telling a life," so the activity becomes "*just* telling a life." Any kind of autobiographical, biographical, or even musical format is a constructed work. There's a structure. We can analyze how autobiography works, just like I can analyze how a torch song works. And my concern and what I'm pushed to do constantly is to find the therapy and then the happy outcome inside the tragedy of the moment. It's very complex because it's really hiding in public. I haven't heard that yet today, and I think it's one of the reasons we're compelled by these stories to hear them and to revisit them. It's highly complex, so I want us to be careful in distinguishing between coding something and constructing something because they're related, but different, processes.

Cristina González: When I'm writing an autoethnography, I am coding, I am keeping a track record of the way that I make my decisions. As John Johnson and David Altheide said, we need to be accountable for the decisions we make along the way, as this is our form of validity in ethnography. And that's what I hold up. When I make the decision to tell this piece and not that piece, if I'm an ethnographer and I'm doing an autoethnography, I can't hide behind, "Well that one just felt right." I have to be able to do what Carolyn described earlier about pushing the end of her story, looking at why she did this and why she would not do that. And that's where I draw distinctions between "just telling a life" and "writing an autoethnography." Nevertheless, "just telling a life" is a major methodological component of autoethnography. If I can't tell my life, *just* tell it without the pushing and questioning, then I don't have anything to turn into an autoethnography.

Erotic Mentoring: Pygmalion and Galatea at the University

JANICE HOCKER RUSHING

When I was a senior in college, I took an unforgettable honors seminar. We met on Tuesday nights at the cozy apartment of one of the students, where we sat amid the bricks-and-boards bookcases on floor pillows and a few rickety chairs, saving the one good armchair for the typically late arrival of HIM—a brilliant fortyish professor, grayed and balding but impressively pumped up, with a goatee and enigmatic smile that cast an image somewhere between Terence Stamp and Satan. He had us read and discuss things this "good" preacher's kid from Texas found devilishly interesting: Betty Friedan's *The Feminine Mystique,* Philip Wylie's *The Disappearance,* Freud's *A General Introduction to Psychoanalysis,* Nietzsche's *Thus Spake Zarathustra* (our group bible), and notes from his own book-in-the-making, *The Marriage Malady.* All twelve disciples were utterly enthralled; we talked among ourselves about the texts during the week, intricately analyzing every word and gesture of HIM, and eagerly awaited the next seminar. These were invigorating times. We were the campus liberal intellectual elite, rebelling against the university's archaic policies toward women, taking turns reading the names of the Vietnam War dead from the steps of the student union, debating the era's treatises on free love and alternative education.

Imagine my incredulous thrill when HE started driving *me* back to my dorm after class, inquiring into my love life, saying he liked the way I looked. Best of all, he said I was smart; in fact, he was so interested in my ideas that he made my papers the centerpiece of an extracurricular study group he formed with the select of us elects and his wife to study things that no one had ever studied before. I quit my voluntary post as leader of a large student congregation at the local church, tried hard to understand Nietzsche, and feverishly wrote weekly, unscheduled papers, anticipating his praise. I gave up my still distant dream to marry a minister like my mother did; in fact, I decided marriage itself was probably equal only to capitalism and traditional education as reasons for the current deplorable state of Western civilization. I found less time for my kind and fatherly mentor in the speech department. I was in iconoclastic, post-Christian, "Big Chill," physically and intellectually activated Heaven.

So why did I not question my professor's antipathy for the physique of the average woman, wandering hungrily instead through the student union snack bar, eyeing the cheeseburgers with fries but dutifully settling on salad with no dressing, striving to conform to his dictum that I diet down to ninety-two pounds? Why did I let him tell me how to dress? Why did I yield to his molding of my every insight to his own standard of rational perfection? Why was I so enamored with his assessment that I was somehow better than the rest that I gratefully delivered my weekly papers to HIM for his own research? Why was I startled to find myself in a confusing and guilty contest with my best friend for his intellectual and erotic attention? Why did he disdain my chosen field as inferior to his own and discourage me from the grad school to which I was headed in the fall? Perhaps I should have thought more carefully about the title of the seminar that began it all: "The Nature of Man."

The Matter of Myth

I've thought a lot about the nature of man—actually, more about the nature of woman—during the academic career I began in earnest at the graduate program my professor warned me against. Always galvanized by something personal, whether I knew it at the time or not, I have invested much of my intellectual energy trying to understand cultural life in terms of myth—in particular, how patriarchy arose and still thrives by burying women's stories, replacing them with versions that make their greatly reduced roles seem "natural." Mostly, I have looked at popular films as a textual critic, unraveling such knots as why I got a charge out of "feminist" Ripley's Amazonian deeds in the *Aliens* series, yet felt insulted by her battle with an oozing, pelvic-shaped feminine monster that the set designer said he modeled after his mother (Rushing 1989); how feminine figures relatively hidden in science fiction films offer clues that could save us from destroying the world with our own machines (Rushing and Frentz 1989, 1995); and how Old Rose in James Cameron's *Titanic* exhumes the rusting "Ship of Dreams," consummating its "maiden voyage" in a distinctly feminine way (Rushing and Frentz 2000). In all these pursuits, myth has helped to unfurl the stories like a rose, revealing that the layers, especially the feminine ones, go very deep indeed.

I have long suspected that the patriarchal bias of U.S. universities is storied in myths that, like those of the culture at large, are built upon the grave sights of their more feminine bones. And so my instinct was to turn again to myth to explore those nagging questions I still have about a professor-student relationship that happened thirty years ago. I felt less sure without the buffer of a cultural artifact to analyze, however, and wondered whether my decades-long immersion in myth would help me here. One day I came across this quote by Albert Camus in the contemplative journal I read every morning:

> I know with certainty that a person's work is nothing but the long journey to recover, through the detours of art, the two or three simple and great images which first gained access to his heart. (Hiles and Hiles 1999: 12)

An image from my childhood appeared, as if an electrode had stimulated my soul.

I am gazing at the large, unframed poster above the twin beds in the room I share with my sister in Dallas. I must be about four or five. It is a fabulously detailed drawing of myths and fairy tales; the figures are intricately interwoven, the characters moving in and out of each other's territories, filling every square inch with color and intrigue. As I study the pictures, I mount a white horse, ride onto a bridge, cross the moat, slide down Rapunzel's hair, find the Holy Grail, wait for a knight to save me from a dragon, rescue Hansel and Gretel myself from the witch's oven. I am fearful and courageous, tentative and exhilarated. For what seems like hours I lose myself in this splendid landscape until my mother calls, and I rematerialize back into "reality."

With a jolt, I realized that much of my scholarly career was prefigured in my interactions with that picture, when, to paraphrase James Agee, I was "disguised as a girl" (Hiles and Hiles 2000: 2). All this time I have been working it out, entering the realm of the imagination, what Joseph Campbell terms "the facts of the mind" (1972: 11), and coming out again, finding as I go that the "fiction" of myth and the "reality" of life are not all that distinct. It feels right, then, to enter this topography of myth again to recollect what Jane Tompkins calls *A Life in*

School (1996). Thus I have begun a larger project, of which my exploration of mentoring is one part. Myth has helped me many times to piece the episodes of my life into a story—as Arthur Bochner puts it, "to make a life that seems to be falling apart come together again" (1997: 429). Furthermore, he says, "there is nothing as theoretical as a good story," especially if both theory and story are conceived as communicative rather than objective, representational activities, and if "we think with a story rather than about it," letting it resonate with our moral dilemmas and ambiguities (1997: 435–36). And what is a myth other than an extraordinary story with a very long shelf life?

Following a myth unconsciously can be limiting, for we merely live out the timeless dimensions without making them our own. As Willie Nelson sings: "Be careful what you're dreamin'/ Soon your dreams'll be dreamin' you" (1974). Becoming conscious of a myth's allure, on the other hand, helps to break its spell. We can personalize it, use and discard what we want, make it our own. Encountered with eyes wide open, a myth mirrors the complexity of a life, offering what Kenneth Burke calls "equipment for living" (1973: 63). In my own attempts to achieve narrative coherence, I have weaved in and out of mythic consciousness many times. I have sometimes unwittingly tried to mold a cultural text or a piece of my self into a template based on some misguided notion of a myth's perfect beauty, to make a static thing without flaw or flow, like the poster in my bedroom if viewed from a safe distance rather than up close and personal. I get tangled up in "fate," and can live the myth *forward* only if I become aware of its grip on me—an enchantment that typically has historical roots not only in my story, but also in my culture's. Outward Bound, that serious boot camp for problem teenagers that believes *Outdoor Living* is therapy rather than a slick magazine, has a phrase for when you get stuck in some pickle like dangling from a rope on a sheer cliff when your foot misses its mark: "The only way out of this is into it."

Reading Pygmalion and Galatea Backward

Fairly sure that the relationship with my honors professor was related to the myth of "Pygmalion and Galatea," I ventured backward into the text. Here is a short form of Ovid's Roman version, the one most of you will recognize:

> Pygmalion was a sculptor from Cyprus who hated women. Refusing to marry, he molded all his genius into a statue of a woman—some say it was of ivory and others stone—so exquisite that no mortal woman could approach its beauty. He then fell passionately in love with her, dressing her in rich clothes and

imagining that she was pleased. But she was unable to respond to his touch, for he loved a lifeless thing. Desperately he prayed to Venus, who brought her to life. Pygmalion named the maiden Galatea and Venus herself graced their marriage. We do not know what happened after that, except that their son, Paphos, lent his name to Venus' favorite city. (Hamilton 1999: 112–15)

This is tantalizingly brief, stopping just where it gets good with a happily-ever-after ending more characteristic of fairy tales than myths. Galatea has no personality here; in fact, she never speaks a word. So I piled up the myth history books on my desk to search for roots. I love this part, playing the scholarly Columbo, goaded by the hunch, "There's something that bothers me here." As I read, a story spanning millennia began to emerge:

"Galatea" was another name for the Great Goddess in her many manifestations, including the Middle Eastern Astarte, the Cyprian Aphrodite, and the Myceneaen Demeter. Celtic tribes from Galatea worshipped her as Galata (gala, or "mother's milk"), and the Gauls and Gaels traced their descent from her. "Pygmalion," a Greek corruption of the Phoenician "Pumiyathon," was a common name for Semitic kings in general. (Walker 1983: 332–33; Frazer 1996: 387)

Galatea was once the Great Goddess? Something big must have happened on her way to becoming a sculpture. Who was this goddess before she turned to stone?

Personifying the reproductive energies of nature, the Great Goddess was supremely powerful all over Europe, the Mediterranean, and Eastern Asia, and she took many male son/lover consorts, whose role in reproduction was not well known. Each year her sacred marriage with a divine consort was simulated on earth by the temporary union of male and female at a temple dedicated to her. This "god-king" or "year king" was sacrificed at the end of his predetermined reign of one to seven years, because it was thought that life sprang from blood, and his was spilt to ensure fertility. In cultures where the royal blood was traced through women, the king held office through his marriage with a hereditary princess, who was the real sovereign, and thus he would lose his throne if his wife died. (Campbell 1976a: 4–6, 1976b: 151–69; Frazer 1996: 385–87; Lerner 1986: 125)

Galatea was apparently powerful when her sexuality was hers and not in the service of Pygmalion. Dating back to the Neolithic period, before Christianity abolished the custom, the goddess's transformative sexuality was worshiped for nearly 2,000 years throughout these regions, including in Pygmalion's Cyprus, in the ritual of "cultic sexual service" or "sacred prostitution":

> In the temple of Aphrodite the woman lay with a stranger thought to be an emissary of the gods. Some records suggest this was required of all women before marriage or once in their lives, and others that it was enacted primarily by temple priestesses. The woman used her body not to attain security, power, possessions, admiration, or devotion from the man. Rather, the ritual's purpose was to unite flesh and spirit and to bring the love of the goddess—an impersonal force—into the human sphere. The fertility of the land and the people depended upon her sexual power. (Frazer 1996: 384–85; Gimbutas 1982; Lerner 1986: 125–31; Qualls-Corbett, 1988: 39–40)

Under the goddess' greater authority, however, the year-king's role was not exactly enviable, and the onset of patriarchy coincided with an ingenious strategy:

> A king who wanted to lengthen his reign simply married his sister or his daughter, the offspring of his or his father's union with a sacred priestess, and therefore a divinity herself. (Frazer 1996: 386; Graves 1992: 72)

And this helps explain a version of the Pygmalion myth that predates the one above:

> Pygmalion was in love with Aphrodite. Because she would not lie with him, he made an ivory image of her and kept it in his bed. He prayed to her for pity, and she entered into his image of her and brought it to life as Galatea. This story probably arose from a ritual of invocation that called down the goddess' spirit into her sculpture. (Graves 1992: 211; Walker 1983: 332–33)

When Pygmalion refused to give up his white ("milky" = Galatea) cult-image, he was attempting to extend his reign by holding on to the goddess's authority.

If we consider that Pygmalion was succeeded by Paphos, the son borne him by one of Aphrodite's priestesses, and then by Paphos' son Cinyras, who also married his own daughter, then Pygmalion was the first king to replace the matrilinear with the patrilinear system of divine descent on Cyprus. Pygmalion's priestess-wife, literally his daughter, was called Metharme, which means "change." (Graves 1992: 211–12)

Tracing this historical line through the myth of Pygmalion and Galatea reveals one route to patriarchal mentorship. Pygmalion emerges from a context of sacred marriage that regards the feminine as authoritative. When he steals the icon of the priestess, he wants to retain her impersonal creative potency for himself, so he *annexes* the feminine for personal and political gain. By the time of the Roman myth on which we base our modern fictional extensions and which seems quite prevalent in the academy, Pygmalion no longer needs to seize a symbol of the goddess because he crafts one himself, and the goddess of love is reduced to one who merely grants his Frankensteinian wish to bring her to life. For her part, Galatea loses her capacity to animate, as "making love" becomes just "making."

Living Pygmalion and Galatea Forward

Thinking about how much Galatea has been reduced over time offered some clues to the doubled-edged feelings I have harbored over my early mentoring. The relationship with my professor was both thrilling and distressing, and though it conformed quite closely to the later Pygmalion myth, I did have a life before him, and must have provided him *something* other than a virgin block of stone to shape. I also knew that sexual-intellectual apprenticeships were—and probably still are, even in these days of sexual harassment policies—very common in the university. I remember thinking one time as I looked up the towering, open central atrium of the Los Angeles Hyatt Regency at all those guest room doors clearly visible from the glass elevator, "This would never work as a convention hotel!" I wanted to understand my own experience within a broader contemporary, as well as historical context, to hear the complexity of Galatea's voices, what other women would have to say about their Pygmalions.

When I hit midlife at the same time as I published a book and made full professor, I crashed hard, finally realizing what a product of the academic patriarchy I was, working almost all the time (but never enough) to prove my worth, my beleaguered body finally crying "Foul!" at my nonstop pace. I looked back on the "body of work" that constituted my curriculum vita with a mixture of fondness and aridity, contemplating the costs of learning to talk the parched talk of academic prose and walk the soulless walk of "institutional depression" (Bochner

1997). I wanted to play, to garden, to just sit. And I had valued men more than women, unwittingly considering "feminine" ways of being and thinking less legitimate than "masculine" ones, even when arguing the opposite case in my teaching and writing. If I spoke to women about their lives in the university, maybe I could get to know them. Suddenly, women became very important to me, not only for how they could illuminate my own story, but also for their friendship.

Five years ago I began intensive interviews with women I knew who were willing to talk. I wrote before I planned to be in their city or at a conference, asking if they would talk to me about such questions as: How did you decide to go into academia? Who inspired you? What is pleasurable and not so pleasurable about being an academic? Is academia a good outlet for expressing your most creative side? What have been the highs and lows of your studies or career thus far? To what extent do you feel you are the author of your own career? The conversation could go anywhere they'd like, and I asked if I could record our talks. Almost everyone was so enthusiastic that I sensed there were nerves out there relatively untouched. Their friends called me. I got unsolicited e-mails. Men asked to be included. We met in our offices and living rooms, hotel rooms, coffee shops, bars, and, in one case, an expensive restaurant where I paid for dinner, because I didn't know the woman and felt grateful. One woman even whispered her story to me at lunch while five others carried on separate conversations. I taped many of the talks, but had to recreate the more spontaneous ones retrospectively.

I always started with something about myself. If I thought the woman could relate, I told her about my midlife burnout. If she were young, I told her how burdened, yet excited I felt as a graduate student or assistant professor. I never asked direct questions about erotic mentoring, but these stories came out anyway. If she "went there," I sometimes told her about me. One day, a man walked by in a bar as a woman was pouring out her story of fifteen years of sexual harassment by that very man and others in her department. He is a good man and a friend, and I couldn't miss his concerned look. I freaked. What if he finds out what I am doing and takes it out on her? Or me? Shaken, I put aside the study for four years, unsure whether I could handle the ethical dilemmas, afraid I couldn't protect the women, and reminding myself I had no training in counseling, yet clearly in some cases that is what I was doing. Perhaps I wasn't really sure I wanted to "go there" publicly myself.

I took up the interviews again a year ago because the nagging questions that had initiated the project had never abated and I got a small grant to fly around the country and meet people of different ages and ethnicities, and from different fields, positions, and countries. Excitement conquered my fears, and I learned to protect others by encouraging them to change earlier drafts of mine that they felt might be too close to home. Out of thirty women I have spoken with thus far, ten told stories related to Pygmalion and Galatea. Their voices carry this myth forward.

These women recreate Galatea as a character who reaches back into her ancestry and ahead into new possibilities. I heard the creative instinct in both the man and the woman in all these stories. The goddess, whether Aphrodite or the early Galatea, can be a force for transformation and the birth of new life. When her spirit is invoked physically, the result can be a literal child. Creative work of any kind comes out of a similar passionate involvement, says Jean Shinoda Bolen, "almost as if with a lover, as one (the artist) interacts with the 'other' to bring something new into being" (1985: 241). When a mentor and student come together with the passion of Aphrodite, a symbolic or "divine child" often emerges—a musical composition, manuscript, theory, or invention. bell hooks, who tells of her own romantic relationships with teachers and a student, thinks of the erotic as "a space of transgression," and urges that, "[r]ather than perceiving desire between individuals (let us imagine here teacher and student) as always and only dangerous, negative and destructive, what does it mean to consider the positive uses of that desire, the way the erotic can serve the interests of spiritual growth?" (1995: 37) At times these women felt their erotic mentoring was "divine," and at others they felt more like a "child." But most did grow from the experience.

I hear five of Galatea's voices echoing in the stories they tell. Each woman lived through more than one role, sometimes at the same time. Their voices narrate a progression from nascent potential to loss of self to its recovery, although not everyone went through all phases, or in this order. The relationship typically began with the woman as a *Maiden Lover,* who reflects Pygmalion's desire for a "soul mate, daughter, or sisterly dream lover who is either the match or the potential match for the perfect relationship" (Young-Eisendrath 1993: 88). Whereas the Maiden Lover springs from romantic love, the *Muse* aestheticizes romance as she inspires the man to re-create himself. Pygmalion owns the *Mistress* as an object of his physical pleasure. He gives birth to the *Brainchild* as a perfect mirror image of his masculine intellect. A woman becomes *Virgin,* or one-in-herself, when she defines herself independently of him. The Maiden Lover is based directly on "Pygmalion and Galatea," whereas the others begin there and intersect with other myths, much like the tales on my bedroom poster. The first four take their names from Pygmalion's projections on to the woman. She may identify with his projection and try to live it out, project her own complementary image onto him, or reject his projection and struggle to define herself.[1]

The Maiden Lover

"I'm sure you could have a heyday analyzing older man, younger woman," ventured Maggie, as she kindly handed me two Tylenol P.M. tablets for the cold that had kept me awake for two nights. "Mixing sex with an academic career happens more often than not. In my case he was thirty-nine, and I was nineteen, twenty." Maggie, a very successful forty-five-year-old associate professor, was talking to me a year after our first conversation. She had called me to say, "Okay, now you want to hear the *real* story?" She had told only her therapist, her husband, and her best friend, Kate, who went through a similar thing at the same time. Though Maggie acknowledged that the nine-year affair instigated by her adviser, Rick, would today be termed "sexual harassment" because of the unequal power dynamic, she has no regrets, and regards herself as "at least as much the aggressor as he was."

Pygmalion sees his Maiden Lover as innocent, beautiful, and full of the latent talent only he can bring out. The middle-aged photographer, Connie, in the film *Guinevere* (1999) tells his twenty-year-old charge, Harper—one of a series of "Guineveres" he loves and mentors—that she can live at his bohemian loft apartment if she works and studies hard, if she "creates something." Not yet confident of herself, Harper whispers softly, "Oh, you're mistaking me for someone with potential." When she feels mirrored by an "artist" who adores her, the woman in love with him is stirred to unfold a part of herself that may have been lying in wait. Harper blooms sensually and cerebrally under Connie's sensitive tutelage when she begins to see herself as he does, symbolized by the beautiful photographs he takes of her. Similarly, Maggie was fascinated that her mentor's wife was "smart, gorgeous, classy, tasteful, and he was still interested in *me*." I remembered feeling the same way when I met my professor's wife, who had precisely the same qualities—could it be that I had them, too? When I asked Maggie why she was so incredulous about this, she answered, laughingly, "Because I'm a dork and a nerd, and I had glasses."

Sarah, a professor with numerous influential publications, also spoke of seeing her own potential mirrored by older men in her field. "Some of these guys were good—they really had the lines down, like, 'I want to talk to you because you're smart.' And I'd go, like, 'Wow, cool! How do you know?' And they'd say, 'I can just tell.'" She admitted that she sought out the attention. "It was so flattering, and it was, you know, you feel like such a stranger in that setting that any type of affection with somebody that you have some admiration for was enough to make me not think about this as much as I should have." In graduate school she had only one female teacher, who was outside her own department, so she was "completely mentored by males. It was almost as if there was this unwritten rule floating through my national association," she said with a touch of acquired cynicism, "that men who were fairly well-known figures felt a license to spend as much time in whatever ways that they wished with the young, dewy-eyed graduate students."

Laura, a fifty-four-year-old ex-professor now flourishing in a second career, described a passionate relationship with her Ph.D. adviser, Al, that she considered more the norm than an aberration: "This was, after all, the early '70s, and all of these professors were having affairs with their students; everybody was." Laura perfectly captured the blissful oblivion of romantic love between a Pygmalion and his Maiden Lover as she recounted the "romantic haze" of her relationship. "This man was only ten years older, but this incredible rush of feeling understood and seen by this power figure—that was pretty heady." She was immersed in the euphoria of feeling different—valued and adored by a powerful and admired man. "I was a confidante, understander, and we felt, as people in those relationships often do, kind of outside the norm—we don't have to follow the rules—this is special, this is different."

For the Galatea absorbed in such elation, the relationship is not only exciting, but "heady," as Kelly also put it, by which she meant something closer to a total emotional-intellectual awakening. Now a thirty-two-year-old Ph.D. student working on her dissertation, she does not remember being sexually interested at first in Joel, her undergraduate debate coach, who had a "huge crush" on her. "But he made me feel smart, and he provided a forum in which I could speak and excel, and he told me I could do it." Still enthusiastic ten years later about this relationship, Kelly related both to being "in her body" and becoming more articulate, "finding her voice." She told of getting up at 5:00 A.M. with Joel and her debate partners, surfing while stoned, then going to rounds with their hair still wet and "kicking ass." They lived "moment to moment," their lives were "packed," and she loved being "on the edge." Returning again and again to her first symbol of academia—a visit to a prospective college where she would have had to live in a gray, institutional-looking, clinical, high-rise dorm—Kelly mused, "I think part of why I wasn't drawn to academia at first is because I didn't think I could be moved there, I didn't think I could be myself. . . . I don't like to conform. . . . I really resist when things are rigid or judgmental. So Joel was showing us a way that we could succeed *and* surf and smoke pot." A talented sportswoman, Kelly clarified that she meant "be moved" in a literal sense, that what she learned from Joel was not to compromise on passion in terms of society's rules. Time and space were not rigid, but fluid. "We weren't bound by the laws of physics and time in a way that linear Western thought wants to tell you."

Like many Maiden Lovers, especially near the onset of the relationship, Kelly's feeling of "an opening up rather than a closing down" closely echoes the sacred prostitute's initiation. In this ritual, the woman enacted the transformative side of the goddess—that which urges change and is similar to the divine madness of the soul in Plato's *Phaedrus*. Such a force transcends the limitations of social constraint and practical reason, producing ecstasy and an enlargement of the personality (Ulanov 1971: 159, cited in Qualls-Corbett 1988: 56). Kelly remembered this time as transformative, and spoke with the fluidity of Aphrodite when she extolled being taken out of social constraints, ecstatically riding the waves of the surf and of her winning debates. (I thought immediately of Botticelli's gorgeous "The Birth of Venus" I had seen in the Uffizi in Florence, with the ocean-born goddess floating ashore on a seashell.) Although she and Joel had a serious flirtation rather than an affair—"he was an instigator, not a partner"—she still thinks of him "really fondly," for "he changed my life; he's one of the most influential people in my life." Kelly probably saw Joel as an Underground Genius, the gender complex Young-Eisendrath sees as most commonly projected on to men by women in their twenties and thirties. The Underground Genius is "seductive, sensitive, passionate, full of dark exotic powers . . . somewhat androgynous and the 'artist type' . . ." He often appears to her as Dionysus—the god of ecstasy who combines sex and power, is exotic and erotic, and attracts crowds of women (1993: 96). *Guinevere*'s Harper obviously sees her photographer this way, as did all the Guineveres before and after her. Her venomously seductive mother nails her daughter's attraction to him as she monologues in answer to her own question, why he prefers a naive girl to an "experienced" woman her age. "I know exactly what she has that I haven't got," she hisses, blowing smoke in Connie's face. "*Awe*." Like most women who felt likewise, Kelly described her debate coach as "passionate," "brilliant," and "incredible."

Although as Underground Genius Pygmalion can facilitate a woman's break from her father, and is usually seen at first as radically different from him, he can transmute into a father figure rather seamlessly. Remember that Pygmalion first broke from the mother goddess by marrying his daughter. I expected academic women, who need a certain fierceness, to be closer to their fathers than their mothers, but more of them felt closer to their mothers than their fathers, particularly when they played the daughter/lover role. Maggie, who pictures her mother as a best friend, said that Rick never seemed like a father figure at the time, but looking back, "I'd curl up in his lap and we'd go over papers." I thought of Guinevere draped over her mentor's lap in a manner half winsome, half seductive, as he called her his "good girl." Rick taught Maggie how to teach and gave her access to important people she otherwise would not have had. "It was a really neat introduction to the field," she pondered. "I think I was able to gain a certain maturity—in the field and for myself—within the safety of his love and support."

Not all were positive about their daughter/lover roles, however, and some were angry or confused about how hard it was to reject them. Amy, a fifty-one-year-old who moved through the ranks in the same department where she is now a professor, grew up without a father, and saw that as a factor in "this 'daughter' thing." She portrayed herself as a reluctant "mascot" to the older men in the department, several of whom pushed unwanted sexual relationships on her: "It was straight out of the 'Mary Tyler Moore Show.'" And Michelle told of being "brought in" to graduate school when she was about twenty by a forty-year-old "nice gentle chair of the department" who "wore Mr. Rogers sweaters. I became this person's student." She also became his "comforter" because "his wife was so difficult and all that," did research projects and took classes with him, and fended off his sexual advances that were covered by his "fatherly" and "emotionally needy" demeanor. When other women revealed that he acted similarly with them, he was dismissed as chair, although he stayed on as professor. Michelle interned elsewhere for a while and when she returned, the graduate coordinator as well as others in the department, all of whom knew about her situation, pressured her into taking another class from him since he was so "depressed" and she was "one of his favorite students." Apparently, the powers in the department considered Michelle to be not only his daughter, but also a dutiful one at that. According to Young-Eisendrath, the Father, Brother, or Guide to the Maiden Lover "feels enabled to be special or unique in assisting, supporting, or encouraging the woman. He may feel that his worth or future depends on her agreement to his plan" (1993: 89). Rather than protect *her* from his inappropriate behavior, "Mr. Rogers's" colleagues protected *him* from feeling his own humiliation.

Perhaps it may seem that the Maiden Lover is merely raw material for Pygmalion's craft, whether this is beneficent or malevolent. It is true that he almost always had more power, and he did sometimes abuse it. But "[i]t is troubling," writes bell hooks, "when focus on the ways teachers can victimize students, especially via erotic engagement, denies the complex subjectivity of the students and makes them into objects by assuming that unequal power means that they are always acted upon and are without any agency" (1995: 38). When I read this, a rather astonishing complexification by such an influential feminist, I thought back to my own question as to what I might have offered my professor. Then I reread how the sacred prostitute, in impersonating the goddess, offered the man a "rekindling of the divine spark of life, a full and complete sense of well-being, perhaps sorely lacking in the world outside the sacred precincts" (Qualls-Corbett 1988: 39). Elizabeth, a fifty-eight-year-old former professor with doctorates in two fields, helped me understand what it is, other than an obvious sexual target, that the Maiden Lover might offer Pygmalion. Women often seek a "magical partnership" with a man, she claimed—one that is intellectually and sexually aflame—and this is not necessarily "bad," even when the man begins as her superior. She alluded to her long-term relationship with Michael, a teacher and later a colleague, as productive and erotically intense for both of them, although it remained unconsummated. She likened it to those of Abelard and Heloise and Marie and Henri Curie.

It is a paradox of the myth, however, that Pygmalion fervently desires Galatea to come to life as a match-mate for him, but when she does, he loses the thrill of creation. Thus he often moves on to another Maiden Lover, who can revitalize him with her youth, beauty, and malleability. One day when Elizabeth and Michael were at work, a younger researcher entered his office and when she left, he remarked, "She reminds me of you when you were young." Their relationship— beginning, middle, and end—flashed before her eyes, and in an instant she left him and their research, never to return to either. "I lost fifteen years of my work," she intoned with flat irony. An unusually reflective person with an immense knowledge of mythology, she believes that the symbolic feminine is the chemical ingredient that makes the mix of elements "fire" for the alchemist when he is trying to make gold. Then it is discarded. She agreed when I suggested that the woman's innocence, beauty, and intelligence are offered up as a sacrificial fire that allows the rebirth of life for the celebrant. What seems to begin as a sacred marriage may sacrifice not the small egos of the initiates, but the woman's sense of self.

The Muse

I arrived at Jessie's professional office in another part of the country for a lunch appointment. She looked at me with incomprehension rather than pleasure over seeing me for the first time in a year. "Oh, no, aren't you tomorrow?" she exclaimed, but then remembering herself, gave me a hug and looked at her calendar. She had one hour, minus time to get to the deli and back. Disappointed, knowing fragments of her rich background, I grabbed a quick cherry-romaine salad, hoping to get at least a shred or two from her life I could use. So much for the tape recorder. But as we talked, it became clear that Jessie knew her own story well, probably from years spent in analysis and a long struggle to make it cohere. She launched into her life story with little prompting from me, and soon I was both absorbed and chagrined for thinking of her as an "informant."

Jessie, forty-nine, is a publishing, private practitioner who left academia after obtaining a Ph.D. at a famous university, then teaching for five years. She related a series of early incidents that delayed the development of her own voice. She called herself the "fourth child in a silent family," where her intellect and ideas were not encouraged. She was "tight" with her mother, but saw her father as an "impediment" who did not have time for her. She eventually fell in love with and married a fellow graduate student, who became the intellectual genius she wanted to be.

Jessie struggled much of her adult life to reclaim herself as the intellectual she now thinks she always has been. In graduate school, her adviser looked like "Jabba the Hut." At first playing the daughter, she "had a warm place in her heart for him" because he was crippled from polio, as was her adored mother. But his wife was not at home when she responded to his invitation to watch opera at his house, and when he tried to push her into sex, she left abruptly. Later she thought her comprehensive exam papers should have received encouragement for publication. But Jabba "came after her" in the orals. Other committee members were "stunned," and although they passed her, no one verbally came to her aid. Nine years later, someone published a paper very similar to hers; it wasn't stolen, she lamented, "It was just an idea whose time had come." This framework "became the paradigm" in her subject area, but it was too late for her.

At forty-five, Jessie had a "midlife crisis" centering around her continuing failure to write or publish her burgeoning ideas. During this time she became passionate about heroes such as those in *The Last of the Mohicans* and other stories, who were "very young and boyish." She needed to develop her "warrior within." "I was successful," she said wryly, so "I tried valiantly for several years to get my *husband*, the 'brilliant intellectual,' to write the book I wanted to write." It was only after prolonged study of her dreams and life that she claimed the book— and her voice—for herself.

Romantic love between Pygmalion and his Maiden Lover can easily coexist with or evolve into a Genius-Muse relationship, as it did with Jesse and her husband, in which she labors as a "midwife to the man's creativity," investing her own artistry whole-heartedly in his development. A Muse is in danger of eventually resenting the ruin of her own talent, inspiration, and ambition, of feeling empty and inferior (Young-Eisendrath 1993: 95–97), although this role may greatly excite her at first with the importance of inciting a "great man." Jessie and her husband evidently had an unspoken contract that she would inspire him, and both would revel in his fame. Visitations by the Muses, or "mountain goddesses," were highly prized in ancient times, for "[t]he man they inspired was sacred far beyond any priest" (Hamilton 1999: 38). The Muses were the triple-goddess (Maiden, Mother, Crone) in her orgiastic aspect. Zeus claimed to be their father as the result of a tryst with Mnemosyne (Memory), but this, like many of his claims to paternity, was a late one, as Hesiod calls them daughters of Mother Earth and Air (Graves 1992: 55). Thus, as in the saga of Galatea, a feminine birthright was forgotten. And a goddess who was once both orgiastic and spiritual, like the one the sacred prostitute imitated, inhabits a woman vulnerable to losing her voice as it is ceded to a man.

Only after she left for a job at another university did Laura realize the extent to which she had served as her adviser/lover's Muse. Perhaps she couldn't have recognized this until after the romantic phase was over. A year after graduating, she attended a convention at which he turned in and presented a paraphrase of one of her dissertation chapters, without her knowledge. Although they were no longer lovers, she still cared for him.

"Were you shocked that he did that?" I asked. Anger tinged her voice decades later as she remembered: "Not only could I not believe it, I *didn't* believe it. I didn't believe that it was my work. I did a little mind game and thought, well, we've talked about these ideas, and I got these ideas from other places . . . but I didn't have enough confidence in my own authority and voice to be able to claim that synthesis as mine. I thought, 'It's really common domain, I guess.' He came up to me immediately afterward, ashen-faced, and said, 'I didn't know you were going to be here. I'm going up for promotion and I need every vita line I can get; I *hope* you understand.' . . . He said something like, 'I should have put your name on it,' and he *implied* that he couldn't put *my* name on *my* goddamn work, because people knew we were having an affair."

Doubting whether I would have had the courage, I asked if she had confronted him. "I said, 'That's all right,'" Laura replied. "I was twenty-eight, twenty-nine years old, I was already shamed about the affair, I was not sure that I had anything original and good. And so by stealing it, which I now see was stealing it, he also was helping nail down the idea that it really *wasn't* mine. But at the same time *he* was ashamed."

Laura thought that "it was kind of just desserts for having gotten involved. I didn't have any real rights. I had anger. But what would I have done? Whom would I have gone to?" Although the department chair "adored" her, she thought he would have protected Al because he was the chair's "rising star son." Besides, the chair had a crush on Laura, too. "And so here his boy had had an affair with the grandkid—that he was attracted to," she said. "It was incestuous." I suggested it was "sort of like getting your pot stolen from your own house—who were you going to go to?" and she affirmed, "Exactly." When Pygmalion steals the priestess's icon and takes it to his bed, she can no longer speak in her own voice, or even recognize her likeness.

Laura recommended a biography that helped her understand cultural pressures for a woman to give away her Muse to a man: Claire Douglas's *Translate This Darkness: The Life of Christiana Morgan, the Veiled Woman in Jung's Circle* (1993). I put off reading it for a year or two, mostly because C. G. Jung is one of my heroes, and it's painful for me to see him exposed. But the book is an even-handed, if passionate, treatment of how the woman Lewis Mumford once called "one of the three best minds at Harvard" (Douglas 1993: 12, 279) let herself be plundered by famous men who loved her. Although Morgan lived before Second Wave feminism nurtured the voices of many contemporary women, her story casts in bold relief the risks of turning the romantic love of a Genius and his Maiden Lover into the aesthetic love of the Genius and his Muse.

Morgan, who was born in 1897, consulted Jung for analysis in the 1920s and worked alongside Henry (Harry) Murray as a lay analyst, research associate, and coauthor at Harvard's psychological clinic from 1927 into the 1960s. She created the fantasies and paintings that Jung mined for a four-year series of seminars, and coauthored with Murray influential works on personality theory and the Thematic Apperception Test (TAT), for which she drew six of the nineteen pictures currently in use. Her patients, lovers, and friends recall her beauty, style, creativity, and analytical skills. However, while her close friends Jung, Alfred North Whitehead, Mumford, and Murray still are remembered, Morgan is not. "She remains at most," Douglas writes, "a footnote in other people's history" (1993: 12). When the article was published on the TAT, Morgan's name preceded Murray's as chief author, but it was inexplicably dropped from all later editions of the test (Douglas 1993: 204). Toward the end of the clinic's productive life in the 1950s, Murray had at least eleven unfinished books, pieces of which he began giving away to new people who caught his fancy—"work on which Morgan and other coauthors had staked the meaning of their lives" (1993: 299).

Douglas attributes Morgan's anonymity to her obsession with romantic love, and to the continual frustration of her yearning for a life larger than what was encouraged for a woman, one that combined orgiastic sexuality with intellectual vitality (1993: 15–16). Morgan went to Jung exhausted and depressed, needing his help regarding Harry, with whom she had fallen in love. Jung valued women and their analytical ideas as few of his contemporaries did, and greatly encouraged Christiana to delve into her inner life, but he may have been infatuated with her himself; whatever the case, he did not adequately differentiate her from his own extramarital "lover, mystical sister, and muse," Toni Wolff, and advised both Harry and Christiana to engage in a similar relationship (1993: 132–51). Christiana recorded in her notebook what Jung told her:

> You are a pioneer woman. Your function is to create a man. Some women create children but it is greater to create a man. If you create Murray you will have done something very fine for the world. (Douglas 1993: 151)

This flattered Christiana's ego and she was excited by the idealism, but she also became further exhausted and depressed. Neither Harry's wife, Jo, nor Christiana and her husband, Bill, first accepted this idea, which Harry openly proposed, but the two did become lovers and collaborators until her death in 1967. Upon starting the affair, she wrote: "I wish that with Harry I didn't have this feeling of a snake in the grass somewhere" (Douglas 1993: 133).

The Mistress

Christiana Morgan's snake rears its head when romantic or aesthetic love is replaced by sexual ownership. This may involve an exchange of currencies that "profits" both partners, although each usually ends up sacrificing what was initially so precious. When the woman's central attractiveness to the man shifts from the Maiden Lover's soul or the Muse's spirit to her body, she becomes a Mistress, even if she is also wife or colleague. The Maiden Lover is "up on the block," with potentially an entire self to be shaped as her Pygmalion finds the beautiful form within. Although she may be reduced to a *femme inspiratrice* as a Muse, at least this intellectual or artistic role has some value within the university. But things of the flesh despoil the ivory tower's purity, and are typically assigned to the "feminine." The Mistress has "been around the block," and so may feel like she is used goods. Revisiting ancient myth and ritual helps clarify how the Maiden Lover or Muse can change into the Mistress. By the middle of the first millennium B.C.E., religious and commercial prostitution flourished in proximity with one another in or near the temples in Babylon. The relationship between these two professions is not completely understood, but there are signs that sacred harlotry was corrupted when temple prostitutes kept the gifts meant for the temple (or the goddess) for their own profit. But commercial prostitution derived most directly from the enslavement of women and the consolidation of social classes. Military exploits made captive women readily available for private sexual use by kings and chiefs, who displayed their wealth in the form of servants, concubines, and harems, symbols of power to be emulated by aristocrats and wealthy men (Lerner 1986: 131–33). Thus, a woman may trade initiation into her own sexuality under the aegis of the goddess for a man's currencies. As Sarah, the professor spoken of earlier who has numerous influential publications, warned, a sexual relationship with a mentor can be "damaging because it really does ingrain you with, the only way to succeed is by being in bed." And a man may enhance his power by owning her body. As one of the women I interviewed, Kate, noted, though she refused a sexual relationship with Ted, she still felt "psychologically owned" by him.

"I got lots of rewards for smiling, drinking with the guys, not appearing to be a 'feminist,'" Amy, the fifty-one-year-old professor, admitted, referring to her role as department "mascot." The "boys' club" in her department was so strong, and the women so few in number that she didn't think she had a choice, but was both bitter and ashamed about trading in her freedom for professional "safety," which turned out to be more like their entitlement to her. She felt comfortable to start a relationship with someone else only after getting tenure, and since her departmental superiors didn't approve of him, she kept it secret for a long time. Clearly resentful years later, she divulged, "I almost had to ask their permission—I knew they'd be angry that 'Marian the Librarian'—me—betrayed them by getting a life."

Likewise, when Kate began dating someone while she was a graduate student, Ted immediately disapproved. When Ted came on to Kate, she said she'd "rather be colleagues and friends." But, like Amy and several other women, Kate took the responsibility herself for the relationship getting out of bounds. Afterward *she* sent *him* a note to make it right. "Everything I said was wrong, and I kept trying to make it right—what it should be. But it could never be right." To make things worse, Ted and Maggie's adviser, Rick, acted as if the two women were in a "horse race" when they neared graduation. Who would get the best job? Apparently a Mistress may still signify "wealth and power," even in the nonworldly arena of academe. Yet the competition between the men was overshadowed by a camaraderie that bound them to protect one another's "property." Kate lamented that she could not get another mentor when she tried; she could not "join the community of scholars because everyone considered me 'his.'" She winced when she recalled the last line of Ted's letter of recommendation for her job hunt, which read, "Kate McCormack is a charming commodity." Feeling that her career was a "bleak wasteland," she considered dropping out of academia to enter business. Once when she was driving, she recalled, "I almost let myself hit a tree."

Laura's anguish over having become Mistress to Al echoes that of Kate, and surfaced as one reason she eventually left her university job. "I don't think I've been free of that until five years after I left academia," she reflected. "It's been a major, major pain and loss of self in my life." What clearly hurt Laura the most was her conviction that her dissertation was not what it could have been, partly because her entire committee knew about the affair with her adviser. "I don't think they wished me ill," she explained. "They were protective, but they didn't know how to separate out the sexual issues from the intellectual issues. Nobody on my committee said to me, 'Laura, this just is not gonna fly,' because they knew I belonged to Al." Although their relationship was "good," especially at first, "the cost in guilt made it not worth it." She learned not to take herself seriously, while at the same time overworking to compensate for her loss of self-esteem. "I didn't feel that my primary currency to anybody was my intellect and my career potential. My primary currency was my sexuality." Clearly having agonized about this for many years, she declared, "I ended up with a degree that felt tainted." Now brilliant in a nonacademic career, she made a stunning disclosure: "I know that I persevered to get a second Ph.D. because I devalued the first one."

A Pygmalion-Mistress relationship can harm a woman's body, as well as her self-respect, if the man perceives her as a powerful threat to his self, or if each blames the other for the loss of romantic or aesthetic love. Young-Eisendrath thinks a man projects the Mistress on to a woman when he fuses sex with aggression, turning women into objects in order to reaffirm his control (1993: 87–88). The case of Harry Murray and Christiana Morgan is far more tragic than any that women have related to me, but its extremes can tell us something about the injurious instincts embedded in such a relationship. Harry considered Christiana his Muse, and used her visions and trances for his own development (Douglas 1993: 305). Although she adored his admiration, his inflated image of her power and "its exaggerated notion that she could carry the entire archetype of the transformative feminine" also weighed her down (306). When Harry failed to finish his books, Christiana lost respect for him. When she also denied the responsibility of her own genius, "then she tried to compensate by getting him to 'thrill her and make her afraid,' by mastering her with whips and chains," writes Douglas. The two of them began experimenting with sado-masochism "as a way to bring some heat into a relationship that was growing increasingly empty and cold" (1993: 264–65). The orgiastic aspect of the Muse descended into violence.

Although Harry promised to marry her after his wife died, he never did, and although Christiana promised to give up her drinking if he married her, she took it up again at their last fateful encounter. In March 1967 the two vacationed on the island of St. John at the cottage of friends. Christiana was intoxicated with the bracing air and the hopes of revitalizing their love, but Harry was intoxicated with Nina Fish, his latest lover, twenty years his junior, to whom he was sending flowers. Sensing defeat, Christiana awoke one morning from an alcoholic stupor to a disgusted and abusive Harry Morgan (Douglas 1993: 312–13). The subsequent events remain in a fog, partly because Harry obscured them with differing reports. "What is clear is that on that sweet and sun-drenched morning, Christiana died," writes Douglas, who obviously interprets her death as a suicide.

> She had taken off the emerald ring Harry had given her thirty years before, wrapped it in her little beach bag, and placed it carefully on the sand. Then she had walked out into the sea. She drowned in the lagoon just below their cottage, the outline of her lifeless body floating unobscured in the tender ripples of the waves. (Douglas 1993: 314)

What these lovers never grasped was that the Maiden Lover, the Muse, and the Mistress, all of which they both expected Christiana to play, are not persons, but types; when they locked themselves into these "agreements," Christiana was locked away from her self, and so destroyed it in the oceanic tides of her despair.

The Brainchild

The Brainchild is the despoiled Mistress's pure sister. She is born, in fact, in immaculate conception, although it is a man, not a woman, who gives birth. Michelle, who was pressured into taking a class taught by her former department chair, intuited this when she called academic mentorship "medieval" and "abusive": "you are of my loins, like you *spring* from me as my student." But the Greek goddess Athena is more the prototype, suggested Joan, a forty-one-year-old writer who employs mythic themes in her fiction. Joan quit her master's program before finishing because the only person who taught her specialty was a man who wanted her to be his cerebral surrogate, as well as his sexual conquest. Athena sprang, fully armored with a mighty shout, from Zeus' *head* after he swallowed Metis, the Titaness who presided over all wisdom and knowledge. Predictably, this version of Athena's birth was a patriarchal adaptation, for Athena was originally the Libyan goddess Neith, who belonged to an epoch before fatherhood was recognized. Virgin priestesses of Neith annually engaged in armed combat for the position of high priestess. After Zeus' co-optation of Athena, she retained her warrior persona, but became his obedient mouthpiece, suppressed her origins and eventually even the awareness that she had a mother, and employed priests, not priestesses, in her service (Graves 1992: 44–47). Metis's feminine and earthy wisdom, literally consumed by Zeus, was recreated as a daughter hatched from his brain.

The Brainchild is a daughter. But she differs from the Maiden Lover in that Zeus/Pygmalion wants his Athena to reflect, rather than complement, his masculinity. She is Henry Higgins' dream come true: "Why can't a woman be more like a man?" Athena was independent, active, nonrelational, achievement-oriented, strategic, and practical—all qualities coded "masculine" today—as well as in Athena's time. "Athena values rational thinking and stands for the domination of will and intellect over instinct and nature." In trials she always sided with the patriarchy, and was typically pictured with a male (Bolen 1985: 75–77).

Zeus/Pygmalion thus holds his Brainchild to a ruthless standard of intellectual perfection. My professor, you may recall, thought speech communication was beneath me. He made a fetish of contrasting "elite" with "nonelite" disciplines and research topics—a demarcation that also extended to people. I wanted desperately to measure up, knowing I would be rejected if I failed. My friend, whom he pitted against me in competition, lost out. I remember my dismay when he belittled her papers and held mine out as the standard she should emulate, as a parent often does with siblings. A strong and beautiful person voted "top scholar" in *his* field, she once collapsed in tears in front of our entire study group at his relentlessly disparaging remarks, which reached beyond the intellectual to make her body and bearing seem inadequate. Egotistical triumph battled with empathic humiliation in my head and heart. But he continued to debase her for crying, a sign she wasn't "elite." *"Why can't a woman be more like a man?"* This marked the beginning of the end of my respect for him, as it finally dawned on me that being his Brainchild spelled the loss of a "sister." I graduated, went to the Ph.D. school he cautioned against, and never spoke to him again.

Along with Artemis and Hestia, Athena was one of the "virgin goddesses," meaning "unpenetrated by a man." This chastity was psychological, and not necessarily physical (Bolen 1985: 35). She must be free of any influences that would interfere with her unstained and rational, armored personality. Sex can be used like a weapon to keep her within this frame, and to lay claim to her as an intellectual emissary. Joan's master's adviser approached her before she graduated with her bachelor of arts degree, remarked how intelligent she was, and announced, "I want to wash you clean of your former [female] mentor." He suggested she study under him, and went on to say, "'I know I could get you into Stanford.'" She remembers "looking at him, pondering the costs, imagining the possibility. And being tempted. Was it a good thing or a bad thing that he was so unattractive to me?" Joan's account made something click for me that I hadn't understood before. Although fueled by mutual desire, my professor's approach to sexuality itself had seemed "clinical," not really romantic or orgiastic. It was more like a purgative, something to be gotten out of the way so that our minds would be free of interference. I thought of Socrates' notion in the *Phaedrus* that one could use this unruly black horse of desire to ascend to the pure heights of reason, where the white horse and the charioteer himself could tame it, keep it in its place.

If the feminine body is anathema to rationality, there are more ways than sex to control it. The Brainchild's "father" may show an obsessive interest in the perfection of her body, an ideal that erases rather than enhances her more feminine characteristics so that she will more closely resemble a man—for example, by dieting away her rounded features.[2] Viewing a picture from a few years back of my professor's wife, also his graduate student, I marveled at what a bony ghost of her former self she was when I met her. Early in Joan's program, her new adviser started making remarks about her body: "You still have a pretty good figure for a woman who's had three kids." She eventually reacted not by trimming her figure to meet his ideal, but by *gaining* thirty pounds to confound it, "eating candy bars, which I never do." If she controlled her own body, she explained, then he couldn't.

Joan's adviser began punishing her with grades and made negative comments to other professors when she did not respond to his attempts to "build her up" the way he wanted her. He encouraged her to submit a paper for an award, then lobbied against it. Her undergraduate feminist mentor advised her to bring the case to the judicial board, but when she heard what it would take, such as the disclosure of specific comments, she felt her only option was to drop out. She didn't want to be seen publicly as a "complainer" and a person who couldn't handle it on her own; apparently, his attempt to make her into a tough Brainchild had at least partially worked. But she never got an advanced degree or an academic job, her original goal. When I asked how this experience affected her, she bit down hard on her memories and answered, "It changed my life."

Playing my professor's Brainchild didn't exactly change my life; I was already headed in this direction. But it did make the ingredients gel, and set a course for my academic success. After all, I got rewards for using my head, and assiduously avoided thereafter anything that would bring me down like my friend. When I wrote earlier in this chapter that I sometimes live a myth without knowing its grip on me, trying to conform to its ideal of beauty, the confession was even then more a concept than a reality. I don't think I fully realized until I wrote this voice—actually until I *rewrote* it—how much it is my myth. I am a Brainchild, and a very good one at that.

The Virgin

In ancient mythology the Virgin is a woman who is not defined by a man. She may be chaste, married, or have many partners; the key is that she is no one's child, product, or object. As Sarah put it, "I don't feel dependent on any of those male elders really any more, although I did at first." For some women, playing Galatea early in their careers helped them to grow. According to M. Esther Harding, the sacred prostitute's ritual made a woman "Virgin" in this original sense because the act was not performed under the social constraints that make the nonvirgin woman, married or not, "trim her sails and adapt herself to expediency" (1971: 125). Pygmalion did ask Venus to bring Galatea to life, and we can at least imagine him stepping out of the way to let his prodigy shine.

"I still think of this as good," Kelly concluded. "I am a scholar because of Joel."

"Did he ever try to mold you?" I asked.

"No," she responded. "He worked against the roles that were confining us. I don't remember him ever disciplining me." Pygmalion can be a true *mentor* rather than a *maker*. The maker retains his privileges to correct, use, and derive pleasure from what he makes. The mentor sends the pupil on her journey with the gifts needed to do the job. The one believes he *is* the god; the other calls down the god or goddess to inhabit the union.

Although a man sometimes helped a woman to become Virgin, it seemed more common that these academic women did it themselves. Elizabeth, the former professor with doctorates in two fields, reflected that, even when the mentor/mentee relationship begins well, "It does sometimes turn out that she leaves him." In the scenario of *A Star Is Born,* the promising protégé eclipses her teacher. Grateful for his initial help, Kelly remarked that, "Now I'm exceeding Joel. I remember sort of outgrowing him at some point. My knowledge became more sophisticated than his ultimately. . . . I wanted him to go into his Ph.D., but he wasn't going there." Most women felt badly if their mentor was bereft upon the loss of his Maiden Lover. Although Maggie's adviser did not try to prevent her from leaving, he still writes notes to her telling her he loves and misses her. She has an image of him as a "sad sack," and thinks he's "never bounced back." Several were also pained if their teachers were resentful of their success.

When Sarah began getting recognition as an important scholar, her former adviser turned from being a "proud father" who introduced her to people, to wanting no interaction at all with her for about two years. "When I was getting attention and he wasn't," she said, "it was hard to even shake hands with him. I think it was really hard on him." Although she refused to tamp down her own work to protect his ego, it worried her greatly, and she kept looking for an "opening" for a healing talk. Eventually they had one and he admitted that it was the first time that one of his grad students so quickly moved into what he viewed as a competitive relationship with him. Now they are good friends again. Repeatedly, the woman took the responsibility for mending a broken relationship; even if she had been hurt, she generally did not want *him* to be.

Sometimes, however, a woman needed to end the relationship in order to become Virgin. Michelle eventually gave up plans to leave graduate school because of "Mr. Rogers," and friends and her fiancé convinced her she "had to get him completely out of her hair." A year and a half later, she gave all his materials back, quit doing research with him, told him she could not interact with him any more, and dropped him from her committee. But it "Made me feel like an idiot that it took me so long to put it all together." Laura got a good job, despite her adviser's attempt to prevent her from leaving by telling prospective employers she "wasn't ready," and realized it was a power-balancing move. "I thought, yeah, you can have all this power, and I'll just leave. Of course, I had to maintain enough civility to get my dissertation accepted and done." Many years after leaving graduate school, Kate got "past being angry" at Ted, and cut off his attempts to hook her emotions.

Most of the women who had lost some sense of themselves in a Pygmalion-and-Galatea relationship were either in the process of finding, or felt they had already found, a stronger self. This may be partially an artifact of age; more of those I talked with were in midlife than in their twenties and thirties. Laura recounted how she told the story of her first Ph.D. to a group of women recently. "My voice broke—literally," she said, but this voicing of her story also helped her to reclaim it. Kate confessed that it was "heartbreaking" to lose the intellectual connection when she ended the personal one with her adviser. She is glad she stayed in academia, and she still loves the work, although "not the field." Nevertheless, she set about creating a sense of community in her discipline that has begun to substitute for her lack of mentorship. Ultimately, becoming Virgin seems to depend more on self-contemplation and reflection, as well as talking with uninvolved others, than it does healing a broken relationship or speaking out to one's former mentor. It also demands a coming-to-terms with what happened rather than a denial of it, a realization that growth and loss often go hand in hand, and an ultimate acceptance of an imperfect life. In the opening voiceover five years after she left her Pygmalion, *Guinevere*'s Harper shares her appreciation for life's ambiguity: "He was my most spectacular and cherished fuck-up."

Breaking the Mold

Though I left my honors professor behind, I have tried much of my career to live up to an imagined collective Pygmalion, who I believe wants me to be the Brainchild that he rewarded. I alluded earlier to a midlife turn in which I began to break Pygmalion's mold—or was it breaking me?—and start to speak, however tentatively, without Athena's overly rational armor. For two years I could write nothing "academic," immersing myself instead in cowriting a science fiction movie script with a woman friend, fighting all the while my suspicion that the infinitesimal chance I'd ever make it in Hollywood didn't justify the time away from scholarly work. I must have been trying out a new voice—if I wasn't ready to use it quite yet, at least our dazzling heroine could. Or maybe I was working on fulfilling the prophecy on a short story that I wrote way before that honors seminar. Rummaging through the attic not too long ago, I discovered my fifth-grade teacher's note scribbled in red on the first page of a yellowed manuscript penned in a childish hand: "I expect to read your stories when I am in my rocking chair."

I didn't make it in Hollywood, but I did return to academic writing with a zest for making myth work for people more than for theory. And so I was more than a little surprised when I received Art and Carolyn's response to the first version of this manuscript, in which they gently asked me to "loosen the ropes of traditional academic writing." I thought I had dropped Athena's shield, but there it was pretty much intact—so obvious when I reread the paper through their eyes—still protecting me from attack. This armor is close to the skin, if not to the bone, and, taking it off, I feel so naked. Suddenly I am back in college, and my honors professor is turning on *me*, not my friend. "You don't have what it takes," he is sneering. "You're not as smart as I thought." I am still standing. "You are not desirable." I am still dry-eyed.

I return to the present and the letter from Art and Carolyn: "Perhaps, in the spirit of your research, you can use a writing voice more in line with that 'real encounter' with the truly feminine that you so persuasively promote." As a loyal

Brainchild I've been imitating Pygmalion's, and especially Zeus's, suppression of the goddess's origins: swallow the mother source whole and deliver through the head a maiden who emerges fully armored, "with a mighty shout." But I have loved myth, that soft and fully rounded underbelly of the harder, more chiseled logic, since I was disguised as a girl. And it is *mythos* from which *logos* was born. Perhaps now, at the tender age of fifty-one, I can begin yet again to claim my birthright, and to speak with a voice that is more Virgin than made.

Notes

1. Young-Eisendrath calls such projections "complexes" or "dream lovers" because of their unconscious quality and their prevalence in personal dreams and cultural myths (1993: 24–27, 71–84).
2. For a mythological treatment of the role of such cultural sentiments in anorexia nervosa, see Woodman (1982).

References

Bochner, Arthur P. 1997. "It's About Time: Narrative and the Divided Self." *Qualitative Inquiry* 3: 418–38.

Bolen, Jean Shinoda. 1985. *Goddesses in Everywoman: A New Psychology of Women*. New York: Harper Colophon Books.

Burke, Kenneth. 1973. *The Philosophy of Literary Form: Studies in Symbolic Action*. 1941. Reprint, Berkeley: University of California Press.

Campbell, Joseph. 1972. *Myths to Live By*. New York: Bantam Books.

———.1976a. *The Masks of God: Oriental Mythology*. 1962. Reprint, New York: Penguin Books.

———.1976b. *The Masks of God: Primitive Mythology*. 1959. Reprint, New York: Penguin Books.

Douglas, Claire. 1993. *Translate This Darkness: The Life of Christiana Morgan, the Veiled Woman in Jung's Circle*. Princeton, N.J.: Princeton University Press.

Frazer, James. 1996. *The Golden Bough: A Study in Magic and Religion*, vol. 1 (abridged edition). 1922. Reprint, New York: Touchstone.

Gimbutas, Marija Alseikaite. 1982. *Goddesses and Gods of Old Europe*. Berkeley: University of California Press.

Guinevere. 1999. Directed by Audrey Wells. Miramax.

Graves, Robert. 1992. *The Greek Myths*. 1955. Reprint, New York: Penguin Books.

Hamilton, Edith. 1999. *Mythology: Timeless Tales of Gods and Heroes*. 1942. Reprint, New York: Warner Books.

Harding, M. Esther. 1971. *Woman's Mysteries: Ancient and Modern*. New York: Harper Colophon Books.

Hiles, Marv, and Nancy Hiles, eds. 1999. *The Daybook: A Contemplative Journal* 34 (Fall).

———. 2000. *The Daybook: A Contemplative Journal* 37 (Summer).

hooks, bell. 1995. "In Praise of Student/Teacher Romances: Notes on the Subversive Power of Passion." *Utne Reader* (March–April): 36–37.

Lerner, Gerda. 1986. *The Creation of Patriarchy*. Oxford: Oxford University Press.

Nelson, Willie. 1974. "It's Not Supposed to Be That Way." *Phases and Stages*. New York: Atlantic Recording.

Nothstine, W. L., C. Blair, and G. A. Copeland, eds. 1994. *Critical Questions: Invention, Creativity, and the Criticism of Discourse and Media*. New York: St. Martin's.

Qualls-Corbett, Nancy. 1988. *The Sacred Prostitute: Eternal Aspect of the Feminine*. Toronto: Inner City Books.

Rushing, Janice Hocker. 1989. "Evolution of 'The New Frontier' in *Alien* and *Aliens*: Patriarchal Co-optation of the Feminine Archetype." *Quarterly Journal of Speech* 75: 1–24.

Rushing, Janice Hocker, and Thomas S. Frentz. 1989. "The Frankenstein Myth in Contemporary Cinema." *Critical Studies in Mass Communication* 6: 61–80.

———. 1995. *Projecting the Shadow: The Cyborg Hero in American Film*. Chicago: University of Chicago Press.

———. 2000. "Singing Over the Bones: James Cameron's *Titanic*." *Critical Studies in Media Communication* 17: 1–27.

Tompkins, Jane. 1996. *A Life in School: What the Teacher Learned*. Reading, Mass.: Addison-Wesley.

Ulanov, A. 1971. *The Feminine in Jungian Psychology and in Christian Theology*. Evanston, Ill.: Northwestern University Press.

Walker, B. G. 1983. *The Woman's Encyclopedia of Myths and Secrets*. San Francisco: Harper & Row.

Woodman, M. 1982. *Addiction to Perfection: The Still Unravished Bride*. Toronto: Inner City Books.

Young-Eisendrath, P. 1993. *You're Not What I Expected: Learning to Love the Opposite Sex*. New York: William Morrow.

Breathing Life into Work

ARTHUR P. BOCHNER AND JANICE HOCKER RUSHING

Editor's note: What follows is an exchange of e-mail messages and letters between Janice Rushing and Art Bochner that took place between February and August 2000. Looking over the entire history of these exchanges, we felt that these messages could serve the useful purpose of demystifying the processes of socialization and legitimation associated with writing and publishing "ethnographic alternatives."

February 5, 2000

Dear Art,

I'm a bit later than I'd like because of the snow piled up around my house and in my office, but I want to thank you and Carolyn for an incredibly well planned and inspiring conference. I've been trying to figure out in the past few years how to make a place for the whole person in research and in this strange land we call academia, and now I see that the new ethnography people are really *doing* it! What I learned at the Couch-Stone symposium gives me courage and a structure for what I want to do—an immeasurable gift.

In *A Life in School,* Jane Tompkins figured out what was wrong with one of the departments she taught in as an assistant prof—I think it was your old stomping grounds at Temple, although in the English department—"no one was keeping house." This is what you and Carolyn did so well, attending to the little creature comforts that make so much difference to people away from home, while also providing intellectual and presentational leadership. Somehow you managed to make the trains run on time *and* infuse the efficiency with warmth and humor. This is much appreciated.

I would like to submit my paper for you to consider for the book you're planning from the conference. I recall you said three copies by March 1. So, thank you again, and now I hope you two will get a well-deserved rest, although in the middle of a semester that may be a distant dream.

Warmly,
Janice

March 3, 2000

Dear Janice:

Thanks for the note. I was very taken with your paper and would like to use it if possible. Actually, I've extended the deadline to April 1 and could extend it a few weeks more if you need more time. We've gotten some terrific papers and Carolyn and I are still writing our own "ethnography of the conference" in which we try to capture the spirit and feeling of what went on and what it might mean to those like yourself trying to locate a place in the academy that feels like "home."

When I thought about your presentation, I couldn't help thinking about Ian Hacking's essays on what he calls "memoro-politics" and "an indeterminancy in the past." In his book, *Rewriting the Soul: Multiple Personality and the Sciences of Memory,* Hacking problematizes the determinacy of our actions and the memories we make of them in language. I think his concept of "semantic contagion" is very relevant to your work, especially when actions, however troubling, disturbing, and traumatic, are placed under terms and descriptions that did not exist at the time the actions took place. I would be very curious to hear your reaction to this notion. Whatever you decide, I know your project is going to be very profound in its effects. It's really great work.

Cheers,
Art Bochner

March 6, 2000

Dear Art:

Thanks so much for the extension of the deadline, your encouraging words about my paper, and your persuasive note. . . . With the extra time, I should be able to get reactions back from the women in my study and feel reasonably confident that I've dealt adequately with the ethical issues surrounding this work. . . .

It's very interesting that you should bring up Ian Hacking's work. Buddy [Goodall] and I have been e-mailing about these issues. He challenges the validity of the women's later reinterpretations of events suggesting that they may not have been experienced as traumatic at the time. . . . My reactions to Buddy were that, yes, of course the women reinterpret the events at a later point in their lives; if they had been experienced as disturbing in a negative way at the time, they probably wouldn't have voluntarily participated in them, but part of the wisdom of experience is how such reinterpretation occurs in the context of a larger life story. He's not content with that, though, insisting on a kind of wisdom of "innocence" that we later tend to lose. I don't think that wisdom and innocence are the same thing. But your comments only make me more eager to see what other thoughtful people say about such things.

Take care,
Janice

March 8, 2000

Hi Janice:

I had a lot of thoughts running through my head after I read your e-mail. . . . To get back to the sexual harassment issue, the question that still bothers me is what are we to believe about the actions of the men who are portrayed as characters in the women's narratives that you present. If I ask you, What were these men doing? And you say they were "sexually harassing" their female students, then, I have to ask, after Hacking, is that what they were intending to do? I think this is where some caution has to enter, because in terms of Hacking's notion of "semantic contagion," I'm just not so sure the idea of harassment existed *then* as it does *now*. As Hacking asks, "How can a person be said to act intentionally under a description that didn't exist?" Looking back *now*, I find what was going on *then* disturbing, as I know you do, but I haven't found a way out of the semantic quagmire Hacking poses. This is particularly true when I ask, as I did in the story I wrote about my father's violent behavior toward me when I was a kid, would he act that way now (meaning now that we have a moral description of that behavior as abusive and bad)? The fact that norms and standards of behavior change (as culture changes), as does vocabulary, sometimes radically, over several generations only makes the case stronger that these meanings and causes may be indeterminate. Wish, I do, that life were simpler.

Looking forward to receiving your "finished" manuscript.

Cheers,
Art

April 4, 2000

Dear Art:

Finally, I have some time to get back to your note; school days have been too rushed for thought lately. . . .

About the quagmire concerning the term "sexual harassment": I have to agree with you that the emergence of the word does indeed make a difference. Some of the men who figure into the women's narratives in the study, as well in relationships I just know about, are lovely people who have no intention of hurting anyone. The development of the phrase may in fact help point out when they may be hurting without intending to. (Obviously, I'm excluding the no-brainer cases such as quid pro quo, and so on.) In other ways the phrase and all the attention it gets create hysteria over relationships that were mutually beneficial. Perhaps it would be best if I took the phrase out of the paper, because so many of the relationships that are being discussed were prior to the "idea" of sexual harassment (although not all of them). What I'm aiming at here is to understand the experiences through these women's eyes and not through what Burke calls a "terministic screen"—although I realize that's impossible to completely avoid. It seems that someone also needs to do a study of the men's experiences, which is what several of the men who read it are saying.

I hope you have spring break coming up soon and some time to enjoy it.

Janice

May 31, 2000 (morning)

Hi Janice:

I thought of you while Carolyn and I were watching a movie, *Guinevere*, on Sunday night. Have you seen it? It reminded me so much of your project. I particularly loved the scene in which Guinevere's mother, who is the same age as her twenty-one-year-old daughter's lover (referred to throughout the film as her mentor), says to the lover, "I finally figured out what you can get from these (young) women that you couldn't get from a mature woman like me. You know what it is? I'll tell you. *Awe!*"

Incidentally, I mailed a letter to you yesterday accepting your manuscript for our book, but asking for some revisions that will provide a bit better fit with the other chapters in the book. Let me know what you think when you get it. Obviously, I love your project. . . . I hope you are well. . . .

Cheers,
Art

May 31, 2000 (evening)

Hello Art:

Funny you should mention *Guinevere*—Tom and I watched it last week and thought it was absolutely superb, and the very scene I picked out as my favorite was the one with the mother that you mentioned! Wasn't she awesome? Actually, everybody in the movie was, and I thought the main relationship was handled so sensitively—really explored the darkness, but was also not judgmental. Loved the ending scene too, when all the Guineveres appear as he dies. . . .

I'm delighted that you accepted my paper for your book, and will be glad to try to make it fit the book better. I've got the rest of my own book outlined, and am working on it whenever I get the chance—happily—I love this work.

Warmly,
Janice

May 30, 2000 (received June 2, 2000)

Dear Janice:

We are writing in response to your manuscript, "Inside Plato's Cave: Pygmalion and Galatea at the University," which you submitted for possible inclusion in our forthcoming book *Ethnographically Speaking*. We love your project and believe that your paper can make a significant contribution, so we are pleased to accept it for the book. In its present form, however, your chapter deviates sharply from most of the others we have accepted, which emphasize alternative forms of representation and/or the autobiographical and reflexive voices in ethnography and qualitative research. We are targeting the book for graduate-level courses in ethnography and qualitative methods. Thus, we are suggesting revisions that will improve your chapter's fit with the others and enhance its appeal to our anticipated readers.

Certainly, the two stories you tell about yourself early in the paper fit well with the autoethnographic emphasis of much of our book and we want to encourage you to put even more of yourself into these stories. When you report your interviews, you have taken a great deal of interpretive license, selecting what you quote from participants, how much, and the conceptual frame in which you embed their words. Thus, your own self-interest, your history and biography, and all that you bring to the project from your own experience plays a crucial rule in the analysis and interpretations you make. Most of our readers are unlikely to be familiar with your scholarship on myth and rhetoric; nor will they know about the many projects you've published in which you link myth to the cultural history associated with the feminine and its representations in popular films. We think it would be helpful for readers to know about this work and to know why you have turned to interviews at this point in your "life" project. Readers also need to know more details about how you participated in the interviews and the nature of your relationships with the participants. In short, we think your subjectivity is all over this paper and we think this is a good thing, but we also believe the paper would benefit from more self-conscious reflexivity and a greater self-presence. How did you respond emotionally to the interviews? What did you learn from these women and from the interviews that you didn't know before? Who were you in the interviews and in what sense may they have been narrating their lives for you (as an audience)?

We want you to expand your discussion of the research project itself. How did you find these women? What did you tell them about what you were studying? How active were you in the interviews? Were the interviews "interactive"? Did you share some of your story with them? Or did you follow a structured protocol? How did you go about analyzing the interviews? How did you select the quotes you used in the paper? So much of the meaning of these quotes is dependent on how you contextualized and framed them that it seems important to know this. What ethical issues concerned you and them? . . .

We think you can probably condense details of the portions on mythology. As it now stands, the theory overwhelms the women's narratives. You are brilliant at telling the plot and detailing the characters in the stories from mythology, but the women's stories are not emplotted in nearly as much detail; nor do we experience these women as characters. One possibility that occurred to us is to tell one story for each of the types or characters you posit—such as muse, virgin, brainchild, giving more detail, characterization, and so on, though we recognize this may be difficult to do. What some narrative ethnographers do is to create composite characters and we think this is an option worth considering. . . .

We intend these remarks to be suggestive, not mandatory. What we are trying to say is that you can loosen the ropes of traditional academic writing, if you so choose. Perhaps, in the spirit of your research (and your own perspective on academia, which we share), you can use a writing voice more in line with that "real encounter" with the truly feminine that you so persuasively promote. . . .

As we look over our notes, it occurs to us that the main issue here is how you want to narrate your project and develop yourself as a character in the story. We've tried to hint at some options for you to consider and to give you our sense that we would like you to write this project in an accessible form, one that is freed of some of the orthodox strictures of academic writing. We hope this appeals to you and, of course, we are open to discussing ideas of yours on these issues as well. . . . Please contact us if you have further questions.

Cheers,
Art and Carolyn

June 9, 2000

Dear Art and Carolyn,

I got your letter on my paper for your book a week ago today, and it's been a *most* interesting week! Your review threw me into a state of turmoil, for sure, but it's turned out to be incredibly beneficial. I quickly got through the "I've failed" stage (which I always do but have gotten much faster at), as well as feeling derailed from the rest of my book project and went on to being really excited about redoing the paper *and* the book. Tom helped me go over every line, both of your letter and the paper, and we both think you were right on about everything you said. You guessed right that I really have been wanting to write more personally, but still have been mostly writing *about* the need to write more personally rather than doing it, retaining more vestiges than I'd like of that old academic armor. So thanks for encouraging me to lay it down a bit, and for getting this to me at just the right time—*before* I've written the whole book!

I knew my paper wasn't a good fit with the autoethnographic folks even before the conference, and was painfully aware of it while there. I think that's the result of moving fairly uneasily from rhetorical criticism into this new thing that is very attractive to me, but I don't know much about. (I studied and wrote about the old qualitative methods while a grad student.) At first I couldn't see how I could redo my own paper to make it fit, because of the multiple interviews, but a form is unfolding that frames it more as my story that the women help to expand. I think you will be much happier with this version, which is coming so fast now I've got about one-third of it rewritten already. As you describe in some of your work, I'm making some significant self discoveries as I *re*write—much more so than in the original writing. So I'll probably hang on to it awhile after I finish to let the process percolate some more. Thanks for taking the time to read this so carefully and to have faith there's more of a story there waiting to get out.

Tom and I are hoping to take our annual trip to Montana/Colorado/ New Mexico July 4–August 2. . . . I hope you two have made it to the beach this summer or wherever you go to have fun.

Warmly,
Janice

June 12, 2000

Dear Janice:

What a fantastic letter. I want to save it and, with your permission, share it with the graduate students in my "writing seminar" next year. It is a great example of the ideal scholarly attitude. You are amazing. I so much appreciate your willingness to take in our feedback, struggle through the process of reimagining and reconstructing the paper, and arriving at such a positive and affirming notion of what you want to do.

To be honest, I was very reluctant to send my comments to you. I consider you a friend and this was, of course, not a blind review. (What does this say about our presumptions about the norm of anonymous reviewing?) Moreover, you've had such incredible success as a scholar. Why would you want to change? (Lots of people asked me the same thing when I stopped doing quantitative research fifteen years ago.) Then again, you did come to the conference. You are doing a qualitative, interview project. You are in that midlife age group who ask, "What matters?" "Where is my voice?" "What do I want to say?" And your work deserves a larger and more diverse audience than one reaches with the *QJS*. Besides, if you're at all like me, you may have reached a point where you say (pardon the cliché): "Been there, done that." So, I thought, why not open the door a bit wider and see if she'll walk in. Well, to see your response—*wow*—no wonder you say "it's coming fast." I can only imagine what you may have held back (again, if you're anything like me) because of the censorship promoted by academic conventions and the voices of the "Others" in our head that tell us don't do or say this or you will be punished.

A couple of years ago I published an essay with Carolyn and Lisa Tillmann-Healy, which we called "Mucking Around Looking for Truth." Your letter reminded me of a passage we quoted from Linda Sexton, who wrote an autobiography of her abusive relationship with her mother, the poet Anne Sexton. Talking about the taboos (personal and professional) that silence writing from the heart, she says: "Though I am no longer a child, to write of these things feels forbidden, to give voice to memories such as these, taboo. . . . If you tell they will not love you anymore. . . ." I know one of the fears I faced when I stopped writing for journals like *Com Monographs* and *Human Communication Research* and started my "second career" was whether "they" would still love me, if you know what I mean.

I'm glad to hear you're taking a vacation. Carolyn and I love the four corners area of the Southwest and have made two very memorable, extended trips there, one a rafting trip down the Green and Colorado Rivers, through a place called Cataract Canyon, that was truly magnificent. We had a nice trip to Vancouver and then to Sanibel Island, but are basically staying close to home this summer due to the precarious health of both of our mothers.

Got to run. Hugs to Tom.

Fondly,
Art

June 13, 2000

Dear Art:

Of course you can use my letter in your writing seminar—I'd be honored! All of a sudden I'm getting with the program here about letting secrets out if there's a chance they'd be helpful to others. Once again, I've endorsed the *concept,* but it's been real hard for me to do it, or to believe that anyone would be interested.

One of the chapters I'm working with is going to be called "Veils and Armor," I think—about the complex mixture of seduction and protection in "wearing" academic jargon. I've known for quite some time that I carry my mother's unfulfilled dreams like a script: She was the valedictorian in a large high school class and voted "most intellectual," and almost finished a master's degree, but continually puts all her talents under cover so as to fulfill her role as a preacher's wife and not upstage my dad, who doesn't want to see her (or me) as smart. She turns eighty in August, and Tom has a life-threatening disease. And I ain't no spring chicken, as they say. So the time must be right for me to drop the sword and shield, and your encouragement is so propitious. Tom and I have a convention paper somewhere on synchronicity in doing academic research (reminds me a little bit—different theory—of your discussion of fortuitous accidents in the paper about your father), and I do believe there are times when several strains in your life come together like magic. Right now I can't take a walk without a little notebook tied around my neck to get the thoughts down.

You're so right about the voices of "Other" in my head. Actually, sometimes they've not been in my head, but right out there, spoken by colleagues

I often admire. Yeah, being loved is bottom line, or in my case, probably even more so, being *respected*. But yes, midlife is the time to find your deepest voice. What is continually amazing is that I don't just find it once and am done with it, or that just when I thought it was the strongest, it has to change. And here I thought I was *post*–midlife and wouldn't go through that again. Guess that's life, huh?

Tom and I got more response on our "Gods Must Be Crazy" paper than anything either of us has ever done—kind of like the responses to your talking about institutional depression—even though we weren't nearly as personal. It must have touched that same nerve of disenchantment with academic orthodoxy that you've mentioned before. Several poignant stories. And I talked to several women in the course of my project who have either dropped out because of it or are seriously contemplating it. It's very real. As one woman put it, "I hate doing the review of the literature part— it's like, find a hole and fuck it!" She has a good sense of humor.

I'm sorry to hear that both you and Carolyn have ailing mothers. That's another aspect of midlife, and it's really hard. I don't like being so far from my parents and siblings; my folks live for part of the year in a cabin they handbuilt so far up in the mountains in Colorado you can't get to it for eight months out of the year, and it's damn hard to even in the summer. But they're still doing it, chopping the wood, and so on. That's spunk at their age.

Today is Tom's and my nineteenth anniversary, so I'm going out on the deck to drink a glass of wine. Again, thanks for opening the door. You and Carolyn are great friends to do that.

Take care,
Janice

June 26, 2000

Dear Art and Carolyn:

Well, here are three copies of my revised manuscript, which I've entitled "Erotic Mentoring: Pygmalion and Galatea at the University." . . . This has been a fascinating journey; I really do see what y'all were talking about in your letter about making this more self-reflexive throughout, and have enjoyed immensely trying to write this in a different (more personal) voice. I may never go back.

Here is a summary of how I tried to deal with your questions and suggestions:

1. I have reframed the rewrite as my own search for answers to that original college experience, that a foray backward into ancient myth and forward into what other women have to say, helps to illuminate. I omitted the first personal vignette and started directly with the "honors seminar," because that seemed like the crux of *this* paper. But I've gone back to and drawn out that college experience now throughout the paper, and also end with it.

2. I gave a short history of my involvement with myth—in terms of what I've written about, what myth means to me personally, and why it's important for this project.

3. I shortened the ancient mythic stuff near the beginning by about half, and tried to unfold it as a mystery I was unraveling. I included only stuff I actually used in analyzing the interviews.

4. I talked about how these interviews came about, how I conducted them, and ethical concerns. I also tried to present in terms of what I learned, and to inject myself more into the process. I am aware that having so many interviews makes it hard to feel these women as characters. I thought really hard about collapsing them into composite characters, like one for each "voice." But I simply couldn't figure out how to do that without violating the reality that each person played more than one role and that they went through a *process*. So I ultimately decided to keep the actual people. But I did, most of the time, try to organize *within* the voices by person rather than by concept, in order to avoid the choppiness and confusion of multiple comments by different people following closely upon one another. . . .

I want to thank the two of you so much for pushing me on this. It will help me to write the whole book in a far more personal way. . . . Hope you're having a wonderful summer.

Fondly,
Janice

August 20, 2000

Dear Janice:

I've now had a chance to read your revised manuscript, "Erotic Mentoring: Pygmalion and Galatea at the University," which we intend to publish in our book, *Ethnographically Speaking: Autoethnography, Literature, and Aesthetics.* Your revision is superb and I am very excited about having it in the book. The difference between this version and the last one, which really was quite good in its own way (form of discourse), is light years.

I have only a few minor comments that I'd like you to think about in preparing the final draft for the book. On page four, paragraph two, first sentence. I guess this is in the eyes of the beholder. In terms of tolerance, I think myth and personal narrative are about equally rejected and under suspicion. Each seems to suffer, in my view, from the privilege given to theory qua theory and the general distrust of stories (as in "it's only a story"). Reminds me of the preface to a family communication text in which the author begins: "You won't find any stories here. This book deals only in facts and theory." Of course, this is a relatively minor point, but I don't think it helps either to say that myth is even below personal narrative in academic ranking. Besides, my inclination has been not to write defensively (as much as possible). Instead, I prefer the tactic of taking for granted the significance of myth and storytelling in the hope, naive as it may sound, of making it into a self-fulfilling prophecy. When you're constantly defending yourself (not you in particular; I could say we), then you're forced into a weaker posture, one that seems to need to be defended. I think you can make many of the same points as you do about myth, without placing your enthusiasm for the merits of myth in the context of your critics' attacks. So I think if you're looking for a place to cut, and I do think the paper could still be cut by one to three pages, I think the issue of the attack on myth is one place to do it. My guess is that most of the readers of this book won't be found among the antagonists against whom you are defending yourself. So think about how you might make the same "positive" claims about myth without framing it within the response to critics.

On page eight, you briefly introduce the topic of "your midlife burnout." This is a topic dear to my heart and one I've been dealing with under the heading "institutional depression," particularly in terms of academia (and perhaps more so among academic women, for example, Jane Tompkins). I have two responses here. The first is that you make me want more details about your burnout here (on page eight). You do return to the burnout in the last few pages of the manuscript and I can appreciate the foreshadowing that is done here, but I think a bit more detail up front would be helpful. In many ways, your whole study appears to be an attempt to recover the passion you were losing for your work and, perhaps, an unconscious calling out to revisit the repressed emotions associated with your earlier experiences as an undergraduate, graduate student, and young professor. It could be that you quit the study for four years not only because you wanted to protect these women (which I definitely believe), but also because you were defending against some of your own fears and uneasiness about what letting all this out might do. I sense, in other words, that you were tapping into some pain of your own—where most of the growth is—and you may not have felt ready to cope with it. Of course, I may be totally off here, or projecting too much of my own story, but I think knowing some of the details of your "crisis" would help us appreciate you and your project more fully. I'm not talking about a lot of detail here but certainly more than you've given on page eight. Let me know what you think. . . .

That's about it. I really love this piece and feel it's going to be regarded as one of the real gems of the book. It's wonderful working with you, Janice. You make the whole enterprise of scholarship feel worthwhile and meaningful.

> Fondly,
> Art

August 20, 2000

Dear Art,

I got your letter about my essay, and as usual, you were able to put your finger *exactly* on what was not quite in line with the direction I was going. I really agree that being defensive about myth is unnecessary; a holdover from the Brainchild—I'm trying to put her in her place, but she goes down kicking and screaming. I can also give a flavor for my midlife crisis that won't take up too much room, I think. . . . Again, thank you for your close and helpful reading—I appreciated Carolyn's comments, too. I'm happy with the way this is turning out, and yes, the whole process has been so positive and so educational.

Right now I'm trying to deal with the shooting in our building yesterday; perhaps you heard about it in the news. A professor was killed by a graduate student who then killed himself. Tom and I were three floors up at the time, and were evacuated. A horrible thing made worse by the fact that John Locke (head of comparative lit) was a good friend. We had been in a study group together for twelve years, and we shared several doctoral students. . . . I'm in shock, and sure didn't feel like starting classes today. I hope you're well, and thanks again,

Janice

August 29, 2000

Hi Janice:

Good to hear that you felt my comments were on target. It's been such a pleasure to work with your manuscript and I'm thrilled that it will be in the book. It's been an education for me too.

Jesus, you know I heard about the shooting from one of my colleagues. She asked me if I knew anything more about it but I was so into my own little mundane world of teaching and getting everything ready for my class that I bypassed the significance of it and your likely connection to it entirely. It's all so frightening. I know sometimes my undergraduates really scare me. Let me know more details when you get a chance. Say hi to Tom.

Cheers,
Art

September 18, 2000

Dear Art:

I'm enclosing three copies of my final draft of "Erotic Mentoring . . ." along with a short autobiographical statement and a disk. Although this one was not nearly as hard as the last one to do, I want to thank you for your careful and thoughtful reading, and for nailing once again exactly what I needed to do to lay down those vestiges of defensiveness and write this thing closer to me. Maybe this will now serve as a constant reminder to me not to keep putting up that shield. Also, many thanks to Carolyn for her encouraging remarks. Would that every author could be so "heard"— in the lines and between—throughout several drafts. . . . I can't wait to see the final book.

Take care,
Janice

Stories that Conform/Stories that Transform: A Conversation in Four Parts

DOUGLAS FLEMONS AND SHELLEY GREEN

Part 3

Publish *and* Perish?

Note: This is the third of four conversations derived from a taped panel discussion titled "Autoethnography and Therapy: Stories That Conform, Stories That Transform." See also pages 87–94, 115–122, and 187–190.

Carolyn Ellis: Let me tell you about a story I wrote once about coping with a minor speech problem. In my first-draft ending, I said that I didn't really suffer the speech problem as a minor bodily stigma. It hadn't really changed its physical presence, but I didn't respond to it anymore. Okay, so that was an ending, but I wasn't really happy with it. I thought, "Well, where do I want to go now?" I started to push further, asking myself, "Am I just so okay with this that it will never bother me again and I never have to think about it?" The answer was no, it's much more complex than that. There will be times when it bothers me again, it's not so set, and now it may bother me because I still have the speech problem but it also may bother me because I made such a big deal about it. What if people now don't think I have a speech problem? Then that will bother me too—here I've made this big deal out of something that shouldn't have been a big deal.

By pushing that first-draft ending, I got to what I thought was a much more complex understanding of the process, and I also worked myself out of feeling, "Well, if I ever have a problem with it again I will have failed because I thought I fixed it and now it's not fixed." I don't have the ending to that story yet—it's still in process.

Shelley Green: But partially that's because you made it public, right? If you announce it to other people, it becomes a different kind of story, and then you have to deal with your relationship with it in relationship with the audience.

165

Carolyn: With how they read it.

Shelley: Right. I talked with my students this week in class about how writing autoethnography, or ethnography in general, becomes an outing process—that you out yourself intentionally or unintentionally—and how uncomfortable that might be. You have to decide if you're ready to be outed or to put yourself out in that way. You have to think about what that will do to your professional identity and your personal relationships.

Laurel Richardson: My book *Fields of Play* has a lot of theory, but also a lot of personal stories, narratives. And I've been struck by how many students and assistant professors have said to me, "Oh, it took so much courage to write that book. How did you have the courage to write that book?" But I didn't see the writing as a courageous activity. I saw it as a healing activity, as all kinds of other emotional activities, but the reader sees a heroic tale: "Oh, this is courage."

Art Bochner: Most of the focus is on the *teller*.

Laurel: And not on the audience.

Art: Right. As Lesa Lockford brought up yesterday, how is the audience invited into the story and where do they live in that story?

Cristina González: One of the most difficult decisions I've had to make over the years has been what stories *not* to tell. I do not want to put on paper a story that makes of me and my experience something that it isn't. To be squeezed into a particular frame would feel like I was incarcerating myself. In a therapeutic session, how do you respond to someone who wants to come and just sit there? Someone who doesn't want to tell you anything?

Jerry Gale: Sometimes a spouse or a child in a family doesn't want to participate in therapy, or they participate by being quiet, because they feel there will be consequences for them, regardless of whether they speak or stay silent.

Shelley: And they may also not want their story told by someone else. Clients feel violated when another person in the therapy room is telling their story without their permission.

Douglas Flemons: What strikes me from hearing you talk, Christina, is that your choice not to tell a story has been a way of protecting your freedom.

Cristina González: Exactly.

Douglas: You have the choice of either telling a story or not telling a story. The story works to the degree that it keeps you from being constrained or imprisoned by either the telling or the not telling.

Carolyn: Every story I've ever told has freed me in all kinds of ways, but it has also constrained me—because I then become "the person who." I am "the woman who had an abortion," I am "the woman who has a minor speech problem," and even if I don't define myself that way any more, or even if I've changed and those are not the decisions I would make at this point in my life, I'm still that person because it's on paper. But the telling is also freeing in all kinds of ways.

Laurel: Cristina, *not* wanting to tell a story seems to me a very strong act of volition over which one has control: I don't want to tell that story, either because I don't want to know of it myself, I don't want to deal with it, or because I don't want anybody else to know about it. But sometimes stories aren't told because they are untellable. I have a friend who has a child with an autism-like illness, but it isn't autism. The doctors don't have a name for it and her child, because of the illness, is unable to speak. The story of his condition isn't my friend's to tell, but her son can't tell it either. And neither can the doctors. And I've got stories of my own life that I don't know how to tell.

Art: This brings out the issue of vulnerability. Laurel, you and Carolyn, especially, have written yourselves as vulnerable storytellers. Cristina, you seem to be saying, "I don't really want to be the vulnerable storyteller in this instance."

Cristina González: In terms of that particular story, yes. If it were in print, I would be vulnerable.

Kathryn Church: I think the tenured professors are the ones who need to be assuming the position of vulnerability and writing the difficult stories. I myself wrote an autoethnographic tale about a breakdown experience and I think there has been a tangible cost to me in writing that tale as a person who has not succeeded in making entry into a university position, who has not been legitimated in those ways that you already are. I think there is a direct link between the telling of that tale and the outcome in terms of my personal and professional life. So, those risks I think we need to lay on the table. My purpose in writing a breakdown experience as a social science text is to socialize the experience and to help people understand that what it is that I have lived through is not just me, it is profoundly social, it is common, it is always among us. And this is why the risk is so important.

Laurel: I tend to use the word sociobiography and not autoethnography because I want to emphasize that Millsian part. And I agree with you that for me it's no risk to write anything I want to write, at least in terms of professional stuff.

Saliha Bava: I am a family therapy intern writing an autoethnography about my experience, and there are stories that I've not told. I know that writing these stories would change that experience, would change the relationship, would change my future. As a family therapist, I make sure I don't pathologize others, but I feel that I risk getting pathologized myself, and that risk is so great that I may just have to pack up and go back to India.

Carolyn: There are people in here who wrote autoethnographies as students who are now professors at universities. Maybe they should be the people talking about the risk, the professional risk. Christine? Lisa?

Lisa Tillmann-Healy: For many of the jobs I applied for, I did not send the bulimia paper with my packet of materials. So I think there are ways that you can still write an autoethnography and not have to have it as a forefront of who you are. Anything we write about is a small part of the totality, and I think it's important to talk about it politically.

Annette Markham: Shelley, you talked earlier about how the role of therapist is somewhat complicated by the institutional norms, by the pressure to heal, by having to have a certain outcome. To me, the whole project of autoethnography is a mirror image of that same struggle. You have an urge to speak or write so that you can come to grips with something. The question is, "Do you put it out there in the public realm?" Is it necessary, if it is therapy, to make it public? Does an autoethnography need to be made public in order to fulfill part of its goals? We are also under some requirements to make what we write public.

Douglas: Well, part of how we define ourselves is to engage in conversations.

Annette: Yes, that's one sense of it.

Carolyn: Part of my healing is hearing the stories of those who respond to mine, so the making public can be self-consciously therapeutic, hoping to open up the conversation so the conversation can continue to be therapeutic for the writer.

Jim King: Even the construction of the text with reference to an intended audience causes such a transformation—because you're framing it in a way and recasting the experience in a way that it is intended for an audience. Now I may chicken out and not send it out after all, but I think the experience of writing it would still be valid.

Carolyn: You try to write yourself into a space that you can live in, and the space we live in has other people in it, other people reacting to us. And so it does become a very social process.

Shelley: I see a dual risk. You need to publish or perish, but then if you're thinking you might publish *and* perish, this creates a really difficult situation for people who are not in tenured positions.

Art: I want to comment on the courage it takes to risk one's career to speak forbidden narratives. It involves incredibly difficult choices; people need to be aware of the potential consequences in making the decision to publish. Obviously it would be wonderful if we could change the orthodoxy of the academy or if we could destigmatize therapy or destigmatize the depressed self, and that ought to be part of our project. I have worked with students who have suffered from the experience of boldly and vulnerably telling their stories. What you say, Kathryn, about full professors or senior professors is an important point, especially those who have a little more latitude to take risks. I hope we can encourage people to do that. I didn't really make the transition from being an empiricist to being an interpretivist or narrativist until I was a full professor, but I can tell you that when I did, I lost a lot of friends.

Carolyn: And gained a few. [laughing]

Art: Exactly.

Lesa Lockford: There are certainly lots of risks involved in these kinds of tellings; I'm not tenured and I certainly feel these things. But I'd like to make a distinction (not my own) between confession and testimony, appealing to the question, "To what ends are we writing these tales?" The confession is done for the self; it is therapeutic, and it conjures up the role of the therapist who is invited to listen in a particular way. A testimony, on the other hand, is made by someone who is standing as a model and saying socially, "This has relevance beyond my self; its purpose is to better others."

Searching for Autoethnographic Credibility: Reflections from a Mom with a Notepad

Elaine Bass Jenks

Some roles are easy to put on, aren't they? Other roles don't feel as comfortable. We feel awkward or inept or, worse, inauthentic, when we try on these roles. Autoethnographer is like that for me. First, I feel a little odd calling myself an ethnographer. I'm a communication researcher, not an anthropologist. Besides, I've always thought of ethnographers as the sort of scholars who dress in khaki shorts with lots of pockets and stand near bamboo huts in order to appear in sepia-toned photographs. Second, I feel awkward calling myself an *auto*ethnographer. It's taken me a long time to write about my experiences, and I'm still not sure my own narratives are appropriate "*data*" for analysis.

Preconceived notions aside, I embarked on my first autoethnographic study this summer. I spent six weeks at a day camp for blind and visually impaired children, conducting interviews and observing communicative interactions between and among blind, sighted, and visually impaired individuals. The "auto" part of this ethnography is that I'm the parent of one of the visually impaired campers. While I may have entered the study with the idea of becoming one of those khaki-clad, sepia-toned researchers, the truth is that I conducted this study as my son's mom. I was granted access to the camp because I am his mom and I was introduced to others as his mom.

No one else's mom came to camp this summer. No one else's mom attended each day, went on every field trip, and knew all the words to the camp song. No one else's mom sat on the side of the pool at 2 P.M. every day during free swim and watched the campers' newest swimming tricks. Even on Family Day, when the other campers' moms *did* come to camp, no one else's mom carried around a notepad.

I believe it is my notepad that made me more than just a camper's mom, that differentiated me from all the other parents, and that separated me from the counselors, the volunteers, and the campers themselves. I believe it is my notepad that brought me autoethnographic credibility this summer.

But the summer is over. And now what I have is a pile of six stenographic notepads filled with my very first field notes. To be perfectly honest, I'm not sure if my field notes are any good. I'm not sure I wrote down the right things. Are my notes filled with others' experiences and void of my own? Or is it the other way around? Did I write too much about my experiences and not enough about others'? And speaking of others' experiences, I'm not sure I had the right to write down what I did. Not everything I wrote is complimentary; should I edit out the negative comments before I write up my study? Further, I'm not sure how many of my notes are useless. What am I going to do with the lists of who helped pass out dessert each day? Will the names of the swimming groups turn out to be important observations? How will I judge my field notes?

This paper is an exploration of my search for autoethnographic credibility though my field notes. I begin by describing some of the practical concerns and theoretical issues present in the literature about writing observations in field notes. Then I describe how my field notes were created. I end with lessons learned about autoethnographic credibility in the field and in life.

Practical Concerns and Theoretical Issues about Writing Observations in Field Notes

As a student of communication, I wasn't taught how to take field notes. But from what I've read (see especially Sanjek 1990a), many others, including anthropologists, haven't been taught how to take field notes either. In fact, those with formal training in field-note-taking techniques haven't always found their education useful when they actually entered the field. Moreover, ethnographers disagree as to just what field notes are (Jackson 1990; Emerson, Fretz, and Shaw 1995). That is, are field notes what is handwritten in a notebook while interaction is being observed? Or are field notes what is typed at the end of the day from the notes written in the notebook? Are other sorts of data, such as journals, diagrams, and preliminary analyses, also considered field notes?

The problems surrounding field notes extend beyond training and definitions. Ethnographers have to decide issues such as who else, if anyone, will see their field notes, how will they protect the confidentiality of their participants, and, most importantly, exactly what is the *field* that is being recorded in their notes (Clifford 1990; Jackson 1990; Wolf 1992; Emerson, Fretz, and Shaw 1995)? Where are the boundaries of the field? Where does it begin and end? When does one start taking field notes? What exactly does one record? When does one stop?

These technical issues about field notes underlie larger theoretical concerns about what it means for ethnographers to write observations about others. In his well-known discussion of "thick description," Geertz (1973) wrote that the writing ethnographers do is "interpretive" rather than "observational." In the following decades, this line of argument was challenged, supported, and expanded by Clifford (1986, 1990), Wolf (1990, 1992), Marcus (1986), and Geertz (1988) himself. Further, the topic of ethnographers observing and writing about others (and the self) continues to be debated (Bochner and Ellis 1996; Denzin 1997; LeCompte and Schensul 1999; LeCompte, Schensul, Weeks and Singer 1999; Angrosino and Mays de Perez 2000; Denzin and Lincoln 2000; Ellis and Bochner 2000; Lincoln and Denzin 2000; Richardson 2000; Tedlock 2000).

Geertz (1973) equated interpretive ethnography with "thick description." What ethnographers produce in thick descriptions, he observed, is their own detailed interpretations of what the participants in their studies are doing—our views of their views. In subsequent work, Geertz wrote that "something is happening to the way we think about the way we think" in the social sciences, describing the increase in the use of "blurred" analogies such as the game, the drama, and the text (1980: 166). He drew attention particularly to the meanings and responsibilities of ethnographic authorship—an ethnography is a text written by a particular somebody, some place.

However, in 1986 James Clifford and George Marcus published an edited book, titled *Writing Culture: The Poetics and Politics of Ethnography*, that directly attacked Geertz and others who support a literary perspective of ethnography. Clifford and Marcus (1986) argue, in short, that a literary perspective still assumes the authority of the ethnographer who is speaking for, rather than with, the participants in a study. Clifford (1986) finds that ethnographies are inseparable from the historical, political, institutional, social, and rhetorical contexts in which they are created and read. Clifford concludes that thick descriptions are not "merely interpretations," but "rhetorical constructions" (1990: 67). While Geertz (1973) does call descriptions "constructions," Clifford's concern is that the term "description" implies a "representational relation to culture" and Clifford believes all description is "always rhetorically (also historically and politically) mediated" (1990: 69). The place of the author in ethnographic writing, then, according to Clifford and Marcus (1986), is to be more aware about the selection of the voices being reported, about how those voices are presented, and about which other voices are being silenced by that selection process.

In a chapter titled "Writing Ethnography: The Poetics and Politics of Culture," Margery Wolf (1992) speaks directly to Clifford and Marcus (1986) by playing with the title and disagreeing with the premise of their text. Wolf (1992) argues that while Clifford and Marcus (1986) have encouraged ethnographers to be more self-conscious (an activity Wolf supports), she believes they are wrong to suggest that experimental forms of writing will solve the problem of ethnographers claiming authority in their descriptions of their fieldwork. Wolf asserts that ethnographers do not purposely omit or privilege certain voices or descriptions. She explains, "As ethnographers, our job is not simply to pass on the disorderly complexity of culture, but also to try to hypothesize about apparent consistencies, to lay out our best guesses, without hiding the contradictions and the instability" (Wolf 1992: 129). Geertz himself speaks to his critics when he argues that whether a text is "author-saturated" or "author-evacuated," ethnographers must still "persuade readers . . . that what they are reading is an authentic account by someone personally acquainted with how life proceeds in some place, at some time, among some group" (1988: 143).

More recent discussions of ethnographers speaking for others have evolved into questions about ethnographers speaking for themselves. Tedlock traces the history of this evolution. She labels the shift from observing others to observing the self as a move away from participant observation and toward observation of "coparticipation within the ethnographic encounter" (1991: 69). Observation itself is a complex phenomenon. Angrosino and Mays de Perez (2000) and LeCompte and colleagues (1999) remind us that ethnographers need to recognize that they are changing what they are observing simply by being who they are. "Different ethnographers . . . might well stimulate a very different set of interactions, and hence a different set of observations leading to a different set of conclusions" (Angrosino and Mays de Perez 2000: 689).

Ellis and Bochner (2000) move beyond the topic of ethnographers affecting their observations to the issue of ethnographers becoming the observed. These authors explain that observing interactions produced by the self (of the ethnographer) involve far more than writing reports in the first person or even "just" writing about one's own life. Autoethnography is "connecting the personal to the cultural" until the "distinctions between the personal and the cultural become blurred" (Ellis and Bochner 2000: 738–39). While autoethnographers write about themselves, their goal is to touch "a world beyond the self of the writer" (Bochner and Ellis 1996: 24). In short, autoethnographers enact the basic assumption of interpretive, qualitative social science that one cannot separate the knower from the known (Denzin and Lincoln 2000). Here, however, the known is the knower's experience.

In the past thirty years ethnographers have come to understand that who they are will affect what they observe, that what they observe will affect what they write, and that what they write will affect how others react to what was said (Angrosino and Mays de Perez 2000; Richardson 2000). Yet, as social scientists, we are all still grappling with the very basic question of exactly how to speak about, for, and with others (Rawlins 1998).

It is not my intent to provide a definitive answer to this question. Instead, I am interested in exploring how the practical concerns and theoretical issues discussed in the literature played out in my actual field notes. The three main issues I want to explore are:

- What did I write down?
- How did others react to my writing down what I wrote?
- How did being a mom who's a researcher and a researcher who's a mom affect the field notes I collected?

Creating My Field Notes

The Notes

What *did* I write down? This question is the easiest to answer and the hardest to explain. After reading about field notes before my study, I had decided that it would be best for me to tape-record my impressions and then transcribe the tapes. I thought I could include more detail by talking my notes rather than writing them. My first contact with the "field" came on the day before the first day of camp. I went to a staff meeting of the camp counselors. I brought my notepad along, but I didn't write anything in it during that meeting because I had decided to tape-record my notes.

When I got home from the meeting, I let the tape run a long time before I said anything. Then I kept rewinding the tape and rerecording my thoughts so that they sounded more coherent. Not feeling comfortable saying my thoughts made me realize that my initial idea to orally record my field notes wasn't so clever after all. I had taken almost as long as the one-hour meeting to record my notes of the event. How could I possibly tape-record my field notes for an eight-hour day? Plus, who wanted to transcribe all those tapes?

But deciding to write field notes in my notepad while I was at camp still left me with the question: What do I write down? Some of the literature offers advice. LeCompte and Schensul (1999) suggest writing down activities, events, settings, behaviors, and conversations. Richardson includes all of these suggestions under her heading of "observation notes" and adds that researchers can also write notes on method, theory, and feelings (2000: 941). Emerson, Fretz, and Shaw (1995) discuss not only what types of observations to write down, but where in the field to write notes. Sanjek (1990a) includes reproductions of actual field notes in his text. While all of these excellent resources discuss what ethnographers might possibly write down, none of these authors answer the question: What do I (*this* researcher in *this* setting) write down?

The next morning I showed up for the first day of camp with a clean notebook and looked around. I decided to begin with the most concrete aspect I could think of, a physical description of the camp. I started with the sign at the entrance to the drive and wrote down what the camp looked like. Then, feeling very anthropological, I drew a map of the camp. But as I looked at my creation, I wondered if anything I'd written on the first three pages of my notepad was connected with my topic of communication and visual impairment.

While drawing my map, I walked away from the camp house and toward the jungle gym. Across the grass, I saw a young boy on the swing set. The boy was calling to someone named Jimmy [all names are pseudonyms], only no one else was around. I said, "Hi, I'm Nick's mom. Do you want me to find Jimmy?" He said, "No" and kept on swinging. As I stood there watching him swing, I was amazed at how unself-conscious he was when he realized he was calling to someone who wasn't there. I, a sighted person, would have been humiliated if I'd been talking to the air. At that moment, I realized that I didn't need to worry about what to write in my notebook. I would just write what happened. And that's what I did.

Some of my initial concern about what to write down was connected to the physical act of writing. While I've written for years in many different places, I had never before written in a "field." At first, I felt awkward continuously writing in a setting where no one else was writing. I also felt very aware that others at camp knew I was the researcher, so I thought I should look like I knew what I was doing with that notepad. Once I actually started writing my observations, my self-consciousness dissipated as I hurried to capture the camp experience in my field notes. But before I started my study, I should have practiced the physical act of writing in a notepad in a setting where I was the only one writing.

Since the camp was structured into time periods, I wore a watch after the first day and most of my notes are listed by time ("10 A.M., walked to the flagpole talking to Mary about the field trip tomorrow"). I found that sometimes when I had a long conversation with someone, I'd write down what we'd discussed ("12:30 P.M., talked with Michelle about Braille") and would fill in the details later that day.

In short, my field notes are a recording of what I saw and heard. I did not record what I felt (though I did note my thoughts at certain moments). When I reread my notes, memories of particular situations are brought forth, complete with my sensations of those moments. I'll illustrate with an example.

One of the camp field trips was to take a ride on a restored, open-air train. I sat next to Doug, a totally blind camper, and across from two sighted teenage volunteers and Patty, a visually impaired camper. At one point during the ride, I saw that we were coming up to a gigantic U.S. flag that looked to me as if it were painted in a field. The train conductor announced that it was a flag made out of red, white, and blue petunias. My notes read:

It's an amazing sight. I say, "I'm not sure how far you can see, Patty, but there's going to be a big American flag in a field in a minute." She leans and looks. "Is it white?" she asks. "Yes," I say.

In the margin of that page, I later wrote:

I wonder why I pointed out the flag to her. If she just saw white on a field, what was the point?

When I reread that portion of my notes, I feel hot with embarrassment. I feel as if I enacted one of the very stereotypes I'm trying to dispel with my research. That is, I, as a sighted individual, viewed a visually impaired individual as missing something. In this case, what she was missing was a flower flag in a field. The unimportance of the object she didn't see just increases my sensation of humiliation. I could have told Patty about the flowers in the shape of the flag because, after all, I didn't expect Doug (the blind camper next to me) to even attempt to look at the flag. I could have told her in a way that sighted people appreciate hearing about things in outer space or deep under water, even though we've never seen them ourselves.

My point here is that my field notes describe what I saw, heard, and, sometimes, thought, but not what I felt. My choice to omit emotions brings me back to my initial hesitancy about calling myself an autoethnographer. Ellis and Bochner (2000: 738, 754) state, "Most social scientists . . . are not sufficiently introspective about their feelings or motives. . . . Not everybody is comfortable or capable of dealing with emotionality. Those who aren't probably shouldn't be doing this kind of research."

As a newcomer to this perspective, I don't understand why emotionality is so central. I believe the reader learns about sighted people's assumptions about visually impaired people from my flower flag example whether or not the reader knows I felt hot with embarrassment. The main point of my example is that sighted people are often the ones pointing out what blind/visually impaired people aren't seeing and that perhaps sighted people should think twice about their choices. The main point of my example is not my feelings. The goal of my example is to attempt to connect "the personal to the cultural" (Ellis and Bochner 2000: 739).

Issues of emotionality aside, my field notes focus on what *I* witnessed. My field notes are clearly my experience of being at camp and no one else's. Yet while I found that I was writing mainly my perceptions, others at camp thought differently. This leads me to the next area of creating my field notes: How did others react to my writing down what I wrote down?

The Physical Notepad

The most intriguing element to me is the reaction of others to the notepad I used. Each day that I attended camp, I carried a five-by-seven-inch notepad that had sixty green, lined pages held together with a spiral wire at the top. The notepad was covered with a plain, gray cardboard back, and a white cardboard front with the words "Stenographic Note Book by Tops" printed in blue and red ink.

The camp started on a Tuesday and on Thursday, the third day of camp, it rained in the afternoon. The campers had an indoor music activity after lunch and then right when the 2 P.M. free swim was about to begin, the sun came out. The campers left the camp room with the sighted, teenage volunteers to go swimming. I was in the back of the camp room finishing my notes on the music session and when I stood up to leave, I realized that the only people still in the camp room were the four (paid, adult, sighted) counselors and myself.

As I stood up, the director of the camp, Mary, said, "What are you finding to write so much about?" By the time I'd opened my mouth to answer, all four counselors were looking in my direction. I felt sort of trapped. The counselors had a right to ask. Yet, at that moment I was surprised and not sure how to answer. What *was* I finding so much to write about? This is what I said to the counselors:

> Well, I'm writing what you do. You have a lot of knowledge about communicating with blind and visual impaired people that you probably aren't even aware of. Like yesterday, when you were passing out camp T-shirts to the campers and Doug [a totally blind camper] asked Mary what color the camp T-shirt was this year. Mary said, "It's maroon." Then she asked, "Do you know what maroon is?" When Doug said, "No," Mary said, "Maroon is a dark red color with a lot of purple in it." I was fascinated that Doug was interested in color and that Mary was able to describe maroon to him. I was amazed by Mary's response. And yet you four didn't seem to find the moment unusual at all.

My comments led into a discussion of what the counselors found unusual when they first started communicating with blind or visually impaired campers, but that they no longer notice.

The conversation ended with my saying to the counselors, "Oh, you can look at my notes if you want to." Inside, however, I was hoping no one would take me up on my offer. Not that what I was writing was secret. It's just that I wasn't sure they knew the extent of the detail I was writing down (Angrosino and Mays de Perez 2000; Denzin 1997). No one did ask to read my field notes. Ever. In fact, after that conversation, no further questions were raised about what I was writing in my notepad. There seemed to be a certain respect, though perhaps it was more of a fear, for the physical pad itself.

For example, when I sat on the side of the pool watching the campers, more than once a counselor or volunteer told the campers not to splash my notebook. I don't think anyone else ever touched the pad. That is, sometimes I left it under my pen on a shelf when I used the bathroom or got a drink from the kitchen. My notepad was always exactly as I left it when I returned. A few times I forgot and left my pad on a table that was used for an activity. Yet, no matter what occurred before I returned, my notepad would be untouched. It was as if everyone (especially the counselors) were sending me a clear (nonverbal) message that they were *not* looking at what I was writing.

The most surprising view of my notepad came during the sixth, and last, week of camp. Heather, a counselor who had talked to me a great deal about my study, said, "Hey, did you fill up your pad yet?" The reason I was startled by her remark is that I had filled up a notepad for each week. I was writing in my sixth notepad when she asked the question. I guess I'd assumed that they knew I had a clean pad each Monday. But her comment made me realize that all six pads looked alike. And since I didn't write the dates of each week on the pad until after that week was over, the front of each notepad looked the same while I was at camp. But rather than explain how much I'd written, I just said, "Yeah" when she asked if I'd filled up my pad.

Answering her question truthfully, but not completely, reminded me that no matter how "close" I'd become to the campers, counselors, and volunteers during the six weeks I spent at camp, I was still a researcher. This leads to the last element in creating my field notes: Who was I in relation to what I was told?

Moms Who Research

Being a camper's mom gave me incredible access to the camp. It gave me initial access through the director of the association for the blind that ran the camp and it gave me continued access through everyone I met during my six weeks at camp. I wasn't a nameless researcher who was studying the other. I was Nick's mom, the parent of a visually impaired camper. I was one of them. Or was I?

Even though being a camper's mom gave me great access to the people I wanted to interview and observe, I experienced many moments of role conflict during my study. For example, sometimes comments were addressed to me in my role as a mom. When I was listening to a discussion among the counselors about a surprise for the campers later in the summer, one of the counselors looked at me and said, "Don't tell Nick." While I said, "Okay" aloud, inside I was thinking, *Of course, I won't tell Nick. I'm just a researcher observing a meeting.* But the counselor didn't look at me and see a researcher at that moment; he saw a camper's mom.

My mom role was always present. Pieces of information were often framed in relation to my son. When telling me about a spring weekend beach trip some of the campers had been on, the person talking to me said, "Oh, Nick's not old enough to go on this trip yet. He'll be invited when he's ten." At other times, information about other campers' visual impairments was given to me in comparison to my son's vision ("Hers is worse than Nick's" or "He can see distances a little farther than Nick").

The most disturbing incident happened near the end of camp. One day, one of the teenage visually impaired campers didn't come to camp. It turned out that the retina in his stronger eye had detached the night before and he had gone into surgery. Unfortunately, this was not the first reattachment surgery he had had in that eye and this time the procedure was not successful. He went from being sighted (though visually impaired) to being blind.

As a parent, I found this situation frightening. When I first found out my son was visually impaired, all I wanted was a medical treatment that would improve his vision. Over the years, however, my hope has become a desire for his vision to stay the same (and not get worse). Yet here I was at the camp witnessing my scariest fear played out in another mother's child.

As a researcher, however, I looked at the situation in a different way. Many of the people associated with the camp, including the camp counselors and the state's educators of the visually impaired, were extremely upset about this teenager's loss of vision. They had known him since he was five years old and felt close to him and his family. Some of the people who knew him were crying when they talked about the unsuccessful surgery.

As a researcher, I found this situation fascinating because this camp focuses on what blind and visually impaired children can do. This is a camp where the campers swim and play baseball (with balls and bases that "beep") and make art projects and sing and go on field trips. This is a place where visual impairment stops no one from doing anything. This is a context where the loss of vision is accepted as the ordinary. Yet, I was witnessing people, who had worked with blind and visually impaired children for many years, mourning the loss of vision.

I wondered if I was being callous watching the situation unfold as a researcher while everyone was upset. I found it disconcerting that I was feeling simultaneously sad about the camper's vision loss, worried about whether this would ever happen to my son, and intrigued by the vision professionals' reaction to the situation.

Other, less upsetting, issues arose because of my role as a mom. That is, I wasn't just a mom in general at the camp. I was specifically Nick's mom. Thus, I had to negotiate my being at camp with my then almost nine-year-old son. After all, no one else's mom was there all day long, every day. The campers ride in vans to and from camp, and my son liked the idea of skipping the van and riding with me to camp. But once we got there, he stayed away from me—except at lunch. For some reason, every day he saved a place for me to sit with him at a picnic table.

One day my son and some other campers were playing around in the pool, dunking one of the smaller teenage volunteers. I wanted to scream at them to stop, but I held my tongue and let someone else stop them a few minutes later. In the car on the way home that day, I told my son that I didn't like what he'd done in the pool. His immediate response was, "You wouldn't have known if you hadn't been there." Of course, he was right. And I never mentioned his behavioral choices at camp again, though I sometimes had to bite the inside of my mouth to keep myself from making "mom" comments.

My son seemed simultaneously pleased and embarrassed that I came to camp. For example, he stayed away from me for the most part, but one day when the other campers were showing me tricks in the pool, he ran up and said, "That's *my* mom. Hey, mom, watch this." (And, yes, all the campers said, "Watch this," even though they couldn't see if I was watching or not.) I've tried to let him participate in my study as much as he wants to. For example, he picked his pseudonym for this paper. But when I asked my son to let me pilot my interview with him, he said, "Mom, you'll know all my answers." When I asked if I could have someone else ask him the questions, he still refused when he realized that I would hear the tape.

My self-image of myself as a mom affected my study as well. That is, in all of the previous (in-depth interview) studies I have conducted, there was no mention of me being anyone's mom (or wife or daughter or friend). I was the interviewer, not a mom. But at camp, all day long, I was a mom in all the ways I've mentioned above. I felt like I was being treated like a typical mom even though I don't think of myself as that sort of mom. I think of myself as a cool and fun mom. I think of myself as the type of mom who serves candy bars for breakfast sometimes. I think of myself as the type of mom who says it's okay to wear something from the dirty clothes bin when I haven't done the laundry. I think of myself as the type of mom who wears shorts and tank tops, not housedresses and aprons. After all, I am not only a mom who researches, I am a researcher who is a mom.

And as a researcher who is a mom, I believe I expend more energy researching a topic that affects my child than I would if I studied a more distant "other." For example, I'm part of communities I never wanted to know about: my state's

Division of the Visually Impaired that takes care of my son's educational needs; my state's Association for the Blind that runs the summer camp; and my state's Association for Blind Athletes that offers sports activities for my son. While I'm grateful for all of these organizations as a mom and as researcher (ever more data to collect), I still ache at the fact that my son needs these services.

Additionally, I believe I expend more energy parenting my visually impaired child than I do his sighted younger brother. From teachers to extended family members to strangers to physical barriers, there are constant unforeseen situations that need negotiating because my son has low vision. Just walking down unfamiliar stairs, especially those without any color differentiation on the edges, can be a challenge. Do I make a third-grader hold my hand? Do I talk him through the situation? Do I even notice the stairs are a problem before he starts to stumble?

Because my son is visually impaired, I also have to decide when to tell people he has low vision and when to let him pass as sighted (Uttermohlen 1997). Does everyone he comes in contact with have to know about his vision? Do I tell the ride operator at the amusement park who sees my son stumble when he gets off a ride, and who says, "Oh, I was clumsy when I was his age too," that my son is partially sighted? Do I explain to strangers in the grocery store (who sometimes stare) why he's standing so close to the shelf searching for the items we need? Do I embarrass people, like the guy at the pool who stood and watched me play catch with my sons and who then announced that, "The reason he's missing the ball is that he's wearing goggles," by telling this stranger that the goggles are protecting my child's eyes from the sun?

My point is that under my upbeat pragmatic approach to my son's visual impairment, there are continuous decisions, a lot of exhaustion, and considerable pain that make being a researcher who is a mom who is researching what she is living a continuing challenge.

Lessons Learned about Autoethnographic Credibility from My Field Notes

Lesson No. 1

Autoethnography has little to do with sepia-toned, khaki-clad anthropologists. As Rawlins says, "Everybody everywhere is simultaneously a potential ethnographer and subject of ethnographic inquiry. Ethnography is . . . a way of being" (1998: 360).

My journey into ethnography didn't begin with these field notes in these notepads during this study. Some of my field notes will never be included in any ethnographic report of the camp I attended for blind and visually impaired children, but none of my field notes are useless. Writing itself, as Richardson reminds us, is a "method of inquiry" (2000: 923). My notepads, then, are filled not just with what I observed, but also with what I know.

Lesson No. 2

One of the aspects of writing field notes that I didn't see mentioned in the literature is that recording my observations at camp made me more aware in other contexts. Stereotypes about blindness are everywhere (Kleege 1999). For example, on the very first page of *The Wounded Storyteller*, Frank writes of Tiresias who was blinded by the gods and whose "wound gives him his narrative power" (1995: xi). On the very last page of the second edition of *Handbook of Qualitative Research*, the editors, Yvonna Lincoln and Norman Denzin, write of awaiting "the visit of yet another blind Homer" to predict the future of qualitative research (2000: 1063). These examples unintentionally perpetuate the stereotypical belief that the blind have special powers in place of their vision. Of course, these examples can be explained as metaphors. But when you're the parent of the referent, the meaning changes.

Lesson No. 3

Rereading my field notes has shown me that I don't agree with Ellis and Bochner's statement that "the real work" of autoethnography begins when "you think you can't stand the pain anymore" because I don't believe "connecting the personal to the cultural" *has* to involve "emotional pain" (2000: 738–39). I do agree with Ellis and Bochner that autoethnography is a place where social scientists can examine "the contradictions they experience" (2000: 738). Real life is messy and even those who write about the self's experience change over time.

Lesson No. 4

I'm a researcher who studies communication and visual impairment. I'm also and simultaneously a mom who has a child who will never see my face clearly even when our heads are on the same pillow. Then again, maybe that's just a sighted person's desire to point out what a visually impaired person is missing. My son always knows it's me. Maybe I'm the one who misses him not seeing me the way I see him. Maybe the point is not who misses what. Maybe the point is that we each see things our own way. Maybe "when we close our eyes . . . we see everything the same" (Kleege 1999: 228).

Lesson No. 5

I went searching for autoethnographic credibility. What I found is that questions of how to speak about, for, and with others need to be continually examined. What I found is that who I am affects what I observe, what I write, and how others will react to what I say. What I found is that I am somewhat reluctant to completely embrace this "evocative form" (Richardson 2000: 931) of self-reflection. What I found is that the act of writing field notes allowed the camp participants (as well as myself) to view me as more than a camper's mom and something other than an outside researcher. What I found is that it was my notepads, each made of two pieces of cardboard, sixty pieces of paper, and one spiral wire, that brought me autoethnographic credibility this summer. Oh, it wasn't the notepads per se. It was the act of writing field notes in a context I both was and wasn't a part of that allowed me to become an autoethnographer.

Acknowledgment

This study was aided by a College of Arts and Sciences Support and Development Award from West Chester University.

References

Angrosino, Michael V., and Kimberly A. Mays de Perez. 2000. "Rethinking Observation: From Method to Context." In *Handbook of Qualitative Research*, 2nd ed., ed. Norman K. Denzin and Yvonna S. Lincoln (pp. 673–702). Thousand Oaks, Calif.: Sage Publications.

Bochner, Arthur P., and Carolyn Ellis. 1996. "Talking Over Ethnography." In *Composing Ethnography: Alternative Forms of Qualitative Writing*, ed. Carolyn Ellis and Arthur P. Bochner (pp. 13–45). Walnut Creek, Calif.: AltaMira Press.

Clifford, James. 1986. "Introduction: Partial Truths." In *Writing Culture: The Poetics and Politics of Ethnography*, ed. James Clifford and George E. Marcus (pp. 1–26). Berkeley: University of California Press.

————. 1990. "Notes on (Field)notes." In *Fieldnotes: The Making of Anthropology*, ed. Roger Sanjek (pp. 47–70). Ithaca, N.Y.: Cornell University Press.

Clifford, James, and George E. Marcus. 1986. *Writing Culture: The Poetics and Politics of Ethnography*. Berkeley: University of California Press.

Denzin, Norman K. 1997. *Interpretive Ethnography: Ethnographic Practices for the 21st Century*. Thousand Oaks, Calif.: Sage Publications.

Denzin, Norman K., and Yvonna S. Lincoln. 2000. "Introduction: The Discipline and Practice of Qualitative Research." In *Handbook of Qualitative Research,* 2nd ed., ed. Norman K. Denzin and Yvonna S. Lincoln (pp. 1–28). Thousand Oaks, Calif.: Sage Publications.

Ellis, Carolyn, and Arthur P. Bochner. 2000. "Autoethnography, Personal Narrative, Reflexivity: Researcher as Subject." In *Handbook of Qualitative Research,* 2nd ed., ed. Norman K. Denzin and Yvonna S. Lincoln (pp. 733–68). Thousand Oaks, Calif.: Sage Publications.

Emerson, Robert M., Rachel I. Fretz, and Linda L. Shaw. 1995. *Writing Ethnographic Fieldnotes*. Chicago: University of Chicago Press.

Frank, Arthur W. 1995. *The Wounded Storyteller: Body, Illness, and Ethics*. Chicago: The University of Chicago Press.

Geertz, Clifford. 1973. *The Interpretation of Cultures*. New York: Basic Books.

————. 1980. "Blurred Genres: The Refiguration of Social Thought." *American Scholar* 39: 165–79.

————. 1988. *Works and Lives: The Anthropologist As Author*. Stanford, Calif.: Stanford University Press.

Jackson, Jean E. 1990. "'I am a Fieldnote': Fieldnotes as a Symbol of Professional Identity." In *Fieldnotes: The Making of Anthropology*, ed. Roger Sanjek (pp. 3–33). Ithaca, N.Y.: Cornell University Press.

Kleege, Georgina. 1999. *Sight Unseen*. New Haven, Conn.: Yale University Press.

LeCompte, Margaret D., and Jean J. Schensul. 1999. *Designing and Conducting Ethnographic Research*. Walnut Creek, Calif.: AltaMira Press.

LeCompte, Margaret D., Jean J. Schensul, Margaret R. Weeks, and Merrill Singer. 1999. *Researcher Roles & Research Partnerships*. Walnut Creek, Calif.: AltaMira Press.

Lincoln, Yvonna S., and Norman K. Denzin. 2000. "The Seventh Movement: Out of the Past." In *Handbook of Qualitative Research,* 2nd ed., ed. Norman K. Denzin and Yvonna S. Lincoln (pp. 1047–65). Thousand Oaks, Calif.: Sage Publications.

Marcus, George E. 1986. "Afterword: Ethnographic Writing and Anthropological Careers." In *Writing Culture: The Poetics and Politics of Ethnography*, ed. James

Clifford and George E. Marcus (pp. 262–66). Berkeley: University of California Press.

Pratt, Mary Louise. 1986. "Fieldwork in Common Places." In *Writing Culture: The Poetics and Politics of Ethnography*, ed. James Clifford and George E. Marcus (pp. 27–50). Berkeley: University of California Press.

Rawlins, William K. 1998. "From Ethnographic Occupations to Ethnographic Stances." In *Communication: Views from the Helm for the 21st Century*, ed. Judith S. Trent (pp. 359–62). Boston: Allyn and Bacon.

Richardson, Laurel. 2000. "Writing: A Method of Inquiry." In *Handbook of Qualitative Research*, 2nd ed., ed. Norman K. Denzin and Yvonna S. Lincoln (pp. 923–48). Thousand Oaks, Calif.: Sage Publications.

Sanjek, Roger. 1990a. "A Vocabulary for Fieldnotes." In *Fieldnotes: The Making of Anthropology*, ed. Roger Sanjek (pp. 92–135). Ithaca, N.Y.: Cornell University Press.

———. 1990b. "On Ethnographic Validity." In *Fieldnotes: The Making of Anthropology*, ed. Roger Sanjek (pp. 385–418). Ithaca, N.Y.: Cornell University Press.

Tedlock, Barbara. 1991. "From Participant Observation to the Observation of Participation: The Emergence of Narrative Ethnography." *Journal of Anthropological Research* 47: 69–94.

———. 2000. "Ethnography and Ethnographic Representation." In *Handbook of Qualitative Research*, 2nd ed., ed. Norman K. Denzin and Yvonna S. Lincoln (pp. 455–86). Thousand Oaks, Calif.: Sage Publications.

Uttermohlen, Teresa L. 1997. "On 'Passing' through Adolescence." *Journal of Visual Impairment & Blindness* 91: 309–14.

Wolf, Margery. 1990. "Chinanotes: Engendering Anthropology." In *Fieldnotes: The Making of Anthropology*, ed. Roger Sanjek (pp. 343–55). Ithaca, N.Y.: Cornell University Press.

———. 1992. *A Thrice-Told Tale: Feminism, Postmodernism, & Ethnographic Responsibility*. Stanford, Calif.: Stanford University Press.

Stories that Conform/Stories that Transform: A Conversation in Four Parts

Douglas Flemons and Shelley Green

Part 4

Healing and Connecting

Note: This is the fourth of four conversations derived from a taped panel discussion titled "Autoethnography and Therapy: Stories That Conform, Stories That Transform." See also pages 87–94, 115–122, and 165–169.

Shelley Green: One of the dilemmas of being a therapist is that we tend to get a little too captivated by thinking, "What could be a corrective story or a healing story?" and deciding that the story that gets told must be corrective or healing in some way, rather than just taking the story for what it is and living with it in its own form. Robert Bor, a researcher and therapist who works with HIV-positive clients in London, tells a story of working with a gay male couple who were sero-discordant. They worked for a couple of years with Rob, and part of their discussions centered on how to protect the HIV-negative partner from getting the disease, how to preserve his health.

And after a couple of years of being very successful at this and building very positive stories around this, the couple came to him after being away from therapy for a while, and they told him a new story. They had stopped practicing safer sex, and their rationale was that they wanted to "infect the ill partner with wellness." This was a very challenging story for Rob to hear, given that it completely went against everything he and the couple had been working on for a couple of years. Of course, all he could think in the moment was, "No, you've infected the well partner with illness!" But they needed him to be able to hear their story about infecting the ill partner with wellness. And so as a therapist and a researcher, he had to sort through his understanding of stories. What's a corrective story? What's a healing story? What's a bringing-together story? Rather than pushing the story I want to tell, how can I listen to the story that needs to take priority? This is our dilemma as therapists and researchers: how to let the story *be,* how to keep from needing to intervene.

Laurel Richardson: The last essay in my book *Fields of Play* is called "Vespers." It is a story about my mother and myself and my family, and it took a great deal of pain and energy to get it written. Recently, a friend of mine told me that he saw "Vespers" as being about my coming to grips and learning to love my mother. And I thought, *Boy, that's really interesting.* And then my husband said, "Well, you know he's right, but the healing here has been toward you, toward your brother." And it was like *snappo,* I hadn't even thought of this piece as having *any* relationship to the problems between myself and my brother, problems that have been healed since I wrote it. Once I could heal my feelings, I guess, toward my mother and the whole family structure, I could then move into having a relationship with my brother again, which had been severely severed for maybe twenty years. And I think this is what I'm trying to say then is that the stories can have lives of their own in healing things. So, was that a corrective story? I don't know if it was corrective.

Shelley: For whom?

Laurel: Yeah, and when.

Douglas Flemons: The thing about the word *healing,* it comes from the same root as the word *whole,* and so to heal is to make whole. It seems to me that the stories that you [Laurel and Carolyn] have described—Laurel's "Vespers," and Carolyn's story about her minor speech impediment—they had a healing effect, but they weren't written with the *intent* of healing. The healing came about as a secondary result. What seemed central to the stories was the making of a connection. Laurel, you made a connection with your mother that then allowed you to make a connection with your brother; Carolyn, you made a connection with something that you'd struggled with such that it no longer was a struggle. The healing that took place was not the primary purpose of the writing.

Carolyn: I don't know if it's the primary purpose, but one purpose for me is to connect with others who read or listen to my story and who then tell me *their* story as a result, as a response. And the dialogue that occurs leads to some sense that things are better. "We are companions, you've felt this way too, this is part of what we're in together." So the idea is not to heal but the idea is to start these kinds of conversations.

Douglas: The conversation becomes a connection, which creates a sense of wholeness or community among you and your readers.

Saliha Bava: I'm thinking of the word *healing* that keeps coming up. There is a therapeutic discourse that says that therapy is about healing. But you are talking about connection. What if therapy is about connection? It changes in some ways the stories we are going to tell and the stories I may write. My own approach to therapy is not focused on "healing" but on establishing relationships in conversations. As a therapist, I come into a conversation that the client is already having with other people, and in autoethnography, also, it's just a conversation that I am having that I'm choosing to talk about in different places of my life.

Shelley: Listening to you talk, I think that maybe the best in therapy and in autoethnography comes about not when we decide, "I'm going into this because I want to heal something," but that we go into it saying, "I'm willing, I'm taking, making the proactive stance to struggle with something privately and publicly and I don't know where this is going to go and I don't know how anyone else is going to respond and I don't know how I'm going to be different in this struggle and through this struggle, but I'm choosing to take on the struggle, and I'm choosing to include another voice."

Jerry Gale: The metaphors you use to describe your therapy affect what you do in the room. What are you doing as a therapist? What's your goal? Is it to heal? Is it to make connection? Is it to fix? These metaphors have real implications in the practices. In both therapy and autoethnography, you have to ask yourself where you're trying to get and how you're trying to get there.

Carolyn: Right, to what end point?

Jerry: And there's the danger of that, I think.

Carolyn: Yeah.

Art Bochner: Well, healing sounds to me like a metaphor of closure. You've sewed up the scar and you're done.

Carolyn: Yeah, I think you should have more questions at the end than you had at the beginning.

Janet Yerby: I like this playing around with language. What's the end of the story or what's the purpose or the goal of the story? Healing without feeling finished, or is it connection? That seems a little different. But when I think of healing, my own healing really is a way that I try to make some kind of connection with something that's happened to me in my past that has jagged edges or that comes out and it's not right and I haven't worked it through. So, I don't like to use the word healing but what I need to do somehow is, as a person who is living in the present, work to see if I can make those connections with events that have happened to me in the past and integrate them. So in a sense there is a lot of talking about something that happened back then at a particular place and time and then trying to get to this no place in time. It is kind of the present that is moving, like the river. I just wondered, can you talk a little bit more about this.

Shelley: Therapists unfortunately often focus entirely on outcome, which really limits us. It helps to stay open to serendipity, to coming up with more questions.

Caroline Joan S. Picart: I've been struck by the dichotomy between the closure of being completely healed and the openness of the unhealed wound. As Carolyn pointed out, it's not, perhaps, a matter of "isness" but of chiaroscuro—an undulating dynamic in which health and sickness have strands that weave into each other and tear away from each other at the same time.

Carolyn: Writing an autoethnography can be self-consciously therapeutic. But it goes beyond the writing—it opens up conversation, and when it works well, the conversation continues to be therapeutic for the writer.

Border Crossings: A Story of Sexual Identity Transformation

BEVERLEY DENT

Sunday, October 2, 1995, at nine in the morning, the bright cloudless sky throws its best light on this late fall day. Flocks of shiny black crows crowd nearby bluffs of tall poplars, calling noisily, taking off, circling, and landing back where they started, the young ones strengthening their wings for a journey they have never made before. The older, wiser ones know that it takes many strong wing beats to propel them 2,000 miles south. They know that not all will return. If the young understood all the hardships they might experience, the threats and the dangers they would meet, would they leave? If each had to fly alone, would any of them go?

I drive south out of Prince Albert, Saskatchewan, in the heart of the Canadian prairie provinces. The highway stretches like a black ribbon. In front of me, the road disappears on the southern horizon; behind me, through the rear view mirror, I see it disappear on the northern horizon. The two vistas represent my split mind. "He" looks back to all that has been and never will be again; "she" looks ahead to all that has never been, but might be. Trinidad, Colorado, the sex-change capital of the world, 1,500 miles straight south—my destination, my Rubicon—awaits.

Behind me is Laurie, the woman Tom married twenty-three years ago. Laurie is the only person I have ever been intimate with, the woman who bore our two children, the woman who has slept with me for most of that twenty-three years. She said, "Until death do us part." She said, "For better or worse"—but not this worse, not this death. Behind me are my son, Bruce, and my daughter, Nancy. Will I ever see them again? Will they ever want to see me—Beverley?

By two o'clock, I am through Regina, the last large center until Denver. The farther south I go, the more complete the harvest. At three o'clock, I stop in Weyburn, Saskatchewan, for Kentucky Fried Chicken. Not so healthy, but I like it. Besides, I am in good shape, and soon I won't be eating much. By five o'clock, I am at the U.S. border, the first hurdle to jump. I am dressed as I have been living— female and feminine, but my driver's license and my ID state that I am a male. I still have a penis. What if the U.S. border guard asks for my ID? Will he accept my explanations? Some guards are very reactionary, especially at small rural crossings like this one.

I have been dreading this moment. My heart pounds while I try desperately to appear unconcerned.

"What is your name?"

"Beverley Dent."

"Where are you from?"

"Prince Albert, Saskatchewan."

"Where are you going?"

"Trinidad, Colorado."

"Purpose of your visit?"

"Medical treatment."

"Okay."

In two minutes, I am gone, but it takes much longer than that to slow my heart. Before long, the sun has set and the whole world is quickly fading into a dull gray, then a deep black. It was warm in the sun; now it becomes cold. I turn on the heater. The headlights cut a narrow swath through the blackness as I continue south into this foreign country. I play tapes—just music, no vocals—trying to distract my mind, quiet it, make it leave me alone, but there is no distracting a mind on a mission.

I am back with Laurie, as she sobbed, "I cannot love you as a woman. I am not a lesbian. I cannot be a lesbian." For twenty-two years I tried to be the man she wanted me to be. It was never quite good enough—for her or for me. Now she would gladly accept that inadequate man, but I can't. And she cannot, or will not try to be what I would like her to be. It seems so unfair. Nothing I have ever done, nothing I have ever been is worth anything now. A life wasted. Near midnight, I find a motel in the small town of Belle Fouche, North Dakota. I should be tired; I should sleep, but sleep does not come easy on this night.

When I told my son, Bruce, what I was about to do, he wanted assurances that this was not a flash-in-the pan, that this was something that affected me deeply and had been carefully considered over a long period of time. Once he was convinced of that, he did not argue. He seemed to accept the inevitable, buried his grief so that I could not see it, and gathered his strength for the rough days to come. He never turned away from me. I still don't know how much he has suffered.

When I first told my daughter, Nancy, she flew to my defense. I was her father, and if I had to do this thing, then it must be something that I had to do. "It should not diminish you in others' eyes," she said then. Twenty-four hours later, after she had a day and a night to think and talk about it, she changed her mind. "I want to ask this one favor of you," she said. "I will never ask you for anything else. Just this one favor. For me, please. Do not do this thing!" I would do anything for her, but I could not go on living my life as a man, not even for her. I could not. When I told her, she screamed, "I don't know you. You don't exist. You're dead!" Then she ran to her bedroom, and I ran to mine. Those horrible words, mere marks on this sheet of paper, forever seared deeply into my memory. I wonder if there is any disease so terrible that it could erase those words? Do some memories last forever? I wonder, as I drift finally to sleep.

Monday morning, I am up early and on my way. A low fog hangs over the land; it is damp and cool as I head into the Black Hills of South Dakota. Up in the high country it snows and the wind whips the snow into a blizzard. Blinded by the white moisture outside the car and the gray wetness of my own tears inside, I often have trouble seeing the road. Why couldn't Laurie try for me, even for one year? "Because," she had said, "I am normal. I don't have to try to be abnormal. It wouldn't be right. You have a responsibility to be normal."

I've heard the same words from my boss, a born-again Christian. "You have to take whatever these people do to you because they are only behaving normally. . . . You have to bend over backwards to please them because you are the one who is not normal!" Those who are different apparently have obligations and responsibilities to those who are "normal," but "normal" people owe us nothing, not even human decency.

Once I am down out of the hills and onto the flat prairie of eastern Wyoming, the sky clears, the sun shines, the temperature rises, and the world becomes a more pleasant place. By six o'clock, I am rolling through Denver and the temperature is dropping again. I drive on into the night, uncomfortable, even afraid, in the darkness of an unfamiliar road in a foreign country. I feel relieved when the signs for Trinidad begin to appear. I take the second exit, spend half an hour surveying the main part of the town, buy a hamburger, and then settle into the Trinidad Motor Inn.

Around noon on Wednesday, I am ushered into Dr. Stanley Biber's office on the fourth floor of the National Bank Building. Dr. Biber has done more sex-change operations than anyone else in the world. I will be number 3,449. Dr. Biber's executive assistant, Marie Pacino, is a slim, middle-aged woman with dark hair. Pleasant and efficient, she takes care of all the details, ensuring that my paperwork is in order, and accepting the large bank draft that I hand over to her. No checks or Canadian cash taken here.

Dr. Biber is pleasant and cheerful, and we quickly settle into a comfortable conversation, despite the fact that this is a critical interview. Dr. Biber has the final say about my transition. I must convince him, as I have already convinced two psychiatrists, that I need this surgery to survive, to be the person I have always known I should be, could be. I am an adult, more than fifty years old. Under the law I am accountable and responsible for my actions. Still, others have more power to determine who and what I should be than I have, even though I am the one who has to pay the price, and the one who has to live with me twenty-four hours a day, each and every day for as long as this life goes on.

By one o'clock I am on my way, first for a small lunch, then up to the Mount San Rafael Hospital, where I am admitted. Two pleasant nurses come in to do my physical exam. They remark that I seem to be in good shape—not too fat, good muscle tone, and good color—although very white. I have been watching my diet, exercising, and riding an old pedal bicycle every day. My experiences with surgery during the last few months have taught me that recovery is much easier and faster if one is in good emotional and physical condition.

Before I had my first surgery, I had to leave home for the last time. After twenty-three years of marriage, I left my wife, my nineteen-year-old daughter, and my twenty-two-year-old son. Left them all, not because I didn't love them, not because they didn't mean the world to me, but because I didn't know how to go on living as the husband and father they knew, and because Laurie didn't know how to live with me if I wasn't that person. The pain of leaving was excruciating. The first thing I did was to drive 300 miles to Manitoba to tell my parents what I was going to do. It was a slow trip. I cried much of the way and had to pull off the road many times. I don't think they really believed me. They thought I had gone mad, so they humored me. My father shook my hand when I left.

Back in Saskatoon on May 3, I had a complete upper facelift. The timing wasn't very wise as I was an emotional wreck, but I survived the operation. The next one, the lower facelift, was six weeks later. My surgeon told me that it could be worse than the first one, but it wasn't. I was better prepared physically, and stronger mentally. The third one, surgery on my neck and vocal chords, in Vancouver during August, was better still, so now I am confident. I know this surgery is going to be rough, but I can do it. I must!

The lab technician takes blood and urine samples. I am checked for everything, including AIDS. If I were HIV-positive, they wouldn't touch me. I was tested a month before at the University Hospital in Saskatoon, and now they test again the day before the surgery. No problem. I've only ever had sex with one person, Laurie, the mother of my two children, and not even that during the past two years. I've never done drugs, and haven't had any transfusions, so there is no risk. I am clean.

A young male doctor, the anesthesiologist, comes to discuss my options. I can have a general anesthetic or a spinal tap. The spinal tap doesn't put one right out, but is supposed to make one's recovery easier. No way! I'm squeamish. I tell him, "I don't want to know anything about anything until after it is over. You put me right out of it!"

After supper all my pubic hair is shaved off, and I am cleaned with Betadine. At ten o'clock, I accept the offer of a sleeping pill. It doesn't work. My mind will not turn off. I tried so hard to be "normal," but I failed. I have never been "normal." I can never be "normal." I am different. I just want to be me, Theresa Beverley Dent. If I cannot be me and live as the person I know myself to be, then why live? What is life if one has to be constantly pretending to be someone else, an illusion, someone else's fantasy? If my family can only love this illusion, is that really love or is it merely the illusion of love? If it is only an illusion, then what am I losing? I am losing the illusion of being loved.

Around 5 A.M., I finally drift off to a blissful sleep. It lasts only minutes. At 6 A.M., the nurses awaken me. Last trip to the bathroom, my last shower for six days, final preparations, then transfer to the gurney, and I am wheeled along the corridor to the operating room. Suddenly I feel terrified. This is it! I can still say "No." I can still walk out of here and go home. My temporary insanity would be forgiven. I could still have the life that I had before April. All I have to do is say "No." But I cannot live like that. I'd soon be spiraling down into that black pit. I would soon want to be dead again. I came within a hair's breadth of killing myself before; the next time, I would succeed. No use going back. I do not say "No." I drift off into the anesthetic darkness.

My Rubicon is crossed.

I am drifting up out of a dull gray fog. I hear someone calling, "Theresa . . . Theresa." Oh, yes, I am Theresa. Theresa Beverley Dent. Yes, I am here. "How do you feel?" I don't know. Oh, yes, I see you now. I'm okay, I guess. Yes, I exist. I must be female now. Others report the ecstasy of the moment; I feel only peace. I drift off again. A little later, I awaken again. There isn't any mist. I see the light. I feel the pain. Whatever isn't between my legs now hurts awful damn bad. At least that is the place from which the pain that spreads out through the rest of my body emanates.

"Are you feeling pain?"

What a question! My eyes must be as wide as saucers, and you ask me whether I'm feeling any pain. A nurse brings me some Demerol, but it seems to take hours before it gives me any relief. Finally, I drift off to sleep—oblivion, heaven. It doesn't last nearly long enough. After sleeping for an hour and a half, I drift back into the world, a world full of feelings—bright, sharp, searing sensations; dull, throbbing, aching sensations. I burn, I freeze, all at the same time. My body sweats with the heat, and trembles with the cold, simultaneously. I am anchored to the bed, lying on my back with my legs spread apart, with rolls of blankets or something wedged between my lower legs to keep them apart. I cannot roll over. I can move my arms and roll my head from side to side; that is all, and it is not enough, not nearly enough. There is no position that is comfortable. Machines are connected to me by wires and plastic tubes. Fluids flow into me and out of me, unaffected by my will. I am helpless. I have no control over anything. I am hardly human. Perhaps only the excruciating pain makes me human. I lie there and pay the price—the physical and mental pain of just wanting to be me.

The next three days are pure hell. My body makes me pay, and my mind joins in. It dredges up the past and causes memories to flow in front of my tightly closed eyes: all that has been, and is no more; all that can never be again. It replays "their" words, my mother, my wife, my daughter:

"Why do you want to mutilate yourself?"

"If you do this terrible thing, no decent person will ever want you!"

"You will live out your life alone and lonely."

"You will go to hell!"

"I don't know you. You don't exist. You're dead!"

I cry. Sometimes I don't even know why I am crying. I don't understand; I didn't expect to feel so out of control. I have no control over anything, not my body, not my mind, not my emotions, not my self.

They told me that I will not be able to get out of bed for four days. I will be confined to the bed so that there is no chance of ripping or pulling the stitches and sutures, which are holding my new body together. I understand. I don't forget, but on the third day, I get out of bed anyway. I drag the machines with me across five feet of floor and into the bathroom, where I sink onto the toilet seat. I don't know why because I can't use the toilet anyway. I don't think I even have the urge. I just have to do something. I don't know how long I have been here. Not long, but now I can't get back. I don't have the strength. So I sit here slumped against the wall, tormented by memories, with no hope, and no will to move. Finally, I pull the little emergency chain. Two large practical nurses come running into the room. I'm not in bed; they turn and see me in the bathroom, the door open.

"What are you doing there? Don't you know you're not supposed to get out of bed?"

The larger one harangues me like some unruly child. I take it silently. What is there to say? She is right, but it doesn't really matter. I am here, in the bathroom, out of the bed.

At this moment, Maria arrives. Maria is a registered nurse and the supervisor on this shift. She is in her mid-fifties, of Hispanic descent, and one of the most loving, caring, competent people I have ever met. Maria is the first of my three angels. In a flash, her eyes and ears take in everything. She dismisses the others, then helps me back to my bed. She bathes me, changes my dressings, touches me gently, gets me some Valium, and speaks to me in her soft, sweet voice. When you are a pariah, as I now am to many people, that human touch is priceless. We talk about our families. She is a grandmother now. I tell her it is Thanksgiving weekend at home in Canada. Fifteen hundred miles is a long way, but I am much farther away than that, and I can never get back home.

Maria comes often now, the Valium helps, and I feel a little better. When the shift changes late this night, the second of my angels comes to me. Joan is the RN supervisor taking over, and most likely she has been briefed by Maria. I suspect that Maria has told Joan that I need emotional as well as physical care. Joan is younger than Maria, in her late thirties, of Native American descent. We talk for a while about her life and mine, about her family and mine. She tells me she has been a nurse in the U.S. military; I tell her I worked as an electronics technician for twenty-four years for the Royal Canadian Mounted Police. She makes sure I am comfortable, medicated against pain, and ready for the night. She pins the emergency cord close to me.

"If you need anything tonight, you pull this, and I will come. I don't care how many times you pull it during my shift, I will come right away."

I pull it twice during the night, both times for medication, and she comes, herself, each time, and quickly.

Another day, another evening, Laurie phones from Prince Albert. Everyone else is home for Thanksgiving. They will have a big turkey and pumpkin pie. Bruce always wants big turkeys, and pumpkin pie is my favorite. I tell her what has been happening to me, and about the hot and the cold that I can't control. She laughs. "You wanted to be a woman, now you know what a woman experiences at menopause when her hormone levels change."

Suddenly I understand. I have been on estrogens for five years prior to this surgery; the doctor instructed me to stop taking them one week prior to my surgery to help reduce the risk of bleeding. In addition, when my testicles were removed, I lost 95 percent of my body's production of testosterone. My body has not only received a terrific physical shock, but also has been dealt a heavy chemical blow. No wonder it can't even regulate my temperature properly. My body is having to relearn basic autonomic functions that it had performed unaided for years. My experiences are starting to make sense, and Laurie's laughter is not malicious. I see the irony, and I laugh at myself.

The pain starts to diminish, but there are other trials in store. The first is having a bowel movement after four days without one. It sounds simple, but it isn't. They pour mineral oil and other things down one end of me, and force liquid up my other end. Finally, after another day, another part of my body starts to function again. Next is my urinary tract. This part is a little different now. For five days, I have been hooked to a catheter to take care of that function. Catheters come out easily; they don't go back in so easily, and certainly not painlessly either. The catheter is removed, and my body is coaxed with copious amounts of fluid to start functioning normally. It won't, so Dr. Biber says, "Give her some beer; that'll work." Right from our first meeting, Dr. Biber has referred to me as though I were already female. So have the nurses and other staff members. That is satisfying.

They bring me the beer. I hate beer. I tell them, "You take that stuff and put it in the freezer until it is almost frozen, then bring it to me, and I will drink it." They do, and I do, and my body blithely ignores it. My situation is getting dangerous now. It is possible for a bladder to rupture under too much pressure, so they say the catheter has to be reinserted.

My third angel is Florence. She is also an RN shift supervisor of Hispanic descent, and nearly fifty-five years old. Florence has a backbone of pure stainless steel, no nonsense; there are things that have to be done, and they will be done—now, not later. "I will explain to you what we are going to do," she says, "and how you can help so that it will be as easy and as painless as possible, but it will still hurt." Self-disciplined, gentle, caring, and very competent. Just like the others, she gets me through the tough times. The next day, the catheter comes out again, and goes back in again. Florence is sympathetic and as gentle as possible, but the job gets done now. My body may delay, but Florence will not. A day later, another part of me starts to function normally, and the catheter is left behind. I can get up and move around now. I start to feel human again. I can eat, but not much.

My three angels are very special people, but it is their human touch that makes them angels. The others are mere technicians; they carry out the mechanical functions to keep my body alive. Maria, Joan, and Florence soothe my tortured soul.

Finally, on the ninth day, I am released, but there is one more irony to accept. Before I leave, I am given two dilators, and am taught how to use them on myself. I am warned that if I do not perform this procedure religiously, I will be back for reconstructive surgery, and if I think that the first surgery was bad, well, I don't want to know how horrible the reconstruction would be. I vow not to return. After coming all this way and paying $18,000 Canadian to get rid of a real penis, I'm going home with two artificial ones. The gods must be killing themselves with laughter.

The trip home will be much different from the trip here. It will take five days to drag myself home. I drive for nearly an hour, then stop at a highway rest station, pull myself out of the car, stretch, and lie face down on the hood of the car. My body relaxes as the heat from the engine penetrates deep into me. After a few minutes, I push myself up off the car and walk around a little. Before I slide gently into the driver's seat, I carefully position the plastic air-filled donut I had been given as I left the hospital. They told me, "This will be your best friend for some time to come." That wasn't an exaggeration. For weeks I do not sit anywhere without it. After gingerly positioning my tender posterior on the donut and adjusting the driver's seat to a different position, I leave the rest stop and drive for another hour, then repeat the procedure.

Five hours and a little more than 200 miles later, I find a motel and collapse on the bed. Four or five hours of rest and I am able to change my dressings, bathe, take care of my body, and take painkillers. The next day I start out again. This time, I will make 250 miles before I am forced to quit. I can't eat much. Nothing tastes good, not even Kentucky Fried Chicken, but I force myself to eat an occasional hamburger, some fruit, and a few chocolate bars. They keep me going. My problems on the return trip are primarily physical. I lack strength and stamina. I tire easily and my body is very tender, but my thoughts are much more positive. I think about future possibilities, little things like being able to wear whatever clothes I want to wear, to grow my fingernails as long as I wish and color them any shade I wish. I plan a new wardrobe. As soon as I get home I will have to change all my documents to reflect my proper sex: female. Fortunately, this is possible where I live; in some jurisdictions it is not possible to ever change your birth certificate. I am hopeful that I will find at least some degree of tolerance at work and in the community; after all, I was a good citizen, good father, good employee, and good friend. At this time, I have no idea how little any of that will be worth.

On the fourth day, I finally crawl back across the border into Canada. I may be crawling, but I have no trepidations about the crossing; I am Theresa Beverley and I am female. The customs officer is female and friendly. One day later, I arrive in Prince Albert, where I hole up in my small basement apartment like a wounded animal in its burrow. It is a long cold winter. My recovery is slow. I have little company. I am away from work for two months; after that, it is another four before I am performing all my duties. For many months following the surgery, I suffer phantom pains from the penis that isn't there. Gradually these pains fade away. The others are much more permanent. I have made my bargain, a Faustian bargain some would say, and I have paid the price in cash and in pain, both physical and emotional. But this was something I had to do. It was this or death. How do I ever explain how strongly I felt about something so foreign to "normal" people's experience?

Long before the first fuzzy pussy willows display their soft gray buds, before the dirty white snow has left the fields, strong black wings appear in the southern sky. Not so pretty as the bluebirds that will follow, or as soft and loveable as the graceful, white pelicans that will glide into the unfrozen river a month later, these dark defiant messengers perch on the top of the tallest bare poplars and confidently declare, "We are back! Let life begin again!"

Acknowledgment

I would like to express my gratitude to Dr. Carolyn Ellis for her generous advice and assistance in preparing this chapter for presentation and then for publication.

Rebirthing "Border Crossings"

CAROLYN ELLIS AND BEVERLEY DENT

ugust 17, 2000

Dear Beverley:

Your revised paper is much improved over the last draft I saw. I enclose an edited version. I wonder about the title "Rebirth." What about "Border Crossings" instead? You also might think of a subtitle, something like "A Story of Gender Transformation." Otherwise readers won't know from the title what the paper is about, which means it's difficult for those doing a search on this topic to locate your paper.

The first part of your paper is quite poetic. I love that you now reflect backward. It adds more context for your story, especially the reflections on your family. These reflections add layers to the text and make it so much richer. Some other parts are not as poetic, and I have tried to help with those. You should go through the paper, after doing all the revisions, with an eye toward making the text as poetic as possible. The description of the plastic surgeries, for example, can be cut a great deal, as I note on the text.

I still encourage you to put in more of your emotional reactions. (Those you've added are wonderful.) Think of describing more fully a scene with concrete detail to bring readers into your emotion. Make us feel with you. For example, what about adding, after "I sit here slumped against the wall," the words "tears running down my face, memories of their words

screaming in my mind"? Also, be sure to add necessary or important concrete details that the reader might be curious about and that will bring us
more immediately into the scene with you. For example, how much did
the surgery cost; what kind of work do you do; what is involved in a "comfortable conversation"; and tell us what you talked to the nurse about.
These details will give us more of a sense of you as well as the experience.
On the other hand, leave out unnecessary concrete detail, such as "They
work twelve-hour shifts." I know it is sometimes difficult to decide what is
necessary and what is not, but try to put yourself into the role of reader.
What do readers want/need to know?

I'm not sure "paying the price" works that well (and you use this several
times in the paper). You at least need to clarify what that phrase means to you.

I still would like a little more sociological reflection in places. For
example, you mention the negative responses of the women in your life to
your transformation. How did men respond? Was it harder for women
than men? Why? I would have thought it would be harder for men, who
would fantasize having their own penises cut off, and be forced to question
the privileged status of male. Reflect on that a bit: Were there gender differences in reactions, and in your expectations of what the reaction would be?
What about your father? He is an unusually silent character here. Or
maybe you didn't think about gender in terms of the response to your
transformation. If not, say you didn't.

I'd also like a little more self-reflection on the sociological significance
of your changing gender. For example, the doctor refers to you with the
female pronoun. How does this feel? What does it symbolize for you? A
male performs the operation, but women take care of you. Do you feel like
one of them then? Do you feel the people taking care of you judge you in
any way? Do you feel more caring as a woman? You think about wearing
clothes and polishing nails as a woman—is this what it means to you to be
a woman? Anything else? These are what I would call ultrafeminized symbols. If those were what was significant to you, can you comment on them?
Why are they significant? When I first met you in Edmonton, I found your
appearance extremely feminized—makeup, lipstick, feminine clothes, high
heels. (I could never wear those damn things.) I am not making a judgment
about your appearance, just an observation. The next year at our conference,
you seemed less dramatically feminine and more "naturally" feminine. Is
this something you're conscious of, or think about a lot?

What about things like equal opportunity, softness and caring of women, less emphasis on domination and control and competition? Were they not in your mind? If not, can you comment on those things not being on your mind, from your position now? Can you comment on the meaning of "woman" when you decided to make this change and your meaning now that you have lived as a woman for five years? I'm not asking you to say things that weren't on your mind, but simply to reflect now on your experience then, and what might have been absent or silent, given what you know now. This might involve playing with time. Perhaps you might say, "From my position now as a person who has lived as a woman for five years, I see that my experience then . . ."

I want you to anticipate forward more than you have as well. Would you feel comfortable commenting on sexual orientation? Do you wonder about sex as you drive home? What it will be like? Who will it be with? If with women, as you are accustomed, then you will now be considered a lesbian. How do you take that in to your identity? If with men, well, now that will be quite a change for you. You must have fears about that. Or maybe you really don't think about these things at all as you take each step, one at a time. Perhaps you were able to deal only with the physical pain. If so, can you at least let us in on what you're not thinking about? These things absent in the text are important.

Finally, I am not pleased with the ending. The last paragraph works and is a nice poetic return to the beginning. The paragraph before the last one is too much like a cliché for me in its discussion of how hard life is, wanting to die, and being the woman you should be. I tried to fix it, but I'm not sure my suggestions work either. You want this to be dramatic but not general and clichéd. It's hard, but I think you'll find the right words.

Beverley, I think this is a wonderful piece. Overall, I like it very much, and now you are in the process of artfully crafting it. Don't think you have to do everything I suggest above, but these are suggestions that occurred to me as I read. It is your piece and you should make it as you see fit. Please get this back to us in two weeks. I am hopeful we are going to be able to publish it, but time is tight so return it as soon as you can. Thanks for working so hard, being willing to share your story, and being so open to feedback. Working with you has been delightful. I look forward to getting your revision.

Warmly,
Carolyn Ellis

August 26, 2000.

Hi Carolyn,

It seems to me that many of your questions about my paper actually relate
to things that have happened or understandings that I have acquired since
the trip to Colorado. I will try to answer some of them here, then we can
decide whether they should be included in the story.

I like your idea of "Border Crossings" instead of "Rebirth" for the title.
I also have added a subtitle as you suggest, though I have decided to use
"A Story of Sexual Identity Transformation" rather than your suggestion of
"A Story of Gender Transformation." Yes, the psychological term for my
"condition" is gender dysphoria; however, I do not like the implication
that I changed only my gender. I changed my *sex*. Some people manage
to adopt the behaviors and live in the roles of the "opposite" sex without
undergoing sex reassignment surgery. It is problematic, but it can be done.
That is a gender transformation. I did that too, but I also changed my sex.
Someday soon I will write a paper on this topic.

Yes, I want to make my writing poetic and I will continue working on
that aspect. It is difficult to put myself in the position of the reader when I
am so very closely connected to this story, and that is another reason why
your comments and suggestions are so valuable. Thanks again.

I use the expression, "It's part of the price" or "paying the price" quite
often in my work. It's a takeoff on the work of the French-Canadian writer
Nicole Brossard, who uses a similar technique in her work. It emphasizes
the theme that we make our choices, then we must live with the consequences. We must pay the price, and often we do not know what the price
will be. What bothers me the most is that so much of the price I have to
pay is the result of social constructions that others impose on those of us
who are different. My theoretical writings deal with that topic.

Let me give you an example. When I made the decision to change my
sex to try to save my life, I knew that there would be a price, a heavy price,
but I had no idea how heavy the price would be. Laurie had said, "No decent
person will ever want you. You will live out your life alone and lonely." I
would be making myself undesirable, even unlovable to almost all people. I
expected to live out my life alone and I thought I could pay that price. I did
not expect to fall in love with a heterosexual woman, as I did after my transformation, in a way that I have never loved before, or to have her say that the

feeling was mutual. For a little while it seemed that the impossible might be possible. For a little while I dared to dream. For a little while I lived with hope. Then one day she woke up, and in the cold light of day decided that she could not go there. In the deep darkness of the first hour of New Year's Day 1998, after having a few drinks, she told me that she did not want me, and that if she *had* wanted someone, she could have married a real man. That was a pain that has had no equal, and one that I continue to pay to this day. It is a price that I never thought I would have to pay.

You have asked about men and whether they have a harder time than women in accepting my situation. They certainly do. What I have done is any "normal" man's (gay or straight) worst nightmare. So terrible is the thought of losing their genitals that they cannot bear to even think about it. My father is gone; he died about two and a half years ago. A few months before he died, he said, "You can live too long." He meant that when you have lived to see your oldest son do what I have done, you have lived too long. Dad died of cancer. He would not permit any treatment. Before he died my father's penis shrank and became useless for everything. He could not even pee properly. In his final days he lamented, "I am not even a man anymore." I will always regret that he felt that a penis was so important that it defined who and what he was. I always saw him as so much more than that. My brothers blame me for my dad's death; not that he wouldn't have died eventually, but they are convinced that he would have lived longer had I not done what I did. That may well be true. My brothers have written me off; they hate me. I didn't expect that price either.

I have mentioned my son, Bruce, named after my father, in the paper. My son and I have always been close and we still are. He has never turned his back on me. He was engaged to be married on September 16 of this year, 2000, but all of that changed during the last week in June. The young woman and her family found me very problematic. She could hardly stand to look at me. Bruce wouldn't tell me, but I have recently learned what I had suspected. I am the insurmountable problem. His relationship is over now. He has made the choice that was forced upon him. He has paid the price for my decision. He never had any choice in that decision. It isn't fair.

I talk to my mother on the phone every week or two, and visit her two or three times a year. She lives in a small town about 300 miles from here. When I visit her, none of her friends ever come around while I am there. I am hidden, denied, like the mad one a family hides in the attic. She always refers to me as Tom, he, him, etc. I am her mentally ill son, but always a son. It will never be any different. She will not try. She will not go to family events, such as a wedding, if I go. She does go if I do not go. She grieves for my father a great deal. She will not say it directly, but I am fairly certain that she would be much happier if it was me in that grave. She would still have my father, and there would not be any division in the family.

You have asked about sexual orientation. As I am writing this, there is a documentary on TV behind me. It concerns four transsexuals who had their operations at a clinic in Montreal. They talk about some of the issues you are interested in. They claim to be orgasmic. I have little sensation in my genital area, and in addition, I have no sex drive. I regard that as a blessing. With so little possibility of finding anyone to love or to love me, I do not need the harassment of a physical need that will never be met. Sexual orientation does not seem to change. I am still attracted to females; however, during the last five years I have met two men who have made me wonder if being with a man is a possibility. Both men are gentle, sensitive, caring, intelligent persons. That is also the kind of women I am attracted to. I was heavily conditioned from birth, just as most others are, so I do not know what might be possible. But it doesn't matter because both of these men are gay. They like me as a friend, but they are sexually attracted only to men, and they have no doubt about my sex. To them, I am definitely female. Perhaps that, too, is one of the attractions. So am I a lesbian now? Without someone to love and love me, the question doesn't seem to have much significance.

From the first moment he met me, Dr. Biber referred to me as a woman. He does that for all his patients. So when he says to give her some beer, it is not the first time I have heard him refer to me that way. Also, I have been living as a female person for six months so it is not the first time I have heard myself referred to with the feminine pronouns. It is pleasing. Remember, I also have heard myself referred to, many times, in other more derogatory ways.

What does it mean to be a woman? What did it mean before? What does it mean now? I am certain that I can and will write a few papers on this subject. No, it isn't just about clothes. In fact that is a small part of the matter, but our clothing is the most obvious signifier of who we are and how we wish to be treated. What we wear also has a strong influence on how we feel about ourselves. You may not like the "ultra feminine" kinds of things, like high heels, but you have always had the option. You could wear them or leave them as you chose and with no fear of condemnation either way. That is a luxury I have not had, so if I, and others like me, tend to pay a lot of attention to these insignificant matters, perhaps you can excuse us. Your appearance is not sexually ambiguous. It doesn't matter what you wear, nobody is going to mistake you for a male. You don't even have to try! If people have any doubt about one's sex, the default is always male; therefore, we have to display more overt cues about our female sex so that people will make that judgment automatically. It's called passing. I find it very important.

The other things, such as equality and the experience of caring and concern, and reduced emphasis on competitive and controlling behavior are also important, but you don't even get to those experiences until you are first accepted as a woman, and your presentation has a lot to do with that. Appearance is really not as frivolous as it may seem.

I always preferred the company of women to the company of men. In our society it is very difficult for women and men to be "just friends." Now, I get to enjoy the company of women as friends, being accepted by women as another woman, being free to walk into women-only spaces, communicating with women as only women seem to talk to other women. The intimacy, the caring, the sharing are all part of what it means to me to be a woman. Changing my sex and changing my gendered behavior were essential prerequisites to gaining these privileges. Now, I don't feel the same pressures toward competition and one-up-manship that are so prevalent in male space. Relationships are far more important to me now than they were before. I used to have to guard myself against exposure of my deviant thoughts and feelings, so I had to keep a safe distance between myself and friends and family. Now, I don't have to do that; I can be open and honest. I don't hide. My new friends know who and what I am, and having lost my old "friends" and family, I really value the ones I have now.

I have written all of this so that you might better understand what it is to be different. That is my purpose in writing, but it is difficult and it still hurts, and new hurts continue to surface. When one is different, as I am, the price is never paid. It is never over. It continues on and on. Still, I would rather be dead than go back to where I was. I like my life and myself much better than before, and that makes life worth living.

I understand now why Lenora raves about her experience studying with you in Florida. I hope that someday I might also have that chance. You are so encouraging and you make me feel that perhaps I really can do more than I ever thought I might. As a result of your questions on what it means to be a woman, I already have another paper running around in my mind. The trouble with this e-mail technology is that I can't give you a big hug and I would certainly like to. Thanks for everything.

Beverley

August 26, 2000

Dear Beverley,

Your e-mail made me cry. Your story touches my heart. I feel deeply for your pain and the rejection in your life. It's hard to imagine that people could react so narrowly, but I know all too well they do.

I've been wondering why it is that your transformation doesn't bother me at all. I don't even think in that way. What you did seems so appropriate: You had a problem and you tried to fix it. In the same way, sexual orientation does not impact how I feel about a person—I think we are all multisexual if we take off the blinders/binders—sexual identity transformation does not change how I feel about a person either. Of course, you are not my husband, my father, or my son, and I didn't know you before your sex change. But I would hope, and have to assume, that I wouldn't feel different than I do now, even in those circumstances.

Art and I are publishing a volume from the 2000 SSSI Couch-Stone Symposium, and we'd like your paper to be included. I think it's important to get your story out in the world, for people to know it, for you to tell it, and for others to react to it. I'd like to celebrate your life, your choices, not hide you away.

As you continue working through my suggestions, remember this is your paper. You decide how to craft the final version. I'll still comment, but I want the final story to come from your heart. Given how your last e-mail affected me emotionally, I'm wondering if maybe we shouldn't publish these letters instead of trying to incorporate all of what you wrote into the story itself. It would show how the paper, and our relationship, developed as we worked together. What do you think?

By the way, I'd love to continue this work with you at University of South Florida, if that could ever be arranged.

Warmly, Carolyn

Autoethnography: Self-Indulgence or Something More?

ANDREW C. SPARKES

A rare sunny day so far this June in Exeter, and I'm stuck in an external examination board meeting. I glance at the clock on the wall—3.30 P.M. We started at 2 P.M., so not bad going; these boards usually take hours. All the marks for the third- and second-year bachelor of science students have been checked, discussed, and confirmed. By now, my attention is drifting and I find it hard to concentrate. That just leaves the last item on the agenda, which is the "external examiners' report." If they keep it brief, I can get finished early today and fit in a bike ride.

Members of the department sit around a large table in a conference room. The left corner of the table is taken up by the external examiners, Professors X and Y. I am sitting next to Professor Y, on his right, so I get only a limited side view of him when he speaks. The head of the department invites comments from both of them. To my delight, Professor X begins by saying that the comments will be brief and he makes a few helpful points before giving the floor to Professor Y.

Again, this external examiner makes a number of supportive comments about assessment procedures and the quality of the students. Regarding the latter, Professor Y mentions that he read a small sample of the dissertations. Most of these were conducted within a traditional scientific framework and he makes positive comments about each. Professor Y then turns slightly toward me as he begins to discuss the only qualitative dissertation he looked at. This was supervised by me and was an autoethnography as defined by Ellis and Bochner (2000). It was written by a mature student and revolved around his experiences of sport, social class, the armed forces, hyper-masculinity, physical burnout, clinical depression, and his recent attempts to restory himself. Professor Y notes that it was "beautifully written, very interesting, fascinating." He fully supported the first-class mark I awarded the work. But then came the sting in the tail, when he said, "even though the dissertation might seem a bit self-indulgent."

Self-indulgent—the word slams into my left ear. I feel my neck and shoulder muscles tense as I move forward from my chair to rest my elbows on the desk. A flush of blood warms my face. By now Professor Y has turned a full forty-five degrees to his right to face me, and is smiling. I know it is a friendly smile and he means no harm. Indeed, in confirming a first-class grade for a work of this kind he is actually being very supportive. But for me, damage has been done. To use a word like "self-indulgence" in front of a department that is dominated by the scientific paradigm is to undermine not only the autoethnographic venture but, by implication, all forms of qualitative inquiry. I think to myself that this is all some might need to confirm their suspicions about the kind of work I do. I feel their eyes on me. They, and Professor Y, seem to be waiting for a response. But I'm not sure how to deal with it in this context.

I want to ask him what he means by self-indulgent. Why not use different terms, such as self-knowing, self-respectful, self-sacrificing, or self-luminous? For me, the dissertation was anything but self-indulgent, and it included many of the characteristics of he*art*ful autoethnography (Ellis 1997, 1999). These include the following: the use of systematic sociological introspection and emotional recall; the inclusion of the researcher's vulnerable selves, emotions, body, and spirit; the production of evocative stories that create the effect of reality; the celebration of concrete experience and intimate detail; the examination of how human experience is endowed with meaning; a concern with moral, ethical, and political consequences; an encouragement of compassion and empathy; a focus on helping us know how to live and cope; the featuring of multiple voices and the repositioning of readers and "subjects" as coparticipants in dialogue; the seeking of a fusion between social science and literature; the connecting of the practices of social science with the living of life; and the representation of lived experience using a variety of genres—short stories, poetry, fiction, novels, photographic essays, personal essays, journals, fragmented and layered writing, and social science prose.

I want to ask him just how aware he is of the new writing practices that have emerged in qualitative research, and how writing differently allows us to know and analyze differently, as well as to make our "findings" available to more diverse audiences (Barone 2000; Richardson 1994, 1997, 2000a). I also want to ask him about the criteria he is using to judge the autoethnography produced by the student. I wonder if he has engaged with the debates on the nature of criteria and the kinds of nonfoundational criteria appropriate for judging alternative forms of qualitative inquiry.

I want to ask him, given that there are now multiple interpretive communities and multiple criteria for evaluating qualitative research, has he thought of the following criteria as possibilities when judging autoethnography: What substantive contribution to our understanding of social life does it make? What is its aesthetic merit, impact, and ability to express complex realities? Does it display reflexivity, authenticity, fidelity, and believability? Is it engaging and evocative? Does it promote dialogue and show potential for social action? Does the account work for the reader and is it useful?

I want to ask Professor Y so many things. In my imagination I do all this and more in a few fleeting seconds to save the day and dissolve the charge of self-indulgence. But meetings like this revolve around quantifiable marks and assessment procedures as provided by university regulations. It is not the place for a long, or even a short, debate on judgment criteria and the nature of autoethnography. I feel my shoulders getting tighter; I feel angry, but know that a confrontation here would serve no good purpose. Anyway, I have a tendency to avoid conflict whenever I can; it's not my way. So, I turn ever so slightly to my left, but keep my eyes fixed on the paperwork in front of me.

"Don't worry," I say with a smile, "I've written a paper about the charge of self-indulgence."

Professor Y laughs and responds, "I'm sure you have."

Some members of the department also laugh. The tension is broken and we move on to the final details of the meeting. My questions are neither asked nor answered. The charge of self-indulgence is left undisturbed.

Before leaving the room, I thank Professor Y for his comments and we exchange pleasantries. But the tension remains in me. The sweat is on my palms.

I had forgotten how painful the word "self-indulgent" can be, and how deep the wound goes when it is applied to the work of your students or to your own work. I'd forgotten how difficult it is to defend against this charge. The word gets to me. I feel guilty about not challenging it. On leaving the exam board meeting I could simply have got on my bike and cycled off the stress. Instead, I went to my office and picked up two papers that I had written. One was a "narrative of self" (Richardson 1994), which I had written about my own body-self relationships over time, called "The Fatal Flaw" (Sparkes 1996). The other was an article that revolved around reactions to "The Fatal Flaw" specifically, and autoethnographies in general, in which I focused on the kinds of criteria used to pass judgment on them and how these might change in the future (Sparkes 2000). Given the need I feel to defend myself and my students, I quite literally armed myself with these papers and returned to the conference room to give them to Professor Y. Jokingly I say, "Here is something to help you sleep on the train," before asking him to read them when he got a chance. To my delight (or was it relief?) he says he will and I want to believe him. Perhaps when we meet again next year, he will think differently about self-indulgence and understand why I feel it so often is misapplied to autoethnographic work.

I return to my office. The sun is still shining but I don't go for the bike ride. For the rest of the afternoon I sit and churn over why the charge of self-indulgence makes me feel so vulnerable. My thoughts go back to 1994 when I first began thinking about using my own personal experiences as the basis for an academic article. I mentioned this to a colleague who, without hesitation, informed me that it sounded like an "academic wank"; that is, a form of public masturbation.

I recall how relieved and elated I felt when I read the comments from two of the six reviewers of my initial submission of "The Fatal Flaw." One said, "By artfully merging the subjective biographical/biological with the sociocultural, the 'personal' does not become solipsistic," while the other said, "The writing is personal without the narcissistic quality that so often mars such work." These and other comments made by the reviewers suggested that they did not see my article as self-indulgent— I had escaped the charge. But the emptiness in my stomach always returns when I read the comments of one reviewer who said, "It is very hard to make good sociology—which is what I think this paper wants to be—from a single case study, especially if it is one's own. We all have stories. Indeed, we all have lived lives, and I'm not sure we're doing scholarship, and sociology, a favor by 'sociologizing' them."

I was simultaneously flattered and nervous when in a book by Coffey (1999), my "Fatal Flaw" article was used for the purpose of discussing self-ethnographies in two chapters. I'm flattered that my article is chosen at all, and for Coffey's depiction of my "ethnographic body narrative" as "extremely personal and highly reflective" (1999: 124), and a "rather different, self-centralized approach to ethnographic writing and tales of the body. . . . The account can be located within a new wave of autobiographical writing that focuses on the body and the self" (1999: 125). Perhaps, Coffey suggests, articles like mine indicate we are now standing on the boundary between ethnography and autobiography. What we might be witnessing is a new form of ethnographic practice, more firmly rooted in a social context and the situatedness of author-self.

Next I get anxious—particularly when, having noted that this move might have positive consequences for the representation of peopled, polyvocal social worlds, Coffey comments, "Yet some would say that such texts are not 'doing' ethnography at all, but are self-indulgent writings published under the guise of social research and ethnography" (1999: 155). Indeed, at one point Coffey asks, "Yet are we in danger of *gross self-indulgence* if we practice autobiographical ethnography?" (1999: 132, emphasis added) Thus, the *universal charge* of self-indulgence seems to slip into place for *all* autoethnographic work regardless of the qualities of any individual venture. For me, this is a dangerous and threatening move.

Self-Indulgence: Internalized Fears and Regulatory Practices

Self-indulgence: undue gratification of one's appetites or desires.
Self-pollution: masturbation.
Self-knowing: knowledge of one's own nature.
Self-respectful: respect for oneself or one's own character.
Self-sacrificing: forgoing one's own good for the sake of others.
Self-luminous: emitting a light of its own. (*Chambers Twentieth Century Dictionary*, 1982: 1229)

According to Charmaz and Mitchell (1997), scholarly writers are expected to stay on the sidelines and to keep their voices out of the articles they produce. In many ways, they are expected to emulate Victorian children: that is, to be seen (in the credits) but not heard (in the text). Thus, "silent authorship comes to mark mature scholarship. The proper voice is no voice at all" (Charmaz and Mitchell 1997: 194). Writing that breaks away from this standard, the kinds of writing found in autoethnographies, thus falls under the rubric of what Church

(1995) calls *forbidden narratives*. Such narratives are treated with deep suspicion and hostility within the academy. Mykhalovskiy (2000, personal communication) asks why this is so: "What is it about personal narratives in social science that people find so offensive? It must be something more than a challenge to scientific objectivity, etc. There is something I think that people really despise about this kind of work that I haven't quite figured out." Certainly, those that produce autoethnographies are acutely aware of this hostile atmosphere and universal charge of self-indulgence that is so often leveled against them.

For example, Jackson (1990), commenting on his own critical autobiographical project, noted the common criticism, particularly in many leftist groups, that this kind of work is too self-indulgent, too introspective, and too individualized: "Or there is the dismissive sneer of 'lifestyle politics,' that reductively fits this kind of autobiography into the polarities of economic/class politics or navel-gazing" (1990: 11). Reflecting on her experiences of presenting a poem about her traumatic relationship with her now-deceased father, Anderson (1999: 63) says, "I offered the paper with some trepidation, as I felt exposed and at risk of self-indulgence." Likewise, Brett Smith, commenting on his use of a narrative of self to explore his experiences of depression, acknowledges "the charge of narcissism and self-indulgence that might be leveled against my project" (1999: 267). More recently, in exploring his thoughts about the powerful imprint left by a father who committed suicide when his son was only ten years old, Gray expresses the following concern:

> Perhaps my biggest struggle throughout the writing has revolved around taking what has always been very private and making it public. Despite my determination to make this happen, I hear voices that tell me this is a very bad, dangerous course to take. These voices say, "This work is narcissistic, and self-indulgent, and you are embarrassing yourself through a melodramatic, emotional self-exposure." When I read the social science literature on masculinity, my fears are confirmed. I encounter writers who express a disdain for autobiographical approaches, an implied suggestion that the genre is populated with narcissistic egomaniacs. Is that me? (Gray 2000: 111)

Of course, writers of autoethnographies and narratives of self (like any other form of representation) need to be aware that their writing *can* become self-indulgent rather than self-knowing, self-respectful, self-sacrificing, or self-luminous. As Hertz notes on the ethical questions that rise in the wake of new self-reflexive forms of ethnography, "revealing oneself is not easy. For example, how much of ourselves do we want to commit to print? How do we set the boundary between providing the audience with sufficient information about the self without being accused of self-indulgence" (1997: xvi). Indeed, as part of his critique of the new fashion of self-revelation in what he calls narrative nonfiction in literature, Morrison (1998: 11) comments, "Confessionalism has to know when to hold back. . . . It takes art. Without art, confessionalism is masturbation. Only with art does it become empathy."

According to Rinehart, the universal charge of self-indulgence leveled against autoethnography and other forms of vulnerable writing is based on a misapprehension of these genres as self-conscious navel-gazing that is "grounded in a deep mistrust of the worth of the self" (1998: 212). This is because, as Krieger argues, the traditional view of social science is premised on "minimizing the self, viewing it as a contaminant, transcending it, denying it, protecting its vulnerability" (1991: 47). For Mykhalovskiy (1996), once the view of the self of the social scientist as a contaminant is in place, then the way is opened to define any writing about one's self as self-indulgent. As a form of academic gatekeeping, he notes, "naming of the work of the writer as work that indulges only that writer's self is peculiarly silencing. . . . They are symptomatic of practices through which the proper academic subject is reproduced; one who is writing, above all else, writes about the other" (Mykhalovskiy 1996: 135–36). More recently, Mykhalovskiy (2000, personal communication) notes, "The whole notion that pleasing the self is a problem, is a problem. I continue to wonder about the charge as a regulatory practice. I know it worked in my case. I've really backed off of autobiographical sociology and am only now tentatively reentering the field." Clearly, as Bochner and Ellis (1996) point out, narcissism and related criticisms, such as, self-indulgence and self-absorption, function to reinscribe ethnographic orthodoxy and resist change. Moreover, this regulation and reinscription contain a number of misplaced assumptions that need to be highlighted.

Challenging Misplaced Assumptions

Freeman (1993) analyzes autobiographical texts that provide exemplars of what a particular kind of life can be like, and the narrative work that goes into reclaiming one's own history. He does not find it difficult to see that such work "might be of value to someone besides ourselves" (1993: 229). Likewise, Church (1995), in exploring the *personal, private,* and *emotional* dimensions of research, observes how this challenges male-dominant conventions concerning what can be discussed in academic settings. She emphasizes that the emotional does not wipe out the *public, theoretical,* and *rational.* Rather, Church suggests, what we experience and present of ourselves as subjective or personal is simultaneously objective and public:

> I choose to foreground my own voice. This is not narcissism; it is not an ego-centric indulgence. . . . Critical autobiography is vital intellectual work. . . . The social analysis accomplished by this form is based on two assumptions: first, that is it possible to learn about the general from the particular; second, that the self is a social phenomenon. I assume that my subjectivity is filled with the voices of other people. Writing about myself is a way of writing about these others and about the worlds which we create/inhabit. . . . Because my subjective experience is part of the world, the story which emerges is not completely private and idiosyncratic. (Church 1995: 5)

Questions about the goals of autobiographical sociology are also raised by Mykhalovskiy (1996). He argues that the claim of narcissism rests upon an individual/social dualism that obfuscates "how writing the self involves, at the same time, writing about the 'other' and how the work on the 'other' is also about the self of the writer" (1996: 133). Consequently, to characterize autobiographical work as self-indulgent is to make claims about its content by invoking a reductive practice that asserts the autobiographical to be only about the self of the writer and no one or nothing else. However, this kind of dualistic thinking, according to Jackson, is mistaken because it "wrenches apart the interlocking between self and society" (1990: 11). In a similar fashion, Stanley (1993) notes that people do not accumulate their life histories in a social vacuum. That is, even though individuals may largely control the processes of recalling and interpreting past events, this process is also a social activity influenced by people with whom the individual interacts. Therefore, the autobiographical project disputes the normally held divisions of self/other, inner/outer, public/private, individual/society, and immediacy/memory. Likewise, Gergen's (1999) social constructionist view of the self as *relational* challenges the dominant ideology of the self-contained individual that underpins notions of self-indulgence.

Drawing on the work of Mikhail Bakhtin, Gergen (1999) argues for a vision of human action in which rationality and relationship cannot be disengaged. Here, our every action manifests our immersion in past relationships, and simultaneously the stamp of the relationships into which we move. Thus, for Gergen, any performance, such as writing an autoethnography, is relationally embedded.

> Recall the way in which our expressions gain their intelligibility from a cultural history. In the same way I cannot make sense if I use a word that I myself have made up, my actions will not make sense if they do not borrow from a cultural background. Thus, when I perform I am carrying a history of relationships, manifesting them, expressing them. They inhabit my every motion. . . . [W]e are always addressing someone—either explicitly or implicitly—within some kind of relationship. . . . We now find that one's performances are essentially constituents of relationship; they are inhabited not only by a history of relationships but as well by the relationships into which they are directed. (Gergen 1999: 133)

Against this backdrop, Mykhalovskiy challenges reductive practices and argues that "to write individual experience is, at the same time, to write social experience" (1996: 141). Indeed, he argues that making connections between individual experience and social processes, in ways that point to the fallacy of self/other, individual/social dichotomies, is the task to which autobiographical sociology is best suited. As one of the reviewers noted about my autoethnography the "Fatal Flaw," "Especially noteworthy are his reflections on a number of 'blurrings' (disease-illness, mind-body, public-private, man-woman, body-emotion, physical prowess-intellectual strength, self-others, conformity-deviance, etc.)." Likewise, in reflecting on her own narrative of self that focuses on identity formation in high-performance sport, Tsang (2000: 47) notes:

> I have claimed these stories to be my own, yet a story of myself, of my identity, necessarily involves and depends upon a story of the Other too. So these stories belong to them as well (albeit not in the same way or invoked with the same power)—the Other being the characters in the stories with whom I interact and compare myself and allude to. These are also the readers' stories, for through reading, readers construct their own meanings and identity with or resist certain elements of a story. How they do so not only reflects back on them and their own values and notions of themselves, but also implicates them as collaborators in the creation of the meaning of the text.

These views receive strong support from Bochner and Ellis, who ask, "If culture circulates through all of us, how can autoethnography be free of connection to a world beyond the self?" (1996: 24). They rightly conclude that it cannot, and so the concerns that some critics have raised about the self-indulgence of autoethnographers become absurd.

Another question Mykhalovskiy (1996) asks is: "To whom does the autobiographical text speak?" Condemning autobiographical texts as self-indulgent, he suggests, reflects the experience of a particular reader that is then generalized to a universal reader. "Here, the charge of self-indulgence is a contradictory reading, which as a specific or particular response invokes a universal reader who shuts out the possibility of the text speaking to others" (Mykhalovskiy 1996: 137). Such a move also seems to imply that the universal reader has universal characteristics and always reads from the same social positioning. These assumptions may inform the production of some texts, but they do not hold for autoethnographies that call on different ways of telling and showing, and invite a different kind of reading.

Barone (1990) notes how paradigmatic texts are designed in accordance with a logico-scientific mode of thought; invoke a universal, passive, unengaged reader; and call for *efferent* readings that focus on concepts, ideas, and facts to be retained and the actions to be performed as a result of reading some work. Such texts have the characteristics of an *industrial tool* that is not meant to be dismantled and reconstructed; its function is to create a seamless, denotative, linear discourse that rearranges the relationship among complex phenomena into a propositional form. According to Barone, the text-as-tool does not prize metaphorical aptness but offers the standard of technical precision. "It is not designed to surprise the reader-as-user. Its modes of fashioning are not designed to challenge the common order. . . . This text offers one verbal version of reality, meant to be taken literally, taken for the only world that can be represented, the real one" (Barone 1990: 315–17).

In contrast, as a way of knowing, narrative implies a *relational world*. As McLeod (1997) notes, a story always exists in a space between teller and audience. The story may be created by the teller, but it is always created in relation to a particular audience, "so it is as if to some extent the recipient(s) of the story draw it out of the teller. . . . Even a story written alone, such as a novel, has an implied audience" (McLeod 1997: 38). Accordingly, Barone (1990) makes a strong case for literary narrative texts that call upon narrative modes of knowing, as an occasion for conspiracy that encourages the reader to engage in the activities of textual re-creation and dismantling. Here, reading is not a passive but an active process that people undertake from multiple positions. This point is emphasized by Tsang (2000: 55):

Even with my stories in print and susceptible to readings and rereadings of the same words, form, and medium, each reader brings different resources to a text and, thus, different tools for making meaning out of my stories. For example, a reader who identifies racially as being white may have a different reaction and set of experiences with which to refer to when reading my stories of racialization than does a reader who strongly identifies as a racial minority. This in turn may be different from someone who identifies as racially mixed, or someone who hasn't really thought about race at all. The stories may summon different experiences from different readers in a variety of ways and with each reading (by the readers).

Therefore, according to Barone (1990), an *aesthetic* reading of the text is called for in which the readers' attention is centered directly on what they are living though during their relationship with that particular text. Similarly, Frank (1995) suggests that readers of personal accounts of illness might like to think and feel *with* the story being told rather than *about* it. In distinguishing between the two, Frank (1995: 23) comments, "To think about a story is to reduce it to content and then analyze that content. Thinking with stories takes the story as already complete; there is no going beyond it. To think with a story is to experience it affecting one's own life and to find in that effect a certain truth of one's life."

Furthermore, as Bochner and Ellis note, a good account is able to inspire a different way of reading, "It isn't meant to be consumed as 'knowledge' or received passively. . . . On the whole, autoethnographers don't want you to sit back as spectators; they want readers to feel, care and desire" (1996: 24). Thus, Brett Smith (1999), in a narrative of self about his ongoing roller-coaster ride with severe clinical depression, sets out to challenge realist forms of representation that strip away the depth and intense emotional experience of the various depressions, flatten people's words and worlds, and provide disembodied and emotionless accounts. Smith's messy text, in the form of short stories and poetry, is intended to evoke the reader's vulnerabilities, ambiguities, and ongoing struggles, as well as the gendered nature of his condition, by inviting the reader-as-*bricoleur* to rupture the traditional pattern of scientific knowing, and to "feel, hear, taste, smell, touch, and morally embrace the world of depressions" (1999: 275). In a similar fashion, Tillmann-Healy (1996) provides a sensual text on the secret but complex relationship she has with her body, food, and bulimia. Here, she pulls the reader away from the abstractions and categories that fill traditional research on eating disorders in a culture of thinness and invites them into the midst of her otherwise "normal" life to experience how she, a bulimic, *lives* and *feels*. Tillmann-Healy (1996: 80) comments: "I write from an emotional first-person stance that highlights my multiple interpretive positions. Physicians and therapists keep readers at a distance. I invite you to come close and experience this world yourself."

As such, authors of autoethnographies seek to produce writerly rather than readerly texts. According to Wilson (1998), readerly texts lead the reader logically, predictably, and usually in a linear fashion, through the research process. Little space is available for readers to make their own textual connections between the stories and the images presented. In contrast, Wilson (1998: 173) notes, "The writerly text is less predictable. It calls on the reader to engage with the text to more deliberately bring to the reading his or her experience as a way of filling the gaps in the text."

This kind of thinking fits with poststructuralist views that stress the interaction of the reader and the text as a coproduction, and reading as a performance. As part of this performance, readers must be prepared to make meaning as they read, put something of their own into the account, and do something with it. To this end, according to Barone (1995), the artfully persuasive storyteller who *trusts* the reader, understands the necessity of relinquishing control, of allowing readers the freedom to interpret and evaluate the text from their unique vantage points, will coax the reader into participating in the imaginative construction of literary reality though carefully positioned *blanks* in the writing. These invite the active reader to fill them with personal meaning gathered from outside the text. Here, the aim of the storyteller "is not to prompt a single, closed, convergent reading but to persuade readers to contribute answers to the dilemmas they pose" (Barone 1995: 66). For example, Tsang, in attempting to convey to the reader a sense of her varied, ambivalent, confusing, but sometimes definite relationship to her own multiple identities, notes, "My belief is that an engaging story can relate this sense to you in such a way that you can identify with it on a personal level, using your own experience to understand and empathize with my experience" (2000: 46). Similarly, Ellis, in reflecting on how she came to write *Final Negotiations* (Ellis 1995), makes the following points:

> My open text consciously permitted readers to move back and forth between being in my story and being in theirs, where they could fill in or compare their experiences and provide their own sensitivities about what was going on. I attempted to write in a way that allows readers to feel the specificity of my situation, yet sense the unity of human experience as well, in which they

can connect to what happened to me, remember what happened to them, or anticipate what might happen in the future. I wanted readers to feel that in describing my experience I had penetrated their heads and hearts. I hoped they would grapple with the ways they were different from and similar to me. (Ellis 1997: 131)

This focus on reader response encourages connection, empathy, and solidarity, as well as emancipatory moments in which powerful insights into the lived experiences of others are generated (Sparkes 1994, 1997). This kind of writing can inform, awaken, and disturb readers by illustrating their involvement in social processes about which they might not have been consciously aware. Once aware, individuals may find the consequences of their involvement (or lack of it) unacceptable and seek to change the situation. In such circumstances, the potential for individual and collective restorying is enhanced. Accordingly, a valuable use of autoethnography is to allow another person's world of experience to inspire critical reflection on your own (Bochner and Ellis 1996; Ellis 1997; Sparkes and Silvennoinen 1999). Here, readers recontextualize what they knew already in light of their encounter with someone else's life. This may not always be a pleasant experience. When an autoethnography strikes a cord in readers, it may change them, and the direction of change cannot be predicted. Indeed, as one of the anonymous reviewers commented in regard to my own autoethnography, "The Fatal Flaw":

> In "tapping" and evoking different levels of experience/subjectivity he constructs a multi-layered text which allows for, rather than specifies, a wealth of insights reaching well beyond the author's particular predicament. It makes you think and feel, and opens up a wide range of questions able-bodied people probably never think about. Actually, this text could be used as a great "sensitizing" agent in the classroom. (See Sparkes 2000: 25)

Autoethnographies can, therefore, become a call to *witness* for both the author and the reader. For example, in chronic illness, as Frank noted, becoming a witness means assuming "a responsibility for telling what happened. The witness offers testimony to a truth that is generally unrecognized or suppressed. People who tell stories of illness are witnesses, turning illness into moral responsibility" (1995: 137). Frank distinguishes between the witness in the traffic court and the illness witness. Both speak on the authority of being there but the latter's testimony is less of seeing and more of *being*; "illness stories are not only about the body but *of* and through the body" (1995: 140). This testimony, according to Frank, *implicates* others in what they witness. Witnessing is never a solitary act, and it always implies a relationship. Ill people tell themselves stories all the time, but they cannot testify to themselves alone; "part of what turns stories into testimony is the call made upon another person to receive that testimony" (Frank 1995: 141).

For Ropers-Huilman, acts of witnessing occur "when we participate in knowing and learning about others, engage with constructions of truth, and communicate what we have experienced to others" (1999: 23). These acts can have powerful consequences:

> Witnessing affects one's persona in its entirety—our bodies, hearts, and souls are changed and renewed by what we witness in our lives. . . . Witnessing is powerful. There are great opportunities and dangers inherent in the process of witnessing others' lives and constructing meanings about those experiences. (Ropers-Huilman 1999: 24)

Witnessing also has a number of *obligations* (Ropers-Huilman 1999). These obligations include recognizing our engagement in active, yet partial, meaning-making; recognizing that, as witnesses, we will change others and our roles as change agents need to be considered with great intentionality and sincerity; we have to be open to change; we have to tell others about our experiences and perspectives; we have to listen to the interpretations of other witnesses; and finally, we have to explore multiple meanings of equity and care and act to promote our understandings of these concepts.

Closing Thoughts

In light of the issues I have raised, I believe that the universal charge of self-indulgence so often leveled against autoethnography (and narratives of self), is based largely on a misunderstanding of the genre in terms of what it is, what it does, and how it works in a multiplicity of contexts. Autoethnographies can encourage acts of witnessing, empathy, and connection that extend beyond the self of the author and thereby contribute to sociological understanding in ways that, among others, are self-knowing, self-respectful, self-sacrificing, and self-luminous.

The lack of understanding surrounding autoethnography, and how it might be judged, is not surprising. As DeVault (1997) notes, sociologists are not accustomed to evaluating personal writing and, for many, the standards for critique and discussion seem "slippery" in comparison with the more familiar criteria associated with orthodox scientific research reports. She suggests that as personal writing becomes more common among social scientists, researchers will need to develop new avenues of criticism and praise for such work. "Presumably, a 'good' story in some contexts, for some purposes, may not be so good for others. Such criteria for evaluating personal writing as sociology have barely begun to develop" (DeVault 1997: 24).

As researchers begin to develop ways to judge autoethnography I hope they can resist the temptation to seek universal, foundational criteria lest one form of dogma simply replaces another. In making a powerful case for understanding research as *experience,* Garratt and Hodkinson (1998) argue against choosing any list of universal criteria in advance of reading a piece of research. They suggest that the selection of appropriate preordained sets of different paradigmatic rules is not a solution: "A more constructive way forward begins with the acknowledgment that the selection of criteria should be related to the nature of the particular piece of research that is being evaluated" (1998: 527). As John Smith (1993) echoes, we need to construct our criteria for judging various forms of inquiry as we go along.

Therefore, as Schwandt (1996) proposes, criteria are better seen as enabling conditions and guiding ideals to be applied contextually. Here, criteria operate in ways that enable adjudication to take place. The reviewer actively deliberates on the extent to which the research embodies qualities such as coherence, expansiveness, interpretive insight, relevance, rhetorical force, beauty, and texture of argument. Such criteria as impact, evocation, authenticity, fidelity, and believability might also be called on in passing judgment, moving the social sciences to incorporate more literary, poetic, and artistic forms of judgment.

For many, myself included, it is no easy task learning to judge differently, to listen carefully and to attempt to grasp what is being expressed and said in research traditions different from our own (Bernstein 1991). Our academic backgrounds, professional socialization patterns, and career structures mitigate against this. It is so much easier to display an indifferent superficial tolerance, or facilely assimilate what others are saying into our own categories and language without doing justice to what is genuinely different, or even simply to dismiss what the other is saying as incoherent nonsense. However, as Bernstein suggests, we have an ethical imperative to attempt to "understand and engage with the incommensurable otherness of the 'Other'" (1991: 66).

Smith and Deemer also emphasize that in any encounter with a production, especially something "new," one must be willing to risk one's prejudices: "Just as in the process of judgment one asks questions of a text or person, the person or the text must be allowed to ask questions in return" (2000: 889). They argue that approaching a novel piece of work requires that one be open, that one be willing to allow the text to challenge one's prejudices and possibly change the criteria one is using to judge the piece, and thereby change one's idea of what is and is not good inquiry. Smith and Deemer are quick to point out that to be open does not mean to automatically accept, and that one may still offer reasons for not accepting something new. They also emphasize to risk one's prejudices "requires one to accept that if one wishes to persuade others, one must be equally open to being persuaded" (2000: 889).

As part of this openness, we need to educate ourselves and others (as producers, critics, and consumers of research) to recognize differences and judge various genres accordingly, using appropriate criteria. Again, it is important to emphasize that this does not involve using criteria as universal standards against which to make judgments. In this sense, as John Smith (1993) argues, the term "criteria" is laden with foundational implications and becomes a touchstone that can be employed to distinguish the good from the bad, the correct from the incorrect. In contrast, Smith points out, "criteria" may refer to *characterizing traits* that have, at best, mild implications as a prescription for inquirer behavior and do not necessarily refer to something held to be foundational. Here, researchers might discuss the characterizing traits of a particular approach to inquiry, such as autoethnography, and simply note that these are the way researchers seem to be conducting these particular kind of inquiries at the moment. The difference here from the foundational view is that reviewers are willing to describe what one *might* do, but they are not prepared to mandate what one *must* do across all contexts and on all occasions.

For John Smith (1993) and Smith and Deemer (2000), once criteria come to be seen as characterizing traits or values that influence our judgments, then any particular traits or values will always be subject to constant reinterpretation as times and conditions change. They have an open-ended quality that can be challenged, added to, subtracted from, modified, and so on, depending on the context and the purposes. This is because a characteristic of research we thought important at one time and in one place may take on diminished importance at another time and place. Therefore, various criteria in list form may act as a starting point for judging autoethnographies, but these may not apply on all occasions and other criteria can be added to or subtracted from them, depending on the circumstances. These lists are challenged, changed, and modified in their application to actual inquiries. As Smith and Deemer emphasize, the limits of modification are a *practical* matter; they are worked and reworked within the context of actual practices/applications and cannot be set down in abstract formulas. "Our lists are challenged, changed, and modified not though abstracted discussions of the lists and items in and of themselves, but in application to actual inquiries" (Smith and Deemer 2000: 889).

Given the conditions described, it is clear that tensions, contradictions, conflicts, and differences of interpretation will persist regarding autoethnographies. However, this should not cause undue anxiety. Rather, as Garratt and Hodkinson (1998) emphasize, such diversity should be seen as an invitation to deepen our understanding and sharpen our judgments of those specific pieces, of the issues they raise, and of research in general. My hope is that many will accept the invitation.

Imaginings: Too Happy an Ending, or a Possibility?

It's a sunny June day again. Again, I'd rather be out riding my bike than sitting in the external examination board meeting. The same faces are here sitting around the table as last year. The main difference is that now I choose to sit opposite Professor Y rather than next to him. His remarks about an autoethnography produced by one of my students last year unsettled me, got to me, stung me, and made me reflect long and hard on the issue of self-indulgence. This year will be different. In my head I've rehearsed my answers a hundred times. I'm ready. If he once again speaks of self-indulgence, I want to be looking at him as I refute the charge.

But all this angst is costing me. In the days leading up to this meeting, I feel the defensive posture I'm so used to taking seep into my bones. Last night I couldn't sleep for thinking how things might go today. I'm tired, my lower back aches more than normal. All this, I realize, because I am still intimidated deep inside by the charge of self-indulgence. Despite my mental rehearsals, I'm still not sure I believe myself.

Adrenalin is beginning to kick in now. The meeting is going very much to schedule and the reports from the external examiners are next on the agenda. I suddenly realize that my mind has been so focused on this item that I can't remember much of what has been said so far. Then I recall giving Professor Y a couple of my papers on autoethnography at the meeting last year and wonder if he has read them. There has been no contact between us since then, and he didn't mention them in the usual exchange of courtesies between us at the start of the meeting. I inhale deeply and try not to look anxious or agitated.

Professor X says his bit. Nothing surprising there. Professor Y begins by adding some supportive comments to reinforce the points made by Professor X. He then moves on to the dissertations he read. Four again this year, three quantitative and one qualitative, the latter supervised by me. I hardly hear what he says about the quantitative dissertations. Phrases such as "well-defined hypotheses," "aware of validation procedures," and "appropriate forms of statistical analysis" slip by me. I know the form.

Then mine. I lean back slightly in my chair and look across the table at Professor Y. I suddenly realize he is wearing the same jacket as he did last year and wonder if this is a bad omen. I become conscious that I am staring at him. I glance down at my notes only to look up sharply as he reads out the title and the name of the student. It's an autoethnography in which a student explores the ways in which, over the years, various relationships between his father and himself have been constructed and deconstructed by their involvement in contact sports. Using photographs, short stories, and poetic representations, it highlights how their involvement in contact sports has limited the forms of communication available to them as father and son, how this shapes and constrains their current relationship within a specific form of masculinity, and how this is a source of worry for the son as their "sporting bodies" decline in the future. For me, it was an outstanding piece of work. I awarded it a first-class grade. But what did Professor Y make of it?

Our eyes meet. I suddenly realize that I don't want a confrontation. I just want to listen. I offer him a small smile and I feel my shoulders drop as the tension in them releases. He begins with an audible sigh and then a long pause as he collects his thoughts.

"Well, where to begin? No easy task this in more ways than one. First, I'm simply not used to this kind of inquiry. I don't get to read it much—actually never—in my line of work and I'm far more comfortable with straight scientific dissertations." Nods from some of my colleagues around the table. "Having said this, in my role of external examiner I feel duty bound to be fair when I make comments. I feel this even more having read the two papers Andrew gave me last year." He looks directly at me.

"Yes, Andrew, I did read them. Not my idea of bedtime reading for sure (laughs), but they certainly got me thinking. They made me realize that I can't call on my usual criteria. However, if I'm honest, I'm still not totally sure how I should be judging this kind of work. Let's say I'm on a steep learning curve. So, I'm looking to you to be kind to me today, I'm moving into unknown territory and that's dangerous for a man of my age." Laughter from colleagues around the table. I smile at Professor Y and realize that he has been just as worried about this moment as I have been.

"Right, let me use a word I didn't know last year. This is an 'autoethnography,' is that right Andrew?" I nod approvingly. "Now last year, on reflection, I wrongly used the term self-indulgent to describe a similar kind of dissertation. I'm much more cautious about using that term now. I still think that writing about your self *can* be self-indulgent but clearly this is not necessarily so in all cases. So let me say right away, I *don't* find this dissertation in any way self-indulgent. I *do* find it very well written, thought-provoking and, dare I say it, 'evocative.' That's another word I wouldn't have thought of using last year (laughs).

"This dissertation really held my attention and I read it all the way through in one sitting. I even read some chapters twice. It's beautifully crafted. There are some wonderfully engaging stories about the relationship between the student and his father through sport, and I couldn't help but see bits of me is some of the stories. After all, I'm a father of two boys, well, grown-up young men now, and of course I've been a son. And sport has been central in all these relationships. So a great deal of what the student wrote about rings true to me, it connects to moments in my own life. At times this is amusing but at other times it's disturbing. His autoethnography makes me reflect on the ways in which, when I was a young boy, my father and I communicated. It makes me very conscious of how I learned that some things could be said but other things were out of bounds, and how I carried these silences into my adult life.

"The dissertation made me think a lot about how I've communicated, and *do* communicate, with my sons now, and how this has been shaped by what happened between my father and me. I was left worrying about what we can and cannot say to each other as father and sons. I'm sure there are things my sons would like to talk to me about but they don't. I *know* there are things I would like to have said to my own father before he died. I *know* there are things I'd like to share with my sons but don't, and this makes me sad. It's something I would like to change over the next few years. In fact, as a starting point, I'd like to share this dissertation with my sons. I'd also like to give it to some other sporting fathers I know. I think many of the issues it raises would resonate with them and be a big help in thinking about how things might be different between them and their sons.

"I could go on, but I'm conscious of time. So I'll close by saying that this dissertation had a big impact on me in a lot of ways. Even though I'm not sure how to judge it, I'm happy to judge it as a first-class piece of work, and support the grade it has been awarded. My thanks to the student for having the courage to write it in the way he did."

And then, the moment is over. The head of the department quickly deals with the final agenda items and closes the meeting. Professor Y has to rush to get his train home but I catch up with him on the stairs as he leaves. We shake hands.

"Thanks for what you said in there. I really appreciated it."

"My pleasure. Who says you can't teach an old dog new tricks?"

"Not me. Have a safe journey home. I'll see you again next year."

"Look forward to it. Who knows, by then I might have written a few short stories of my own."

We depart. He for the train station, I for a bike ride.

Notes

1. For examples of this debate and suggestions for appropriate ways of judging alternative forms of qualitative research see Blumenfeld-Jones (1995), Bochner (2000), Clough (2000), Denzin (2000), Ellis (1995, 1997, 2000), Garratt and Hodkinson (1998), Gergen and Gergen (2000), Lather (1993), Lincoln (1993, 1995), Richardson (1994, 2000a, 2000b), Schwandt (1996), John Smith (1984, 1988, 1989, 1990, 1993), Smith and Deemer (2000), Sparkes (1995, 1998).
2. For other criteria in action and a rejection of this orthodox scientific view see Sparkes (2000).

References

Anderson, Yvonnne. 1999 "Therapeutic Narrative: The Final Say." *Auto/Biography* 7: 63–68.

Barone, Thomas. 1990. "Using the Narrative Text As an Occasion for Conspiracy." In *Qualitative Inquiry in Education,* ed. E. Eisner and A. Peshkin (pp. 305–26). New York: Teachers College Press.

———. 1995. "Persuasive Writings, Vigilant Readings, and Reconstructed Characters: The Paradox of Trust in Educational Storysharing." *Qualitative Studies in Education* 8: 63–74.

———. 2000. *Aesthetics, Politics, and Educational Inquiry.* New York: Peter Lang.

Bernstein, Richard. 1991. *The New Constellation: The Ethical-Political Horizons of Modernity/Postmodernity.* Cambridge, U.K.: Polity Press.

Blumenfeld-Jones, Donald. 1995. "Fidelity As a Criterion for Practicing and Evaluating Narrative Inquiry." In *Life History and Narrative,* ed. J. Hatch and R. Wisniewski (pp. 25–35). London: Falmer Press.

Bochner, Arthur. 2000. "Criteria against Ourselves." *Qualitative Inquiry* 6: 266–72.

Bochner, Arthur, and Carolyn Ellis. 1996. "Talking Over Ethnography." In *Composing Ethnography,* ed. C. Ellis and A. Bochner (pp. 13–45). Walnut Creek, Calif.: AltaMira Press.

Charmaz, Kathy, and Richard Mitchell. 1997. "The Myth of Silent Authorship: Self, Substance, and Style in Ethnographic Writing." In *Reflexivity and Voice,* ed. R. Hertz (pp. 193–215). London: Sage.

Church, Kathryn. 1995. *Forbidden Narratives.* London: Gordon & Breach Publishers.

Clough, Patricia Ticento. 2000. "Comments on Setting Criteria for Experimental Writing." *Qualitative Inquiry* 6: 278–91.

Coffey, Amanda. 1999. *The Ethnographic Self.* London: Sage.

Denzin, Norman. 2000. "Aesthetics and Practices of Qualitative Inquiry." *Qualitative Inquiry* 6: 256–65.

DeVault, Marjorie. 1997. "Personal Writing in Social Research." In *Reflexivity and Voice,* ed. R. Hertz (pp. 216–28). London: Sage.

Ellis, Carolyn. 1995. *Final Negotiations.* Philadelphia: Temple University Press.

———. 1997. "Evocative Autoethnography: Writing Emotionally about Our Lives." In *Representation and the Text,* ed. W. Tierney and Y. Lincoln (pp. 115–39). New York: State University of New York Press.

———. 1999. "Heartful autoethnography." *Qualitative Health Research* 9: 669–83.

———. 2000. "Creating Criteria: An Ethnographic Short Story." *Qualitative Inquiry* 6: 273–77.

Ellis, Carolyn, and Arthur Bochner, eds. 1996. *Composing Ethnography.* Walnut Creek, Calif.: AltaMira Press.

———. 2000. "Autoethnography, Personal Narrative, Reflexivity: Researcher As Subject." In *Handbook of Qualitative Research,* 2nd ed., ed. N. Denzin and Y. Lincoln (pp. 733–68). London: Sage.

Frank, Arthur. 1991. *At the Will of the Body: Reflections on Illness.* Boston: Houghton Mifflin.

———. 1995. *The Wounded Storyteller: Body, Illness, and Ethics.* Chicago: University of Chicago Press.

Freeman, Mark. 1993. *Rewriting the Self: History, Memory, and Narrative.* London: Routledge.

Garratt, Dean, and Phillip Hodkinson. 1998. "Can There Be Criteria for Selecting Research Criteria? A Hermeneutical Analysis of an Inescapable Dilemma." *Qualitative Inquiry* 4: 515–39.

Gergen, Kenneth. 1999. *An Invitation to Social Constructionism.* London: Sage.

Gergen, Mary, and Kenneth Gergen. 2000. "Qualitative Inquiry: Tensions and Transformations." In *Handbook of Qualitative Research,* 2nd ed., ed. N. Denzin and Y. Lincoln (pp. 1025–46). London: Sage.

Gray, Ross. 2000. *Legacy: A Conversation with Dad.* Harriman, Tenn.: Men's Studies Press.

Hertz, Rosanna. 1997. "Introduction: Reflexivity and Voice." In *Reflexivity and Voice,* ed. R. Hertz (pp. vii–xvii). London: Sage.

Jackson, David. 1990. *Unmasking Masculinity: A Critical Autobiography.* London: Unwin Hyman.

Krieger, Susan. 1991. *Social Science and the Self: Personal Essays on an Art Form.* New Brunswick, N.J.: Rutgers University Press.

Lather, Patti. 1993. "Fertile Obsession: Validity after Poststructuralism." *The Sociological Quarterly* 34: 673–93.

Lincoln, Yvonna. 1993. "I and Thou: Method, Voice, and Roles in Research with the Silenced." In *Naming Silenced Lives,* ed. D. McLaughlin and W. Tierney (pp. 29–47). New York: Routledge.

———. 1995. "Emerging Criteria for Quality in Qualitative and Interpretive Research." *Qualitative Inquiry* 1: 275–89.

MacDonald, A. (ed.). 1982. *Chambers Twentieth Century Dictionary.* Edinburgh, Scotland: WER Chambers.

McLeod, John. 1997. *Narrative and Psychotherapy.* London: Sage.

Morrison, Blake. 1998. *Too True.* London: Granta Books.

Mykhalovskiy, Eric. 1996. "Reconsidering Table Talk: Critical Thoughts on the Relationship between Sociology, Autobiography and Self-Indulgence." *Qualitative Sociology* 19: 131–51.

Richardson, Laurel. 1994. "Writing a Method of Inquiry." In *Handbook of Qualitative Research,* ed. N. Denzin and Y. Lincoln (pp. 516–29). London: Sage.

———. 1997. *Fields of Play: Constructing an Academic Life.* New Brunswick, N.J.: Rutgers University Press.

———. 2000a. "Writing: A Method of Inquiry." In *Handbook of Qualitative Research,* 2nd ed., ed. N. Denzin and Y. Lincoln (pp. 923–48). London: Sage.

————. 2000b. "Evaluating Ethnography." *Qualitative Inquiry* 6: 253–55.

Rinehart, Robert. 1998. "Fictional Methods in Ethnography: Believability, Specks of Glass, and Chekhov." *Qualitative Inquiry* 4: 200–24.

Ropers-Huilman, Becky. 1999. "Witnessing: Critical Inquiry in a Poststructural World." *Qualitative Studies in Education* 12: 21–35.

Schwandt, Thomas. 1996. "Farewell to Criteriology." *Qualitative Inquiry* 2: 58–72.

Smith, Brett. 1999. "The Abyss: Exploring Depression through a Narrative of Self." *Qualitative Inquiry* 5: 264–79.

Smith, John. 1984. "The Problem of Criteria for Judging Interpretive Inquiry." *Educational Evaluation and Policy Analysis* 6: 379–91.

————. 1988. "The Evaluator/Researcher As Person vs. the Person As Evaluator/ Researcher." *Educational Researcher* 17: 18–23.

————. 1989. *The Nature of Social and Educational Inquiry: Empiricism Versus Interpretation.* Norwood, N.J.: Ablex Publishing.

————. 1990. "Goodness Criteria: Alternative Research Paradigms and the Problem of Criteria." In *The Paradigm Dialog,* ed. E. Guba (pp. 167–87). London: Sage.

————. 1993. *After the Demise of Empiricism: The Problem of Judging Social and Educational Inquiry.* Norwood, N.J.: Ablex Publishing.

Smith, John, and Deborah Deemer. 2000. "The Problem of Criteria in the Age of Relativism." In *Handbook of Qualitative Research,* 2nd ed., ed. N. Denzin and Y. Lincoln (pp. 887–96). London: Sage.

Sparkes, Andrew. 1994. "Life Histories and the Issue of Voice: Reflections on an Emerging Relationship." *International Journal of Qualitative Studies in Education* 7: 165–83.

————. 1995. "Writing People: Reflections on the Dual Crises of Representation and Legitimation in Qualitative Inquiry." *Quest* 47: 158–95.

————. 1996. "The Fatal Flaw: A Narrative of the Fragile Body-Self." *Qualitative Inquiry* 2: 463–94.

————. 1997. "Ethnographic Fiction and Representing the Absent Other." *Sport, Education and Society* 2: 25–40.

————. 1998. "Validity in Qualitative Inquiry and the Problem of Criteria: Implications for Sport Psychology." *The Sport Psychologist* 12: 363–86.

————. 2000 "Autoethnography and Narratives of Self: Reflections on Criteria in Action." *Sociology of Sport Journal* 17: 21–43.

Sparkes, Andrew, and Martti Silvennoinen, eds. 1999. *Talking Bodies: Men's Narratives of the Body and Sport.* So Phi, Finland: University of Jyvaskyla.

Stanley, Liz. 1993. "On Auto/Biography in Sociology." *Sociology* 27: 41–52.

Tillmann-Healy, Lisa M. 1996. "A Secret Life in a Culture of Thinness: Reflections on Body, Food and Bulimia." In *Composing Ethnography: Alternative Forms of Qualitative Writing,* ed. C. Ellis and A. Bochner (pp. 76–108). Walnut Creek, Calif.: AltaMira Press.

Tsang, Tosha. 2000. "Let Me Tell You a Story: A Narrative Exploration of Identity in High-Performance Sport." *Sociology of Sport Journal* 17: 44–59.

Wilson, V. 1998. "The 'Last Blue Mountain'? Doing Educational Research in a Contract Culture." In *Doing Research about Education,* ed. G. Walford (pp. 64–76). London: Falmer Press.

ETHNOGRAPHIC AESTHETICS: ARTFUL INQUIRY

PRELUDE

"Collage"

The Hard Road Home: Toward a Polyphonic Narrative of the Mother–Daughter Relationship

KATHRYN CHURCH

Preamble: The Walk

THE SCREEN door bangs softly behind us as Ross, my partner, and I leave the house. It is unexpectedly cool in Toronto this summer, a welcome turn of events for our early morning walks. We duck under the Rose of Sharon tree that is bent almost double over the sidewalk, its branches heavily laden with rain-soaked purple blossoms. As we head in the direction of Withrow Park, I make a mental note to call a pruner.

The only people out and about are animal owners who, plastic bags in hand, take advantage of this greenspace known locally as "doggy heaven." I adjust the peaked cap that Ross bought me to sit more firmly over my unruly hair. "Alphie's Gym," it announces, optimistically. Emboldened by this allusion to working out, I swing into a stride that should carry me over our route. We walk in silence across the bottom of the park. As we turn to head south into a series of connected lanes, Ross punches me gently on the arm.

"What's the matter?" he asks, clearing his throat. "You seem preoccupied."

Surprised, I glance up. The sunglasses he wears as pollen protection make his expression difficult to read. He looks, I decide, like a more substantial Richard Gere.

"Sorry!" I reply. "It's not you. It's this chapter that I'm working on for Art and Carolyn. I'm stewing over the revisions."

"Tell me about it," he responds wryly, reminding me that he has his own revisions to worry about. "No, really," he presses, "Tell me about it!"

"Oh!" I say, laughing. "I thought you meant . . . no . . . well, it's layered. Even though I make my living at it, I find writing difficult. When I actually complete something that has a beginning, middle, and an end, I become deeply committed to that particular construction simply because it exists. I'm threatened by the thought of altering it—as if the original is so fragile that it won't sustain change."

I pause for a moment, feeling the constriction of my breathing, the sudden tightening of my jaw.

"You come by that honestly, Kath," Ross replies. "Where you come from, women weren't supposed to have a voice, spoken or written. It makes sense that the words feel fragile."

More silence as we pass a property that houses two large, overprotective dogs. Today they're indoors, sparing us the way they howl and throw themselves against the fence.

"There's more to it than that, isn't there?" asks Ross.

"Well, yes," I say, smiling at how well he knows me. We make a sharp right turn onto Simpson as I struggle to express the rest of it.

"Art and Carolyn's feedback was thorough, compassionate, insightful. It's rare to be read in this way. But I am struggling with the core suggestion for revision. Art felt that the framing device for the paper should be what he called the 'dialectics of separation and identification' in relation to my mother. This is what will resonate with most women. He suggested that I connect with the mother/daughter chapter in a book by Nancy K. Miller called Bequest and Betrayal [1996]."

"Okay," says Ross. "I'm with you so far. Have you had a chance to read what he suggested? Can you see connections between Miller's work and your own?"

"Miller argues that the primary tension between mothers and daughters is a confusion of boundaries, and for daughters, a lot of anxiety about resembling the mother. She cites Adrienne Rich's [1976] argument that the mother stands for the victim or the martyr in ourselves. That strikes me as an insight that might be more relevant to women of my generation, women with 1950s mothers, than women in succeeding generations. But that's just a guess on my part."

The walk has warmed me up as well as loosening my tongue. I pause to tie my cotton sweater around my waist as we turn right onto Broadview. Between there and the right turn onto Victor, I retrieve my train of thought.

"Miller discusses Jessica Benjamin's [1995] work to the effect that the one thing mothers and daughters want from each other is recognition—of a particular kind.

Each wants to be recognized as like the other and yet as distinctly her own person. This is where things begin to get sticky for me but I haven't quite unpacked how."

"So, that task lies ahead of you," notes Ross, as we hit Logan Avenue on our return.

"It certainly does," I sigh, thinking about all the other work that remains undone. "I forgot to tell you that Miller's book focuses on memoirs by daughters about mothers who have died—if you get my drift. As daughters, all of these biographers felt the need to separate from their mothers. They left home and cut themselves off. After their mother's deaths, they wrote about what they left behind. They made reparation by writing and in that way, as authors, they returned home."

"That sounds something like you," says Ross, hopefully.

"The circle is too tight," I argue. "I left but also stayed in close touch. I returned but in many ways I'm as distant as I always was. Everything that runs one way about my life as a daughter seems also to run the other. I can't quite grasp it!"

"You'll have to try, love," he counters gently. "Do the rewrite and see what happens."

We are on the final stretch now and panting a bit. As we enter "lone pine alley" I have a final thought.

"It's quite a different project to come to terms with your mother when she is alive and to do it publicly as I have."

"Indeed," Ross agrees, as we stumble back up our steps.

But his mind has moved on to the complexities of the day that looms ahead. I am left alone to write.

The Chapter: Revised

My mother graduated from Vermilion School of Agriculture and Home Economics in 1949. While this formal training was important, Mom actually learned to sew from her mother who learned from her mother whose sister was also a dressmaker. Skills were passed from women of one generation to women of the next. This lineage, embodied so fully by my mother, ends with me. I cannot sew. I can only write. But there are continuities. With my words, I take up the threads of their lives.

—From the exhibit "FABRICATIONS: STITCHING OURSELVES TOGETHER"

Introduction

A feminist sociologist departs Toronto for her childhood home in central Alberta, Canada. In an unorthodox act of research, she designs a museum exhibit that features the work of a local seamstress. I am the sociologist. My mother, Lorraine, is the seamstress. The exhibit, titled "Fabrications: Stitching Ourselves Together," is a three-dimensional biography of her work featuring twenty-three wedding dresses that she sewed for family, friends, and neighbors between the years 1950 and 1995.

My initial idea was to do a one-woman show in a church basement or a community hall—small venues scattered liberally throughout the town in which I grew up. I soon enlarged the scope of the project by forming a partnership with the nearby Red Deer and District Museum. Its staff collaborated with me on exhibit design, production, and management. "Fabrications" opened there in July 1998, welcoming roughly 8,000 visitors, mostly women, in nine weeks. Building on this popularity, the museum organized a national tour of "Fabrications," including a ten-month stint at the Canadian Museum of Civilization in Hull, Quebec, where it drew 88,000 visitors. Currently at the Glenbow Museum in Calgary, the exhibit will go up at the Museum for Textiles in Toronto in 2001.

To promote this project, I have given radio interviews, public speeches, and academic lectures. My mother and I were featured in a national radio documentary and filmed for a segment of a television series. Our story has been written up

Canadian Museum of Civilization opening, March 1999

in local and national press. An edited version of the exhibit text was published in a national women's magazine (Church 1998) and I recently coauthored an article for the Canadian Museums Association (Church and Martindale 1999). Interpretation Canada gave "Fabrications" awards of excellence in the interior exhibit and Web site categories (Church, on-line). My mother was named "ambassador" for the town of Lacombe and recognized by the Red Deer Museum with a Volunteer Recognition Award. The city of Red Deer recently gave Mayor's Recognition Awards to me and to the museum staff.

I begin with this summary to highlight the success of "Fabrications" but also to problematize it. For most of my life I have felt uneasy in relationship to my mother. Yet, as a result of our collaboration on the exhibit, we have become one of the most famous mother–daughter pairs in Canada. My mother is a shy person, someone who prefers the background to the limelight. Yet, during the past three years, she has made her way from the privacy of her basement sewing room to the public grandeur of the country's premiere museum.

These two difficult dances—the movement I initiated toward rather than away from my mother and her intersecting movement through the exhibit toward me and the world—are the subject of this chapter. Collaborating on "Fabrications" has changed the ways in which I relate to my mother. What were the turning points in this journey? What can I tell of the story? What do I feel must be left out of the public account?

Theorizing the Project

The driving force of my life has been a refusal to be like my mother. From early on, I perceived her as someone who was enslaved: by her body, her house, her marriage, and her children. My own body was light, quick, and flexible—perfect for hanging from trees and riding bikes, for swimming like a fish, and skating like 1950s Canadian figure skater Barbara Scott. The only girl in a family of boys, I grew up in a landscape and culture that celebrates physical movement. My first feminism was competitive sport. When I graduated from high school in 1972, I was named best female athlete.

As a young adult, I was determined to undo the relations of marriage, family, and womanhood embodied by my mother. I married young but picked a partner who was committed to similar kinds of unraveling. I kept my own name just in case, a decision that shocked the ladies at church. But that didn't matter because education became my new religion. I spent fifteen years at university, becoming the first person in my extended family to earn a doctorate. And I remained childless, my most explicit refusal to reproduce.

All of this only increased the distance between my mother and me. From my home in Toronto, I could not communicate to her the complexities of my journey. By herself, she could not see them or me. Given how crucial this disconnection was to my becoming a big city woman, it didn't trouble me much until I turned forty. Then, at life's midpoint, I suddenly felt a pressing desire for my discarded women's history. I channeled that desire into giving birth to "Fabrications."

One way I explain my energy for this project is to connect it with the arguments, dilemmas, and experiences that structured my doctoral work. These are present not in a linear way but as a weaving together of intersecting tales. For sixteen years I have worked in the fields of community mental health and economic development, focusing primarily on the psychiatric survivor movement. It hasn't been easy. The members of this movement are poor, badly housed, and often badly served by the service system that purports to help them. They tend to be traumatized around issues of power and are badly stigmatized. Working as an ally but "outsider" to their movement (Narayan 1988), I found myself suffused with guilt, constantly struggling to establish trust, and suffering in terms of career development from stigma by association. "Why am I doing this?" I kept asking.

Answers were difficult to find and, in the course of searching, I developed a debilitating physical illness that had a powerful emotional overlay. As a result of what felt like radical changes in my appearance—specifically because of a lupus-like rash on my nose and cheekbones—I experienced a breakdown between identity and ocular presence. When I looked in the mirror, I did not recognize myself. I lost my sense of having a face that I could turn to the world. At some level, I fused with my survivor colleagues. For several years afterward, I struggled with two major implications of this experience for my research and my life (Church 1995).

The first was recognizing the importance of beginning from "I" in my intellectual work, from my own story in relation to power and (medical) authority. Against the grain of traditional academic practice, I amplified the private, personal, and emotional dimensions of my project. In doing so, I was forced to confront the ways in which academia is split: public from private, subjective from objective, personal from social. I wrote my findings in ways that I hoped would blur the lines between these dualities, to show how the subjective and personal are simultaneously objective and public.

The second was recognizing that service providers have a lot of work to do—individually and collectively—if we are going to be part of a mental health system in which psychiatric survivors have an equal say. At its best, our work makes connections for users of services between their subjective experience and the objective conditions in which they live. "But how can we do that for them," I wondered, "when we aren't doing it for ourselves?" Ultimately, we need to become connected to the sociality of our own subjectivities. As Peter Lyman admonishes, we need "to learn from the history that we live. Not from the formal chronicle of events, but from the subjective feelings and thoughts with which we experience the events of our everyday lives" (1981: 55).

After my doctorate was complete, I went looking for new ways to explore the history that I live. Why had I hung in with psychiatric survivors when many other researchers would have quit? Some of my reasons had to do with abstract notions of democratic rights, equality, and social justice; some had to do with relationships and personal loyalties. But a big part of the process was a search for the roots of my own oppression: growing up female in a patriarchal culture reinforced by fundamentalist Christian ideology; growing up on the periphery of the country immersed in my parents' conservative frontier consciousness.

Having identified these as places of long-standing hurt and powerlessness, I wanted to pursue them closer to the source. My illness created a tangible break with the small town prairie woman I was raised to be and the compliant femininity I was taught to perform. In that space, I hoped to do an exhibit that would illuminate my mother's work, her material and symbolic construction of femininity. I wanted to return to the place where my notions of womanhood were created in order to enter into and to understand them differently.

Bringing My Mother Back In

British feminist theorist Valerie Walkerdine writes about the contradictions she lived in using education to transform working-class social relations, and the effects that this had on her relationship with her mother.

> There was no way then that my success could have done anything other than take me out of my class, for to have stayed within it, I would have to reject school and being clever. However, inside that history is a suppressed history and struggle through which I was constituted as a pedagogic subject. What is suppressed is another knowledge which had to be countered as wrong and which I had to learn to abandon. In rejecting this, my mother too had to be rejected and classified as stupid. (1987: 6)

For years, I lived this same dilemma. In the process of legitimating myself to the world, I delegitimated my mother. I rejected her. Although never overtly, I, too, classified her as stupid.

The whole difficult dynamic began to shift for me one evening during a rare visit home in May 1996. My mother was sitting at the dining room table, thumbing through her "sewing scribblers," a series of ragged schoolbooks that originally belonged to my brothers and me. In the unused pages, over a period of four decades, she kept a record of her sewing projects: sketches, measurements, scraps of fabric. I knew these scribblers very well, having lived with them for many years as a taken-for-granted feature of daily life. But in that moment of watching Mom engrossed in their pages and sensing the memories evoked, I suddenly *saw* them. The social scientist in me recognized Mom's scribblers as original data, a priceless case history of domestic sewing in a prairie community (and one, it turns out, that she was preparing to throw out). In that moment, the idea of an exhibit sprang into my mind.

My mother had created an extraordinary body of work—a significant portion of which we eventually assembled as "Fabrications." As her labor and mine came together in the same conceptual and relational space, I expanded and shifted my sense of what she had been doing and how she had been doing it. Interviewing her "brides" became a crucial part of this process, quickly revealing the special role that my mother occupied in their lives. Like the sales personnel in bridal stores, my mother watched them use their dresses to absorb the bridal identity (see Friese 1997). The important difference is that she wasn't a paid stranger. She accomplished her task in the context of noncommercial, collaborative, and personal relationships. "I would not have gone to just anyone for my wedding dress," emphasized one bride. "And I never thought of going to her as going to a seamstress. It was a totally different relationship. It was knowing a great seamstress as a personal friend that made it special."

Mom had a history with most of the brides for whom she sewed. Sometimes the wedding dress was the culmination of a number of projects the women had worked on together: riding and dance costumes, graduation and other special occasion garments. The process went smoothly because of this familiarity. A kind of "knowing" developed on both sides. In the course of making a dress, the women deepened their knowledge of my mother and her work. Explained one bride:

> I had known her before but I really got to know her in the process of making the dress. I felt that I paid myself for appreciating her that much better. I love

her now! There is such a connection there that wasn't there before. It was superficial; now it is deep. She is part of me. Part of her is in that dress and that dress is in me.

The brides felt known in return. "She knew what kind of a person I was," one declared. Another told me that Mom "figured out what I wanted and made it happen. She had the capacity to get into and draw out my unspoken images and desires for the dress."

The women of my mother's community fed her sewing activities with a nineteenth-century desire for special attention and advice with respect to their clothing (see Gamber 1997). In return, she had a way of making them feel right at home. As one put it, she was "very good, very caring, very loving about the dress." My mother affirmed these brides at a time of significant transition in their lives. A big part of that was helping them feel good about their figures. She was complimentary about all of the bodies that, in various stages of undress, passed before the full-length mirror in our upstairs bathroom. Seemingly mundane acts such as complimenting a woman on her small waist sometimes went to the heart of female self-loathing. At least one bride experienced my mother's positive attention as a welcome balance to the verbal taunts about her body that she absorbed as a child.

The brides relied on my mother's advice. As one put it:

I valued her input and suggestions, her ability to create from the ideas that I gave her. She had a better eye than I, the ability to see the finished product. She could suggest things that I would think were too hard to do. She was open to challenging things when I wouldn't have bothered. That she had the confidence to make the suggestion and then carry through with it was amazing to me.

These women left everything in my mother's hands, feeling very assured that the dress was going to look great. Said one: "Never do I recall feeling oh, oh, what will happen? What will it look like? Will she do this? I felt very confident of her abilities." These women trusted Mom as a professional but their relationships with her remained personal. "We had fun together," reported one woman. Another remembers my mother serving waffles when she and her bridesmaid came for a fitting. In ways that were both simple and complex, dressmaking was a social process. Facilitated by class and racial homogeneity, the end result for the brides was a tremendous sense of comfort and safety.

Here I am, nine years old on Easter Sunday. This navy coat is part of a "line" that my mother started a few years earlier with a little blue duster. Underneath I wore a plain white blouse and a navy-and-white checked skirt.

I, too, am one of Mom's brides, but I recognize only part of my experience in this collective account. My mother and I did many sewing projects together and, for the most part, we agreed on a basic "look." How could it have been otherwise? I had been her model since I was a child. Over many years, Mom educated me into her sense of fit, color, and style. I became an active participant in the process but not an independent one.

The brides startled me with their stories of how Mom facilitated their desires and fantasies. As her daughter, I had fewer degrees of freedom. The expectation that I would reproduce the pattern of her existence was very strong. It was transmitted through clothing, with the work of her hands shaping the way I was entered into the world. In one of our interviews, Mom talked about how startled she was when she discovered that, in sewing for other people, she was giving input rather than just following instructions. The thought of being so instrumental made her uncomfortable but she was oblivious to the powerful ways that she had stitched me into existence.

Here I am at seven years old astride a big red combine parked in my grandparents' farm in northern Alberta. Dressed in worn jeans and a red cardigan, I have a firm grip on the steering wheel. I like the claim I make on that typically male place.

Miller points out that the classic adolescent moment for daughters is a "conflict … over sexual autonomy, a violence located around the body." This tension, the kind that "explodes in outbursts of rage over clothes," was present between my mother and me (1996: 79). Sewing created a deep but problematic connection between us. While we came to know each other through years of dressmaking, I also needed to hide from her, to distance myself. If I was to move into a public, active, and sexual womanhood (feminism rather than femininity), I needed to control my own "wardrobe." I wasn't always able to voice how I might have liked to look and be otherwise. But part of me resisted—in ways that were active, substantial, and sustained.

The two outfits pictured in this chapter capture the basic tension of my childhood years. They point to clothing and my mother's intense involvement with domestic sewing as the terrain on which we struggled over the kind of woman I would become. Through clothing, I was bound to Mom in highly visceral ways. As I grew older, I felt constrained by the way she structured my life and self through garments. She didn't draw out unspoken images and desires so much as create them in me. I have been identifying, deconstructing, and replacing them ever since. Even now, when I have achieved a style of dressing and being in the world that suits me, I carry this subliminal heritage.

I used the exhibit to work with this ambivalence. The brides' enthusiasm for my mother, her skill and attentiveness, laid down an emotional trail of crumbs that helped me discover/recover my love for her. As I studied her work, I felt surges of pride and, even more unfamiliar, of identification. Unexpectedly, I saw myself in Mom's record keeping and in the natural way that she linked garments to women's stories. I saw myself in the trust that she built through careful listening, in her attempts to translate other people's visions into reality, and in corresponding attempts to have her say as a woman with considerable expertise.

I have built my knowledge of psychiatric survivor communities in the same intimate way that my mother built her knowledge of women's community: conversation by conversation, project by project, layer by layer. The spheres that my mother and I inhabit are different but our ways of working in them are remarkably similar—right down to our inability to value ourselves by charging what our labor is worth. The difficult insider/outsider relationship that I have to academia stems from my unconscious retention of her ways of knowing: the poetry of her hands and her eye for beauty; her sensitivity to color and texture; her lateral, relational approach to the world. Mom's methods are alive and well in my autobiographical approach to social science, and in my ongoing struggle to construct (but not own) knowledge from the margins.

Going Public

My mother and I were having lunch in the Co-op Cafeteria of a local shopping mall when I first spoke to her about doing a one-woman show of her work. The way she tells the story, she said "a definite no!" to my idea. I don't remember it that way. I remember her silence, the tiny noise she made in her throat, and the way her eyes slid away from mine. "A hair-brained scheme that won't amount to anything." She didn't say the words but they hung in the air. I know her starting point: disbelief, a refusal to envision possibilities based on a lifetime of disappointments.

Secretly, I didn't feel very confident about the idea either, or my skills in pulling it off. But I was sufficiently curious to draft a short description of what I wanted to do and post it on a number of e-mail discussion lists. The response pleased and amazed me as scholars from all over North America urged me forward. This was the point at which my mother first began to grapple with the public interest in what she had been doing in her basement for forty years. Several months of network-ing later, I called to tell her that the Red Deer Museum had agreed to partner with us. "I must tell you," she confessed slowly, "that when you first told me about this I thought it would never happen. It was beyond my imagination. Maybe I don't consider my sewing as something outstanding that I have done."

That phone call was a turning point. It was the (small) moment in which our pattern of mother–daughter conversation began to change. Previously, Mom talked primarily about my brothers, their wives, their houses, their vehicles, their yards, and especially their children. The topic was fraught with anxiety about sep-aration and divorce, new partners and remarriage, and the fate of those precious grandchildren. I was a funnel for her grief, rage, and confusion over two house-holds broken by the departures (about fifteen years apart) of daughters-in-law who did not take up wife and mother in the old ways. Helpless to change any of that, I couldn't seem to make my own life visible or interesting to her. However, with the emergence of the exhibit project, we began to have new things to say to each other. Over time, what I am most conscious of is this shift in the substance of our conversation, a muting of the painful domestic dramas in which she was embroiled and the emergence of a constructive dialogue about a mutual project.

One of the first steps that I took in developing "Fabrications" was to contact the women whose wedding dresses were made by my mother. As with my e-mail correspondents, their response to my letter of enquiry was positive. "What a neat idea! What a wonderful project!" the women exclaimed almost with one voice. "What a wonderful tribute to your mother, a gifted seamstress and special friend and neighbor, for her many years of hard work. Lorraine will be thrilled and excited." In fact, from a deeply ingrained modesty and a strong class-based sense of place, Mom was finding it difficult to tolerate the implication that she had done something special. She joked that she wouldn't want her name publicized because it would mean too much new business. But she also acknowledged that it would be a shame not to take credit for what she had done.

The brides' speedy enthusiasm for the project left me excited and uneasy. While I intended no "dishonor," I wanted an exhibit that would penetrate beyond a simple display of artifacts. I wanted to critically analyze what was going on in the construction of these dresses—for Mom, for her brides, and for myself as someone who had been captivated and captured by the process for many years. By reinforcing its meaning solely as "tribute," the brides introduced a tension into the project. Could I air my questions and opinions in highly conservative central Alberta? Would I hurt or offend anyone? Did that matter?

The next step was to interview Mom and her brides, locate and retrieve the wedding dresses, and begin planning with museum staff. To accomplish this, I spent a month in Alberta during the winter of 1997. Throughout that time, my mother continued to be consumed with the unexpected complexity of her domestic scene: one grown but not yet flown grandson living in her basement, two small, active grandsons dropped off daily for childcare. In her late sixties, she was in effect still nurturing a young family. From next door where I was house-sitting for the neighbors, I attempted to moderate my demands on her but kept slipping into rage over her situation and my inability to command more of her attention.

We did manage several long conversations about her early life and the evolution of her work. I learned much that I had not known but the most compelling part was teaching myself to attend to what she said. As her daughter I tended to tune her out, but as a researcher her words were vital to me. Slowly, almost fearfully, my disregard flipped over. These sessions were often interrupted. One day she said, rather abruptly, "Look, I've got to go get some lunch ready or I won't have a husband." As if my father would up and leave her after fifty years of marriage because his soup was late! Other days, overcome by small town claustrophobia, I would get in my father's Pontiac and bolt down the road to the city to let off steam.

This somewhat bumpy start to our joint project was capped by a social event. At the end of my visit, Mom and I hosted an evening tea for some of the local women whose dresses would appear in the exhibit. Also present was Wendy Martindale, the executive director of the Red Deer Museum, who came to meet people and answer questions. A high-profile person in the area, her face and her comments frequently appear in the local papers. At the time, the big issue was the museum's controversial acceptance of a grant to research local gay-lesbian history. The tea was crucial for Mom. Having Wendy in her home was an act that linked her private world to a public space that she viewed then as beyond the scope of her life.

For both my mother and me, one of the strongest and most frightening aspects of inventing the exhibit was crossing the line we each drew between private and public aspects of our lives. A primary task of the project was to imagine ourselves as public people. I understand "imagining" in this context as an active piece of work on enlarging and revisioning the self. For my mother the change was more pronounced. Sometimes I felt that she experienced the interest that I generated around her as a genuine threat. At one point, she expressed concern at what people would think of her because of the exhibit—as if there was an element of shame in her sudden visibility. "I am," she said, "the mouse behind the door." Living the contradiction between this reading of self and the one I was constructing through the exhibit was not easy and she often retreated to the domestic. More than once she exclaimed that it simply could not be her life and work that people found compelling. "You are doing this!" she accused. It was difficult for me to understand why this was a problem for her—even though I had my own troubles being more visible. And so we struggled, alone and together, to make sense of ourselves in the context of our collaboration.

A major turning point, and our biggest risk, was being featured in a radio documentary. Typically, I got us into it by networking my way to the executive producer of Canada's public radio morning show. I then had to call Mom and tell her what I had done. It is interesting that she didn't refuse outright. Perhaps her confidence was growing; perhaps she was just curious. I didn't tell her that what we were about to do scared me silly. It has always been my role to be adventurous, to seem certain.

Mom and I were interviewed separately. For me the process was oddly familiar. Telling my story evoked my therapy voice, that low, strong timbre that reveals painful, sometimes delightful emotional truths. I didn't hold much back and my sense is that Mom didn't either. I don't know for sure because I spent the two hours of her interview waiting and fretting in her basement. After it was over, she didn't ask me what I had said and I didn't ask her. We both spilled our guts to the producer and settled in to await the outcome. Well, "settled" is probably the wrong word. Many nights I tossed and turned, remembering outrageous bits and pieces and wondering how they would be used. I suspect Mom did the same.

The morning that "Behind the Scenes at the Red Deer Museum" finally aired, I sat with Ross and listened while the tears ran steadily down my cheeks. What hit me hardest was the strength and clarity of my mother's voice, this woman who just the previous year was convinced that no one would be interested in her world. Yet there she was telling—and hearing—her story. "The morning the tape aired," she recounted later, "I listened alone in my kitchen. I couldn't believe the impact my own voice had on me."

I am not suggesting that her words were easy for me to hear: far from it. Asked about my doctoral work, Mom confessed that when she read my dissertation, she "cried for days."

It was one of the things she has written that I could read and understand. Then she started getting personal and it was mostly in describing me. One of the things that hurt the most was that she said I had limited education. It certainly was limited compared to what she has. But at the time, it was more than a lot of girls had. So that one hurt. I can be honest about that. I thought perhaps I hadn't been the best mother that I should have been and we weren't as close as we should be. (June 1998)

The show's producer had already confronted me with this information, capturing my gaping response for a national audience. "She didn't tell me," I explained, my throat swelling. "I didn't know that she had cried for days. I wish we could have talked about it, why it hurt. Maybe we could have cried together and that would have been good."

So there I was for all to see: the arrogant, insensitive daughter who had wounded her gentle, hardworking mother with her sharp words, who had made her feel like a bad mother. It felt like a familiar rebuke. The primary rule for being a good daughter in our family was *do not, under any circumstances, hurt your mother.* It was understood that her sacrifice for her children was total and thus demanded unquestioning loyalty. Unfortunately for us, the loyalty I bear my mother—profound and sometimes tortured—is a questioning loyalty.

All my life I have asked unsettling questions. And I have learned to protect my mother from them through silence and distance. The quest built into the exhibit was to be closer as she grows older while remaining open about my life and vocal about my perceptions and analysis. The radio documentary fulfilled this desire. But it also highlighted my perilous stumbling around in Mom's class wounds, and her precipitous flights from any hint of conflict. Our closing remarks illustrate the tension.

"I feel that we have become closer since we started doing this project," Mom stated.

"I want her to feel my attention to her life," I declared. "Whether we move any closer as two very different women to understanding each other's lives, I don't know. But with the exhibit, and her collaboration in it, I know that we have tried."

Embodying Correction

The night that I committed myself to the idea of an exhibit, I woke suddenly in my parents' house, the small town stillness punctured occasionally by the whistle of passing trains. That's when it hit me.

All of her life my mother has struggled to be accepted, to be loved by the people around her, the people she loved. And in this struggle, I had rejected her.
The biggest message I have sent to her if not in words, then in actions, is that
nothing she does is good enough. I have been correcting her—me in my
arrogance—all of my life. My life is a message to her about the inadequacy
of her life. It is an embodied correction in the face of which she is speechless,
powerless. This is our terrible dilemma: to love and to hate each other for
what we have made of each other. (Journal entry, May 1996)

By returning home to collaborate with Mom, I wanted to dissolve this sense
of embodying correction, to integrate what she represented in order to strengthen
my woman's life and my scholarship. What I didn't anticipate was that I, too,
would be corrected—by my mother and by central Alberta visitors to the exhibit.

When I interviewed her, one of the first things Mom did was to challenge the
original narrative about her that I had fixed in my mind. Early on, I had written her
in as a seamstress who supplemented the family income through a kind of cottage
business that she ran out of her basement. My mother denied this identification. Her
sewing, she argued, was not about earning extra income. Indeed, Mom often gave
her dresses as gifts and, if forced to name a price, rarely charged more than $20.
Thus, her work was not a business. It was about love and service, a way of connecting to family and community. She was not a seamstress; she was a housewife and a
mother who sewed because she loved it, because she couldn't deny her creativity. So,
conflicting points of view emerged. What was I, her feminist daughter, to do in this
situation? Should I correct her again? Should I remake her in my image and get her
to see herself as the independent businesswoman that I wanted her to be?

After weighing my options, I remembered that a big part of the reason that
I had come home in the first place was to learn my mother's life on her terms, to
refuse any further corrections of her life. My commitment as an ethnographer
was to portray what I heard and perceived in such a way that the women I interviewed would actually recognize their lives. I was there to celebrate what Mom
had done, not to subject her choices to my feminist critique. At that point I went
deeper into core elements of feminist method: biography, subjectivity, and emotionality. Knowing that our differences are lived much more broadly than just
two lives, I wrote the argument between Mom and me about her work and
women's work generally into the exhibit text.

"Fabrications" was very successful for the Red Deer Museum. Significantly,
it drew new visitors, people who had not previously made a link between their

lives and the work of that institution. It was as if the exhibit shouted "1-2-3-we-see-you!" Blushing with excitement, a whole community of women stepped out of hiding. In their wake, they left a stack of comments in the scribblers that we put out for them. Here, most visitors reinforced the meaning of the exhibit as a journey of reconciliation. They portrayed me as an exceptional daughter who was lucky enough to appreciate her mother's value before it was too late. But there were dissenting comments, too.

In central Alberta, sewing is a natural part of women's careers as wives and mothers, a situation they live with honor, care, and love. As one visitor put it: "The exhibit speaks clearly of the value of women's natural role and talents far beyond the price tag." And she left me a quote from the Bible: "Who can find a virtuous woman? For her price is far beyond rubies" (Proverbs 31:10). Mom reminded several visitors of their own mothers: "same era, same solid Family Values, a woman totally dedicated to and fulfilled with being a wife, mother, and seamstress; a wonderful role model." Or, as another put it: "a woman with a servant's heart; something we truly need to get back to in today's broken world." For these viewers, my persistent questions about Mom's earnings and the value that society may or may not place on her labor revealed my "feminist bias."

Several women explicitly attempted to correct this error on my part, suggesting that my struggle and dissatisfaction were a direct result of my failure to take on a woman's traditional and natural role. From their point of view, if I was unhappy, if I broke down, if I became ill, it was my own fault. A note from one reads:

> To me it is very telling that Kathryn is the one who has suffered so emotionally. While her mother seems happy, content and, yes, fulfilled. Her life's contributions making gowns that expressed each woman's personality and made them all very happy is a direct contrast to dissertations and discussion of abstract ideas and questioning women's place in society. Perhaps there is more value in giving and it produces a more peaceful psyche than questioning past values.

Another short comment reads:

> I think and pray that eventually Lorraine's daughter will come to understand what a Real Woman her mother is.

My first reaction to these comments was relief. "Thank God!" I exclaimed to Wendy over the phone. "We've done our job after all." In spite of the hide-and-seek, some of my hard-won feminism actually was visible. Controversy meant that, although some people would read the exhibit only as a celebration of traditional skills and values, it wasn't completely congruent with that discourse. Later, the irony hit me. What our "family values" visitors failed to perceive was that, if all women lived my mother's life, there would have been no exhibit for them to visit.

Women in significant public roles opened the doors to this project. We brought it to life with our skills in social science research, writing, community organizing, networking, public speaking, public relations, museum management, fund-raising, artifact conservation and storage, computer graphics and layout, e-mail communication, exhibit design, production, installation, promotion, and sales. The network evolving over more than three years included professors, camerawomen, documentary producers (film and radio), magazine staff, illustrators, historians, and Web writers. "Fabrications" was built on the diverse strengths of contemporary women both in and out of the home.

In attempting this bridging, my dilemma was whether I could celebrate what my mother represented without reproducing it, whether she and I could be visible together without One wiping the Other out of the picture. My mother needed the exhibit to be "safe" while I needed it to be "unsettling." In my mind, the exhibit was a commentary on two generations of women, their constraints and possibilities. It was an outgrowth not only of my success in living a life different from my mother's, but also of my failure as a small town seamstress's daughter to achieve an academic subjectivity, its material benefits and social power.

However, I was not always able to keep the project poised on this edge. The artifacts themselves consistently slipped away from me (and into my mother's arms). The wedding dresses that we recovered for display pulled everyone who saw them into a set of narratives about love, hope, purity, innocence, heterosexuality, and fidelity (see Ingraham 1999). If a single dress is potent for one woman, a roomful is simply overwhelming. I was seduced by how they looked, how they felt, and how they made me feel. I found it difficult to think around them and about them except in highly prescribed ways. And that struggle showed up in the display. In spite of active attempts to "distress" (dis/dress) it, the design we developed lacked the unsettling quality that I had hoped for it. Like the dresses, the exhibit remained resolutely inviting, beautifully serene, and slightly otherworldly.

Afterwords: The Deck

The sun is sinking behind a cluster of tall trees. Out the kitchen window I can see the top of Ross's head over the back of a lawn chair. I am amazed at his hair, gone almost white now, and a far cry from the auburn curls he sported at seventeen. And then I smell the cigar. Occasionally this summer, he has allowed himself a contemplative smoke. I pad over to the backdoor, bare feet cool on the hardwood.

"If you stub that out for a while, I'll join you," I tempt him.

"Anything to lure you out for the mosquitoes," he teases, reaching for the ashtray. "Who was that on the phone?" he asks, as I slip into a chair beside him.

"Mommy Dearest," I reply. I know that he won't get the allusion.

"What's up in her world?"

"Ahhh, so glad you asked. A community development worker phoned from Hanna, Alberta, wanting to know whether Mom and I would be special speakers for an event she is organizing in March. She claims that she can get 100 local women to come out and listen to us talk about 'Fabrications.' Mom was practically on the ceiling with excitement. That's interesting, isn't it? Considering how reluctant she was in the beginning."

"Where the hell is Hanna?" he asks, but my mind has slipped to remembering our press conference during installation week in Red Deer. Here I learned how extensively my mother was making her own sense of our project. "One thing I realize," she declared from a podium in the gallery, "is just how perceptive Kathryn was as a child. There was a lot going through her mind. There is a larger lesson here for parents. I hope the exhibit helps people realize that we have to learn to communicate, especially with those we love." Later that week, she took the microphone to deliver remarks to 160 people at the gala opening. What a remarkable turn of events. For years I tried to draw her into my world without success. Having given that up to reenter her world, suddenly, there she was: a public face, a public voice.

"You know," I blurt out, "the gala opening in Red Deer was one of the few times in my life that I have felt perfectly balanced."

"Was it?" he queries, somewhat startled. "Well, it was a huge night in your Mom's life, too."

"She's much more comfortable with 'Fabrications' now, and with her own public profile. I think that she knows that it isn't going to hurt her."

"It would be more accurate to say that you have decided not to hurt her with it," he points out.

"There's that," I agree. "I can't remember whether I told you about the speech she gave last autumn when we were in northern Alberta."

"Tell me again," he suggests, indulgently.

"Well, she gets up in front of an audience of fifty at the local museum and she tells them she's a bit worried about the dresses. I'm wincing and wondering, 'Oh-oh, What's she fretting about now?' But she went on to talk about her creations as pampered guests in exotic locations, about how they had been spruced up, fawned over, and celebrated to an extent that she felt they would be traumatized when it came time for them to return to their shoeboxes."

"How'r ya goin' ta keep 'em down on the farm?" he quips.

"After they've seen Ottawa?!!" I finish, incredulous. "My Mom, the comedienne."

"Who knew?" he grins. And we laugh into the growing shadows.

"And where are you in all of this?" he broaches, curious.

"To be honest, the complexity of my own perspective remains largely hidden—from my mother and from the public. I began this project out of both pleasure and pain, and these contradictory feelings continue to shape my experience. I find myself publicly celebrating not just my mother but also a whole generation of women who did skilled domestic labor. And that's great. I'll admit that part of me clings to that role. But another part feels betrayed, restless, and even ashamed of my performance as the 'good daughter.' I had hoped that I could use the exhibit as a vehicle for persistent questions that I carry about women and their place in society. But, it's damned difficult to celebrate and question at the same time. I'm trained to reveal the darker things in life. Instead, here I am struggling to do social analysis from love!"

Frustrated at not being able to see Ross's expression in the dark, I go and search out a candle. It flickers cheerfully on the table in front of us as I continue what is turning out to be a rant.

"I have found it difficult to strike a good balance between my mother's voice, the voices of the brides, and my own voice. As a daughter, I have struggled to foreground my own critical analysis. I have agonized over whether, in those places where I stepped back from what I think, I gave up too much: my hard-won separation from these lives lived, my break with the pattern of women's lives in central Alberta, my feminist politics."

"Where do you think you've stepped back?" he probes. "Give me an example."

"Well," I splutter, "the most obvious is around the role of women. I do not believe that there is a natural role for women as wives and mothers within which we find a kind of peace that is otherwise lacking. As my 'husband,' you know this. From the beginning of our marriage twenty-five years ago, I have understood at least intellectually that roles are social constructions. As such they can be and, indeed, in this case,

have been significantly transformed. What women are is not given. We actively stitch ourselves together against a larger pattern of constraints and opportunities. The end product is a shifting multiplicity of legitimate forms. Asserting this through the exhibit has been more problematic than I expected. I remain trapped by fears that my attempts at deconstruction will hurt some of the people I love."

"Those feelings are a big part of the gendered nature of this project, aren't they?" he observes.

"They are," I confirm. "But it is around class that I feel the most limitations. To put it bluntly, there are deep structural divisions between Mom and me. Miller [1996] gets at this phenomenon quite nicely through Annie Ernaux's story [1991]. With her shopkeeper mother's help, Ernaux used university education to move into a bourgeois professional class. Her mother wanted her to remain unchanged by this but education altered both their material and their class relations. It gave Ernaux new words for new ways of being in and interpreting the world. Ultimately, that process—what Ernaux calls her 'passage into the dominant world'—ruptured and displaced her relationship with her mother."

"I can see why this resonates with you," says Ross. "You have made your own difficult passage into the dominant world with similar ruptures and displacements."

"You know it," I reply. "You were there. The separations that education opened up between Mom and me were very present when I started this project. In fact, they made the exhibit both necessary and possible! They have persisted and continue to be present as the national tour nears its close. Although it is a message people don't like to hear, structurally, there is no resolution here."

"So, the dialectic between identification and separation continues?" he asks.

"I relate very differently to Mom now than I did when we first started," I acknowledge. "I consciously take pleasure in her creativity, revealed so clearly in the luminosity of those dresses. I have a sense now of our common creativity—even sensuality—that really strengthens me. Collaborating on the exhibit has taught me my mother's legitimacy. I can't tell you how important that is to my emotional life. It's a piece that was never there before. Beyond that I take pleasure in the dialogue that we are having about our lives as women in a male-dominated society. It has been very satisfying to bring forward the story of an (extra)ordinary woman, and an invisible social history of women and domestic labor. This is 'therapeutic' but not healing."

"Why are you hedging?" he counters.

"Because so many people want this story to be a variation on what Art Frank calls a 'restitution narrative' [Frank 1995]. They want to minimize or resolve the mother/daughter alienation, treat it as a temporary interruption, and get the players to reconcile, *to live happily ever after. I value difference—not conflict—but difference too much to do that. For some time, politically, it has been much more important to me than resemblance. Like my work with the psychiatric survivor movement, I see 'Fabrications' as a political project in naming and working together across difference [Narayan 1988]."*

"Then how would you characterize the narrative that you are writing with and about your mother? Is it a quest?"

"It has elements of a quest narrative but my hope is that, as I work on it over time, it comes closer to what Doug Ezzy calls a polyphonic narrative [2000]. He uses the term to refer to many voices, stories, and values that are woven together in openly contradictory accounts. Polyphonic narratives leave room for uncertainty. I like that."

Ross gives a small grunt of assent. It suddenly occurs to me that I have worn him out.

"I'm going to turn in," I say. "Enough of me for one day."

"I'll be up in a minute," he replies, "just as soon as I finish my smoke."

Softly, I blow out the candle and leave him in the dark.

Note

I am grateful to Ross Gray, Eric Mykhalovskiy, and Nina Bascia for intellectual and emotional assistance in the preparation of this chapter, to Sharon Rosenberg for our conversation about theorizing from love, and to Art Bochner and Carolyn Ellis for the comments that set this final draft on a fruitful course. My gratitude as well and as always to Lorraine Church for going public "just once more."

References

Benjamin, Jessica. 1995. *Like Subjects, Love Objects: Essays on Recognition and Sexual Difference.* New Haven, Conn.: Yale University

Church, Kathryn. 1995. *Forbidden Narratives: Critical Autobiography As Social Science.* Amsterdam: International Publishers Distributors.

———. 1998. "The Dressmaker." *Elm Street Magazine* (Summer): 54–62.

———. "Fabrications: Stitching Ourselves Together." Access at http://womenspace.ca/Fabrications

Church, Kathryn, and Wendy Martindale. 1999. "Shall We Dance? Looking Back Over a Community-Museum Collaboration." *Muse* 17(3): 43–50.

Ernaux, Annie. 1991. *A Woman's Story,* trans. Tanya Leslie. New York: Four Walls Eight Windows.

Ezzy, Douglas. 2000. "Illness Narratives: Time, Hope and HIV." *Social Science and Medicine* 50: 605–17.

Frank, Arthur. 1995. *The Wounded Storyteller.* Chicago: University of Chicago Press.

Friese, Susanne. 1997. "A Consumer Good in the Ritual Process: The Case of the Wedding Dress." *Journal of Ritual Studies* 11(2): 51–62.

Gamber, Wendy. 1997. *The Female Economy: The Millinery and Dressmaking Trades, 1860–1930.* Urbana, Ill.: University of Illinois Press.

Ingraham, Chrys. 1999. *White Weddings: Romancing Heterosexuality in Popular Culture.* New York: Routledge.

Lyman, Peter. 1981. "The Politics of Anger: On Silence, Resentment and Political Speech." *Socialist Review* 11(3): 55–74.

Miller, Nancy K. 1996. *Bequest and Betrayal: Memoirs of a Parent's Death.* Bloomington: University of Indiana Press.

Narayan, Uma. 1988. "Working Together across Difference: Some Considerations on Emotions and Political Practice." *Hypatia* 3(2): 31–47.

Rich, Adrienne. 1976. *Of Woman Born: Motherhood As Experience and Institution.* New York: W.W. Norton.

Walkerdine, Valerie. 1987. Surveillance, Subjectivity and Struggle. Minneapolis: University of Minnesota Press.

Living the Hyphenated Edge: Autoethnography, Hybridity, and Aesthetics

CAROLINE JOAN ("KAY") S. PICART

MY POINT of entry into conversations concerning autoethnography is rooted personally, as a body and entity marked by multiple hybridities, but also professionally, as a philosopher concerned with metaphysical and ethical questions of "truth" in relation to narrativity, or in the language of Nietzsche, "perspectivalism," particularly in negotiating what Trinh Minh-ha characterizes as the battle of "warring fictions" (1991).[1] I am also a visual artist and a dancer, interested in the hermeneutics of color, form, and movement; the language games of bodies, gestures, and rhythms; fluctuations across the realms of two- and three-dimensionality; the poesy of abstraction agonistically and intimately intertwined with lived experience. Thus, in this piece I weave across, theorizing about structures of narrativity and the politics of the gaze as mediating the deconstruction and reconstruction of truths. Also, I experiment with performing a poetic, visual, and multivoiced text that sinuously weaves in the interstices of the autobiographical and theoretical.

My attempt is a risk-filled experiment. Like many who live in the survival-rich realm of the hyphenated edge, I find myself working in the liminal spaces of several worlds: as a philosopher and scientist trained in the Philippines, England, and in the United States; as an artist who has had exhibitions in the Philippines, South Korea, and various parts of the United States; as a dancer trained in the body languages of ballet, Hawaiian, Philippine, Korean, and ballroom dances; and as a woman of mixed heritage—with French-American blood on my father's side, and Spanish-Chinese blood on my mother's side, yet growing up in the Philippines, a country known for its history of colonial conquests; its geographic and cultural splintering because of its composition as an archipelago; and its adoption of English as an "official language" alongside "Filipino." Hybridity, to me, is not only a theoretical concept, but also a practically lived and constantly negotiated reality that demands that every "center" remain permeable, fluid, and multiple. In the words of Stuart Hall:

> The diaspora experience . . . is defined, not by essence or purity, but by the recognition of a necessary heterogeneity and diversity: by a conception of "identity" which lives with and through, not despite, difference: by *hybridity*. Diaspora identities are those which are constantly producing and reproducing themselves anew, through transformations and difference (1990: 235).

I challenge comfortable binaries through the use of intertwining genres, polyphonous voices, multilayered modes of looking and being in an effort to revision what narrativity, as (auto)ethnographic, entails. Hybridity, as an operative principle that blurs the borders of the "pure" and "impure," is as much an artistic and epistemological force as it is a political stance to me. By "political," I mean that the form of art/writing I create aims to diffuse beyond the now too easily pronounced "personal is political" mantra in order to show that the personal is most intensely and intimately political when it engages the difficult work of addressing larger questions of signification and valuation, while being aware of the temptations toward solipsism, sentimentalism, and Truth. As an illustration of how my own work as an artist and theorist receives its impetus from the lived experience of multiple hybridities and diasporas, I juxtapose the text and images from an art video, "Inside Notes from the Outside,"[2] which I have rewritten in CD-ROM format, in the attempt to explore contested cultural and spatial constructions of "insideness" and "outsideness." The use of the CD-ROM format is crucial to the presentation of the text, as the vibrant fluctuations across sound, color, and images are essential to the performance of this narrative experiment.

Filling Blankness with Layers of Black

Dot. Dot. Dot.
Form darkens,
deepens, draws shape;
achieves texture, creates substance.

Point. Line. Plane.
Animate converging with inanimate,
diverging
within a confluence
of meaning.

Shadow. Shade. Sketch.
Eternal dance of stillness
ensnared within
forms of motion.

Whorl-like images
within the labyrinthine shell
of substance.

An experiment
in the metaphysics
of light and shadow.

I sit, my legs tucked underneath me. I hunch over the pale film upon which a form begins to congeal. Slowly, slowly does it harden beneath small hard dots linking with thin lines that threaten to waver and wander, anchored in place by the outline of the form gaining form. Faintly, faintly does the fine impress of its breath suffuse the blank sheet. Carefully, carefully does it allow the peril of enfleshment, for corporeality may either grant it the language of form, gesture, mood, and texture, or render it mute, locked in the space of the pseudoform, the incomplete gesture, the simulated mood, the apparent texture.

Slowly, slowly do the hovering forms become opaque upon the translucent sheet. Softly, softly do shadows and shades fall across the unfurling plane: a fissure in the fabric of the three-dimensional. Gently, gently does the pen's fine point scratch the sheet's smoothness—filling, filling, filling blankness with layers of blackness. Forming a face framed in shadow, a figure held within interlocking

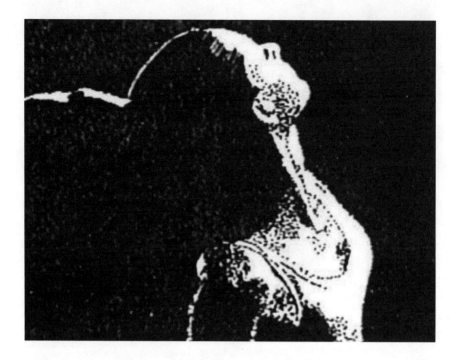

squares of sunlight streaming through a windowpane, the graceful arc of hair swung back in the abandonment of dance.

An artist once remarked that my pen and ink sketches frozen images—portraits seemed more like marble busts rather than live human faces. But it is through the solidity of the fine points of darkness converging that I find the interplay of light and shadow meaningfully captured. The art of fine point sketching, to me, lies in the capturing of the expressive potential of a movement, a look, a pose, made possible through the skillful imposition of expressive stasis. Tangible faces, arms, and legs are but media for the expression of the intangible, be it called a mood, an emotion, or an idea. Moods, emotions, and ideas, hazy and fluid as they are, are glimpsed in the starkness and solidity of the arrested gaze, movement, or pose.

Color is a different matter. Color, to me, evokes movement and plasticity. Color vibrates with warmth, gently subdues, violently assaults. Whenever I experiment with color, I require a more intimate contact with my medium. Very little can compare with the sensation of color melting upon color, oozing into the paper's fine pores and clinging to the tips of my fingers as I experiment with the movement of texture and tone. (See *The Assault of Color* in photospread.)

Most of my color studies have been inspired by Monet's fascination with the splintering of light on the undulating surface of water; the impressionist rever-

ence for the truthfulness of the roving, fleeting gaze; the expressionist passion for the raw, sundering power of unmediated emotion; the surrealist longing for an active reality stretching beyond the confines of the familiar and the banal. (See *Glimpses of the Numinous* and *Visions of Home* in photospread.)

Yet the interplay of fixity and fluidity, light and shadow, form and color—all dissolve in the wholeness of the experience that evokes an awareness of the beautiful. The to-and-fro motion linking stasis and movement, texture and tone, form and substance is the artist's entry point into the numinous—his/her transcendence of the existential chiaroscuro or of the ambivalent interplay of being and nonbeing.

I sit, cast in shadow, my hand bathed by the halo of my desk lamp, a form slowly congealing beneath my slowly disappearing hand. It is a humbling experience . . . but also a piercingly beautiful one.

Inside Notes from the Outside

There is always the silence—the barest of pauses. Then the silence congeals into a hard glint in the eye; a faint twist of the lips; the echo of a cold, metallic ring that vibrates in a voice.

"Oh. Filipino."

Two short words that fall—ensnaring me in a trap.

Suddenly, the fulcrum of the conversation dissolves. I forget to pursue a point. But it no longer matters. The essential point has been made.

The center is no longer what he wants to know; it is what he wants not to know. It is not what he says that speaks so eloquently and forcefully. It is what he does not say.

Our eyes meet as we comb our hair, peering into a mirror. We share a public place to enact a private act. The act of combing into place what must be combed; tucking in what must be tucked in; smoothening what must be smoothened out.

Our reflections undergo movements that mirror each other: now bending forward, then turning around—brown hands stroking thick, dark hair.

Brown eyes meet brown eyes. First, there is the shy recoil; then the return. A smile dangles on strings of silence.

"*Pinay ka ba?*" ("Are you a Filipina?") The question inevitably comes up: sometimes shyly whispered; at other times, loudly expressed.

However, the initial onrush of warmth is often deftly sliced by the next question: "*Anong pangalan mo?*" ("What is your name?") For my name reveals the guilt of my lack of racial purity. My father has French-American roots; my mother, the hint of a Spanish-Chinese heritage.

I feel the coldness in the pit of my stomach again as the next set of questions falls, like shadows of steel bars, across us. They are questions loaded with silent presuppositions, accusations, and condemnations. They are searchlights that attempt to probe into my educational status; my economic position; my possible usefulness. They are quiet sentences that scream, tear, and ravage, leaving me mercifully numb.

It is over. Long before we had bared our teeth at each other's images in the mirror, that silence had claimed us.

A name defines, identifies, embodies. Through it, one gains a face, a body, a voice. But your name also grants others the power to gain access to you; to construct, deconstruct, and reconstruct your face, body, and voice to suit what they think your name must mean. A name then becomes a means by which a face, a body, a voice may be erased: an invisible yet systematic mechanism of defacing,

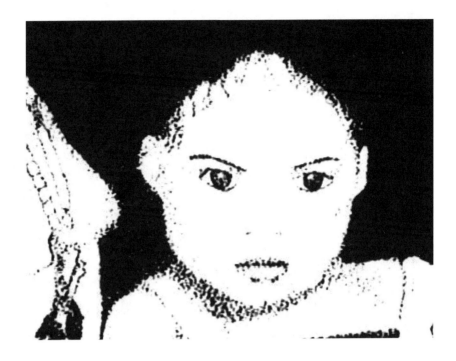

disembodying, and silencing. A force through which the politics of naming and being named distinguishes the empowered from the powerless.

I bear the name of a country famed for its white-sanded beaches lined with palm trees and its mountains of green and brown jutting out and falling against a sky of deep blue. I bear upon my forehead the Cain-like mark of a country named by its young, sweet-looking whores, self-effacing maids, and submissive illegal workers. I am made and unmade by a country of warm, friendly smiles; swarms of bloated bellies and hard, stringy arms burnt by the sun; ancient Spanish-looking churches; patched-up houses of wood, rubber, and plastic; tiers of sprouting green forming an amber-tinged stairway to the sky; almost perfectly cone-shaped volcanoes that tower like sleeping giants, occasionally awakening to breathe dark fire and red mud on slumbering towns, leaving behind a void of white-gray sand and human ghosts whose shrill cries mingle with the moaning of the wind; armies of jeepneys swathed in paintings, plastic figures, and streamers, and altars of red lightbulbs in front of images of Christ or the Virgin Mary and stickers of a driver's prayer—that cough out dark smoke as they scuttle, helter-skelter, through roads of potholes, stones, and mud.

It is a name that names and unnames me—a set of notes that sits, trembling, laughing and weeping on the borders of my voice, the curves of my body, the shadows that line my eyes.

Echo and Narcissus

Let not your silence
speak to me
with its many tongues;
its ghostly breath
of blood, fire and ice;
its fingers of poison and honey.

Let not your silence
touch me
with the unruly grace
of soiled clothing
flung over an armchair,
the suspended ecstasy
of the stillness
between notes;
the cruel vastness
of a darkness
momentarily held at bay
by a trembling flame.

Speak—Speak—
That all that
tumbles, cavorts,
taunts, cajoles,
threatens and consoles
in your silence
may be still.

"Echo and Narcissus" is one of the few drawings I have created that took only a few hours to finish. But they were hours intensely and passionately spent on an all-consuming concentration. I emerged drained, exhausted, and spent from the work.

Conventionally, it is Narcissus who is the focus of much narrative, political, literary, and psychological speculation. It is Narcissus who is viewed as the archetypal object of universal desire; the cold and haughty embodiment of unattainable beauty who mortally falls in love with his own visage; the immortal symbol for the human desire of assimilating all that is other.

Yet it is less Narcissus than Echo who fascinates me. It is the lover, and not the beloved, who is wrenched into and sojourns through the depths and heights of the darkest and most profound spiritual realms. It is Echo, this woman who fades into a voice, whose portrait haunts me. It is Echo—this diminutive admirer who skillfully crafts a confession of love from fragments of Narcissus's speech in spite of the verbal handicap of mere repetition wrought on her by the jealous Hera—who speaks to me. This diminutive, disembodied voice has become, to me, emblematic of the power and impotence (see figure in center of volume) of female intelligence, passion, and devotion: refractory feminine properties across various cultures—occasionally virtues, occasionally vices.

Notes

1. A more theoretical exposition of this position in relation to issues of feminism and multiculturalism may be found in: Caroline Joan S. Picart, "Inside Notes from the Outside: Narrativity, the Gaze and Post-Modernity," in *This Bridge Called My Back*, vol. 2, ed. AnaLouise Keating and Gloria Anzaldua, forthcoming.
2. This video was produced through grants from the Institute of Race and Ethnicity, University of Wisconsin System and the Office of University Research, University of Wisconsin-Eau Claire.

References

Hall, Stuart. 1990. "Cultural Identity and Diaspora." In *Identity: Community, Culture, Difference*, ed. Jonathan Rutherford (pp. 222–37). London: Trade Paperback, Lawrence & Wishart.

Minh-ha, Trinh. 1991. *When the Moon Waxes Red: Representation, Gender and Cultural Politics*. New York: Routledge.

The Visitor: Juggling Life in the Grip of the Text

Karen Scott-Hoy

> Somewhere between the two (objectivity and subjectivity) is a
> region where you are partly blown by the winds of reality and partly
> an artist creating a composite out of the inner and outer events.
> (Bateson 1977: 245)

Introduction

THREE YOUNG ni-Vanuatu men, dressed in T-shirts and shorts, stroll down the main street of Port Vila, Vanuatu. One is wearing a cap, sneakers without socks, the laces untied. Another has a piece of red and yellow cotton fabric tied around his forehead. With their heads tilted and the sunglasses perched at an angle on the end of their noses, they laugh and slap each other on the back as they move toward the market house. They draw people's attention to themselves through their behavior, stance, dress, and by wearing sunglasses.

Several women, wearing brightly colored island dresses, sit on woven pandanas mats by their craft stalls on the opposite side of the road, their arms wrapped around their knees. As the wind sweeps across the sunny marketplace, they raise their hands or use a cloth to shield their eyes from dust and glare. The long journey from the village in the open taxi truck has left their eyes red and sore. One woman's husband has forbidden her to wear the sunglasses provided by the eye doctor. The other two women feel too much fraet (fear, embarrassment) to wear sunglasses.

My husband, Stephen, an optometrist, and I spend up to several months each year in Vanuatu, a small island nation in the Southwest Pacific, conducting primary eye clinics. We do not charge for the eye examinations, although on the advice of pastors and chiefs, we charge a small fee for the glasses dispensed. Purchasing their own glasses enhances their self-worth, which would be diminished by receiving them as "charity" or "foreign aid." However, when glasses are donated to the project by our patients or suppliers, we donate the money back to local projects in Vanuatu.

While conducting the eye clinics, we were confronted by many ni-Vanuatu (Vanuatu citizens) who suffered from eye disease and damage, which wearing sunglasses may have prevented. Although many had been advised to wear sunglasses, both at our clinics and by others, still they did not. I wanted to know why they were not following this advice.

I began asking them about their eye problems and how they perceived people who wore sunglasses (Scott-Hoy 1997). Sunglasses appeared to be a symbol of *waetman*'s (European) culture, and the *fraet* (fear, embarrassment) of being labeled *flas* (showing off) when wearing sunglasses reflected a struggle to maintain a stable cultural identity in a changing world. The more I explored, the more I saw that visiting health professionals, of which I was one, were part of the problem. We operated from a worldview that was very different from theirs. Even the question that triggered my research—"Why won't they wear sunglasses?"— implied, "Why won't they *comply* with our advice to wear sunglasses?" This question assumed both that I had the right to advise and that my advice was "right." I soon began to question both assumptions.

To really work *with* the people in preventing eye problems, I had to examine my own worldview, not just theirs. Similar to other agents of change, I was "coming to see that the problem is more 'us' than 'them' . . . it is with ourselves that we have to start" (Chambers 1997: 32), so I became a more consciously self-reflective practitioner. I kept asking myself questions, perhaps even more than I asked the ni-Vanuatu. My focus swung from them, to me, to the world I was sharing with them.

My first attempt to represent my research project took the format of a traditional ethnography. Soon I was left feeling that something was missing, that somehow I had misrepresented the experience and betrayed the people. Writing the traditional ethnography I seemed invisible, yet in absolute control. That was not how it appeared to be in the field, or how I felt it should be. I had concerns about questions of identity and selfhood, voice and authenticity, and cultural displacement. I had learned *from* the ni-Vanuatu, not just about them. I was as much the taught as the teacher. That knowledge did not appear to be present in my first ethnography, because I was not present. I wanted to be there, alongside the people, for that's how I felt it was. I wanted to use a form of representation, which would not violate my desire to be alongside the people. Further, as I felt accountable to the people of Vanuatu, I wanted to re-present what I learned in a way that was appropriate for them, that would answer why it mattered, and to whom. I turned to autoethnography, a blend of ethnography and autobiographical writing that incorporates elements of one's own life experience when writing about others, a form of self-narrative that "place[s] the self within a social context" (Reed-Danahay, 1997: 9). Autoethnography as a product and process, "a method and a text" (Reed-Danahay 1997: 9), enabled me to more fully explore and portray my attempt to work with the people of Vanuatu in establishing a preventative eye care project.

Visual Representation

As I thought more about how to represent the research, pictures formed in my mind, which was not surprising, as I often painted when I wanted to think. My oil paintings were interpretations of my experience of life, of my knowledge of the world. It occurred to me that ethnographies are interpretations too, not just records of human experience (Denzin 1997: 284). Usually ethnographers had "language sit in for life" (Bochner and Ellis 1996b: 20). They translated their visual observations into words, and had "language doing the work of eyes" (Tyler 1986: 137, cited in Ball and Smith 1992: 6) but my paintings employed an aesthetic language that did not rely on words, and so could "speak" to my linguistically varied audience.

I knew the paintings wouldn't "say" the same things to everybody and that different people would see different things in the paintings, but the question was: Did that enhance, or detract from, the goals of the research? The knowledge I was seeking was "the kind that helps an audience use other people's sorrows and triumphs as a way to reflect on or recontextualize their own, enhancing their capacity to cope with life's contingencies" (Bochner and Ellis 1996b: 28). Increasingly, I felt that "visual art with its elements of aesthetics, economy of statement, and individualized expression, conveyed information and points of view in emphatic and convincing ways" (Sharf 1995: 72), and that painting could be both a "natural" and verisimilar method of portraying my experiences and interpretations.

I realized that viewing a painting involved more than "seeing"; it involved understanding, and the starting point for understanding and interpretation was not "an act of an individual conscious mind but enactments, performances, or a kind of praxis" (Schwandt 1999: 455). The audience entered the "created" world of the painting through connections they felt with images, people, or places depicted in the painting. Once inside this world, the audience was privy to interaction and relationships, heard what the artist/Other had to say, and entered into a dialogue with the artist/Other. Understanding and interpretation thus became practical-moral activities, not so concerned with grasping the content, as in engaging in a dialogue with that which is to be understood (Schwandt 1999: 455).

The Art of Storytelling

Since my paintings included images of worlds of which some audience members may not have had previous experience or ready connections, I needed to incorporate points of access for my audience. One such point came through the telling of stories emerging from the paintings. *Storian,* the Bislama (the lingua franca) expression for chatting or storytelling, had been a major part of my experience and research method. Vanuatu had a long oral tradition, but with the coming of the *waetman,* the ni-Vanuatu entered a world of written text, as missionaries began to write down stories, chants, and songs. However, the texts created by the missionaries, social scientists, and colonial administrators appeared final, objective, and neutral entities that had no history, no parentage, no people, but plenty of authority (Manoa 1995: 19). The art of storytelling, which had been so prominent in the oral tradition, was lost in the transition to the written word.

How could I rediscover the *art* of storytelling, yet write down the stories? My paintings seemed to have many of the qualities that textualization erased. I needed to free myself from "the grip of the text" (Schwandt 1999: 454) in order to begin to bridge or navigate the divide between ni-Vanuatu oral and Western academic textual/written cultures, but I needed to record the stories to provide a point of access for my audience.

Barone and Eisner (1997) suggest that the *art* of storytelling lies in the writer's ability to create a virtual reality and make use of expressive, contextualized, and vernacular language in the telling of the story to promote empathy. These stories have aesthetic form, allow the presence of ambiguity, "long to be used, as well as analyzed, to be revised, and retold rather than settled and theorized" (Bochner and Ellis 1996a: 4), and bear the personal signature of the teller. All these characteristics give the stories orality, and connect the stories to a life-world (Manoa 1995: 3).

Prompted by the images of the paintings, I tried to record stories that could be read aloud to others and bring the audience in as participants. I left these stories open so the storytellers could add their own experience to, and interpretation of, the paintings. So began a process that had a life, a passion of its own, which provided an experience of an experience as the storyteller and audience interacted with each other, the stories, and the paintings.

As I began to show my paintings, I was asked to tell my stories, first to friends, relatives, and visitors in my home, then later to colleagues and others at conferences. Each time I told a story it felt different, as my voice gave the stories rhythm, inflection, subtlety, dynamics, and life.

Performance

It became hard to tell the stories sitting or standing still. They seemed to have too much energy, and to instill that energy in the teller. So, while telling the stories I added movements, gestures, changes in position and posture. These movements drew attention to the body that was telling the story, invited debate about the body's impact on the experience and the experience's impact on the body.

I showed my audiences objects, "props," which served to connect the "real" and "created" worlds, and stimulated the audiences' imagination, or triggered questioning. I watched for, and responded to, audience members' reactions as they followed my movement in and around the paintings, and as they laughed, muttered agreement or dissension in response.

Pauses became important. Silences slowed down and held the audience's attention as I endeavored to take the audience with me, the artist, through the action and passion of life performed, into "a jointly felt and shared field of experience" (Denzin 1997: 94). Gradually, from the seemingly "natural" role of artist/storyteller in my home, I had constructed a performance that provided my audience with another point of access to the "created" world of the paintings as "another's experiences came alive for the self" (Denzin 1997: 95).

I began to ask why I had chosen certain props. Why did the audience find certain parts of the story sad, funny, or boring? What was the performance doing for them and me? How could I record the performance? Indeed, could it be captured at all? Once again, as artist, performer, storyteller, and sociologist, I faced questions of how to retain the *art* of storytelling, and yet record the story as I sought to show how "the sociological imagination engages some of the things that matter in everyday life" (Denzin 1999: 156).

Soliloquy: *The Visitor*

The soliloquy, *The Visitor,* which I present below in written form, begins with the artist telling her audience about a previous visitor. As the performance continues, the audience assumes the role of the visitor, as I, the artist, tell a visitor about a visitor. It becomes apparent that the audience and the artist have at times played, and still play, similar roles to the visitor. Although the artist, I was also a visitor in this "created" world, just as I had been a visitor in the "real" world, as a cross-cultural health worker. The "real" and "created" worlds thus were connected through visits and revisits. Through coperformance, the audience and I discover that we are all sometimes visitors seeking to understand the visited. This requires an openness to experience, and a willingness to engage in a dialogue with that which challenges our self-understanding. Such dialogue requires that we listen to the Other and simultaneously risk confusion and uncertainty both about ourselves and about the other person we seek to understand (Schwandt 1999: 458).

Some of you may find it helpful to read *The Visitor* aloud. You also may want to move around the room with the artist and make the experience come alive for you. For others, that may feel too awkward and uncomfortable. Perhaps you can better hear the artist's voice, and picture the scene in your head, since within your imagination the characters are not bound by your own physical qualities. Either way, it is important to try to picture yourself alongside the artist, as I speak, and when the script directs, take time to look at the painting so that you, like the visitor, form your own interpretation and understanding of the painting. Let the painting speak to you. Listen to the artist's story, and endeavor to engage in dialogue with the artist.

The Visitor

Scene: A lounge room. In the center of the room, the artist is seated at a desk writing a letter. The oil painting, titled What's Eating You?, *is propped against a stool, next to the desk. To her right is a bench containing an array of souvenirs, including a bright pink-and-yellow, intricately woven basket and a carved wooden mace about eighteen inches long. A second oil painting leans against the end of the bench. To her left, a third oil painting is leaning against a chair. (See photograph in photospread.)*

Artist: You know I was just reminded of a visitor I had yesterday. I was busy writing a letter to my friend in Vanuatu when a rap on the front door caught my attention. Tentatively I opened the door and showing good "Aussie" hospitality I invited the visitor in. My entrance hall is dominated by what was a planter box in a bygone era and now, topped with a large highly polished slab of red gum, holds an impressive display of "dust collectors." The visitor seemed intrigued by the collection and admired several items.

[Artist moves to her right and picks up a carved rosewood ceremonial mace displayed on the bench.]

These are my memories, triggers around which I tell and retell stories. I recollect "little fragments that have no beginning and no end" [O'Brien 1991: 39]. As I look at, touch, and smell each object, I am transported back to the time and place it was bought.

[Artist runs her fingers sensuously over the mace. As if suddenly remembering her visitor, Artist places the mace down on the bench and moves to where the visitor had admired another object, a basket.]

And that? We were given that woven basket at a circumcision ceremony several years ago. I recall the silence of the ceremony followed by the sound of the pigs as they were killed. It still makes me shudder. The pigs sound like human babies as they cry out. . . . And the sound of the skulls being broken when hit with the maces. Ugh.

[Pause]

I remember the woman who gave me the basket. I can picture her and her daughter: their bodies wrapped in red-and-yellow material, and swirling grass skirts, colored feathers and tinsel twisted around their black curly hair and their dark brown faces painted with bright red, green, and yellow patterns.

[Artist puts the basket back in its place on the bench.]

I did a painting of that day. It's called "And Daughter." It hangs just around the corner from the hall, on the way into the kitchen, so I pass it many times a day and smile and wonder what that little girl is doing.

[*Artist returns to the center of the room.*]

Yesterday, when the visitor arrived, several oil paintings were propped around the room drying. I'd been very busy painting my experience as a health worker in Vanuatu.

[*Artist walks across to the painting on her left, which is propped against a chair. Artist turns to face the painting momentarily, then turns toward the audience.*]

I love to paint. I love the feel of the palette knife moving the thick, glossy paint across the canvas. I love the anticipation, the sense of creativity, and the feelings captured and displayed. Even a painting of a tree is not just a tree. It is how I felt about seeing that tree. It is how small I felt, how huge the tree. It is an interpretation of my experience of that tree. Paintings are lived experiences interpreted and depicted.

[*Pause*]

Being a researcher in Vanuatu is not dissimilar to being an artist. You need to be sensitive to the texture, features, tones, and perspectives of the social settings. You need to be intuitive, creative, and reflective [Wolcott 1995].

Most human beings come to know the world as it is for them through a process of picturing [Ball and Smith 1992; Barone and Eisner 1997; Chaplin 1998; Fyfe and Law 1988; Harper 1998; Van Manen 1997] and as I thought about the experience of being a health worker in Vanuatu, pictures formed in my mind. Sometimes they were realistic visualizations of places, people, and events. Other times collages of superimposed images, faces, colors, and textures.

[*Artist turns to face the painting leaning against the chair and looks into the painting. Artist turns back to face the audience.*]

To translate these pictures into words was to rationalize, and lose some of the spontaneity and fluidity of the images. Words also "miss the fullness and the uniqueness of our private worlds. Words fall short because language is essentially social. It is only through the collectivity of language that we can access experience, the experience of others as well as our own. And so the essentially unique and private qualities of inner experience will ultimately be beyond our linguistic reach" [Van Manen 1997: xiii]. Through the medium of oil paintings I was able to tap into deeply personal experience, using a consciousness that did not rely on words.

[*Artist moves to the painting leaning against the end of the bench on the opposite side of the room.*]

The results often surprised me, as I looked at the finished paintings. I had captured thoughts and events of which I was not actively conscious at the time. The act of painting took me back into experiences that were buried under my conscious reasoning. So the painting process taught me things about the experience, about the culture I had begun to absorb and know, and about myself. [*Artist speaks as she returns to stand behind her desk in the center of the room. Artist looks down at the papers on desk. Artist looks up at the audience.*]

Did you know that Vanuatu has three official languages? English, French, and Bislama. Most of my research was conducted in Bislama, the language of inter-island communication. I was constantly struggling to translate what I had learned into English, and vice versa. It was hard to understand some concepts and expressions that lost meaning in the translation. Through painting I could capture meaning without linguistic constraints. Through their nonverbal language, the paintings could speak to each sociolinguistic group.

[*Artist momentarily looks around the room at the paintings. Artist faces the audience once more.*]

After a while the visitor asked me how I knew what to paint. I asked myself the same question. In going to the field I had learned much about the people of Vanuatu, their culture, their perceptions of eye health, preventative measures, and sunglasses. I had kept field diaries and taken many photographs, yet I used none of them in creating the paintings. Rather, I sat. I looked inside my mind. I drew. As I drew, moments came to mind, and strong feelings accompanied them.

[*Artist moves in front of the desk, where she stands with her back to the audience as if in front of an easel. She imagines and reenacts the creative process.*]

I chose colors.

[*Artist squeezes paint from the tubes onto the palette.*]

I painted.

[*Artist makes large sweeping movements at the canvas. Artist steps back from the easel, and then moves in as if to correct the image with sweeping motion.*]

I cried.

I clenched my fist.

I danced around the room, expressing the energies the act of painting released.

[*During the dance Artist ends up facing the audience. Artist suddenly becomes self-conscious and draws a deep breath. Artist stands tall and moves purposefully*] *behind the desk. Artist sits up straight, facing audience, hands folded on desk, feet firmly together on the floor.*]

It's a good thing my art room is away from the house and private. One could get a reputation for being a bit funny, behaving like that, I mean. [*Pause*]

Creating the paintings helps me reenter the experience and move around inside it, exploring the experience from within, then from without. My mind's eye opened up the experience and brought back the events, linking them by common themes, images, or words. When I looked at the paintings, I did not just see the people depicted, but sensed the experience. I jotted down thoughts that came to mind while painting. I went back to my field notes and photographs to fill in blanks, and reconstruct events. I began to write stories. These stories became a way of further involving the viewers of the paintings. I did not want my audience to be just spectators; I wanted them to *feel* the paintings. [*Artist moves across the room to stand facing the painting leaning against the bench to her right. Artist turns and faces the audience.*]

Looking at the painting I felt the excitement, the disappointment, the fear, the relief. I could smell the musty air, feel the humidity, and hear the voices. I wrote some more. Yes, I know I said language was confining. But these words were not coming from my linguistic, rational mind; they were coming from the paintings. They were words and stories *of* me, not from me. I wrote poems and autoethnographic stories. Are you familiar with the term autoethnography? The visitor wasn't. So I had the visitor listen to what Ellis has to say:

> Autoethnography is an autobiographical genre of writing and research that displays multiple layers of consciousness. Back and forth autoethnographers gaze, first through an ethnographic wide-angle lens, focusing outward on social and cultural aspects of their personal experience; then they look inward, exposing a vulnerable self that is moved by and may move through, refract and resist cultural interpretations. Concrete action, dialogue, emotion, embodiment, spirituality, and self-consciousness are featured, appearing as relational and institutional stories impacted by history, and social structure, which themselves are dialectally revealed through actions, feelings, thoughts, and language. (1999: 673)

I read that to the visitor, who just stood looking into the painting, which was propped against this bench completing its drying process.

[*Artist turns away from the audience and looks into the same painting still leaning against the bench. Artist turns back to audience.*]

I don't think the visitor heard much of what I said. Too transfixed, transported into, and exploring the world of the paintings, I guess the visitor was.

[*Pause*]

I asked the visitor to take a seat while I went into the kitchen to put on the kettle. When I returned the visitor was standing in front of another painting, *What's Eating You?* (See painting in photospread.)

[*Artist moves across the room and stands facing* What's Eating You?, *which is propped near the desk in the center of the room. Artist turns to face the audience.*]

The visitor looked away from that painting and looked at me curiously as if trying to work out what sort of person would paint something like that.

I explained that the title of the painting is *What's Eating You?* and is one of a series I have created to show what it's like to be a health worker in Vanuatu.

[*Pause*]

Looking at the Green Monster about to eat someone, the visitor wondered if it meant the person was being consumed by jealousy. Or was jealousy only a green-eyed monster?

[*Pause*]

The visitor said it didn't really have the feel of a threatening monster as the teeth weren't jagged and pointed, and it wasn't drooling, or frothing at the mouth.

[*Artist turns toward the painting and points to the teeth in the painting. Artist turns back to face the audience.*]

I could see what the visitor meant, but the size and color of it I found revolting. Here, green seemed the color of greed, or of parasitic, life-sucking mold, not natural, grassy fields. And the grip of the bony, green hand on the sandwiched person frightened me.

[*Pause*]

The visitor commented that eating the person in the sandwich appeared to be a perfectly normal action for the monster. A perfectly normal action! I said that I found it scary that the green monster didn't appear to see what it was feeding on. After all, its features were more human than monster. Didn't that imply it should recognize those similarities, and not prey upon its own?

The visitor suggested that maybe it just hadn't looked . . .

[*Artist covers her eyes.*]

. . . Or maybe the bigger creature chose not to see the smaller creature.

[*Artist drops her hand quickly to her side.*]

Either way it didn't seem fair.

[*Pause*]

The visitor said with a sigh, "I have felt like that—at work. Every day big companies devour little companies . . ."

I was surprised that this painting, dealing with my experience of cross-cultural health work, had stirred up in the visitor feelings similar to mine, even though my visitor's feelings had been evoked by very different experience.

[*Pause*]

The serene look on the woman's face intrigued the visitor—the upturned eyes, almost looking heavenward. Dressed in the long robe, barefoot , and arms outstretched, she reminded my visitor of the way Christ is sometimes depicted.

I gasped. I had not consciously sought to portray that, although I did feel a sense of martyrdom at the time I painted her. It had felt as if she was the one making all the sacrifices for the cause. But wasn't that more feeling sorry for herself, than being Christ-like? I wondered, but did not say.

[*Pause*]

The visitor commented how the woman in the painting was focused on the task of juggling those balls. She kept doing it even in the *face* of danger, the visitor said, and reached out as if to touch each of the balls.

[*Artist also reaches out while speaking as if to touch each ball.*]

I knew that the woman juggled those balls, which I saw as her responsibilities, because they were all important parts of who she is, not just what she *does*.

[*Artist points to each ball, beginning at the bottom left of the painting and moving clockwise.*]

Mother with her children.

Researcher, writer at the computer.

Friend, Lover, wife.

Businesswoman with the Eye Bus.

Health worker with the ni-Vanuatu women.

[*Pause*]

I urged the visitor to look again at the balls. Were they not like bubbles about to burst, seeming to have a transparent glistening quality? How volatile were those bubbles?

[*Artist turns to face the painting,* What's Eating You?, *and looks at it a few moments. Artist turns to face audience.*]

Perhaps they look more like crystal balls—sort of glimpses into the past, present, and future life of the woman. What would happen if she dropped one?

Would her future fragment?

[*Pause*]

Yesterday, the visitor stood in front of this painting, willing me to tell a story of what the painting portrayed, of Vanuatu, of my research and of me. As I shared the story, the visitor became more than a spectator.

[*Artist turns to face painting,* What's Eating You? *Artist holds out her hand as if taking the hand of the visitor and steps toward the painting.*]

Together we stepped into the other's world. We heard and felt the struggle, related personal understanding to the one described and pictured, and were challenged to go out and do something about it.

[*Artist turns to face audience.*]

Oh, you'd like to hear my story too? Well, look deep into the painting and I'll begin. Then maybe you, like the visitor, will tell me yours?

[*Artist sits at the desk in the center of the room. Artist picks up the papers and reads.*]

What's Eating You? A Story of Turning Points

"What's eating you?" Stephen, my husband, asked as he placed his arms tenderly on my shoulders.

"I feel like the meat in a sandwich," I replied in a tone that indicated I was truly sorry for myself.

"Hope you've got sauce with it," he replied with a smile, trying to jolly me out of the mood.

I swung around to face him, eyes flashing with anger and hurt. "Just like you to say that. It's easy for you. You just go off to work, in your Eye Bus, doing one task at a time, having time to yourself in the evenings. I'm left here trying to write my thesis, juggle four kids going to basketball practices, music lessons, tenpin bowling, gymnastics, doing homework, mediating arguments, overseeing office work, fixing broken spectacles, keeping up with the housework, shopping, cooking meals, sorting out the stuff getting to Vanuatu . . ." I paused as I struggled to keep control of my emotions. ". . . And still try to be a loving wife." My voice trailed off as the tears began to flow out of the guilt I felt for venting my frustrations on an undeserving other. It seemed that I could often muster the energy to be polite to strangers and guests, but the family got the brunt of my frustrations and pent up anger.

"Charity begins at home." It didn't always in this house and that in turn contributed to guilt and anger that I directed inward toward myself and then outward toward those I loved. In the business of life it was easy to lose sight of priorities, to neglect the importance of stillness, to overlook the perfume of the roses, to forget to just be. Why was it that women in our society assumed so much? Seeking to juggle motherhood, career advances, body image—after all, we still want to resemble supermodels—and community involvement. Was it that we selfishly wanted it all? Perhaps it was something subtler; something that was infiltrating our home as it had our society.

Living in a world of juxtaposed images, news, sports, movies, sitcoms, medical dramas, commercial advertising, beamed in through television, radio, and the Net, we "saw" some people have it all in their virtual worlds. Was my life what it should be? How could I tell? I wondered if these virtual people became our measuring sticks. With less extended family interaction, and decreasing contact and support from neighbors in communities, were these virtual people becoming our neighbors? TV characters that we not only identified with, but also knew better than any real person. Especially on days like today I felt so tired of the effort involved in living. I wanted to enter an unreal world to escape the pressures of mine for a moment. I realized I resented the demands being made of me by my world, my family, and myself.

Stephen tightened his grip on my shoulders as my head fell back against his chest. "I'll get you a cup of coffee," he said gently.

As I watched him leave the room, I realized just how much my life course had been changed by marrying into optometry. I turned to look out the window. A car came to the edge of our drive, braked, slowly turned around and went back up the road. I live at the turning point. Here, the long, black snake of carefully planned, smooth road ends. The surface becomes rougher, gouged out, and distorted by the run-off from the "real" road. Where the dirt road leads cannot be seen. Cars stop and turn back. Yet, those who turn back never experience what lies beyond. They don't hear the kookaburra's laugh, see the intimacy of couples walking hand in hand, or watch the joy of a boy playing with his dog. But they don't get chips in their paintwork, dents in their bodywork, or clouded windows, either.

"Life is full of turning points. Points of time where we choose to go on or turn back," I wrote. My fingers moved automatically across the keys of my ergonomic keyboard. Deep in thought I did not hear Stephen return.

"My, my, we are philosophical." Stephen's voice startled me. Returning unnoticed, he had been reading over my shoulder. He placed the coffee mug on the desk next to me.

"Don't you ever feel like turning around and going back?" I asked.

"Sure I do," he said, as he sat on the edge of the bed across from my desk.

" I guess it's a good thing we can't go back in time, " I mumbled, cradling the warm mug in my hands. Visions of all the things I'd do differently, if only I could, flashed through my mind. For more than six years we had worked in partnership with the people of Vanuatu, in clinics, in schools, in workplaces. I had listened, suggested, acted, and learned with them. Still I questioned whether we were true partners. This was especially so on days like today, when I felt so alone, so pulled in all directions, so sandwiched between worlds.

"I've spent most of the day sending faxes back and forth, trying to find out how the Preventative Eye Care program is going, but nobody replied. It's so frustrating. Until I hear from them, I can't go on. I need their input. I'm hanging here in limbo. I feel like I'm not worth anything."

"Why would you think that?" Stephen asked, taken aback by my logic.

"Well, these people know us. We've been there many times. We've shown our commitment, our integrity. They wanted me to draw up the proposal. They chased me for it in the beginning. Now I need their help, I can't even get an answer. They must not value me at all," I replied.

Stephen waited, sensing there was more.

"Then I find the people I thought were having a hand in supporting me are really just manipulating me. They saw me coming and gobbled me up." I paused and was grateful for the coffee as an excuse to swallow hard, before going on. "I guess I can't blame them. It's my fault. I should have seen that we are imposing something from our culture that they just don't want. I've wasted years of precious time and money. Risked our lives, all for nothing." The tears began to flow again.

Stephen moved over to my chair by the computer and drew my head gently against him. "You know that's not true. And you know you're not the only one who has this trouble. It isn't personal. The surgical eye team had the same trouble. Remember?" He was looking directly at me as I nodded my head.

"Maybe it isn't personal. Maybe it's racist! Maybe they just don't want to talk to White people," I spluttered back.

"So how do you account for them not getting back to their own people? The research coordinator never got a reply from the department when they applied for a person to assist you. And if you think back, there's plenty of examples we've come across."

I knew he was right, but it didn't change the way I felt.

The next day I wandered into the office adjoining our home. The phone rang and the receptionist answered it. "Hello, Optometrist. How may I help you?" She reached out and began looking through the patient record cards on the desk.

I picked up the bundle of mail alongside, and sorted through it. There was a blue envelope with a stamp depicting a large pink hibiscus, and bearing the word Vanuatu. My heart leapt. Sending letters was not easy from the islands. You had to have cash to purchase pens, paper, and stamps, and in a rural community, largely dependent on subsistence living, cash was sometimes hard to find. Periodically boats visited the island to purchase bags of copra, the flesh of the coconut, which people had cut, dried, and packed in hessian bags, but if the copra boat hadn't called for sometime, cash would be running low. Then, after writing the letter you needed to find someone traveling to a village that had a post office, and ask them to post the letter for you. That made letters like this very special.

I put the other mail to one side, carefully slit open the envelope and removed the thin blue sheets, and read:

> Dear Stephen, Karen and boys,
> Greetings in the name of our Lord Jesus Christ.
> Hello from Vanuatu. Concerning my family, everybody is well . . .

It was from one of the ni-Vanuatu eye health workers we had trained in a recent workshop and who had assisted in our clinics. How wonderful it was to hear from her!

> We are still working together with the aid post nurse. People came to the dispensary to have their eyes checked and bought some glasses from us.

Here was the encouragement I had been lacking yesterday, well, had been lacking for months. As I read about her efforts to use her new skills, I was encouraged by her ingenuity. Tapping into the existing health areas, although logical, was difficult to achieve because of all the government red tape. I knew that only too well. She had used her social networks and made a niche for herself.

I arranged with some people from up top to check their eyes.

I smiled as I read the words. Originally from "up top," from the mountains, but having married, she now lived in her husband's coastal village. I remembered how someone had told me that the coastal people thought the people from "up top" were not as smart as they were. The equivalent of "hillbillies" I guess. How wrong she was proving them to be. I read on.

And when I got to their villages, nobody waited.

So it wasn't just us. It happened to insiders as well. We had often traveled long distances and arrived at villages to find the people had not waited and had gone to their gardens. Sometimes we would wait while people made their way back down to the village. Often this waiting time became special, enabling us to *storian,* to discuss life with the people. Other times, we would just move on to the next village with a mixture of disappointment, anger, and resignation churning inside. I turned back to the letter again.

I'd like to learn a bit more to help my own people.

I knew the deep longing she was expressing. I had felt it many times and I wanted to be able to help her fulfill her desire to learn more. We had limited time for training people, as the demands for direct service were so great. And when we made time, trainees' attendance was hampered by social obligations, funerals, feasts, and weddings, or bad weather, which prevented travel or required cleanup time, or lack of finances, or myriad other reasons. For people to learn more, we needed a coordinated effort from the bureaucracies, that more often than not seemed to either run away from the challenge of, or place stumbling blocks in the path of, those training their own people.

This letter was a reminder that the people at grassroots level really felt the desire that many, though not all, of the bureaucracy seemed to have lost. I was sure that many of the bureaucrats also had felt this passion once. Why was it that now they had the power to bring about change, they appeared to have lost this passion? Did absolute power *really* corrupt absolutely? Or was it that they were now part of a system that belonged to a different culture, one so different, that it alienated them from their people's needs, or buried their passions deep in a mire of political intrigue and protocol? I looked back at the pale blue handwriting.

Remember I brought back lots of reading glasses and a few distance glasses and also a few sunglasses.

Yes. I remember. By the flickering light of the hurricane lantern, eyeglasses and sunglasses, left over after our last clinic, were transferred from our plastic containers into cardboard boxes, which were taped and tied closed, ready for the journey to her island. Education brochures were packed, and posters carefully rolled, so that she could distribute them. We had then walked along the wet, muddy, potholed street to a small restaurant, where we shared a meal together as a special treat. Saying good-bye was always an emotional time. Even now, recalling the parting from her brought a large lump to my throat and burning in my eyes. Not knowing when you would see each other again was not something you forgot.

The sunglasses are all gone. I could see that people now like the sunglasses. I want more sunglasses, if you send some, send plenty of sunglasses. I'm looking forward to hearing from you again. God bless you all,

Much love . . .

My vision blurred as I read the closing words of the letter. I wiped my eyes and read again:

People now like the sunglasses. . . . send plenty of sunglasses.

My heart was beating as fast as if I had just read that I had won the lottery. I wanted to run outside and shout it aloud so that it reverberated from the hilltop. This didn't just mean that people liked tinted glasses—it meant all our hard work was paying off, that there was hope that the number of eye injuries, sun-related diseases, and discomfort could be reduced. To me, it meant following our hearts and not turning back had led to something that was good.

Later that night, snuggled under our warm feather quilt in the deep comfort of an electrically heated waterbed, I thought of our friends in Vanuatu, in their homes built of cane and coconut leaves. Cotton blankets would cover them as they slept on thin foam mattresses, atop woven pandanas mats on crushed coral floors, and as the sea breeze blew in through the open windows.

"Stephen?"

"Hmm."

"Have you got any optometry books I could send to Vanuatu?"

He mumbled and pulled the quilt up higher.

I knew that reading wasn't the *kastom* (traditional) way of learning in Vanuatu. To learn by example was preferable, but I couldn't be there. How could I get books and sunglasses over there? It was so expensive to mail heavy items. Shipping was risky. Things seemed to get lost or stolen if there was no one to collect them when they were off-loaded at the wharf. Airfreight, the most reliable method, was way outside my budget. I tossed and turned, unable to fall asleep. Finally, I snuck out of bed, pulled on my dressing gown, padded into the dining room, and began to write. It was a letter of encouragement, as much to me as to her.

> *I have arranged for some sunglasses to be sent up to you from Port Vila. They should arrive in the next couple of weeks. . . . I am really encouraged by what you are doing. . . . As soon as I know the date we are returning this year I will write you. . . . Give our love to your family.*

My eyes were heavy now, my mind more peaceful. The letter was finished. I folded the crisp, white paper and slid it in the envelope, addressed it, and propped it up on the table.

As I climbed back into bed, I heard a car coming down the road. As the tires crunched onto the gravel road, the sound of the engine dropped in pitch. I waited, hearing the soft ticking of the engine. Would they go on, or turn back? The tires squealed as the car went back up the street.

I closed my eyes and prayed: "Lord, maybe I don't know what lies ahead, and maybe I won't always have a safe, smooth road to travel, but may some of those bumps in the road serve to jolt me out of my normality, cause that rush of adrenaline, so that I am more alert and able to see, in a new way, the things around me. Thanks for the people who travel with me, for their encouragement and sharing. Thank You that I didn't turn back."

Juggling life's responsibilities, dreaming of possibilities and risking being gobbled up by jealousy, greed, and self-interest is part of the road traveled by a cross-cultural, eye health worker. It is a journey, that today at least, I feel glad I have chosen to take.

[*Artist folds the papers and places them on the desk. Artist walks slowly over to the painting* What's Eating You? *Artist turns slowly to look into it, then turns to face the audience.*]

And so now do you, like my visitor, know what's eating her?

What's eating me?

What's eating you?

[*Artist turns to face the painting,* What's Eating You? *The light on the painting gradually dims, leaving the room in darkness.*]

Note

Special thanks to Carolyn Ellis and Bob Smith for their careful reading and helpful comments on an earlier version of this chapter.

References

Ball, M. S., and G. W. Smith. 1992. *Analyzing Visual Data.* Qualitative Research Methods. Series 24. Thousand Oaks, Calif.: Sage.

Barone, T., and E. Eisner. 1997. "Arts-based educational research." In *Complementary Methods for Research in Education,* 2nd ed., ed. R. M. Jager (pp. 75–76). Washington, D.C: AMERA.

Bateson, G. 1997. "Afterward." In *About Bateson,* ed. J. Brookman (pp. 235–47). New York: Dutton.

Bochner, A. P., and C. Ellis. 1996a. "Taking Ethnography into the Twenty-First Century." *Journal of Contemporary Ethnography* 25(1): 3–5.

———. 1996b. "Talking over Ethnography." In *Composing Ethnography: Alternative Forms of Qualitative Writing,* ed. C. Ellis and A. P. Bochner (pp. 13–45). Walnut Creek, Calif.: AltaMira Press

Chambers, R. 1997. *Whose Reality Counts?: Putting the First Last.* London: Intermediate Technology Publications.

Chaplin, E. 1998. "Making Meanings in Art Worlds: A Sociological Account of the Career of John Constable and His Oeuvre, with Special Reference to 'The Cornfield' (Homage to Howard Becker)." In *Image Based Research*, ed. J. Prosser (pp. 284–306). London: Falmer Press.

Denzin, N. 1997. *Interpretive Ethnography: Ethnographic Practices for the 21st Century.* Thousand Oaks, Calif.: Sage.

———. 1999. " Performing Montana." In *Qualitative Sociology As Everyday Life*, ed. B. Glassner and R. Hertz (pp. 147–58). Thousand Oaks, Calif.: Sage.

Ellis, C. 1999. "Keynote Addresses from the First Annual Advances in Qualitative Methods Conference: Heartful Autoethnography." *Qualitative Health Research* 9(5): 669–83.

Fyfe, G., and J. Law. 1988. *Picturing Power: Visual Depiction and Social Relations.* London: Routledge

Harper, D. 1998. "An Argument for Visual Sociology." In *Image Based Research: A Sourcebook for Qualitative Researchers*, ed. J. Prosser (pp. 24–41). London: Falmer Press.

Manoa, P. 1995. "From Orality to Literacy and to Orality Again: A Story of Story." *Directions: Journal of Educational Studies*, special edition (November): 3–22.

O'Brien, T. 1991. *The Things They Carried.* Toronto: McClelland and Stewart

Reed-Danahay, D. 1997. *Auto/Ethnography: Rewriting the Self and the Social.* Oxford, U.K.: Berg.

Schwandt, T. A. 1999. "On Understanding Understanding." *Qualitative Inquiry* 5(4): 451–64.

Scott-Hoy, K. 1997. "Dialogue Not Monologue: Preventative Eye Care and Research in Vanuatu." *Pacific Health Dialog* 4(2): 138–45.

Sharf, B. F. 1995. "Poster Art As Women's Rhetoric: Raising Awareness about Breast Cancer." *Literature and Medicine* 14(1): 72–86.

Van Manen, M. 1997. *Researching Lived Experience: Human Science for and Action Sensitive Pedagogy*, 2nd ed. Ontario, Can.: Althouse Press.

Wolcott, H. 1995. *The Art of Fieldwork.* Walnut Creek, Calif.: AltaMira Press.

If the Color Changes

The Assault of Color

Glimpses of the Numinous

Visions of Home

Jesters and Heroes

The Visitor

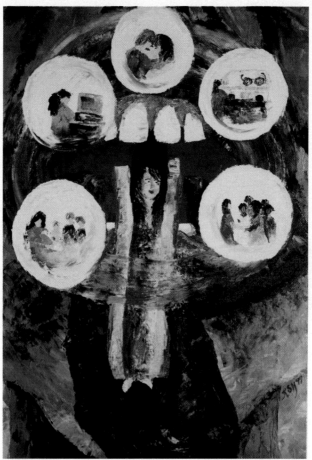

What's Eating You?

"If the Color Changes" (1996–1997)

Mel Bochner

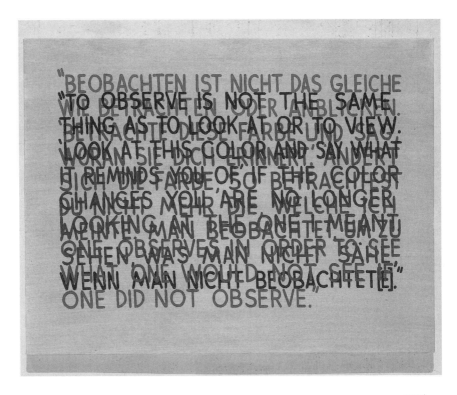

The Griot's Many Burdens—
Fiction's Many Truths

PAUL STOLLER

I magine three West Africans emerging from a Motel 6 near an exit on the Indiana Turnpike. Dressed in billowing robes, they are headed to Chicago. For them, any place outside of New York City is "the bush." Indiana, however, is considered "the deep bush."

"We go now," Dabé announced. "Before too long, you'll see Chicago, little brothers. Chicago. We should get there about 10 A.M. We'll go directly to the place."

"What place?" Nouhou asked.

"The convention center, south of what they call the 'Loop.'"

"The Loop?" Issa wondered. "Why would there be a loop in a city?"

"You'll see."

They headed west through a flat countryside of farms and small towns that eventually gave way to the urbanscape of Gary, Indiana: steel mills and chemical factories hugging the shore of Lake Michigan; warehouses with broken windows; trash-strewn streets clogged with dump trucks and tractor-trailers. To the west they saw the curve of Lake Michigan and the Chicago skyline.

"In the name of God," Issa cried. "It is beautiful, Dabé. What a beautiful city!"

"That is Chicago?" Nouhou asked with wonder.

"Yes," Dabé proclaimed.

Soon after they paid a toll at the entrance to the Chicago Skyway. They were driving high above an unimaginable tangle of railroad tracks, diesel engines, trucks, and barges. Several freighters had docked at industrial ports. Issa and Nouhou had seen bits and pieces of New York's factories, but they had never seen so much industry from so high a vantage.

"America has power. She is very, very rich," Nouhou proclaimed. "I have never seen such wealth."

"In God's name," Issa said, "how can there be so much?"

"Little brothers," Dabé said, "Chicago is different. Black people in Harlem don't have much money. Many Black people in Chicago do. They come to Black Expo and spend very much." Dabé pointed to the right, toward the looming Chicago skyline. "See the tall buildings?"

Issa and Nouhou nodded.

"That's the Loop."

"But I see no loop," Issa protested.

"Right," Dabé responded. "A train loops around those tall buildings. That's the real loop."

"America is a strange place," Nouhou said. "Loops, railroad cars, barges, factories."

Griots are West African bards who take on the social burden of words. Griots are the repositories of history and culture. Through their public performances, the recitation of noble genealogies and epic poems, they convey the lessons of culture from generation to generation. The burden of the griot is to talk social life (see Hale 1990, 1999; Stoller 1997).[1]

The apprenticeship of West African griots is long and arduous. Griots, who are usually patrilineal descendants of specific families, must study with masters for as long as thirty years before they are deemed ready to recite poetry, to talk social life. Early in their apprenticeships, Songhay griots, for example, must master a body of rudimentary knowledge—in their case, the words of Songhay history. But this knowledge is insufficient, for griots must also master themselves in order to embody the power of history. This means that they must learn to dispossess their "selves" from the "old words" they have learned. The words of history, they come to realize, are much too powerful to be "owned" by any one person or group of people; rather, they are possessed by the forces of the past. Put another way, griots don't "own" the "old words" they put to memory; the "old words" own them. By decentering themselves from "old words" and the forces of history, these griots are infused with great dignity; they are ready to impart sociocultural knowledge to the next generation (see Hampaté Ba 1981; Bird 1971; Stoller 1997)

In recent times, however, the categorization of the griot has changed. For several Songhay elders, ethnographers are griots who express social knowledge through the written word and the filmic image (Hale 1999). For many Songhay people, the French filmmaker Jean Rouch is a griot, for the images in his films, some of which are documentaries, some of which are films of fiction, enable the young to uncover their past and discover their future (see Stoller 1992). For the great Senegalese filmmaker and novelist Sembène Ousmane, West African novelists and filmmakers have become an increasingly important kind of contemporary griot. Their burden, like the burden of their forebears, is both to create images that express the social tensions of contemporary social life and to impart treasured cultural knowledge to the next generation.

Words and images, then, are considered precious resources in many African societies (see Chernoff 1979; Stoller 1989b, 1997). In July 1977, when, after a year's residence, it was time for me to leave the Songhay village of Mehanna, an elder said to me, "*Ni go g'iri fagaandi*," which literally means, "You will bring boredom to us." The elder's statement, which is the way Songhay people typically say farewell, implies that he would miss my talk. Among most Songhay, silence is equated to the absence of social contact, which, in turn, triggers a state of social boredom. Talk is a primary foundation of the social personality among the Songhay people of the Republic of Niger. It is more through external expression than internal monologue that a person constructs the composite of his or her social self. It is through external expression that lessons are learned, that history is told, that change is understood. For most Songhay people and many other Africans, spoken words are sacred and stories are treasured. This lesson is evident in the works of such celebrated African writers as Chinua Achebe, Amos Tutuola, and Ngugi Wa Thiong'o, whose novels feature more external talk than internal monologue.

In this chapter I discuss how my implication in things African has compelled me not only to write ethnographic works that feature narratives and dialogue, but also, most recently, a novel, a contemporary form of griotic expression. In that novel, *Jaguar: A Story of Africans in America* (1999), I employ both external dialogue and internal monologue to explore the tribulations of contemporary African men and women who struggle with issues of desire, regret, familial obligation, and social dislocation—subjects well suited to fiction. In the end I suggest that the greatest literary burden for contemporary griots—novelists, filmmakers, musicians, and, periodically, anthropologists—is to articulate the truths of fiction in imaginative stories that, to borrow from Chinua Achebe, begin as adventures in self-discovery and "end in wisdom and human conscience" (1989: 8).

What, then, is the burden of the anthropologist/griot? For me, the use of narrative and dialogue has been an attempt to maintain representational fidelity to African ways of talking social life—the charge, as it were, of the griot. By the same token, I have attempted to maintain representational fidelity to anthropological ways of writing social life. This means that narrative has been juxtaposed with or embedded in theoretical ruminations and social analysis in my ethnographic works (see Stoller 1989a, 1989b, 1992, 1995, 1997). And yet, the constraints of ethnographic writing, I have discovered, can sometimes muffle the drama of social life as it is lived. This tendency pulls the reader away from the excitement and trauma of lived reality and limits the depths of characterization. And so in telling the story of *Jaguar,* I wanted to write a text in which the drama of social life was presented in the foreground, in which the personalities of the characters were developed both through inner reflection and outward expression—in words and action. These expressive goals are best achieved through fiction.

Jaguar is the story of Issa Boureima, a young, hip African street vendor who sells knock-off designer bags and hats in an open-air street market on 125th Street in Harlem. Faced with economic hardship in West Africa, Issa left his home in Niger and his new wife, Khadija, to seek his fortune in the United States. Devout Muslims, the couple has entered a "modern" marriage: Khadija is permitted to run her own business, and Issa has agreed not to take additional wives. Issa quickly adapts to his new surroundings, however, and soon attracts several girlfriends. Aided by a network of immigrants, he easily slips through the gaps in the "system" and extends his stay in the United States indefinitely. Following a circuit of African American cultural festivals across the United States, he marvels at African Americans' attitudes toward Africa and wonders if he'll ever return to Niger. Meanwhile, Khadija also struggles to make it—to become a "Jaguar, a savvy entrepreneur"—as she combats loneliness, hostile in-laws, and a traditional male-dominated society. The eventual success of her dry goods shop and her growing affection for a helpful Arab merchant make her wonder if she'll ever join Issa in the United States. In Jaguar, the characters continuously confront the human costs of transnationalism. They know little about the wired dynamics of the global economy, but every day they must confront and adapt to the forces that it unleashes.

On 125th Street in Harlem, Issa and his compatriots use talk to recreate the comforting character of an African market.

Issa walked over to some older men from Niger. For them, the passage of time may have tarnished the sleek image that the younger Jaguars cultivate, but it hadn't diminished their energetic resourcefulness. One of them, Daouda, had made his pilgrimage to Mecca more than fifteen years before his arrival in New York City. Out of respect, the Jaguars called him El Hadj, the traditional title for one who had made that journey. Since his arrival, Daouda's waist has steadily expanded as his hairline has relentlessly receded. El Hadj sold sunglasses. "Thank God for summer sunshine," he would often say.

Issa greeted El Hadj. "El Hadj," he said, pointing at the older man's belly, "you seem to be eating well lately?"

"How can I eat well, young brother, without a good woman from Niger to make the good sauces."

"Then why do you look so well fed?" Issa asked.

"Burger King and McDonald's."

Issa nodded with complete understanding.

"Big Macs and Whoppers." El Hadj patted his substantial belly. "If you eat enough of that, your stomach fills up, and you forget for a while about peanut sauce and millet porridge. You forget about the good women who prepare those things. But only for a little while." El Hadj laughed. "One day I'll be back with my two wives in my village, if God wills it. How is the market for you today?" El Hadj asked Issa.

"So far, very good for a weekday. And for you?"

"Not so good today. I need to learn more English so I can work better."

Issa had already learned enough colloquial English to get along quite well in Harlem and other parts of New York. "You should study somewhere," he suggested.

"Where?" El Hadj asked.

"Ask around. Someone will know."

"But you need papers to study English, do you not?"

"Not always," Issa answered. "I'll try to find something for you."

"If my English were better, I'd do more business. Maybe I'd be able to go home sooner. If I had good English, I'd get papers and go and find some work in the bush."

"Where in the bush is there work?" Issa asked, always seeking new information that might lead to better opportunities.

"They say there is work in Greensboro, North Carolina, a place where there are many fine bushwomen—clean women—who seek African men for sex."

"In God's name," said Issa, "North Carolina is the deep bush, but there can be no such women there."

El Hadj Daouda laughed but disagreed. "Everybody says: deep bush, good work, good women." For some reason, El Hadj talked incessantly about sex in West Africa and New York—and Greensboro, North Carolina! Besides sunglasses, he also sold pirated videos, maintaining a small table of such cassettes throughout the busy summer months.

Indulging in his favorite pastime, making more conversation, Issa asked El Hadj where he got his videos.

El Hadj scratched his head. "I'm trying to remember the word in English." He scratched his chin. "It bothers me," he said, "that I don't remember exactly. Too many days exposed to the hot sun and dirty air." He looked skyward. "Ah. I remember now. I get them from what they call Mafia. As long as there are no busts, I have an unlimited supply—very cheap. No problem," he said in English.

In Niger, Khadija's illusion of harmony and respect—values of the past—is shattered by gun-wielding teenage soldiers.

The entire cargo of the Mille Kilo (a bus) lay spread out on the ground. More gun-wielding teenagers rifled through every suitcase, opening every box, package, or container—no matter how small. One of them grimaced as he opened a jar of cold cream and tasted it. Another rushed off to the hut, carrying a small cloth satchel. "Drugs! I found drugs!" he cried excitedly. He emerged a few moments later, dejected, and walked back to the inspection. In his eagerness he had mistaken medicinal tree bark for controlled substances and had been scolded by the sergeant. Knowing that the inspection would take much longer, Khadija sat next to an old man under a tree. A young girl, carrying a tray of cooked greens stuffed with peanut paste, approached them.

"Leaves. Cooked leaves."

"How much?" Khadija asked.

"Ten francs each."

Khadija bought six of them and offered three to the old man next to her. He was slight, and his bearded face has been creased by a lifetime of farming millet under the hot sun. He wore a turban around his cap. A dusty, long, white billowing robe covered his dirty drawstring pants. "I give thanks, my child."

"God is strong," Khadija said.

"God is strong," the old man agreed," but sometimes I wonder why we mortals have to suffer so much."

"What do you mean, Baba?" Khadija asked, addressing the old man as "Father" out of respect for his advanced age.

"Look at the way the owners of power treat us. They prevent us from traveling. They look through our things. They treat us contemptuously."

"It is difficult," Khadija acknowledged. "But it seems much worse now. When I was a child people treated one another with more respect."

"Do you think so, daughter?"

"Yes, I do."

"I'm not so sure. Old men like me like to say that if we adhered to our Songhay traditions, life would again be sweet. In truth, my daughter, the peasant's life has always been hard. It was no different in the time of my grandfather. The only difference has been in who rules us. In the old times, it was the kings of Songhay who pummeled us. Yesterday, the French broke our backs. And now it's the iron-fisted soldiers and rich merchants who steal from us and make us suffer."

"It is sad that you feel that way."

"How else can I feel? I am a simple old man. I wanted to travel to Niamey today, and some young boy with a gun insults me. They throw my things on the ground and soil my clothes. Is this the way to treat an elder?"

"No, it is not."

"As our ancestors said: Our only strength is patience. Patience is the world."

In Niger, Issa never experienced racism, but does so regularly in the New York subway. He is both troubled and amused by the way that White and Black Americans categorize him.

Issa entered an uptown subway. As he settled down next to a young White woman, her body visibly stiffened. She arched her shoulders and shifted her handbag away from him. When Issa glanced at her, her face froze into a pale mask with pursed lips. Why do so many White people think that all young Black men are criminals, Issa wondered. Racism in the United States presented a dilemma for him. If White people knew that he was an African, and a French-speaking businessman, it might be different. But people, he concluded, are locked into stereotypes. At 72nd Street, the White woman hurriedly gathered her things and left. At 110th Street, an old Black man sat next to Issa and looked him over.

"You're one of those African brothers, aren't you?"

"Yes, sir," Issa said respectfully.

"Where you goin'?"

"125th Street."

"Me too."

The incident amused Issa. Most White people lumped him in the category of "young Black man." Most Black people lumped him in the category of "the African," thinking him incomprehensibly exotic.

"Do you sell up there?"

"Yes, sir."

The screech of the train's brakes ended the conversation. Issa helped the old man to his feet.

"Thank you, son."

At a rest stop on the Indiana Turnpike deep in what West Africans call the American bush, Issa reflects on his invisibility in the United States.

Americans never ceased to amaze Issa. How many times had he seen parents coaxing their children to finish their meals. More often than not the parents failed, and a large amount of food had to be thrown away. In Niger, children often went hungry and so ate every scrap of food offered to them.

Families streamed by Issa's table headed for a meal at Pizza Hut or Roy Rogers. Dabé had gone to use the telephone and had left Issa alone with his Coke and half-eaten Roy Rogers hamburger. Issa didn't like the hamburger but was determined to finish it—as a matter of principle. A bee buzzed over the open lid of Issa's soda. He felt invisible, a common experience for him in the United States.

Issa and Dabé had been on the road for more than two weeks and now were finally returning to New York, their van empty, their pockets bulging with cash. As a traveling Jaguar, Issa had made more money than he could have ever imagined. He had been able to send lots of it to his family in Tarma, who, he had heard, sang his praises in the streets of the village. They said that Issa was a great Jaguar who had explored the farthest reaches of the American bush. They said that he owned large cars and big houses. They've said many things, Issa thought to himself, sighing quietly.

Issa might have conquered the American bush, but he felt somewhat deflated by his success. He spent more time on the road than in Harlem, and he missed his friends. Although Issa was always surrounded by people—the crowds at convention centers, outdoor festivals, hotel lobbies, and highway rest stops—he felt increasingly alone. Having no kin in the United States, he missed his family in Niger. Alone at night in some highway hotel room, his thoughts drifted to Khadija. He would see her face and imagine her, with no small measure of pride, tending her shop. During such moments, he longed to smell the aroma of roasting mutton, to taste the zest of Tarma sauces, to listen to old men's evening stories, to breathe the air of his homeland. And yet, he realized that if he settled in Tarma, life would quickly bore him. Young Jaguars like him, he told himself, need change, challenge, and adventure.

Out of the corner of his eye he saw Dabé slowly walking toward him and wondered if he would ever return home. Sometimes it's hard, Issa said to himself, to be an African in America.

As I see it, the truth of fiction, to borrow once again from Chinua Achebe (1989), is a powerful way of bringing into relief the multiple realities of contemporary social worlds. A famous Songhay healer, the late Adamu Jenitongo, once told me: "Never forget that there are many paths that lead to illumination." Having written *Jaguar*, I realize now, as perhaps you do as well, dear reader, that there are many expressive paths that lead to ethnographic illumination.

Notes

This essay could not have been written without the generous support of many institutions and the critical insights of many friends and colleagues. Field research in New York has been funded by the National Science Foundation's Law and Social Behavior Program (1994–1998) as well as by the National Science Foundation's Cultural Anthropology Program (1999–2001). Fieldwork in Niger has been funded by the Fulbright-Hays Program (1976–1977), the Wenner-Gren Foundation (1976–1977, 1984), the National Science Foundation, a NATO Postdoctoral Fellowship (1979–1980), an NEH Fellowship (1989–1990), and West Chester University's Faculty Development Fund (1981, 1982, 1984). Funds from the National Endowment for the Humanities (1992–1993) and the John Simon Guggenheim

Foundation (1994) freed me from teaching responsibilities, affording me time for reflection and writing. The critical comments and sage advice of friends and colleagues have improved the quality of my essays, including this one, and books. I especially thank Jasmin Tahmaseb McConatha, T. David Brent, John Chernoff, Alma Gottlieb, Philip Graham, John Homiak, Patricia Smith, David Napier, Kirin Narayan, and Jean-Paul Dumont for their efforts on my behalf. This chapter features narratives adapted from my recently published novel, *Jaguar: A Story of Africans in America* (1999).

1. There is much confusion over the origin of the word "griot" (see Hale 1999). No matter the origin or use of the word, the griot plays an increasingly important role in West African societies, especially in those groups that comprise Sahelian West Africa. Throughout the Sahel, griots are seen as masters of the word. This means more than that they are poets or the people who transmit culture from generation to generation; it also means that they possess *nyama*, which has several definitions. Sory Camara (1976: 11) translates it as "all powerful spirit." Among Mande-speaking peoples of Mali and Senegal and among the Songhay of Mali and Niger, some words possess *nyama*, a force that can be manipulated only by those who are heirs to its dangerous force.

References

Achebe, Chinua. 1989. *Hopes and Impediments: Selected Essays.* New York: Doubleday.
Bird, Charles. 1971. "Oral Art in Mande." In *Papers on the Mandigne,* ed. Carleton C. Hodge (pp. 15–27). Bloomington: Indiana University Press.
Camara, Sory. 1976. *Gens de la Parole: Essai Sur la Condition et le Role des Griots Dans la Societe Malinke.* Paris: Mouton.
Chernoff, John Miller. 1979. *African Rhythm and African Sensibility.* Chicago: University of Chicago Press.
Hale, Thomas. 1990. *Scribe, Griot and Novelist: Narrative Interpreters of the Songhay Empire.* Gainesville: University of Florida Press.
———. 1999. *Griots and Griottes: Masters of Words and Narratives.* Bloomington: Indiana University Press.
Hampaté Ba, Amadou. 1981. "The Living Tradition. Methodology and African Prehistory." In *General History of Africa,* vol. 1, ed. Joseph Ki-Zerbo (pp. 166–206). Paris: UNESCO.

Stoller, Paul. 1989a. *Fusion of the Worlds*. Chicago: University of Chicago Press.

———. 1989b. *The Taste of Ethnographic Things: The Senses in Anthropology*. Philadelphia: University of Pennsylvania Press.

———. 1992. *The Cinematic Griot: The Ethnography of Jean Rouch*. Chicago: University of Chicago Press.

———. 1995. *Embodying Colonial Memories*. New York; Routledge.

———. 1997. *Sensuous Scholarship*. Philadelphia: University of Pennsylvania Press.

———. 1999. *Jaguar: A Story of Africans in America*. Chicago: University of Chicago Press.

Beirut Letters ·

LAUREL RICHARDSON AND ERNEST LOCKRIDGE

The Letters: September 15, 1999

Ernest's Letter

S eptember 15, 1999

Dear Sister and Brethren,

Returned safely—alleluia!—a couple of weeks ago from the sun-drenched oven of Beirut. I'd have written sooner, but promptly came down with a respiratory infection, which by all odds should have been some exotic Med-bred bug, but more likely derived from the steam room of my local health club where I deposited my carcass the day after arriving home to bake out the humours of foreign travel.

Our beautiful Helen is now married to that exceedingly handsome Phoenician, Jean-Paul, whom she met in Mali, West Africa, whilst she was in the Peace Corps and Jean-Paul was operating the colonial wing of the family empire. Jean-Paul's family, the Fayeds, and their circle of Lebanese Christians identify themselves as "Phoenicians" to further distinguish themselves from the bomb-happy Hezbollah and the Palestinians. My exotic new in-laws are bosom friends of the Christian family that once ruled Lebanon somewhat in the manner of Draco, said friendship having, during Lebanon's civil war, drawn a rain of cannon and mortar upon the Fayed's reinforced concrete villa cum bunker and upon their charming suburb north of Beirut where my youngest daughter's 60,000-smacker wedding took place.

These staggering spondulics are only my "guesstimate," mind you, and savvy wife Laurel's, based upon extensive experience with wedding expenses in this country, and do not include the "Bejeweling Ceremony," minutes prior to the marriage ceremony, when the groom's family bedecked my daughter in Wampum—veritable ropes of pearls—sufficient to purchase numerous miserable old Manhattans (the Island). All of which reduced my own measly contribution—the 3500 simoleon wedding dress, personal clothing, and travel expenses, numerous miscellaneous expenses too numerous to enumerate—to a piffling trifle. Following a lavish cathedral wedding hallowed by the participation of a full half-dozen Marianite priests, we attend the lavish reception on the shores of the Mediterranean, vintage champagne effervescing in the hot twilight, banquet table groaning with earthly delights. Atop Grand Tetons of rice on three massive oval platters repose in crumbling languor a goat, a sheep, a shoat. We eat, we drink, we gyrate. Festivities wind down with the release of white doves, then nonlethal fireworks whose reflections bedazzle even the wrinkled old face of the wine-dark sea.

I did treat the bride and groom, my brand new in-laws and family members, the bride's sisters, my wife, my furious ex-wife to an arak-drenched lunch a couple of days later in the Druse-controlled mountains surrounding Beirut. In a castle. Or a palace. Whatever they call those elaborate Casbahs that once concealed the harem from the plebeian gaze, from desires more common to commoners than to Grand Emirs. Perhaps my American Express Corporate Card bill—I await its arrival with the purest of objective scientific curiosity—will inform me of the correct nomenclature. Ah, I have it! We lunched ourselves silly in the equivalent of a defunct Lebanese *Playboy* or *Hustler* mansion!

The Fayeds are immensely gracious and attractive, and as nice as anyone. Jean-Paul's father, Pierre, a handsome fellow, radiates bonhomie and robust good health, though due to countless bouts with sub-Saharan malaria his health is precarious. His sole functioning kidney was purchased from an East

Indian émigré whom Pierre is now supporting along with the man's family. Jean-Paul's mother and sisters are beautiful. Lebanese women, the well-to-do ones, are beautiful. Well-to-do Lebanese men are handsome and charming. Odd, isn't it, how attractiveness here goes hand in hand with prosperity. Beirut follows the shoreline like the endless scrolling of a Krazy Kat cartoon landscape. Reminders exist that this is a war zone—the bullet-pocked garden wall, the bomb-gutted apartment building, the disemboweled motion picture theater—but such touristic thrills are rare. Our drivers made no drive-by of the Beirut Power Plant, knocked out of commission by an Israeli air-strike a few days before our visit. Beirut is hot as hell or Waco. Jean-Paul drives us on a freeway devoid of lane-markers amidst a pack of hyperaggressive drivers violently jockeying bumper-to-bumper. Through this rampage Jean-Paul maneuvers his Mercedes calmly, effortlessly, perfectly attuned to the local rhythms. Men, women, and children rendered intrepid by poverty stand along this racecourse hawking the drooling carcasses—glisteningly denuded of their pelts—of goats, sheep, rabbits. Exotic items are for sale off road, in a hubbub of squalid pleasure domes whose marquees tease the Middle-Eastern tourist in strange syllables, a foreign language redolent of the snake, the Infidel. "Dallas!" sings their Siren song. "Vegas!" "Santa Fe!" The Saudi pilgrim to Beirut parks his wives at the Beirut Hilton then hastens the few short kilometers to this Beirut Mecca and here savors the rarest and most-prized fruits of the Great Satan, forbidden to the hometown boy back in his homely old Riyadh. Here at last his strenuous tongue is afforded unrestrained license to burst joy's grape against his palate fine. Alcohol! Prostitution!

Our own little pilgrimage was perhaps no more "interesting"—as the Chinese proverb has it—than it had to be. Even so, we are relieved to be back home in our charming, prosperous, and as yet unbombed suburb, Worthington, just north of Columbus, Ohio, where the Worthington police look out for our safety by routinely pulling over outsiders on suspicion of not being Worthington residents. In Lebanon, Syrian peacekeepers man the ubiquitous roadblocks, young men scanning Jean-Paul's new Mercedes with their ruthless, watchful eyes and cradling battered AK-47s, arms and the men giving every appearance of having been thoroughly battle tested—their presence no less reassuring, however, than the Columbus police, a rogue body that for years has brutalized and strip-searched the citizenry with impunity, official misbehavior so barbaric that even the U.S. Department of Justice has at last been forced into taking notice. All about

Beirut loom billboards portraying old Dr. Assad, Lebanon's current peace-bringer, eyes shrouded in black sunglasses, and from the thin black line of his mouth extrudes a word-balloon explaining in Arabic that "it is not Syria's will but Allah's that we are grinding your country beneath our boot heels and feeding the miserable remnants to our swine." The Syrian president appears ludicrously untutored in the debonair department, contrasting starkly with our own jolly madcap, Boy Clinton, that irrepressible rake who oozes charm through every pore as he rains ordnance upon Afghans, Iraqis, Sudanese, and Serbs. Lebanese natives, Christian and Muslim, are not much given to criticizing their Syrian liberators; open mouths have dissolved in night and fog. Still, I consider my lovely daughter safer in Beirut than in, say, Washington, D.C., where she resided prior to her apotheosis.

The newlyweds will reside in Mali for six months out of each year. Like the Hutu butchers of Rwanda against whom the United Nations failed to intervene because the United States virulently opposed any such intervention, the Taureg insurgents of Mali are creatures of French foreign policy. Fortunately Jean-Paul is well-armed, and the evening before we bid Beirut good-bye I issue a paternal directive. "Look, Helen, forget all the crap you may have heard regarding guns and just have Jean-Paul teach you how to shoot."

"Okay, Dad."

"Promise me!"

"I promise, Dad."

On the morning of our departure, Beirut International is so utterly clean, so given over to a Platonic Idea of Cleanliness, that it is devoid of toilet paper. Here, too, are the young, hard-eyed Syrian soldiers, one cadre after another scouring our passports to shake loose the flimsiest ink-fleck of evidence that we have once in our lives ever visited Zion, which would provide them with an excuse to detain us on the spot. The sole drama of this sort occurs on the second leg of our return from the Middle East, at London-Heathrow, where Western authorities search our luggage with a thoroughness I had hoped impossible, prying into all containers, twisting our prescriptions' adult-proof caps, unscrewing and squeezing our ointments, burrowing into zipper compartments, x-raying our bags when full and when depleted, a process so precise in its filtering and refiltering of our little cache of personal belongings that an earring from Laurel's favorite pair magically vanishes into thin air!

We are not x-rayed, nor are we probed in our persons, merely "patted down," although said "patting down" does occur twice: 1) whilst the polite and pleasant young English fellow, Colin by name, is ransacking all of our luggage, and 2) at the departure gate as a humorless brace of Continental airline thugs, Americans, further savage our meager carry-ons. So beaten down are we, however, so powerfully conditioned by decades of living beneath the iron claw of our own beloved government here in the West, that Laurel and I, docile fellow travelers, maintain a steady, purring drone of tameness for our would-be captors. All during their pillaging and pawing, we keep insisting aloud to our assailants and one another that, actually, we feel no outrage, no! We feel, well, *reassured* by these Byzantine precautions. And I must admit that our subsequent flight westward over the Atlantic does *not* explode—a la, say, TWA 800. Has the U.S. Navy taken the day off?

Airborne, I speculate aloud that the authorities mounted all this entertainment because my exotic, surly demeanor, plus the black scorpion tattoo upon my forehead, had succeeded in arousing their darkest suspicions. Laurel demurs, "It's that Lebanese stamp in our passports, Ernest."

We agree, however, upon the wisdom of postponing those side trips to Baghdad, Belfast, and Belgrade.

Thine,
Brother Ernest

Laurel's Letter

To: BFK123@aol.com
From: Richardson.9@osu.edu
Subject: Home Again
Date: September 15, 1999

Betty, Dear Friend—I'm home. Safe, but not sound. My body and soul have been traumatized by this trip. Something's seriously wrong with my shoulder. I can't raise my arm above my waist without excruciating pain. I've been at risk physically, interpersonally, militarily. The risks overlap and merge. Marginalized, stressed, dissed—so happy, so happy to be back home.

My shoulders were up to my ears for the weeks before we left. The massage therapist worked on my neck, but without much relief. The U.S.

prohibits direct flights to Lebanon so we had to change airlines—airports, too—in London.

I don't like flying, and there's so much of it; I get so tired, my body exhausted by time-zone changes—eight of them, each way—foreign waters, foreign foods. And the possibility of war, of course. That, too. The State Department has raised the travel-advisory level: "Don't go. The U.S. Embassy cannot protect you."

Most stressful though was knowing I would be immediately arrested in Beirut should the authorities discover I had been to Israel. I have a new passport, of course, without the Israeli stamp, but for all I know the Lebanese keep computer records of Israeli tourists. Maybe their computer knows I am a Jew; a Jewish child who had trees planted in Israel in her name; a Jewish adult whose support of Israeli independence is recorded in Tel Aviv.

My mind settles on Jewish friends who live daily with feelings of vulnerability. I remind myself that my name is "Richardson" and that I look like my gentile father. If the Lebanese authorities ask me, I'll have to deny my heritage. I'll have to lie. I shudder thinking about it, preparing for denial and deceit.

No one who isn't Jewish seems to understand what I am talking about, how unsettling this is for me. It is as if I am no longer "half-Jewish," but now "entirely Jewish," enduring the defining "Jewish experience" of being at risk because one is not a gentile. I think of my Jewish mother, whose witnessing of the pogroms led her to marry a gentile so that her children would never face *the* Jewish Experience.

So why *did* I go to Beirut? You know why. I assessed Ernest's needs as greater than my fears, and I love him. Before we left I was telling everyone that my daughter, Helen, was getting married in Beirut. I liked how exotic it sounded, how important I felt, and how rehearsing nonchalance lulled my fears. I think I had almost convinced myself that it was true—that my daughter was getting married.

Within minutes of us getting into her fiancé Jean-Paul's Mercedes 500 SEL at the Beirut airport, Helen said she wanted her "real" mother and dad to ride in the car with her to the wedding, walk her down the aisle, and for them to sit together during the ceremony. After a pause, she said those were the customs in Lebanon. In the rear view window, I saw Jean-Paul raise his eyebrows, swallow, and shake his head "no." Oh, I thought, this is familiar—Helen as conduit for her mother; Helen finding ways to protect her mother, lessen the turmoil.

Turning to look at me in the back seat, Helen said, "It's not that I don't want you here, Laurel."

I nearly choked on her words. Why would she even think to say she didn't want me here unless she didn't want me here?

"Laurel's been my wife for twenty years and she's not come half-way around the world at great personal, physical, and financial expense to be treated badly," Ernest said. The tension in the car was palpable. I almost cried. I had come to the wedding—not for Helen's sake, after all—but for Ernest's sake. You know how tense and awful everything gets when the girls are around their "real" mother; how Ernest never knows what will set things off; how he's viewed as an accessory, like a wallet, useful when full. Already, it was starting and my presence was the catalyst.

But the marginalization of Ernest was already in the scheme of things, I think, whether I was there or not. We were assigned a seventh-floor room; Ernest's children, grandchildren, and ex-wife 15th-floor rooms. Helen left us a bottle of drinking water and baklava, telling us to enjoy ourselves and she'd see us the next day. This was early afternoon.

Two hours after arrival—and after having our passports checked and rechecked by seven or eight guards, Lebanese and Syrian rifling through the pages, turning them on edge, looking for watermarks, erasures, anything out of the ordinary, I suppose, and me feeling more and more paranoid with each rifling—here we were on our own, hungry, in an Arabic speaking hotel on the Mediterranean in the Christian sector of north Beirut. Beastly temperature; marooned. Everyone else was at a party at the groom's house in a village forty minutes inland, a way up into the mountains.

We nearly missed the wedding. No driver came to take us to the village until late in the afternoon, barely in time to taste the sweets and witness the "bejeweling ceremony." Jean-Paul's parents, Marianite-Catholics, live in a stone fortress enfolding four sumptuous living rooms, five baths, a lookout tower, and a private well and generator, which they were using because the power had not yet been restored from the last Israeli bombing. Surrounding the house are acres of innocent looking flower beds; beyond them an electrified fence. Under the full width and breadth of the house is another house, their bomb-shelter, intended to protect them from Israelis, Syrians, and Moslem Lebanese. The people who were to be our protectors were themselves at risk.

Speaking French, Jean-Paul's father explained the Lebanese wedding customs to Ernest: the bride rides to the church with her father only; he gives her to the groom at the door of the church; the wedding couple walk down the aisle together. Would that be all right with Ernest? Of course, it was. And, of course, I felt vindicated.

Villagers lined the streets to see the bridal car, completely covered with flowers, and to get a glimpse of the bride, as if she were a royal, not merely marrying into wealth. Helen was beautiful, Jean-Paul handsome, and the cathedral wedding mass lovely and long. Six priests, three languages, flowers everywhere. The oldest priest told Jean-Paul to remain faithful to his wife and told Helen she couldn't get divorced. At the reception—Perrier water flowing like wine, food for the multitudes—a whole lamb, pig, goat, salmon, unnamed fish—a three-foot sword brandished by Jean-Paul to cut the ten-layer wedding cake, a pair of doves set free, and fifteen minutes of fireworks over the Mediterranean. After dancing with Helen, Jean-Paul's father asked me to dance and the band to play jazz in Ernest's honor.

If it weren't for Ernest's oldest daughter's insistence, though, that Helen phone us the next morning and my insistence that Ernest and I wanted to be included in whatever was happening, we would have missed the sightseeing; we would have been marooned in our hotel and missed seeing Lebanon. That was the plan. To appease Ernest's ex-wife we would be excluded from the post-wedding festivities.

The temperature was over 100, the humidity close to 100 percent. Our camera records the soppy air. In four air-conditioned Mercedes, the families drove north through Lebanon's porno district, where Saudi men frequent clubs with American names and symbols—Black Paradise, Las Vegas Babes, Girls-a-Go-Go, Dallas. Here they find proof that the American way is the way of the devil. Some of the men have brought their wives. They are sitting on hotel steps in purdah, bodies and heads covered in heavy, black wool garments. I catch one woman's eyes. I see pain. I no longer think the dress is simply custom; I feel its misogynist origins, its practice as abusive.

We stop at Biblos, the palimpsests of Phoenician, Roman, and crusader civilizations visible beneath the contemporary Lebanese culture. I remember my fourth-grade report on the library at Biblos, and the purple dyes and sailing ships of the Phoenicians, the ancestors of the Lebanese, and feel centered through this remembrance. I loved fourth grade and I loved purple cloth.

But then Syrian guards, young men with assault rifles, flanked by Russian tanks, stop us. Check us. What must it be like for Jean-Paul, a descendant of the powerful Phoenicians, to placate a Syrian plebe? Up into the mountains we go, up and up. The houses grow more grand. Syrian politicos have taken these houses as their own. More Syrian soldiers. More checking. I imagine how it would feel to be stopped by foreign soldiers in my own country; how worried I would be about my sons. Through Druse territory, past the Cedars of Lebanon, and finally to Mir Amine, once a sheik son's palace in Beit Edine and now a resort. Jean-Paul's parents seat us with the best view of the mountains, and they sit across from us. Ernest picks up the bill, gladly.

Everyone keeps asking me, isn't Lebanon beautiful? I lie and say "yes." But it looks scruffy to me, pale and unfinished, brown and coarse, like the dreariest parts of California.

A stop at the emir's palace to view the royal baths, swords, and footstools, and down we go southward following a back road. A Lebanese soldier carrying an American rifle sitting on an American tank recognizes Jean-Paul and waves us on. I think perhaps this is the very soldier that Jean-Paul's parents "bought" to fulfill the compulsory military service of Jean-Paul. We reach beyond the southern boundary of Beirut. More Syrian guards. My tension rises. We are in Hezbollah territory. We drive through Palestinian refugee encampments. The road is narrow and rough. People are driving too fast. Men try to sell us live chickens and live rabbits, and dead foxes and dead rabbits; gaunt children watch us pass by, uninterested. I see the awful displacement of the Palestinians—how they are not wanted by the Lebanese, Christian or Moslem, how they are pawns in others' political games. I feel Israel's complicity.

We drive into downtown Beirut, past bombed-out buildings, walls still studded with mortar shots and into the glare of Max and Erma's, McDonald's, T.G.I.F, Baskin/Robbins, Hard Rock Café. We could be anywhere. It was night. We were in Beirut.

But during all of this I kept saying to myself over and over again, "To think that we were going to be left out of this day! To think the plan was to exclude us!" I couldn't shake the outrage or the anger at myself for perseverating in my outrage, focusing on the insult, making that the emotional center of the outing.

I don't like being marginal anymore. I just don't like it.

I'm having nightmares, too. In them, I'm a passenger in a truck, rented car, or taxi. The vehicle breaks down in an uninhabited spot of land or, sometimes, on a highly congested road. I can't speak the language, I am in physical danger, and I can't decide whether to continue to my destination or turn around and head back. It is scary, this dream-text.

I am exhausted thinking about the contrasts—sea and mountains, rich and poor, Jewish and gentile, Christian and Moslem, mothers and stepmothers, lies and truths, American guns and Russian guns, now and then.

All of my academic theorizing about breaking down oppositions, deconstructing binaries doesn't help me now in any practical sense. Or has it? Has it already? Do I glimpse that the oppositional pairs upon which my language—my Self—is built—requires seeing differences within a vision of nondifference?

You can tell I'm home again—at home, again—using my life as entry to the realm of the untheorized.

Meanwhile, Helen will make her life in Lebanon, while I am only comfortable in the Lebanon of my past—my fourth-grade studies of Phoenicia.

My shoulder hurts. I can't type anymore.

Thanks for listening.

Love,
Laurel

The Conversation: October 15, 1999

Laurel: When I read your letter to your brothers and sister, I was struck by how different it was from my letter about the Beirut experience. I thought that the two letters offered a good example of how the ostensibly same experience is reconstructed differently through the process of writing, and that they along with a conversation about their construction would make a good presentation for the 1999 Couch-Stone conference. I'm not sure where the conversation will take us, but, here we are, conversing.

Ernest: I suppose that this letter that I've written can be seen as a little cantata—whistling in the dark a little cantata—because I am really very uneasy about where my daughter is and where she is going to be living. In a way, I think I was trying to—in a horsing around manner—to put the best face on it by implying that she is in no more danger in any absolute sense living in Beirut or Mali, West Africa, than she would be living in this country, and that the powers in these foreign countries are really no more evil than our own very evil powers-that-be here in this country. And—I'm not quite sure the extent to which I truly believe what I'm about to say—I don't know much about, for example, Dr. Assad, whether he eats sheep eyes like the Iraqi guy whom we supported for so long and then demonized during and ever since the Gulf War. But I do know an awful lot about Bill Clinton, and if you remove the checks and balances in this country and I was forced to make a choice between Dr. Assad and Bill Clinton, it would be a hard choice. [*Laughter*]

So, I think there are some truthful notes in this little song I've whistled, but I think the emotional energy beneath this is the energy that one musters to whistle in the dark when one is really very uneasy about something.

Laurel: It is interesting that you're talking about the fear you have regarding your daughter and your daughter's life, because that, of course, maps on to my mother's fear for my life as a Jewish child, and wanting me to avoid whatever might endanger me, and my coming to a total understanding of that—or as total as I have now, at least—based on putting myself at risk in a country that doesn't welcome Jews.

So as different as our texts are—totally different in terms of writing style, apparent language choices, strong male voice-soft female voice—however one might want to talk about the stylistic differences—what's driving both of them is the same emotional issue, the issue of safety of daughters.

Ernest: That's true. If Helen were Jewish, it would be really impossible for me to imagine that she could live either in Beirut or in Mali. Mali, of course, is a Muslim country, and I think I'd just be in constant terror for her safety, that she'd be found out, that something terrible would happen to her. It's sort of possible to think about her living there, in large part, casting it in your terms, I suppose because she is not Jewish.

Laurel: Another parallel in the letters is that each of us began with our bodies—with the discomforts in our bodies. Being back home is being back home in our bodies. Locating ourselves in our bodies. Of course my shoulder has not stopped hurting, and you've been off and on ill with respiratory infections since returning, so in some ways we're not yet "at home."

Ernest: I think that partly what we are doing here, both of us, is trying to write ourselves into mental and physical health. When I was writing this—and

by the way, this is not my usual narrative style, this horsing around here—
I put myself figuratively speaking on the couch and tried to think about,
analyze, even just purge some of the things that are still bothering me. In
your letter you write overtly about family problems which underlie my letter, but which my letter only implies. There are lots of very difficult emotions that went into the writing of both of these letters.

Laurel: Yes, when I started the letter I was furious. I was writing from anger,
which has subsided now. I wrote without self-censoring; I wrote to get to
my emotional state, to enlist the healing power of writing.

You know, I've always liked the epistolary form, but as we continue our
conversation, I find myself entranced with its power for poststructuralist
theorizing. In a letter, you get the sense of a particular person writing to
particular people; there is claim to authorship and authority—not over the
"facts" but over the emotional state of the writer. Because of the letter's conventions, the reader/listener knows that you are not trying to reconstruct a
travelogue or write an ethnographic report. If you're a little bitter, a little
exaggerated, so what. You're trying to convey to particular people the emotional experience, and the epistle is an excellent form for doing so.

Ernest: I agree with that. I'd add that my audience here are painfully aware of
most, if not all, of the important aspects of the personal problems under-
lying all of this. They did not come to this particular wedding, but they came
to the weddings of my other two daughters, and they are very aware—deeply
aware—of the long, painful, terrible family history from which these children
have successfully emerged, so there is no real necessity for me to lay any more
of that bare to them. They know about it, they don't want to *hear* it. And I
don't know whom I'd lay that bare to [*laughter*] in writing at this point in
my life. But that awful history underlies my letter.

Laurel: I truly believe that writing can be a method of discovery and therein lies
its pull for me. I have a hard time nowadays writing about that which I
already "know." I want writing to move me someplace new in terms of my
knowledge about myself, the world, or how things hang together. To sit at a
desk and to really be engaged in the process requires that I not know where
the writing it taking me. And I think you have the same sense.

Ernest: Oh, absolutely. I had no clear ideas about how I thought and felt about
this whole experience until I worked on this letter.

Laurel: I suppose it's this American individualism, or something, but I like saying
I did this myself. My truth was not constructed through my conversation with

someone else—a therapist say—but rather through my conversation with my multiple selves, my history, and so on. It's a very different sense of owning what I claim to feel and know—for me, it is anyway.

Yet, it is clear that you and I have been to Beirut, together. We went to the same places and saw the same things. We agree on the contours and general facts, as we always have throughout our marriage, even though you are a novelist and I'm an ethnographer. We rarely disagree but our perspective differs; we have different takes, different ways of claiming knowledge—

Ernest: —or what is important to us at a particular time, because it would never even occur to me to disagree with your feelings of vulnerability as you state them. I'm being hyperbolic in my letter. It's a mode I'm familiar with and a mode familiar to my brothers and sister and close friends and one I chose to adopt here. Your letter I don't see as being hyperbolic. The only example of hyperbole would be when you say that "no one understands" and what I think you mean is "I feel this very strongly." Of course, I was very aware of that and I was also a little paranoid because there were people who could have caused you a great deal of trouble . . . I didn't mention it . . . [*Laurel laughs uncomfortably*] There you are, you didn't even think about that until now and I was thinking about that the whole time. That with a little imagination someone could have caused us an enormous problem by leaking out the fact of your—

Laurel: No, I never even thought of that. . . . Hmm. Back to the present. During the process of preparing for the conference, we shared our letters back and forth, and each of us did some rewriting. The letters got enriched, not substantially changed in terms of style, form, or sense of audience, but in the concrete details. The process was very similar to the way focus groups work.

Ernest: I think that in my case what I chose to do once I read yours was to intensify the contrast between my take and yours, and so the final draft emphasizes a little more the parallels between being in the United States and being in Beirut. Paradoxically, it may be a good deal safer for us in Beirut than it is here. In Beirut your passport, the fact you are an American citizen, can give you, if not immunity, special consideration on the part of the authorities. They're at least going to think twice before they strip-search you, before they haul you in, before they shoot you through the head. That's not true in, say, Columbus, Ohio, where we can just imagine the special consideration our American citizenship will get us from our own vicious, rogue police force. And so I am not just putting this stuff in here to be literary. It's a way of refocusing on this country—and I say again our exceedingly evil powers-that-be.

Laurel: It's interesting how you've moved to the macro-level to look at the similarities between the political-military structures in different countries. . . .

Ernest: In these letters, I'm the sociologist—the political-scientist, and you're the novelist. [*Laurel laughs*] You're the novelist of manners and I'm the political-sociologist. We've done a little role swap. You're writing about the day-to-day details of the interpersonal situation and I'm giving a ho-ho-ho hyperbolic political science lecture.

Laurel: Yet in our conversation now you seem more emotionally accessible, whereas my focus has shifted somewhat to the macro level.

Ernest: Well, this has been an opportunity for each of us to address issues we may have de-emphasized in our letters, or left out altogether. Here we are rereversing ourselves back into our original roles, perhaps. How's that?

Laurel: It's true about what you're doing in your letter, but what I'm doing in mine is also sociology . . . definitely symbolic-interaction. Just as you're seeing the similarity of political life in Mali, Lebanon, and the United States, I'm seeing the similarities of life in terms of the emotional costs and emotional experiences of peoples such as the woman in purdah, the Palestinians, Jean-Paul, Jean-Paul's parents. Through linking of experiences, I'm broadening my abilities to recognize others that I think of as the "other" as not the "other." It does not surprise me, then, that I end my letter with a nod to poststructuralism—the other as myself that I come to understand through a vision of nondifference.

I'm doing a different kind of labor than you are, but I think the two letters are very complementary. Together they become a macro-micro analysis. Yet, they cannot be one paper. Which is back to a recurrent issue of mine: There is no way for us to write together.

Ernest: Yes, but we've done it and we're doing it right now.

Laurel: Only as dialogue.

Ernest: "Only" as dialogue?

Laurel: As two separate voices. There's no way to create one text in which both our voices are merged.

Ernest: But isn't that what we've been doing all along—here and elsewhere? In dialogue?

Laurel: Anything more you want to say?

Ernest: Yes, this. I certainly have a deep liking and respect for my son-in-law and his people, and deep sympathy for the situation they are in. I don't mean any of the little asides to be taken as flip, ironic judgments against them. I thought for a while whether I should mention the kidney or not, and then decided to do it. These people bring home to me how it must feel to live in an existential world close to the bone where one makes life-and-death decisions, but also where one is in a world where you have more choices regarding life-and-death decisions. Regarding buying a kidney from somebody—by the way, the person who sold his kidney was very poor and is no longer poor and he and his family are now being taken care of by my new in-laws, but if you were in a situation either to die or to purchase someone's kidney, what would you do? If you were in a situation where your choice was to let your child die, or purchase a kidney—a choice we don't have in this country—what would one do? I'm not making any flip judgments about people in this situation. And I really did give my daughter that advice, to learn to shoot, folks.

The Metaconversation: August 15, 2000

Laurel: Carolyn and Art have sent us a letter with some questions they'd like us to think about regarding our conversation. Should we have a conversation about our conversation? A metaconversation?

Ernest: Yes. Their questions look interesting. Let's see, first they want to know "whether the conversation was helpful, illuminating, difficult, therapeutic, or what."

Laurel: That's easy. I found our conversation both illuminating and helpful because of the interplay between the personal and the political.

Ernest: I thought it was fun. I enjoyed it. But illuminating, too. I can't quite recall the extent to which I was consciously aware while writing my letter what all was going on in my mind. For instance, I think I was aware of whistling in the dark, of a sort of manic defense regarding my daughter's safety, but I probably didn't get it fully under heel until our little conversation.

Laurel: I gasped when Ernest said that there was someone at the wedding, in our immediate circle, who might have it in for me. The structural possibility of the Lebanese government doing me in was all I had focused on—I had ignored the more immediate danger. So, I think we've had parallel illuminations. Macro issues have come home into our lives. The conversation was fun, too, but I'm not sure about therapeutic.

Ernest: I wouldn't call it therapeutic—unfortunately, because it didn't cost $125 an hour.

Laurel: [*Laughs*] Here's another question. Carolyn and Art want to know about the conversation as a "metaethnographic and relational strategy." Great! Indeed, the conversation is ethnographic and indeed it's relational. Ethnographically, I think there are methodological parallels to what ethnographic teams do—such as the Glaser and Strauss folks, who pass their notes back and forth to each other, and how a mentor works with a student, reading over field notes. And I think the conversation strengthened our relationship vis-à-vis the experience. Experiencing, writing, conversing, rewriting, conversing, writing. These activities strengthen our relationship because, although we agree on what we see, the actualities of what is going on, we have a different edge, a different take on the experience. "Validity" has a human face. The differences within the similarity make us interesting to each other.

Ernest: Different, but complementary. In some way, too, the same. But I agree with what you've just said. I just enjoyed talking about the letters, and I also took it on faith that having a conversation of this sort would somehow shoehorn reading a couple of personal letters into a scientific conference.

Laurel: Which leads to the next question—how our "different emotional style or form of writing" helped us "cope with our emotionality."

Ernest: These are wonderful questions, and I'm not sure that any further discussion on my part is going to do anything to narrow down or simplify, or make me any friends. I was writing after I'd become thoroughly distressed by Clinton. Not just his predatory sex life but, more seriously, his jaunty killing binges, deploying our latest technologies in pulverizing helpless foreigners to pull attention from his impeachment or merely Monica's pathetic little autobiography. Whatever the late Dr. Assad's flaws, people around the world could probably sleep unconcerned that he'd murder them in their beds as a distraction from some home-grown scandal. I remember thinking, while we were there in Lebanon, *Well, here's as good a place as any for Clinton to send a few cruise missiles—a helpless country, people who can't fight back, what could suit him better?* Fortunately for us, he was occupied at the time bombing the Serbs. So–"emotional style or form of writing"? Well, is it truly any exaggeration to inscribe a parity between our home-bred perils and those of Lebanon? Is Dr. Assad truly more dreadful and downright disgusting than our very own Boy Clinton? On further reflection, I'd call my letter's style, such as it is, "heightened," not "hyperbolic."

Laurel: In their letter Art and Carolyn write that, for them at least, the issue of your daughter's safety takes a "backseat" to your "alignment of life in the U.S. with life in Beirut and [your] anger about Clinton, the Columbus police and the 'iron claw' of our government."

Ernest: I know. That comment's precisely why I'm still nattering on about this stuff. To any reader of these letters—you don't know my daughter, you probably don't know me. Everyone, alas, knows all about Bill Clinton. I suppose it's almost inevitable that references to so public a figure are going to hog the front seat. Though in Clinton's case the backseat would be more appropriate. But I hope my letter embodies a more general sense of authority run amok. I've been aware of this phenomenon throughout most of my life, having come into an awareness of the world around me during World War II. Now, in my sixties, maybe I've simply had my fill, had it up to here so to speak. We're raised to believe that we're "better" here, that our leaders are "nicer," more moral and humane than, say, those sheep's-eye munching Middle-Eastern despots who devour their own people. But as we all know we've supported their regimes when it suited the needs of our "leaders," and the murderous regimes of plenty of other "monsters" about the world, too. Just look at, say, El Salvador and Guatemala. So in this sense I suppose Clinton's merely the latest in a parade of predatory creeps with way too much power. And maybe this sort of venting is therapeutic after all. And by the way, if any of this "alienates" anyone in my "audience," that's just tough.

Laurel: There is this question of audience—one of my favorite issues—and what we did to write for different audiences. The original audience for our letters was our family and our close friends. But when the letters were submitted to the conference, they were more artfully, carefully constructed. Stuff was taken out that was too revealing, and some explanatory and background stuff was put in. Taking audiences into account does not complicate the writing task. There is always rewriting. You're always writing for audiences, so you just think rhetorically. What does your audience need to know? It makes the writing interesting for me.

Ernest: If we had had this kind of conversation prior to our writing of the letters, it would have made writing them more difficult and probably the result would have been pretty wooden.

Laurel: That's a good point, because I think that we each used the letter as a way to come to terms with the experience, rather than talking it out with each other. So, looks like the writing was therapeutic for me, too, after all.

Ernest: We didn't write the letters in order to have a conversation about them or to present them to a conference. We wrote them to friends and family.

Laurel: But when I read them together I thought they, along with a conversation about our different takes on the experience, would make a good performance piece for the Couch-Stone conference.

Ernest: Originally we had thought about going out and experiencing something for the express purpose of writing about it—presumably writing differently, Laurel through the eyes of a "sociologist," and me through the eyes of a "novelist," and then analyzing the results to see how we did it differently. Then we realized that in fact we had already done the primary research. We'd already—if we were, say, geologists—collected the rock samples. So why not use *them*? And perhaps make the project smell less of the lamp?

Laurel: I think of what we're doing as "natural sociology"—a term my dissertation adviser, Edward Rose, coined in 1960. He'd be happy with this work of ours, and I like that here I am doing the unusual and at the same time honoring my sociological roots. That the two do not have to be antagonists.

Ernest: In the early '60s I was in graduate school at Yale, studying for my Ph.D. in English, immersed in "new criticism" but all the while champing at the bit to begin a career—not as a professor or "new critic"—but as a novelist.

Laurel: Now, I think we're getting to the unspoken conversation. I see it in Carolyn and Art's question as to whether this form of writing can achieve the goal of merging voices. Ernest, you said that that's what we have been doing all along. Although I didn't agree, I couldn't articulate why, and so let it go, thinking we were at an impasse. But hurrah! Now, I've had a revelation! If I were to adopt your point of view—that we are writing "together"—I would have to revise my deeply held and heretofore unconscious notion of what I think of as a text. You are accustomed to "writing-in-characters"—presenting characters and characters' points of view—and narrators, partial, omniscient or unreliable, even. So, as a novelist —I'm speaking for you now—

Ernest: That's okay.

Laurel: —you're used to having multiple voices in a text, each having different points of view, and these different from the narrator and possibly from you, the author. Although there might be "characters" in my texts—people I've interviewed or observed, they're always not me—always, not solely my constructions. And I would never willfully be an "unreliable narrator."

Ernest: Of course.

Laurel: You and I have different ways of knowing and of expressing what we know, different core sensibilities, so that although we can have one aesthetic, intellectual unity, our voices must remain separate, distinct.

Ernest: I couldn't have said it better.

Laurel: [*Laughter*] This is interesting.

Ernest: I don't think a single voice is necessary. I worry that you have some sort of romantic ideal.

Laurel: It may be some romantic ideal, but—get this!—it's a romantic idea about science and the single voice of science. [*Hearty laugh*] I may be exploring here the deepest level of my resistance to my own new ways of writing. It's the idea that we can tell "a" truth together. So it is not a romantic vision that we can be one unified and homogenized voice, but my romanticization of the scientific way of knowing. Wow! That's a wonderful insight for me.

Ernest: And a relief to me.

Laurel: [*Hearty laughter*] What, you don't want to be One?

Ernest: I know that one of the things that attracts me to writing, especially fiction, is the independence of it. It's a place . . . here is one place where, even given the, put it this way, the Iron Maiden of Language and Culture, one can experience, at least, the illusion of being independent and in control, and that's a tough one to feel you're under intimate pressure to relinquish.

Laurel: Whew! I think we're both feeling better about the cowriting because of this conversation. Unquestionably, Carolyn and Art's questions have brought us to a new understanding of our relationship to each other and to our work. I really like this. Thanks, Carolyn and Art.

Ernest: Yes, thanks.

Babaji and Me: Reflections on a Fictional Ethnography

MICHAEL V. ANGROSINO

Literary Ethnography: Background Issues

THIS CHAPTER is about my short story, "Babaji" (Angrosino 2000), which uses a literary form to depict the experience of doing fieldwork, and which has been published in a literary journal's special issue devoted to literary ethnography. My purpose here is to discuss a few matters relating to the emerging craft of literary ethnography in general, and to the writing of "Babaji" in particular.

The anthropological tradition of ethnographic writing has flowed in two parallel streams during the last several decades. The more prominent, to be sure, has carried putatively scientific (that is, objective and value-neutral) accounts of the people, activities, and events that make up what Sir Edward Tylor (1871: 1) long ago called "that complex whole" of culture. By contrast, the other is composed of material of a more subjective nature. This approach has been facilitated because the typical anthropological form of ethnographic research has long been one of participant-observation immersion over an extended period of time in an "exotic" setting. The intensely personal nature of such fieldwork tempts anthropologists to be relatively forthcoming about what their experience means to them as individuals, beyond what it may have yielded in terms of substantive data or theoretical constructs. There is thus ample precedent for anthropologists producing memoirs of their field experiences, and for doing so in styles that are more literary than expository (Tedlock 1991).

Nevertheless, as Margery Wolf (1992) has pointed out, it remains necessary for anthropologists to demonstrate that they are capable of producing standard scientific ethnographies before they can be indulged by the profession in their literary pursuits. Cultural anthropology has always been considered the "softest" (that is, the most humanistic) of the social sciences, and its practitioners have labored long and hard to achieve recognition as legitimate contributors to a rational, explanatory, predictive study of the human condition. The process of experimentation collectively labeled "alternative ethnography" (Banks and Banks 1998; Ellis and Bochner 1996; Richardson 2000; Tedlock 2000) has captured the imagination of ethnographers from sociology, communication, education, cultural studies, women's studies, ethnic studies, and others. This form has begun to make it acceptable even for insecure cultural anthropologists to affirm that their status as legitimate experts on culture is not necessarily compromised just because they write in an evocative and allusive style in which fully drawn characters (including that of the ethnographer) replace abstract "types" as representations of social reality. Indeed, social scientists in general (and not just the stigmatized and professionally marginalized "postmodernists" among them) have come to question the assumption of the fixed nature of sociocultural truth. The inherent ambiguity of motives and actions as demonstrated by the conflicts of fully drawn characters (as opposed to generic types) may therefore be seen as a better reflection of that shifting truth than the presumably bounded and quantified representations of traditional ethnography.

As an anthropologist, I continue to try to paddle in both streams of ethnographic writing, albeit with an increasing preference for fictionalized writing as a way to represent cultural reality in all its multiplex ambiguity. The fictional "alternative ethnography" with which I am perhaps most associated derives from my latter-day research among adults with mental retardation (Angrosino 1998). With the story "Babaji," however, I return to the scene of my first independent and "exotic" fieldwork, conducted three decades ago when I was doing research for my doctoral dissertation. This work dealt with the adaptations made by people from India who had been brought to the West Indies as indentured plantation labor in the nineteenth century following the emancipation of the slaves. The Indian community constitutes approximately 50 percent of the population of Trinidad, the site of my fieldwork. At the time of my fieldwork in the immediate postindependence period, the Indians were feeling threatened by the politically dominant African-derived Trinidadians (popularly referred to as "Creoles"). As a result, they were intent on asserting their traditional and distinctive culture against the temptations of creolization.

I have continued my personal and professional association with the Indian community in Trinidad, and have continued to write about the evolution of their culture (Angrosino 1975, 1976a, 1976b, 1976c, 1983, 1995, 1996). Only once before, however, in an essay titled "Son and Lover" (Angrosino 1986), did I use literary storytelling techniques to enhance my presentation. But in that case, the narrative was bracketed by sections heavy with scholarly citations and freighted with theoretical analysis. In "Babaji," by contrast, my explanations and interpretations are expressed obliquely, in the way the characters talk and interact; the people and their actions invite the reader's engagement and participation without a scientist's exposition to guide them.

From Traditional to Fictional/Alternative/ Interpretive Ethnography

What *do* I mean when I say that the story "Babaji" is fiction? Babaji was, indeed, a real person and, as the story says, the one who did the most to introduce me to the forms of Hinduism practiced in Trinidad. And I was, indeed, deeply affected by his death. But as a well-trained ethnographer of that era, I did not allow my personal emotions to surface in the dissertation. That document, which was subsequently published as *Outside Is Death* (Angrosino 1974), includes a dispassionate, objective account of a "typical Hindu funeral." The details in my mind were those of the rites held for Babaji, but the published account was meant to stand as a generic example of social process. It is altogether likely that as a callow stripling, I was not able to deal with the emotions stirred up by Babaji's death, and my way of coping was to find refuge in the objective practice of my professional craft. Now, after thirty years of coping with loss and regret, I am ready to return to that scene. I do not mean to suggest that I have reached a point of satisfactory resolution with regard to the death of a loved one—but I am ready to admit that my confused, and sometimes even downright silly and contradictory responses, are valid expressions of my state of mind and do not need to be submerged under a surface of calm professional control.

And so in my "fictional" story I revisit the account of Babaji's death and funeral, dealing more with my emotional response than with the traditional ethnographic particulars—even though all those particulars are present, albeit not set out in the dryly objective style of the depersonalized dissertation account. In any case, Babaji himself is more of a spiritual than an actual presence in the tale. The action turns on my reaction to Babaji's son, Romesh. My relationship with the real Romesh did not seem at all important at the time. But the character of this bond has come to seem so expressive of both the general condition of Indian culture in Trinidad and the anthropologists who study it and the particular emotional circumstances of Babaji's death, that I have taken the literary license of bringing it front and center. In the story, Romesh is depicted as a highly assimilated Indian who no longer lives in his father's rural village. He lives instead with his Christian wife in the wicked, cosmopolitan capital city, Port of Spain. I have fictionalized Romesh in the sense that he has become the mouthpiece for attitudes I detected among a number of other Indian intellectuals. For example, I attribute to him a diatribe in which the now world-famous Trinidad Indian author V. S. Naipaul is quoted (erroneously) as mocking the Indians' tendency to bask in the antique glories of their ancient culture.

That speech, including the incorrect citation (which I was gracious enough not to point out to the speaker), was actually part of a conversation I had with someone else on another occasion altogether. So Romesh became the repository of many of the qualities I disliked about other Indians who I believed had turned their backs on their own people. He therefore looms much larger, and plays a more decisive role in my retelling than was the case in real life. But a single representative figure is much easier to deal with in a short story than an entire cast of supporting characters.

In the story, the highlighting of Romesh's attitude allows me to depict myself by contrast. I come off as something of an arrogant prig, convinced that I was a far more faithful conservator of traditional Indian culture than Romesh was. I show myself as incensed that the villagers accepted his belated and rather perfunctory attendance at the various funerary rites as if they were genuine expressions of his cultural solidarity with them. I did not, I assure you, think of myself in that way thirty years ago—and there was certainly no single person in real life like the fictional Romesh against whom I could direct my self-righteous indignation. But that reconstruction allows me to get at what I think to be an essential paradoxical truth about anthropological fieldwork—we strive for a comprehensive understanding of the culture we are studying that far exceeds the knowledge of any one real-life member of that society (who, by necessity, is an expert on only his or her small part of the local universe), and yet we ache for acceptance by the people and shrink from any intimation that we are superior to them in the appreciation of their own life ways.

In the story, I come to a realization that both Romesh and I are taking positions that allow us to play on the supposed sympathies of the people we are trying to impress. But no matter how much we want to be part of the neatly defined little world of the village, we are, at best, interested visitors, inclined, as I say of myself, to see a paradise in other people's purgatory. We only become ourselves—and act out our real grief over Babaji's death—in the odd moments when we are no longer being observed. I end up feeling a kind of emotional kinship with Romesh, and begin referring to him as "Boysie," the affectionate nickname used by the villagers that, until that point, had grated on me because it conferred on this disdainful outsider an insider status that I coveted for myself. That change came about because we eventually resolved our conflicting emotions in essentially private, improvised acts. Thus did the professional observer learn a basic lesson in symbolic interaction: that he, too, had been observed, and had modified his own behavior so as to fit in with the expectations of the group. But my brief moment of off-stage epiphany, like that of Romesh, is quickly followed by a resumption of the center stage mask.

The Craft of Literary Ethnography: Some Reflections

And what of the mask I don to play literary ethnographer thirty years after the fact? I like to describe it in terms of the "seven loving lies" the poet Andrew Hudgins (1996) ascribes to all autobiographers. First, the story seeks narrative cogency, dispensing with unnecessary exposition, explanation, and qualifications. Of course, what is considered "unnecessary" is a decidedly subjective judgment; not only might my readers differ with my decision, but I might make different choices were I writing at different times in my own life. Nevertheless, the point remains that literature in one way or another seeks to shape and make coherent the usually ragged, messy stuff of real life. "Babaji" is thus a more linear tale than the real event; thirty years of reflection are compressed into a fortnight's action and the tale has a definite "three-act" structure, including something of a resolution.

Second, the story strives for texture, which is the degree to which a narrative resonates not only with readers' experience, but also within itself. One typical texturing device is the planting of a seemingly innocuous detail early in the narrative that turns out to have both narrative and emotional significance later on. The matter of Romesh's local nickname, Boysie, is such a texturing device. At the beginning, I am fairly sure that the reader will not pay attention to the fact that I refer to the character as "Romesh" even though everyone else calls him "Boysie." The emotional significance of the variation becomes clear only at the end, when I too refer to him as "Boysie" under circumstances that make it clear how and why my estimation of him had changed.

Third, the story operates on the basis of fictional convention. That is, story-telling norms take precedence over "real" development. One simple device I use in "Babaji" is the character of a taxi driver who is the main purveyor of gossip in the rural district where the action takes place. In real life, people tend to "hear things" in ways that they can't always pinpoint. But in a story, it helps to clarify how the elements of the narrative are acquired. A taxi driver, who by definition is someone in touch with many different people in a fairly wide territory, makes a useful figure whose presence helps explain why characters removed from one another seem to know what the others are up to.

Fourth, a piece of autobiographical literature is an act of emotional evasion, or, to put a more positive spin on it, of self re-creation. As noted above, I see myself in quite a different light now than I did at the time of the events described. I may, indeed, be overcompensating—more inclined to see my foolishness where once I was too much inclined to see my professional competence. But stressing my self-righteous blindness serves a narrative purpose—it clarifies the dilemma of the "natives" whose culture I am trying to depict—in a way that a more favorable self-image would not. But on the other hand, the writing and public presentation of the story is emotionally cathartic for me—it allows me to deal with several decades worth of accumulated guilt, and so my rather negative self-portrait is quite expressive of the persona I now adopt with regard to the events and people of those bygone days.

Autobiographical fiction operates in a context of extended consciousness, a kind of emotional foreshadowing: the narrator, in this case, knows at the beginning what he (I) could have known only at the end. The story begins on a note of rueful regret; indeed, the opening paragraph is written in a mock-Faulknerian style evocative of social and cultural loss and decay.

> I remember the hush of the tropical midafternoon in the days when it was still an interlude of dozing respite for those unreconciled to Trinidad's transformation from plantation to industrial culture—and for young anthropologists in thrall to the presumed mystique of the timestopped rhythms of the Caribbean sugar estates that made the village seem to be, for just an instant,

the one calm point in a heedlessly racketing world. It was at such a heat-heavy moment that Babaji the Nawh died. (Angrosino 2000: 28)

But as the events of the first part of the story unfold I had no reason to feel that way—it was only after the funeral rites described near the end of the story that I could have had reason to rue the situation of the Indians, set adrift as they were on the tides of the world system economy.

The storyteller makes use of interpretation—not in the explicit way of the expository science writer, but in a more metaphorical sense. The literary writer searches for "thematic order" rather than logical coherence as defined in technical circles. Thus the actions of all the main characters in the story—me, Romesh, his sister, the *pandit*—speak to the same issue: how we deal, in our various ways, with loss and regret. Incidents are therefore chosen for inclusion in the narrative to the extent that they reinforce that theme. A scene in which any one of the characters is seen acting in a carefree, giddy manner—which might actually have happened at some point or another during the long fortnight during which the story unfolds—would be thematically out of place.

Linked with interpretation is the tendency toward impression, the attempt to evoke feeling in addition to substantive information. My description of the village quoted above captures a tone of regret because I chose to describe it at a moment of stillness in the dead calm of the tropical afternoon—not at a time when everyone is out and bustling about. In a similar way, I describe the beach where the last part of the funeral ritual takes place, but not in terms of Caribbean tourist brochures. The main image of the beach is the presence of the scavenger birds—called *corbeaux* in Trinidad.

I was looking through my photo files recently when preparing for a class lecture, and saw that I had taken a picture of a spectacular sunset over that particular stretch of beach. The photo is beautiful, awash in a glowing lavender half-light. Of course, the beach itself is not visible in the picture, and my heart sank anew when I recalled how ugly it was—steaming beneath the mid-morning sun, the harsh cries of the *corbeaux* echoing across the scattered hillocks of fetid trash—on the day the mourning for Babaji was to be ended. (Angrosino 2000: 35)

And I include a description of the sugar cane harvest—not, strictly speaking, germane to the narrative, but evocative of the harsh life of the Indian peasantry.

The fields had been set afire to clear away the weeds and drive out the vermin in anticipation of the crews going out to cut the cane. The flames cast a lurid, pearlescent pink and orange glow over the nighttime sky. Wisps of charred vegetation fluttered in the breeze and settled on the yard in front of the house like a shiny black snowfall. I thought it was a moment of magical beauty, my aesthetic pleasure tempered somewhat by my realization of what it must be like to work in those burning fields. (Angrosino 2000: 31)

Nevertheless, although the story "fictionalizes" my experience, I firmly believe that it is the most truthful piece I have ever written about the Indian world of Trinidad, and about my role as an ethnographer therein. It is not, of course, for me to say whether I have adequately conveyed that truth through my writing, but I hope the story will at least be accepted in a spirit of reflective dialogue, and in the assumption that such a dialogue is at least as valid a way to deal with "that complex whole" of culture as are the more objective pronouncements of this particular participant observer.

References

Angrosino, Michael. 1974. *Outside Is Death: Alcoholism, Ideology, and Community Organization among the East Indians of Trinidad.* Winston-Salem, N.C.: Medical Behavioral Science Monograph Series.

———. 1975. "The Case of the Healthy Hindu." In *Symbol and Society,* ed. Carole Hill (pp. 44–57). Athens: University of Georgia Press.

———. 1976a. "The Indian Cinema in Trinidad." *Third World Review* 3: 36–50.

———. 1976b. "Sexual Politics in the Indian Family in Trinidad." *Caribbean Studies* 16: 44–66.

———. 1976c. "V. S. Naipaul and the Colonial Image." *Caribbean Quarterly* 22: 1–11.

———. 1983. "Religion Among Overseas Indians." In *Main Currents in Indian Sociology,* vol. 5, ed. Giri Raj Gupta (pp. 357–98). New York: Advent.

———. 1986. "Son and Lover: The Anthropologist As Non-Threatening Male." In *Self, Sex, and Gender in Cross-Cultural Field Work,* ed. Tony Whitehead and Mary Ellen Conaway (pp. 64–83). Urbana: University of Illinois Press.

———. 1995. "Metaphors of Ethnic Identity: Projective Life History Narratives of Trinidadians of Indian Descent." *Journal of Narrative and Life History* 5: 125–47.

———. 1996. "The Indo-Caribbeans: Evolution of a Group Identity." *Revista/Review Interamericana* 26: 67–108.

————. 1998. *Opportunity House: Ethnographic Stories of Mental Retardation.* Walnut Creek, Calif.: AltaMira.

————. 2000. "Babaji." *Green Mountains Review* 12: 28–38.

Banks, Anna, and Stephen P. Banks, eds. 1998. *Fiction and Social Research: By Ice or Fire.* Walnut Creek, Calif.: AltaMira.

Ellis, Carolyn, and Arthur Bochner, eds. 1996. *Composing Ethnography: Alternative Forms of Qualitative Writing.* Walnut Creek, Calif.: AltaMira.

Hudgins, Andrew. 1996. "An Autobiographer's Lies." *American Scholar* (Fall): 541–53.

Richardson, Laurel. 2000. "Writing: A Method of Inquiry." In *Handbook of Qualitative Research,* 2nd ed., ed. Norman K. Denzin and Yvonna S. Lincoln (pp. 923–48). Thousand Oaks, Calif.: Sage.

Tedlock, Barbara. 1991. "From Participant Observation to the Observation of Participation: The Emergence of Narrative Ethnography." *Journal of Anthropological Research* 47: 69–94.

————. 2000. "Ethnography and Ethnographic Representation." In *Handbook of Qualitative Research,* 2nd ed., ed. Norman K. Denzin and Yvonna S. Lincoln (pp. 455–86). Thousand Oaks, Calif.: Sage.

Tylor, Edward. 1871. *Primitive Culture.* New York: Harper.

Wolf, Margery. 1992. *A Thrice-Told Tale: Feminism, Postmodernism, and Ethnographic Responsibility.* Stanford, Calif.: Stanford University Press.

Men Kissing

Lisa M. Tillmann-Healy

MEN KISSING—it strikes me as wonderfully subversive. In the United States, we tolerate little boys who sloppily smooch their fathers and brothers, but when our little men reach a certain age, such displays induce a cultural squeamishness. Verbally and nonverbally, subtly and not so subtly, we send the message: "You shouldn't do that anymore—especially in public." Our little boys become adolescents whose physical contact we conspire to confine to fields, courts, and rinks. Many grow into men who keep other men at arm's length, communicating to the next generation of little boys, "Kissing me(n) is not appropriate; it's not masculine; it's not *right*."

Three years ago, I'd never seen men kissing—not even in a film. This weekend, I'm surrounded by male lips pecking, smacking, and lingering on Mayor Dick Greco (Ball Fields, that is, near the University of South Florida in Tampa).

Along with a smattering of women, more than 300 men come from places as distant as Toronto for the third Gasparilla Softball Classic. The atmosphere is much like a class reunion, only the males don't greet with stiff, distant handshakes. I watch as an Atlanta Heretic puckers for a Virginia Outlaw, and a Birmingham Cub plants one on a Fort Lauderdale Hot Spot.

Four softball fields occupy most of the terrain. Between them sits a sand-cushioned playground with a swing set and jungle gym. Atop the twist slide, the tongues of two Atlanta Trojans are engaged in an enthusiastic tango.

Players inhabit the eight concrete-block and metal-fencing dugouts as the stands fill with spectators, duffle bags, and jugs of Gatorade. Square and triangular banners in a variety of plaids and polka dots line the bleachers. Underneath, an Atlanta Thunder cups the unshaven face of a Cincinnati Comet, laying a smooch dead-on.

The Florida sun tries to warm this early February morning while a cool breeze teases the back of my neck, whipping and turning my pony-tailed hair. As I move toward the concession stand, little packs of silver-foiled Hershey's Kisses entice me, but I settle for a cup of coffee instead. Initially smitten by the robust, roasted scent, my nose crinkles when the bitterness of day-old espresso meets my mouth. Loading down the foam cup with Dixie sugar and Sam's Club faux creamer, I spot partners and Cove teammates Tim and Rob in line for the men's room. Lip-locked, they gently cradle each other's heads.

Nearby, the rest of our team stretch out. Scanning the group, I ask, "Where's Gordon?"

"State Fair," reminds my husband, Doug. I'd forgotten that Gordon's stuck all weekend at a promotion booth. His business partner thought they could scope out clients there; his teammates, however, find that notion ridiculous. Gordon, you see, sells hairpieces. What an image—our leftfielder peddling rugs amid the Zipper and Scrambler, livestock pageants, and fruit judging.

"Peanuts, popcorn, get your hair here!" quips Al, turning to steal a public kiss from the cheek of his lover, new both to him and to this gay community. Neil's cheek blushes when Al's lips take their leave.

Laughter, layers of it, can be heard all around—hooting, howling, snickering, snorting, giggling, and guffawing. Spontaneous laughter responds to a struggling player's surprisingly powerful line drive. Solicited laughter follows cheers of "2-4-6-8, do it like you masturbate. Whack it! Whack it! Whack it!" Despite the analogy's androcentrism, I smile, wondering how women can play softball "like we masturbate."

In addition to the sometimes-campy performances, other markers of gay culture appear. Someone hangs a large rainbow flag on the fence behind center field, and several vehicles parked in the lot display pink triangle decals and stickers. Community-identifying buttons, jewelry, and T-shirts also help transform this city park into a gay space, where men and women can be collectively "out."

When I approach, Jeff and beaux un-Velcro their mouths and wave me over. I sit next to them on the hard, patchy ground of clover and browning grass. Prickly burrs await anyone not careful about where she places her butt. I discover this immediately.

Thorns removed, I begin examining the contents of a plastic bag received upon registration. The first item provided is a tournament schedule. On the second page, the legend of pirate José Gaspar gets a bit of much-deserved revisionism. "Surreptitiously," it reads, "Gaspar would sail into town. 'Arrrr!' he would growl, while looting the guava trees. Erect went his member as his eyes fixed on the soon to be possessed jewels."

There are other surprises inside: a voucher for one free well drink at Rascals; some Banana Boat Baby Sunblock 29; two LifeStyles lubricated condoms, red; an ad for Solar's Pirate Fest claiming, "A Pirate's Treasure Is His First Mate's Body"; from Barnett Bank a "Mightygrip," useful for safely unscrewing light bulbs and mayonnaise jars; a string of reflective Mardi Gras beads; and a Tootsie Roll Pop, chocolate— my favorite. The mix is eclectic and colorful, much like those gathered here.

When people begin filing past, our Cove team heads to field one for opening ceremonies. The Tampa Gay Men's Chorus has been invited to sing the Canadian and U.S. national anthems. Before they begin, my husband warbles unevenly, "Ooooh, Canadaaaaa!"

"I know that off-key voice," calls someone from behind. We turn to find Terry, a former teammate who moved to Georgia last year. I watch Doug and Terry embrace. They don't retain rigid, military postures or slap each other nervously on the back. Jaw-to-jaw, they share a moment of reunion before Terry puckers and plants.

"Jealous?" he teases, peering over my husband's shoulder.

"Grateful," I respond. How beautiful these sights of unashamed men kissing.

Epilogue

"Men Kissing" is based on events that occurred during one day of fieldwork for my Ph.D. dissertation, a narrative ethnography of a community of gay men in Tampa and of the friendships that have been cultivated between those men, my husband, Doug Healy, and me.

When Doug moved to Tampa in 1994, his trainer at work was David Holland, a man who would alter the course of our lives. Doug and David became friends almost instantly. For a couple weeks, Doug and I had a recurring conversation about whether David might be gay, a question David all but answered by inviting us to meet him at Tracks, a gay nightclub in nearby Ybor City.

Neither Doug nor I (both twenty-three at the time) had ever had an openly gay friend before. In fact, both of us had grown up in the rural Midwest with rather conventional ideas about sexual orientation and identity. "Alternative" sexualities had been almost invisible to us, and the pictures that were presented tended to be cropped and blurred, linking nonheterosexual desires and behaviors with deviance, threat, and sin.

Despite our limited exposure to gay people and cultures, we agreed to meet David at Tracks. As it turned out, this was only the beginning.

In November 1994, David mentioned to Doug that he played softball. When Doug asked if his team needed players, David told him that the team (sponsored by a bar called The Cove), and indeed, the whole Suncoast Softball league, were gay-identified. If that didn't bother him, David said, Doug could join under a league provision that allowed each team to field two straight players.[1] At the start of the next softball season, Doug became The Cove's right centerfielder.

For the next year, ours was an innocently personal journey—a straight couple venturing outside the boundaries of their small-town socializations. But in the fall of 1995, the journey took an unexpected turn.

I was enrolled in a graduate course on qualitative methods at the University of South Florida. When my intended study fell through, the softball field emerged as an alternative fieldwork site. What started as a class project on gay male friendship blossomed into a dissertation on the (inter)personal and social implications of friendship across sexual orientation (see Tillmann-Healy 2001).

The events described in "Men Kissing" took place in February 1997, about a year and a half into my fieldwork. In a seminar on ethnography, I was assigned to go into the field and write about "the spirit of a place." For me, the theme of men kissing captured that spirit.

My project falls under the rubric of narrative ethnography (see Tedlock 1991), which is both a way of practicing fieldwork and a way of writing about fieldwork experience and relationships. As a method, narrative ethnography explores the character and process of the ethnographic dialogue between researcher and participants—a move from studying "them" to studying *us*. As a mode of representation, narrative ethnography employs techniques more often associated with fiction and new journalism than with social science, such as thick scenic description, reconstructed dialogue, dramatic tension, and temporal shifts (see Denzin 1997).

Because narrative ethnography centers on the mutual and reciprocal relationship between researcher and participants, a high degree of reflexivity is required. Narrative ethnographers must recognize both self and others as historically positioned and locally situated (Denzin and Lincoln 1994) in cultural categories such as gender, race, and sexual identity. Fieldwork, in turn, involves communicating about, through, and across these categories.

Although my position in "Men Kissing" is more as observer than participant, I do not claim (and make no attempt) to be dispassionate or apolitical. For narrative ethnographers, objectivity and neutrality, synonyms for estrangement, are both unachievable and undesirable (Jackson 1989). We take instead a *purposefully ethical stance* toward fieldwork and participants (Punch 1994), conducting our projects *with* and *for* our research communities, not merely *in* and *about* them (Fine 1994). Ideally, suggests Denzin (1997, 2000), such work sparks conversation and action directed toward greater social accord and justice.

The criteria by which we judge narrative ethnographies are different from those used to evaluate traditional social science. Moving from factual truth to narrative truth (Bochner 1994; Spence 1982), projects can be assessed by their personal, relational, and cultural consequences (Jackson 1989). Says Robert Coles (1989: 47), "There are many interpretations to a good story, and it isn't a question of which one is right or wrong but of what you do with what you've read." The best stories, according to Bochner (1994), enlarge our capacity to cope with life's struggles, deepen our ability to empathize with others, and expand our sense of community.

Readers of these works are positioned differently than in traditional research. Narrative ethnographers write for those who wish to be engaged on multiple levels: intellectually, emotionally, ethically, and aesthetically; to confront texts from their own experience; and to participate as coproducers of meaning. Narrative ethnographies embrace, in Denzin's terms, a "dialogical ethics of reading" (1997: 247).

Because narrative ethnographies remain open-ended, encouraging multiple interpretations, readers are invited to offer personal, analytic, and critical responses. Texts thus become sites of political empowerment and resistance (Bochner 2000). Ideally, by interacting with the work, readers find something to take in and use, both for themselves (Coles 1989) and for social change (Denzin 1997).

What you take away from this story largely will depend on what you bring to it. Practitioners of qualitative research might be moved to reflect on methodological questions raised by "Men Kissing." For example, what are the opportunities and challenges associated with my position as a young, White, female, married, middle-class, educated, heterosexual researcher who studies a collective of gay people, most of whom are White, middle-class men younger than forty? How might my status as a (young) woman mediate and/or exacerbate potential problems associated with studying a (marginalized) group to which I don't belong? Am I reflexive and dialogic enough? In the context I describe, how ethical is my ethnographic gaze? Do I sufficiently go *beyond* voyeuristic gazing to practice what we might call ethical *engagement*?

"Men Kissing" also can be examined as a literary text. Readers of ethnography are encouraged to assess the effectiveness of this ethnographic short story as a short story. What are the strengths and limitations of presenting these events in this way? How might the text have looked and felt had another form been used, such as ethnographic poetry (see, for example, Austin 1996), a layered account (see, for example, Ronai 1995), ethnographic fiction (see Angrosino 1998), or ethnographic drama (see, for example, Ellis and Bochner 1992)? Is reading this a "sensual" experience; does it offer "a taste of ethnographic things" (Stoller 1989)? Does the plot have enough action and suspense? How well does "men kissing" work as a unifying theme? What other themes are possible? To what possible effects? What responses do the characters evoke, including my character? What can "Men Kissing" move us to think, feel, and do?

Readers who identify with feminism and/or queer theory should interrogate the work's ethics, politics, and implications. Feminist respondents might question whether the scene described adequately challenges orthodox masculinity. Further, what is the place of women's experience in "Men Kissing"? What roles are possible for women in general and for lesbians in particular in this gay (male) space (as described by a straight woman)? Is this story sufficiently "queer"; does it contest heteronormativity and heterosexism and undermine the binary construction of hetero- and homosexuality (see Stein 1999)?

Both feminists and queer theorists could ask: In what way(s) and what context(s) is men kissing (as an act and a story) subversive? Are there ways in which this (as an act and a story) could reinforce rather than disrupt and transform the gender (and sexual) order? Are there ways in which men kissing (as an act and a story) could feed rather than counter the backlash against gay visibility? Does this text "normalize" male intimacy, affection, and sexuality (and is the move from margin to center desirable?), or merely put it on display? How might we use this text to usurp the power of sexual shame (see Warner 1999)?

Whatever your interpretations, it is my hope that this text helps us envision— even if only for a moment—a place beyond the closets of heterosexism and homophobia and a day when such stories no longer will need to be written, when there will be nothing left for men kissing to subvert.

Notes

This story was originally published in *Between Gay and Straight: Understanding Friendship across Sexual Orientation* (Tillmann-Healy 2001).

1. In 1999, this rule was relaxed. There no longer is an official limit on the number of straight players a team can have on its roster or can field at one time.

References

Angrosino, Michael. V. 1998. *Opportunity House: Ethnographic Stories of Mental Retardation.* Walnut Creek, Calif.: AltaMira Press.

Austin, Deborah A. 1996. "Kaleidoscope: The Same and Different." In *Composing Ethnography: Alternative Forms of Qualitative Writing,* ed. Carolyn Ellis and Arthur P. Bochner (pp. 206–30). Walnut Creek, Calif.: AltaMira Press.

Bochner, Arthur P. 1994. "Perspectives on Inquiry II: *Theories and Stories.*" In *Handbook of Interpersonal Communication,* 2nd ed., ed. Mark L. Knapp and Gerald R. Miller (pp. 21–41). Thousand Oaks, Calif.: Sage.

———. 2000. "Criteria against Ourselves." *Qualitative Inquiry* 6: 266–72.

Coles, Robert. 1989. *The Call of Stories: Teaching and the Moral Imagination.* Boston: Houghton Mifflin.

Denzin, Norman K. 1997. *Interpretive Ethnography: Ethnographic Practices for the 21st Century.* Thousand Oaks, Calif.: Sage.

———. 2000. "Aesthetics and the Practices of Qualitative Inquiry." *Qualitative Inquiry* 6: 256–65.

Denzin, Norman K., and Yvonna S. Lincoln. 1994. "Introduction: Entering the Field of Qualitative Research." In *Handbook of Qualitative Research,* ed. Norman K. Denzin and Yvonna S. Lincoln (pp. 1–17). Thousand Oaks, Calif.: Sage.

Ellis, Carolyn, and Arthur P. Bochner. 1992. "Telling and Performing Personal Stories: The Constraints of Choice in Abortion." In *Investigating Subjectivity: Research on Lived Experience,* ed. Carolyn Ellis and Michael G. Flaherty (pp. 79–101). Newbury Park, Calif.: Sage.

Fine, Michelle. 1994. "Working the Hyphens: Reinventing Self and Other in Qualitative Research." In *Handbook of Qualitative Research,* ed. Norman K. Denzin and Yvonna S. Lincoln (pp. 70–82). Thousand Oaks, Calif.: Sage.

Jackson, Michael. 1989. *Paths toward a Clearing: Radical Empiricism and Ethnographic Inquiry.* Bloomington: Indiana University Press.

Punch, Maurice. 1994. "Politics and Ethics in Qualitative Research." In *Handbook of Qualitative Research,* ed. Norman K. Denzin and Yvonna S. Lincoln (pp. 83–97). Thousand Oaks, Calif.: Sage.

Ronai, Carol R. 1995. "Multiple Reflections of Child Sex Abuse: An Argument for a Layered Account." *Journal of Contemporary Ethnography* 23: 395–426.

Spence, Donald P. 1982. *Narrative Truth and Historical Truth: Meaning and Interpretation in Psychoanalysis.* New York: Norton.

Stein, Edward. 1999. *The Mismeasure of Desire: The Science, Theory, and Ethics of Sexual Orientation.* Oxford, U.K.: Oxford University Press.

Stoller, Paul. 1989. *The Taste of Ethnographic Things: The Senses in Anthropology.* Philadelphia: University of Pennsylvania Press.

Tedlock, Barbara. 1991. "From Participant Observation to the Observation of Participation: The Emergence of Narrative Ethnography." *Journal of Anthropological Research* 41: 69–94.

Tillmann-Healy, Lisa M. 2001. *Between Gay and Straight: Understanding Friendship across Sexual Orientation.* Walnut Creek, Calif.: AltaMira Press.

Warner, Michael. 1999. *The Trouble with Normal: Sex, Politics, and the Ethics of Queer Life.* New York: Free Press.

INTERLUDE

High Noon:
A "Fictional" Dialogue

CAROLYN ELLIS AND DOUGLAS FLEMONS

CAROLYN ENTERS the Dolphin bar to find her partner, Art Bochner, and Douglas Flemons, a professor of family therapy at Nova Southeastern University, having a drink together. It's the second day of the SSSI Couch-Stone Symposium, shortly after the end of an informal noon forum at which Mary and Ken Gergen and Art Frank engaged in dialogue with about thirty conference participants. The session focused on qualitative inquiry, art, personal narrative, and ethnography.

Douglas: [*Looks up to see Carolyn entering, a broad smile covering her face*] Hey, that was a provocative session.

Carolyn: [*Takes a seat in the booth beside Douglas*] Yeah, I was really glad to see the graduate students so engaged and eager to participate.

Douglas: [*Points to his and Art's glasses of red wine*] Want a drink?

Carolyn: [*Looks at her watch, then speaks to the waitress*] Sure, it's after noon. Give me a Kahlua and cream. Why not live it up? Everything's going so well. Dare this conference organizer relax a bit? Let's celebrate.

Art: Douglas and I have been talking about how energetic and exciting the conference has been so far. Of course, I'm biased, but . . .

Carolyn: [*Interrupting, ironically*] You, biased? Really!

Douglas: Seriously, people seem so engaged. The dialogue between the audience and the speakers during this last session was terrific.

Art: I was impressed by the forthright positions taken by younger scholars and graduate students. They weren't at all shy about speaking their minds.

Carolyn: It probably helped that Mary, Ken, and Art Frank assumed such an inviting posture. They expressed a genuine interest in what the students had to say.

Art: And offered helpful feedback as well. [*Pauses, then continues*] How would you characterize the kind of talk they were doing? Isn't there some sort of term for it?

Carolyn: You and your categories.

Art: Come on, help me out.

Carolyn: Okay, what comes to my mind is a conversation of the "yes-and" variety, rather than these "yes-but" interactions we so often hear at academic conferences.

Douglas: I think I know what you mean. Fritz Perls, the great Gestalt therapist, once said that in a "yes-but" statement, you might as well ignore everything prior to the "but." The "but" negates everything that comes before it.

Carolyn: You can say that again. That kind of talk can be very discouraging and intimidating. I'm reminded of a conference Art and I attended a couple of years ago—remember, Art? There was a noon session, set up much like this one was, you know, for dialogue between keynoters and participants, except it turned into a disaster. The "yes-but" form of conversation dominated. Just about everyone left angry.

Douglas: Really? What happened?

Art: Well, it didn't start off badly at all. Everybody was sitting around, talking with animation about the effects of postmodern ideas on their work . . .

Carolyn: When out of the blue, this man stands up and starts making a speech about truth and science.

Art: Let me tell you, he didn't waste any time offering niceties before his "but"; he cut straight to negation and criticism.

Douglas: "But-no" rather than "yes-but"?

Carolyn: Exactly. He refused to back down, back off, or allow anyone else to change the subject.

346 | CAROLYN ELLIS AND DOUGLAS FLEMONS

Art: That demand to be heard above and beyond everyone else—that's what we've tried to avoid at this conference. It seems there's usually someone at every academic meeting who has this overwhelming need to show how smart he or she is, even if it hurts other people and promotes a negative tone.

Carolyn: You said he or she? I don't know that I've ever heard a woman do this.

Art: Touché. Well, maybe once or twice I have, but usually it's the male voice. I have to admit I feel some empathy here, because I've acted this way myself before. I certainly don't feel proud.

Carolyn: It's the way a lot of us were trained to be academics and it's a difficult socialization to transform, especially for men.

Art: But you're not suggesting that we should just agree with each other all the time, are you? Can't disagreement and criticism be useful and healthy?

Douglas: I certainly heard some valuable disagreements at this last session about what we social scientists are, or should be, up to.

Carolyn: No, I'm certainly not against the expression of differing viewpoints or perspectives. In the last session, Art Frank said he considers the goal of social science to be theory, and I took issue with that. I said that theory is one goal but not the only one.

[*Laurel Richardson sits down beside Art. After greetings, the conversation is halted while Laurel orders an herb tea and others ask for another round of drinks.*]

Art: Laurel, we're weighing in on the purpose of social science and the socio-emotional climate of academic conferences.

Laurel: Sounds like a heavy conversation.

Carolyn: Oh, it is, but it's also a playful one. I was saying that social science isn't just about producing theory.

Art: What the devil is "theory" anyway? It's become such a large and vague category.

Douglas: Great question. Of course, you don't get out of theory simply by saying your work isn't centered on producing theory, right? Someone who wants to throw out theory is left holding a particular theory about the problems with theory.

Carolyn: I was just thinking how defensive I must have sounded in my response to Art Frank, despite my effort not to invalidate his position. I tried to offer my ideas respectfully, but I'm not sure that there wasn't some sting to them.

Art: I don't think that Art felt you were attacking him. He seemed pretty open to different possibilities for conceiving the role of theory and what we should do with theory. But then his shtick is theory and he's a damn good theorist, so if you say, the hell with theory, yeah, that might not sit well with him. Myself, I liked Mary Gergen's response when she said that theory becomes a problem when it becomes an *over*standing, rather than an *under*standing. The "theory" overshadows the experience it's meant to explain. Her message fit with what several of the graduate students were saying in the session about how the evocative, artistic representations they prefer keep you closer to the experience and in a more feeling and embodied way than abstract theory.

Carolyn: Well, art and performance do offer a way out of privileging the head as the repository for understanding. You can't have knowledge without emotional understanding, at least I can't. If Art Frank's shtick is theory, I guess mine is body-based knowing. [*Laughing*] What's yours, Art? Gees, there are too many "arts" in this conversation.

Art: It seems to me that both theory and art—as in artistic—are ways of patterning experience. The artist, just as much as the social-science theorist, creates a work that translates or transforms "raw" experience into some kind of representative or evocative pattern, abstracted from but connected to the "data" that inspired it.

Douglas: Either way, the goal is understanding, though some conceptual artists, for example, shift the "object" to be understood to the viewer. The question becomes what and how we see and understand and frame art when we see and feel it.

Laurel: I'm not so sure why understanding should be the goal. There are more interesting or pressing reasons—political, transformative, therapeutic, and so on—for conducting research. I, myself, am not after understanding per se.

Carolyn: Oh, Laurel, I love how you turn things around! You help me see that seemingly obvious things aren't so obvious. You know, sometimes I learn more when I think I understand less. Sometimes I understand less when I've finished writing a story than when I started. Maybe I should say that my goal is emotional connection between me and my readers, rather than understanding.

Art: I think you have to distinguish between top-down understanding—the original meaning of the word—and bottom-up understanding.

Laurel: That's still limited too much to the head. Like Carolyn says, you have to account for body-based or body-enhanced knowledge.

Douglas: If you think of understanding as a reductive process, then not understanding opens up opportunities for renewed curiosity. [*Carolyn and Laurel* *nod in agreement*] Gregory Bateson used to talk about the problems of "explanatory principles." When you think you've got a handle on something, got it explained, you stop being curious about it.

Art: We search for explanations—theories—but once we have them, too often our inquiry in that area stops.

Douglas: Sort of like when my kids were first learning language. They were perpetual curiosity machines, so full of wonderment. They'd wake up in the morning and start pointing at stuff, wanting Shelley [my wife] or me to connect a name to whatever object they were looking at. They pronounced their question differently—Eric would say, "Wadaaaat?!"; Jenna, "Badaaaah?!"—but both of them were in search of understanding. The thing is, as soon as they heard the name of what they were pointing at, the *instant* they "understood" it, they'd lose interest and point at something new, once again demanding to know what it "was."

Carolyn: As your children get older, I assume the name of a thing will generate more questions, such as: How is it useful? Does it bring meaning to my life? How will it help improve the life of others? And that these questions will generate more complex interest in the thing, and then even more questions. That's what I want from my projects—I want the answers I come up with to generate more questions than when I started.

Douglas: But that doesn't happen to everyone. I had a client a while ago, an artist, who would throw herself completely into the creation of a painting. While she was doing preliminary sketches, working out technical and aesthetic problems, and then doing the actual rendering, she was totally absorbed, totally fascinated by the process of realizing her vision. And then the moment she was done, she lost all interest in the piece. When she was finished, she became totally bored by what she'd created and wanted nothing more to do with it.

Art: I have to fight against that myself. I want to get into the next project, not dwell on the past or what I've just finished.

Douglas: Perhaps instead of "understanding," we should talk about "making sense" or "grasping." We'd at least be appealing to sense-based or body-based meaning.

Carolyn: That's what I was trying to get across to the intruder at that conference a couple of years ago. Laurel, remember the guy?

Laurel: How could I forget?

Douglas: Made an impression, eh?

Laurel: Oh, yes.

Carolyn: There he is, lecturing us all about truth and science . . .

Art: Taking the logo-centric position that multiple perspectives are well and fine for mushy, quasi-science, but *real* science yields singular truths, singular interpretations.

Carolyn: I wanted him to get out of his head, so I start swaying, and others around me start swaying with me, and I say, "Can your body get in on this position of yours? Try moving. Say these ideas with your body. Come on. Dance it."

Douglas: I can imagine how much he must have loved and embraced your suggestion.

Carolyn: Yeah, right.

Art: See, he began his soliloquy by saying that he wanted to stir things up. He thought we were all too harmonious, too, too . . . how did he put it?

Carolyn: Something about how we were stroking each other, being too supportive, you know like rubbing each others' backs and not being critical enough. He felt the need, he said, to introduce disharmony so we could learn from him the truth about science. He seemed to be saying that you only learn from argument, criticism, and conflict.

Laurel: So then Carolyn starts swaying, but the guy will have none of it. Someone else in the audience tells him, "At least kick your foot."

Art: Probably a professional mediator or something.

Carolyn: It was an attempt to melt some of the tension in the room. It was feeling pretty icy in there about then.

Douglas: And?

Carolyn: Well, so, he kicks his foot nonchalantly [*Demonstrates*] and keeps the floor. "I don't want to dance," he says. "I want to establish the importance of scientific truth."

Douglas: Hmm. The dance of truth. Or was it a dance of confrontation?

Art: What would that look like?

Carolyn: And what would it *feel* like? I see him dressed in black.

Douglas: Right. Didn't you say the session was at noon? So we'd need to put him in a cowboy hat and boots and give him a six-shooter. We could call his dance "High Noon." [*Laughter*]

Art: And call *him* Jesse James.

Carolyn: That would cover the confrontation part of it, but how about his appeal to scientific authority?

Laurel: Give him a six-shooter in one hand, a pencil, and a notebook in the other . . .

Art: And call him Jesse Herbert Mead.

Carolyn: Would the note-taking evoke science or storytelling?

Art: Exactly. Now, that's my shtick. What we do and what reporters and novelists do isn't all that different.

Douglas: We could cover both by calling him Hunter S. Mead.

Art: Or George Herbert Thompson. Or would it [*Looking at Carolyn and Laurel*] be Margaret Thompson?

Carolyn: Oh, for Margaret Mead? Rich. Very rich.

Laurel: Okay, but now we've lost the confrontation part.

Art: Hunter Thompson hasn't exactly been shy about stirring up trouble.

Douglas: How about Hunter S. (aka Jesse James) Mead?

Carolyn: And leave it ambiguous about whether it's George Herbert or Margaret. I like it. Makes me want to dance! [*Looks at Art*] Wanna join me?

Art: Absolutely. Meet you upstairs tonight when the Quivering Rhythm Hounds Band cranks up. Don't forget your paper and pencil.

Laurel: And your six-shooter.

Douglas: This image sure captures the difference between the session we were just in and the High Noon one a few years back. Today, the talk was about reaching across not only interdisciplinary lines, but across the humanities/ sciences divide. But it sounds like Jesse James wanted to keep divisions in place, to protect science from the encroachment of human contingencies, emotions, and the fallibility of language.

Carolyn: More than that, the way I saw it, he wanted to widen the division. And then build an impenetrable wall between them, keeping science inviolate so it could properly discover the Truth.

Art: Somehow I got the impression that he didn't really believe in these divisions himself. What he believed in was the necessity of arguing the case as if harmony and emotional supportiveness were the greater dangers that had to be defended against.

Douglas: So what happened next?

Carolyn: Well, Jesse, or Hunter S. or whoever he was, kept talking, and as he talks, I'm feeling the room being taken over by this critical social science voice, by his "It's-right-against-wrong," debating tone, and I don't know what to do.

Laurel: I just haven't the patience anymore to go through these old arguments, just like I don't have the patience to deal with folks who want to knock qualitative research or feminism or Unitarianism or veganism, and so on. The arguments are so old already and so boring. That's the trouble with this kind of negative energy—it exudes and enters, so you have to take your own energy and knock it away. Oh, how tired all that makes me. Like being back in the sociology department from which I chose to retire early. I'm getting tired just talking about it now. [*Laurel sighs and turns attention to her tea*]

Carolyn: It seems these divisions are endemic in departments. As Patricia Geist's performance showed so well yesterday, no wonder we're "Dis/enchanted by Academe."

Art: And suffering from institutional depression.

Laurel: Isn't that the truth?

[*All four sigh and peer into their drinks*]

Douglas: [*Interrupting the silence*] I want to go back to the intruder. Carolyn, were you able to get him to lay down his six-shooter?

Carolyn: Nope. He's shooting up the place with his words. I try interrupting again, but without the suggestion that he dance. I tell him, "Stop, stop! You're interrupting what's happening here!" Others also try to voice their concerns, but he continues his monologue, unabated. I feel like I've gone from a participant to an audience member, watching, speechless, while the "star" performs. I don't want him to do this, but I don't know how to stop him, and I don't want to start sounding as argumentative and confrontational as he sounds to me. I look around and see and feel the energy draining out of everyone. The once animated and passionate crowd now sits slumped in their chairs with sad, defeated looks on their faces, as if they know the discussion we had been having was too good to last.

Art: I didn't know what to do, either. Soon Carolyn looks at her watch, nods to Laurel, and they quietly get up and leave. I stay awhile longer, and now I'm good and angry.

Carolyn: I waited a few minutes before leaving, though. At first, I didn't want to give the impression that I was walking out just because I didn't get my way, but then I realized I didn't care. Laurel and I had already planned to meet for lunch, and I figured there was no point in sticking around, so we left together. Actually, I rather liked the ambiguity of our joint action.

Laurel: And I certainly didn't want my limited time with Carolyn to be spent as an audience to Jessie James.

Carolyn: [*To Laurel*] Remember what our friend Jim said to us afterward? [*To Douglas*] He'd been at the session and had seen us make our getaway, and he came up to us at lunch and told us how much he loved that we'd walked out. He thought Jesse James's intrusion was like a rape, and he thought it was great that we'd refused to participate.

Art: Later, after Carolyn told me what Jim had said, I asked him if rape wasn't too strong a term. He said not at all because the people in that room had been forced against their will to do something they didn't want to do. Then they had only two choices: participate in his language game or leave!

Laurel: I told Jim that I left because it was lunchtime. He said he liked his "rebellious women" story better, so he was going to continue thinking of it that way. He's right in a way. If I hadn't had a lunch date, I would have left, regardless. [*Laughter*]

Art: When Carolyn and Laurel left, some other people followed. I was incensed. I stood up and said to Jesse, "Don't you see what's going on? Several people have left since you started talking, people I care deeply about. This is not the kind of conversation they want to have. They find the questions you're raising profoundly uninteresting."

Douglas: Did he respond?

Art: Oh yeah. He said something like, "Who cares if a few people don't like what I'm saying? We need to be open to alternative points of view, otherwise this is just inverted hegemony. What's wrong with coming up with one right way of viewing something? It's time we reconciled the hard sciences with the social sciences."

Douglas: Ironic, eh? Severing interpersonal relationships in the service of forging a theoretical rapprochement.

Art: Right. There was no awareness of the relational context and no sensitivity to the emotions people were feeling.

Douglas: So you stood up for Carolyn. Protecting her?

Carolyn: I feel ambivalent about that portrayal. Unlike the parts given to women who surrounded the Wild West Jesse James, I don't need that kind of protecting from Art. But maybe that *is* what was happening, because for that moment I'm not so sure that our old Jesse didn't pull Art into his frame.

Art: You mean into his O.K. Corral? Maybe so. But what I did, I did as much for me as for Carolyn. Anyway, shortly after that I left, too.

Douglas: You left out of anger?

Art: No, I left because it was past time for the session to be over. I was hungry. [*Laughter*] Then later, I recall feeling really bad about my response to him, as if I had intentionally insulted him because I was feeling hurt that the whole session had deteriorated so quickly.

Carolyn: It's a dilemma.

Douglas: What?

Carolyn: How to respond to that voice from the outside, criticizing, punching holes. It demands that we respond in the same voice. I don't want to privilege or speak in that voice. I want to ignore that voice because it doesn't work if you don't speak back to it, if there is no audience. Yet I don't want to be seen as excluding voices in the same way I've accused mainstream social science of doing. Or [*Long pause*], maybe I just don't want to be seen as backing down from them. I mean I'm pretty committed to defending my position too.

Art: [*Ironically*] No kidding!!

Carolyn: [*Smiles*] And you're not? Anyway, the interaction opened up much to think about . . .

Art: Yes, if we just ignore voices that are different from ours or are antagonistic, then what do we have? We end up with something akin to separate cliques or gangs who define each other as enemies. And that's what leads to the kind of aggression that was so bothersome at that session. For me the question becomes: How do we allow the voices of difference into our conversation? Is it possible to have dialogue between parties with contentious constructions of reality?

Laurel: All this makes me wonder what might have been opened up if Jesse James hadn't shown up. What did we miss out on?

Art: Good question. What happened in the session today was very different. The dialogue and sharing were marvelous.

Carolyn: Yeah, they were. And you just know that if Jesse had been here in the room, he would have wanted, as he said back then, to throw a snake in the room, to stir some disharmony into all our "mushy, nondiscriminating mutual support."

Douglas: I'm reminded of an interesting story told by the American Buddhist Jack Kornfield about a group of "seekers" living together in a spiritual community. For several years, they had been having to deal with one of the members of the group, an obnoxious man who never pulled his weight with the chores, and he insulted everyone, including the teacher. Despised and resented, the man finally left the community. The remaining members could scarcely believe their good fortune. Elated and distinctly relieved, they went about their lives with a renewed sense of spiritual peace. Their joy was short lived, however. After far too few blissful days, the man showed up again, as demanding, lazy, and disrespectful as always. The others went to their teacher, requesting that he refuse to allow the man to rejoin the community. To their astonishment, the teacher revealed that he had *paid* the man to return! Pressed for an explanation, he told them that the man was like yeast for bread, necessary for their learning about patience, compassion, and loving-kindness.

Carolyn: I don't know, Douglas. Can't we can learn patience, compassion, loving-kindness, and how to live with differences in other ways? Can't we model them for each other and learn through experiencing them from and in our relationships with others? Why do we need to be insulted and invalidated to learn them?

Douglas: The challenge is to feel compassion for noncompassionate people. Maybe this is the first step toward Art's goal of allowing, even embracing, difference. Or if not compassion, then at least curiosity. Would we be having this conversation if Jesse hadn't swaggered into that session a couple of years ago? What better way to learn about relationships than to experience what happens when they're breached?

Art: What are you suggesting?

Douglas: Perhaps we should all contribute to a "High Noon" scholarship fund, so we can financially compensate conference attendees who are willing to disrupt sessions and stir up trouble.

Art: Hmm. We could write up a contract, giving each year's scholarship recipient the honorary title of Hunter S. (Jesse James) Mead—and laying out his or her responsibilities,

Laurel: Such as dressing in black denim.

Carolyn: And showing up at the dance in cowboy boots, ready to two-step.

Douglas: And trying people's patience and tolerance.

Art: And giving us all permission to write about the fallout.

Douglas: That brings up a good point. What about the original Jesse James?

Laurel: What about him?

Douglas: I presume that since the High Noon Scholarship hadn't been established back when the incident happened, you didn't pay him for his trouble, and you didn't get him to sign a release form, allowing us to write about what happened.

Art: Yeah, but on the other hand, who could come to a conference with a bunch of reflexive ethnographers and not be aware that your participation might one day get woven into some kind of account?

Douglas: Even if you weren't aware that you might later be written about, it's not so clear to me that you shouldn't be held accountable. It reminds me of something the novelist Anne Lamott once said: "If my family didn't want me to write about them, they should've behaved better."

Carolyn: Hey, I'm not that concerned about the ethics of including the intruder's participation—after all, it was a public forum. I think we *should* write about ourselves as academics. We don't scrutinize our own actions enough.

Art: But what if Jesse doesn't want to be written about or feels he would be harmed by what is written?

Douglas: Yeah, that's a tough one.

Art: You could give him an opportunity to add his voice, you know, tell the story from his point of view.

Laurel: Or you could always fictionalize the telling.

Carolyn: That's a good idea. I'm not sure that just because people don't want to be written about that we should close up shop. You have to weigh what can be learned against what harm could result. Sometimes it's a very tough call and you struggle with what is the right thing to do. But regardless, Jesse doesn't have the moral high ground here.

Douglas: And we want to make sure not to hand it to him though our actions.

Carolyn: You're right. But what concerns me more is handing him center stage again. I think we're giving the gunslinger too much space in our text.

Douglas: But haven't you gotten anything out of this conversation?

Carolyn: [*Speaking very passionately*] Oh, sure. Our conversation has brought me to a different understanding, a different sense-making, of what happened. My body feels different. It's heightened state lets me know how important and complex I think these issues are. What happened wasn't just a matter of someone holding the floor as I thought before; it's a matter of how we talk to each other and respond to difference. How do we change the conversation? These are issues at the heart of our work and this conference.

Art: What makes me still feel sad, though, is precisely the issue you've hit on, Carolyn. We haven't yet learned how to change the conversation. The "yes-but" still rules for the most part, because we have this realist mentality that we can resolve the differences that divide us through argument and evidence. So when these conflicts occur, we aren't able to recognize and appreciate the differences and make people who genuinely see things differently feel nonetheless welcomed into our conversation. The result is blaming and antagonism and a lot of hurt feelings.

Douglas: Carolyn, maybe you should be the first one to apply for the High Noon Scholarship. You look great in black.

Laurel: [*To Carolyn*] Let's apply for it together. But if we get it, the conference organizers can't give us men's names. I've had patriarchy up to here.

Carolyn: How 'bout we bust things up as Thelma and Louise?

Laurel: Okay, but I'm not driving off any cliff. Let's get that straight up front.

Carolyn: Deal. But I rather like the idea of a convertible.

Laurel: Convertible. Interesting word, that. From the Latin, *con-*, altogether, and *vertere,* to turn: "to turn about, transform." Fits for me. I'd rather change things than "understand" them.

Art: [*Holding his glass up for a toast*] Here's to being convertable! [*Laurel, Douglas, and Carolyn join in*]

The End

Note

Special thanks to Arthur Bochner and Laurel Richardson for being coconstructors of and characters in our story. Thanks, too, to Ward Flemons for tracking down the Jack Kornfield story.

Between the Ride and the Story: Illness and Remoralization

ARTHUR W. FRANK

MAX WEBER'S (1958) problem still looms: Can we find a vocation that affords us honor in disenchanted times? The ghost of Weber reminds us that the work of showing how our times are disenchanted is central to the social scientific vocation, but then I part company with him. Weber saw disenchantment deriving from the absence of legitimate charismatic leadership; for him the fate of the times was to be "resolute" in facing that absence. My experience is that charisma has not left the scene unless one looks only for the kind of political and religious movements that were Weber's central interest. I remember seeing charisma in a New Zealand hospice as I watched a patient's reaction when a young physician knelt in front of her, so that the patient did not have to look up as they spoke. I see charisma in people with cancer who lead support groups until months and even weeks before their deaths. Unlike Weber's leaders, these people would not understand themselves as charismatic. The charisma of their acts lies in their capacity to enlarge the sense of human possibility among those who feel affected by them. Such acts elevate the mundane and reenchant local worlds; the reenchantment is no less significant for the limitation of scope. In the presence of such acts I ask the same question that observers of Weberian charismatic leaders ask: Where did that person's power come from?

But then Weber's ghost returns. Even to those like me who see the world filled with—to coin a Weberian oxymoron—mundane charisma, the fate of our times is the increasing sphere of what is disenchanted. The disenchantment that concerns me occurs in and around illness. What I have learned from illness during the last fifteen years is that suffering is caused not only by physical pain, financial loss, strained relationships, and sheer disruption, not to mention the ultimate fear of death, as real as these are. People certainly suffer for these reasons, but they also suffer because being ill is a profoundly disenchanted, and disenchanting, business. This idea has not escaped others' notice. In a book that inspired my work, Arthur Kleinman (1988: 244, passim) called for the "remoralization" of medicine, and my own work has been about the remoralization that ill people must do to survive demoralized medicine.

One of the most recent and best testaments to the need for medicine's remoralization is Margaret Edson's Pulitzer Prize-winning play, *Wit* (1999). Vivian Bearing, a distinguished professor of English, is dying of ovarian cancer. Although temporal intervals are not specified, the play takes place over about a year, from her diagnosis to her death. Vivian often speaks directly to the audience while individual physicians or the medical staff speak their dialogue in the background. Thus after her oncologist, Dr. Kelekian, has broken the news by simply entering the room and telling her, "You have cancer" (in the production I saw, he looks down at the chart as he says this), he goes into a monotone description of medical details and the proposed treatment, and she carries on her own monologue. Vivian has some success establishing a relationship of mutual recognition with Kelekian—they find common ground in complaints about their students—but her demoralization becomes intense as she goes for various tests. The first technician, after asking her name, asks (without inflecting it as a question) "Doctor." She answers, "Yes, I have a Ph.D." "*Your* doctor," he replies (Edson 1999: 16). In her next encounter she tries joking, but the joke only produces confusion. After the test the technician is annoyed because another technician has taken her wheelchair: "Well, how are you going to get out of here?" he asks. "Perhaps you would like me to stay," she answers (1999: 17). Later in her treatment, when she goes for a test she makes no attempt to establish any relationship with the technician; when he asks her name she speaks by rote, "B-E-A-R-I-N-G. Kelekian" (1999: 42) In the production I saw, that line is delivered with a heavy sense of defeat; all the wit of the earlier exchanges has been extinguished. The medical system has neither time nor interest in whom people are; at most, the amount of chemotherapy that Vivian infuses will be the subject of a medical journal article (1999: 43). Of course I also am writing a journal article, which may be an example of what Vivian is fond of calling irony (1999: 8).

Wit has moments of remoralization, especially in Vivian's relationship to her primary care nurse (she is being treated in a setting where she has a primary care nurse). If disenchantment is our fate, remoralization is our possibility. This chapter extends that remoralization project by asking what disenchants contemporary life in general, how illness crystallizes this disenchantment, and how stories as a form of interaction can remoralize the world.

The Ride

When I seek a name for how society disenchants, I call it the ride. The ride promotes itself as making life better, but others interpret rides as increasing disenchantment. One version of illness as a ride is offered by Albert Robillard (1999), describing his experience of being a patient in an intensive care unit. Robillard's ride involves "the displacement of the self by the screens."

> The displacement was not only characterological, involving finding the truth about who you are in the screens, but spatial as well. Most of the monitor reading, so at least you thought and hoped, took place at the nursing station. The placement of careful and continuous reading of the monitors there may have been a panoptic dream, but it effectively removed the critical reading of factors concerning life and death, as well as televised bodily behavior, to a remote, unseen location. Additionally, the actions derived from this information were formulated in an invisible place, a site beyond personal influence. (Robillard 1999: 49)

On the ride, the reality (Robillard's body) is transformed into an image (the monitor). The ICU ride, like most rides, instructs people to look to the image in order to understand reality; the ride is about the primacy of sign values. The image then receives its privileged interpretation away from the primary reality, "in an invisible place, a site beyond personal influence." In the image is "the truth about who you are" (Robillard 1999: 49).

The ride sweeps people along, reducing the world to its signs. In *The McDonaldization of Society* (1996), George Ritzer uses medicine as an ongoing illustration of how the fast-food model is applied across a diversity of social settings. McMedicine as a ride poses three core questions to its (patient) customers: Can you pay for it? Can you stomach what you can pay for? And how quickly do you forget that there are other ways of eating? The power of the ride is how effectively it can reduce life's possibilities to its menu. As Robillard (1999) testifies, the ride seeks to tell people who they are and how they feel.

Specific rides are real, from intensive care units to fast-food restaurants, but I mean The Ride as a trope for everything that is not The Story, another trope based on but exceeding the real telling of stories. At first I imagined the ride and the story as ends of a continuum, but I now think of them as the ever-shifting foreground and background of a single gestalt. Rides are powerful but not hegemonic. Robillard becomes absorbed in the monitor screens, but he remains capable of critical reflection: "I began to think of how my body and my person were fragmented by the monitors" (1999: 62). Eventually he transcends this fragmentation by redefining the monitors as a source of relationships.

> There was a learning process in my looking at the nurses looking at the monitors and talking about what they saw. I was directed to look at and read the monitors from the attention given to them by these same nurses. It became a coordinated looking and reading. (Robillard 1999: 62)

Unfortunately, Robillard, like Vivian Bearing in *Wit*, is more successful telling this story to his readers in his book than he is converting his "coordinated looking and reading" into dialogues with his nurses. The nurses remained more interested in the ride than the story: "I could not tag them with my face, gaze, or identity, thus pulling them into conversations" (Robillard 1999: 63).

Here are three scenes of disenchantment, representing the medically underserved, the overserved, and the hyperserved. These scenes also illustrate the shifting gestalt that comprises the moral attitudes of the ride and the story. The first scene is actress Helen Hunt's diatribe against managed care in the film *As Good As It Gets* (1997). The punch line is when Hunt says that her insurance company is more interested in denying her claims than in curing her son's breathing problems. The same point is given longer and more tragic development in *The Rainmaker* (1997), in which Matt Damon plays a neophyte lawyer who successfully sues a medical insurer because its denials of treatment claims precipitated a young man's death. The making of these films suggests the public salability of narratives of disenchanted medicine.

The quality of the ride, and the source of disenchantment, in both these films is ambivalent. Both films present themselves as critiques of disenchanted medicine: They criticize how illness becomes a ride when medicine is more concerned with terms of reimbursement than with the care of suffering. Against this disenchantment, the films present themselves as remoralization projects. But then the gestalt shifts and the films themselves can be viewed as rides. Matt Damon wins his law suit; at least among the jury, a righteous sense of disenchantment has a cash value. When Helen Hunt's son eventually gets the best medical care, his breathing problems disappear; he's transformed. His former illness disappears as an unnecessary glitch in an otherwise workable system. With Jack Nicholson's economic clout behind him, he could be fixed.

Viewed in this second gestalt, both *The Rainmaker* and *As Good As It Gets* are disenchanting in their view that suffering is accidental, a mere moment in some larger scheme of things. Some accidents are brutal, but all prove fixable to some degree. The films thus presume the understanding that is implicit in any ride: Bad things seem to happen or happen only for a while; really, riders understand, it's all under control. Jack Nicholson may ask the psychiatrist's waiting room of patients—and by implication the audience—whether they dare consider that their present lives might be as good as it gets, but the film's message is that life gets a lot better. Anybody's life can be changed, and in both films money is a primary medium of change. Or, almost anybody's life can be changed. In both films, those who have no insurance at all, and thus no one to sue, effectively disappear. The ride often includes a disappearing act. Vivian Bearing disappears into research data to the oncologists who neglect her "Do Not Resuscitate" order and call a code because, as one exclaims, "She's Research!" (Edson 1999: 64). Robillard (1999), as an identity to whom one might speak, disappears to his nurses, who are swept along in the images on their screens just as the films' viewers are swept along by its images.

In a second scene of medical disenchantment, illness has disappeared entirely. Getting off a plane in Nashville, I was attracted by a high-resolution, back-lit billboard. At first I thought it must be advertising some nearby resort: I saw pictures of plush hotel rooms and landscaped grounds. I thought it odd that one side of the billboard was dominated by a close-up of a man who must be the hotel manager, but that didn't surprise me. As I got closer I realized the man was a cosmetic surgeon and the billboard was advertising his spa. The facilities were designed for longer stays so that patrons would be able to recuperate in comfort and not risk going back into public while the marks of surgery were still visible.

If the images from the intensive care monitor claim to show the truth of how the patient actually is, and the films show the destitute ill-insured patients that audiences do not want to be, the billboard's ride is promising its viewers how they could be, or at least how they could look. The surgeon had surrounded himself with Greco-Roman busts, which apparently signified classical perfection and, as images, were blank enough to allow any viewer to project on them his or her own face and body. The ride to becoming that face and body seemed to require only paying the price.

Yet everybody has a story. In Kathy Davis's (1995) study of cosmetic surgery, women who are choosing (a recurring verb in the interviews) surgery speak for themselves, and their choices are embedded in stories about who they are. In the lives that Davis interrogated, surgery becomes part of a complex personal story. Davis's interpretation of her respondents' stories is contested (Bordo 1998), and in that contest the gestalt constantly switches. First it's a ride: The foreground is medicine as commodity, and patients are consumers pursuing a commodified image. Then the foreground becomes stories of individual decisions to have surgery not in a spa and at considerable sacrifice. Then the stories can be interpreted as rooted in internalized beauty ideals that articulate capitalism with patriarchy, and cosmetic culture is a ride again. This instability does not make the contest between the ride and the story less real. The women Davis interviewed are making moral decisions consequential both for themselves and, if their accounts become legitimated, for medicine and society.

The ethos of medical overservice is nicely articulated in a third scene that—at least at present—departs from medicine.[1] In a recent interview a British cybernetics expert, Kevin Warwick, described experiments in which he has a computer chip implanted under his skin. The chip allows him to control appliances, such as doors and lights, simply by moving in certain directions. Warwick's work is part of what many see as the ultimate goal of computerization—the computer working in and through the body. The premise of the ride is best expressed in Warwick's explanation of why he undertakes this work: "I was born human. But this was an accident of fate—a condition merely of time and place. I believe it's something we have the power to change" (Warwick 2000: 145). For Warwick, being born human is inherently disenchanting; the ride is changing this accident.

What Robillard (1999) learns in intensive care is that the body is no accident; when bodies are reduced to digital images there is no interaction. Time and space are not "mere" conditions but are necessary for dialogue between persons: "The institutionalized, naturalized, socially consensual order of conversation has a rhythm, a time order, that assumes an intersubjective coordination of physical human bodies" (Robillard 1999: 63). On Robillard's account of the embodied prerequisites of interaction, Warwick's ride will end in profound disenchantment because it deprecates time, space, and the body as mere accidents to be changed.

One of the many issues Warwick raises is how much of the ride any of us want to refuse. I find it easy to be derisive of Warwick's chip implants because I can perfectly well turn on the lights and open the door without them. I have to acknowledge that I appreciate having lights to turn on and doors to open, and these devices once transformed the natural (darkness, cold) into accidents of time of day, climate, and season. As clear as the difference seems to be between Robillard's project of embodied conversation and Warwick's project of the computerized body, the line between the ride and the story is never easily drawn—but again, that difficulty does not render the moral choice of how to live any less pressing.

The need to make practical decisions about which rides to get on and which stories to tell is perhaps clearest when the ride proclaims an end to disenchantment as its political project. Former Delaware governor Pete Du Pont now chairs a "nonpartisan, public policy research institute." Du Pont's op-ed column, "Wealth Creation Benefits Society" (1999), immediately puts its readers on a ride that recalls a succession of other rides:

> The pace of change is accelerating. We are in the midst of a digital revolution, and, let's admit it, we are in a new era.
>
> One innovation follows another—personal computers, fiber-optic cables, fax machines, the Internet, cell phones, CDs, DVD players . . . the wonders never cease. And the best technologies are yet to come.
>
> Big social changes often occur under the radarscope but are equally important. For example: Almost one in two U.S. households own individual stocks or mutual funds today. . . . Wealth creation for many market participants has been spectacular in the 1990s.

Du Pont's "new era" epitomizes the ride; his "wonders" are the toys of the electronics warehouse store. Du Pont's language attempts to generate a sense of charismatic change: *revolution, new era, innovation, wonders, big social changes, the best yet to come.* The "spectacular" ride is "wealth creation," and here the ride shows its politics. Citizens have become "market participants" and the fruits of their participation are commodities: computers, fax machines, music and video players. Most of these "wonders" are media for the advertisement of other commodities, and many require an additional chain of commodities for their operation (software; music, game, and video disks).

Du Pont's prose does not give its reader time to think about whether his or her life is better as a result of being permeated by commodities already defined as wonders. Instead Du Pont or his speech writers create a discursive ride that sweeps the reader along. When Du Pont gets to his political agenda—cut taxes, privatize Social Security, eliminate health insurance by instituting medical savings accounts, benefit the "growing investor class"—the reader is not expected to question how those policies would actually work, just as she or he was never offered space to question whether having a computer, fax machine, and cell phone has actually made his or her life better.

A significant indicator of our cultural preoccupations is that Du Pont's most specific recommendation addresses health. "Most individuals would accumulate tens of thousands of dollars in medical savings accounts over their lifetimes," he writes, "a fund to provide for their medical care in old age and an estate for their heirs." This ride to medical affluence never says who would need less medical care and/or at what lower price, thus generating any new wealth in society as a whole. Du Pont's ride—and the logic of medical savings accounts—offers itself to people who expect to have good health and who expect not to need significant medical care before old age, when unspent deductible payments will have compounded.[2] The ill are tacitly placed outside the ride; they have no admission to Du Pont's theme park of electronic gadgetry and market-generated affluence. Like the other one in two households who do not own stock and have not been part of the 1990s wealth creation, they have no voice or visibility.

Many people are swept along on Du Pont's ride, but like any ride it is not hegemonic. The distinguished lay ethnographer Dave Barry provides a compelling countervision to Du Pont's utopia:

> The other essential tool of the "information economy" is the cellular telephone, which enables businesspeople, wherever they are, to attempt unsuccessfully to return each other's voicemails. . . . As far as I can tell, none of these people has ever actually reached the person he or she wanted to talk to. But they keep trying! They are in the airport right now, pacing and shouting to nobody. This kind of productivity would be impossible without information technology.

And it's just the beginning. Some day, our economy will become so advanced, so purely informational, that we won't even walk around. (Barry 2000)

At first I feel reassured that if as popular a humorist as Barry can laugh at Du Pont's future, the hegemony of rides cannot be taken too seriously. But the same people who laugh with Barry can also support Du Pont's politics. Rides are not hegemonic, but neither do the stories that are told within rides necessarily undo the real power of those rides to condition people's sense of possibilities and of moral action.[3] Robillard (1999) could transform the monitors in the intensive care unit into a story, but he could not get his nurses to talk to him. That talk is the core of my other trope for moral being and acting, the story.

The Story

Sooner or later, the ride wants from us. Rides want us to consume them for someone else's profit, and as Ritzer (1996) has shown with reference to fast-food restaurants, consumption involves increasing amounts of work. The ride not only wants our money and our effort; it wants our assent to its world: Du Pont wants his readers to accept his reality as their own and vote accordingly. Du Pont claims to want for his readers, but all he wants for them is to become capable of consuming more. Consumption is fueled by disenchantment, which it claims to remedy, and the ride's ultimate disenchantment is with various accidents of being born human, as Warwick says. On the ride these accidents can all be fixed, at least for some, and the others are rendered invisible. Riders seem invariably if tacitly isolated from their invisible fellow creatures, producing the isolation Robillard experiences.[4]

A story also wants assent to its world, but how assent is achieved and what it requires differ from the ride. Whereas the ride wants from us, the story wants for us. The story wants for us in relation to others; thus the scope of "us" expands through the medium of the story. The story wants what Robillard (1999) wants in intensive care: conversation based in a mutual recognition of identity.

Here are five premises that seem to guide the story, and again my specific stories are about illness and trauma.[5] The first premise is expressed by Charles Taylor, writing about the emergence of the distinctly modern sense of *self*, which he argues was a new idea in the late eighteenth century.

There is a certain way of being human that is *my* way. I am called upon to live my life in this way, and not in imitation of anyone else's. But this gives a new importance to being true to myself. If I am not, I miss the point of my life, I miss what being human is for *me*. (Taylor 1991: 28–29)

Taylor is well aware that this idea of the self entails a risk of self-enclosure, so it must be immediately complemented by a second idea.

Taylor, like Robillard though in a different idiom, understands human life as being valuable because of its "fundamentally *dialogical* character." "We define [our identity] always in dialogue with, sometimes in struggle against, the identities our significant others want to recognize in us" (Taylor 1991: 33). Thus the point of our unique lives, which we seek not to miss, lies beyond those lives themselves: "So the ideal of self-choice supposes that there are *other* issues of significance beyond self-choice" (1991: 39). Thus, for Taylor it's not sufficient to say that the point of your life is being on the ride, because rides present themselves as self-choices. When rides are taken, they should be used as occasions for dialogical recognition, a good deal of which occurs in Erving Goffman's (1961) famous ethnography of merry-go-round riding.

These first two premises—ways of thinking about the self and its relation to other selves—say nothing specific about illness. The illness story begins when life suffers a *disruption* (Becker 1997) that renders its previous "point" either forgotten or no longer viable. What is disrupted are not only one's plans but also, more fundamentally, the basis of the self that Taylor—following the interactionist tradition—grounds in the self's need for others' recognition. The ill and disabled are typically denied this recognition. Robillard (1999) argues that this denial goes beyond fear of the condition that the ill person represents. He offers particular insight into others' reactions to his own body, paralyzed by what he prefers to call motor neuron disease:

I surmise that in the perception of others one sees the full range of bodily instrumentalities and potential instrumentalities, calling out and institutionalizing, moment by moment, one's own capacities and instrumentalities; the sight of the paralyzed, the crippled, the lame is a sharp denial of this commonsense, reciprocal knowledge. (Robillard 1999: 72; see also 63)

Those whose disrupted lives fall outside others' commonsense, reciprocal knowledge must use stories to establish new terms of common sense and new relations of reciprocity within a community that affords recognition.

The fourth premise is that the interactional dynamics of this withdrawal of social recognition are part of a more extensive political economy of *censorship*. In one of Jean Baudrillard's early works he describes how the logic of consumer capitalism guarantees every desire its respective object of satisfaction. Baudrillard writes that "all the things which do not fit into this positive vision are rejected, censored by the satisfaction itself . . . and, no longer finding any possible outlet, crystallize into a gigantic fund of anxiety" (1998: 177, emphases omitted). Kirby Farrell (1998) describes this fund of anxiety as "post-traumatic culture," which is simultaneously obsessed with life's horrors but also seeks to contain these as exceptional and avoidable instances. *As Good As It Gets* and *The Rainmaker* both can be seen as products of post-traumatic culture, obsessed with trauma but containing it within plot structures where it can be fixed.

My fifth point is the story itself. The story expresses the teller's particular *call of suffering*—the disrupted life that finds no interpersonal recognition. Storytelling is a form of ethical action because it joins those who suffer to those who feel called to respond to this suffering. Although there is considerable philosophical support for this idea (Levinas 1989), I prefer to make the point with a story. Eduardo Galeano describes a physician, Fernando Silva, working late on Christmas Eve in the hospital in Managua. On his last rounds he hears footsteps behind him, turns, and finds a child he is caring for.

> In the half light he recognized the lonely, doomed child. Fernando recognized that face already lined with death and those eyes asking for forgiveness, or perhaps permission. Fernando walked over to him and the body gave him his hand.
>
> *"Tell someone,"* the child whispered. *"Tell someone I'm here."* (Galeano 1991: 72)

The story, as the trope I oppose to the ride, gives voice to what is censored by the logic of satisfaction. Stories tell those things that defy commonsense, reciprocal recognition, yet seek to be heard, seen, and recognized. "I had known the pain," wrote Audre Lorde about cancer, "and survived it. It only remained for me to give it voice, to share it for use, that the pain not be wasted" (1980: 16). Not wasting the pain becomes the point of Lorde's life, at the moment when that pain threatens her sustaining what has been the point of her life. The story is always marked by pain, compounded by censorship of that pain. Stories call to be heard through that pain and censorship.

Another recent film, *Life Is Beautiful* (1997), offers a story about stories. The hero's happy life is disrupted when he and his young son are sent to a Nazi camp. Immediately he knows the point of his life is not only to keep his son alive but also to turn the experience into a story that his son will be able to live with. So he works to maintain the illusion that the whole camp is a big game—a ride—in which it's possible to score points and the winner gets a tank, because his son's favorite toy had been a tank. The death camp becomes an occasion for this man to achieve the point of his life, which is to make possible a life for his son. He not only makes it possible for his son to survive, but he also gives him memories—a story of what his father did—that will allow him to live in a post-Holocaust world and still believe that life can be beautiful. The hero's character is contrasted with a doctor he has known before the war. The doctor colludes with the Nazis, is unable to hear the hero's plea for help, and eventually goes mad. The doctor misses the point of his life.

Some argue that the movie compromises too much: the horror of the Holocaust is contained and turned into a ride for the audience. But if the camp is not shown in all its brutalities, the Nazis are not harmless buffoons either. The hero has to suffer, endure, and eventually die to sustain the story that is the point of his life. For me, his death prevents the film from containing disenchantment as rides do. Instead the film seems an example of remoralization, although the objections to the film show that specific instances of what counts as remoralization and what counts as disenchantment will always be contested. The story accepts such contests as extending its conversation, while the ride seeks to deny such contests.

Stories are told by a self that has been disrupted out of its place in society's moral order and seeks a new place, but the story also compels recognition that the moral order itself requires reevaluation. The story joins these two levels of remoralization; the personal is political.

Mundane Charisma

If the fate of our times is to participate in a contest between the ride and the story, not the least complication of that participation is that we can rarely choose the ride *or* the story. There seems little possibility of living in this world and not participating in rides, but to adapt Weber's terms, we can practice to be *on* the ride without being *of* the ride. We can, while on different rides, listen for the story that is also being told even as people are being swept along. We can also refuse those aspects of the ride that censor certain stories. We can seek to recognize "all the things which do not fit"—my version of Weber's "inconvenient facts"—rather than participate in their (usually tacit) marginalization.

Everyone has a story, and whether any story is on the ride without being of it will remain contested. As Taylor (1991: 78) writes, "The nature of a free society is that it will always be the locus of a struggle between higher and lower forms of freedom." I would add that the struggle is not only between higher and lower forms; the struggle will be over which are higher and lower forms of freedom. The distinction of the ride and the story is only one way to conceptualize this struggle over which are higher and which are lower. Participation in that struggle is part of our fate.

"We" in the above paragraphs are simultaneously social scientists, politically engaged citizens, and variously suffering, disrupted bodies. The great Weberian temptation is to lapse into resigned cynicism about living in a disenchanted world. One antidote to this cynicism is greater recognition of mundane charisma. My own search for mundane charisma has been among the ill. Robillard (1999) and Lorde (1980) exemplify this charisma for me. Like the dying boy in Galeano's story, they remind others that the ill and suffering are there—not invisible—and they call on others to recognize what it's like to be *there*. They are living post-traumatic lives, but their trauma becomes the source of their work, and their work becomes a source of community with new possibilities of role taking and common sense.

Let me tell a final story. When I was in the hospital undergoing diagnostic tests to figure out what kind of cancer I had, one test was extracting bone marrow. I treated the experience as a very unpleasant ride. The last part of the test involved observing whether certain blood markers changed after the extraction, so when the physicians had left a technician came in to take blood. We got to talking about blood taking, tests, and hospitals. Then she said something extraordinary to me. "Remember," she said, "everyone who touches you affects your healing."

Rides touch us in one way and stories in another. Which parts of life are disenchanting and which are remoralizing will remain contested, but the differences are real, and our vocation is the continuing struggle to tell one from the other.

Notes

1. In personal communications with medical researchers and entrepreneurs, the most bullish forecast I have heard about chip implantation involves using these to follow up broad-spectrum genetic testing for disease risks. Implanted chips would monitor protein levels and thus fine-tune the risk information from DNA. Techno-optimists forecast implementation within five years.

2. Proposals for medical savings accounts differ, since the concept is more proposed than actually implemented. In general, individuals are required to carry private health insurance with high deductible payments, for example, $2,000. Thus catastrophic costs are presumably covered. Individuals then receive the deductible amount each year, either as an employee benefit or a payroll deduction; note that the unemployed are excluded. Money not spent on medical costs during the year can be kept in a medical savings account. Thus only good health can lead to what Du Pont predicts, "a fund to provide for their medical care in old age and an estate for their heirs." For a critical discussion see Taft and Stewart 2000: 8–9.
3. This point summarizes Bordo's (1998) objection to Davis (1995). Women may be able to tell moving stories about their strategic use of surgery as part of a personal quest, but their actions still affirm the capitalist, patriarchal beauty system that makes such surgery compelling.
4. Much of Robillard's frustration with a variety of treatment experiences could be glossed by saying that while he is ostensibly the one on the ride, he eventually realizes the ride is not for him. Throughout *Wit,* Vivian Bearing struggles with the realization that she is being used as part of her physicians' ride; again the line at her death, "She's Research!"
5. For specific stories of illness, see Frank 1995, 1997a, 1997b, 2000.

References

As Good As It Gets. 1997. Directed by James L. Brooks; screenplay by Mark Andrus and James L. Brooks.

Barry, Dave. 2000. "The 'Haves' Know What NASDAQ Is; The 'Have-Nots' Are Eating Yak." *Calgary Herald* (May 21), D14.

Baudrillard, Jean. 1998. *The Consumer Society: Myths and Structures.* 1970. Reprint, London: Sage.

Becker, Gay. 1997. *Disrupted Lives: How People Create Meaning in a Chaotic World.* Berkeley: University of California Press.

Bordo, Susan. 1998. "*Braveheart, Babe,* and the Contemporary Body." In *Enhancing Human Traits: Ethical and Social Implications,* ed. Erik Parens (pp. 189–221). Washington, D.C.: Georgetown University Press.

Davis, Kathy. 1995. *Reshaping the Female Body: The Dilemma of Cosmetic Surgery.* New York: Routledge.

Du Pont, Pete. 1999. "Wealth Creation Benefits Society." *Calgary Herald* (November 11), A23.

Edson, Margaret. 1999. *Wit.* New York: Dramatists Play Service.

Farrell, Kirby. 1998. *Post-traumatic Culture: Injury and Interpretation in the Nineties.* Baltimore, Md.: Johns Hopkins University Press.

Frank, Arthur W. 1995. *The Wounded Storyteller: Body, Illness, and Ethics.* Chicago: University of Chicago Press.

———. 1997a. "Illness As Moral Occasion: Restoring Agency to Ill People." *Health* 2: 131–48.

———. 1997b. "Enacting Illness Stories: When, What, and Why." In *Stories and Their Limits: Narrative Approaches to Bioethics,* ed. Hilde Lindemann Nelson (pp. 31–49). New York: Routledge.

———. 2000. "Illness and Autobiographical Work: Dialogue as Narrative Destabilization." *Qualitative Sociology* 23: 135–56.

Galeano, Eduardo. 1991. *The Book of Embraces.* New York: Norton.

Goffman, Erving. 1961. *Encounters: Two Studies in the Sociology of Interaction.* Indianapolis: Bobbs-Merrill.

Kleinman, Arthur. 1988. *The Illness Narratives: Suffering, Healing, and the Human Condition.* New York: Basic Books.

Levinas, Emmanuel. 1989. "Ethics As First Philosophy." In *The Levinas Reader,* ed. Seán Hand (pp. 75–87). Cambridge: Blackwell.

Life Is Beautiful (La Vita è Bella). 1997. Directed by Roberto Benigni; screenplay by Vincento Cerami and Roberto Benigni.

Lorde, Audre. 1980. *The Cancer Journals.* San Francisco: Spinsters/Aunt Lute.

Rainmaker, The. 1997. Directed and screenplay by Francis Ford Coppola. Based on the book *The Rainmaker* by John Grisham. New York: Doubleday and Company, 1995.

Ritzer, George. 1996. *The McDonaldization of Society.* Rev. ed. Thousand Oaks, Calif.: Pine Forge Press.

Robillard, Albert. 1999. *Meaning of a Disability: The Lived Experience of Paralysis.* Philadelphia: Temple University Press.

Taft, Kevin, and Gillian Stewart. 2000. *Clear Answers: The Economics and Politics of For-Profit Medicine.* Edmonton, Alberta: Duval House Publishing.

Taylor, Charles. 1991. *The Malaise of Modernity.* Concord, Ontario: Anansi.

Warwick, Kevin. 2000. "Cyborg 1.0." *Wired* (February): 145–51.

Weber, Max. 1958. "Science As a Vocation." In *From Max Weber,* ed. C. Wright Mills and Hans Gerth (pp. 129–56). New York: Oxford University Press.

The Metaphor Is the Message

Laurel Richardson

My dearest friend has moved into an assisted-living facility 500 miles away from me. She had a little stroke; she has severe migraines. I call her often. I called her today because I wanted to converse with her about Art Frank's chapter. I told her about what I considered the emotional center of the piece: When someone gets ill, finances, mobility and independence are lost; but also lost is the familiar sense of self. The Self is disrupted; the community through which one knows oneself dissipates.

"That's exactly how I feel," she said. "I feel as if my lives have disappeared."

"Lives?" I asked.

"Yes," she said. "My colleague friends. My political friends. My union friends. My Sedona friends. I'm not in those lives anymore. I am not invisible here at this home; but this is not *my* life."

She concluded, "I'm so glad someone is writing about this."

I, too, give thanks to Arthur Frank for turning my attention to illness, and the management of illness in a commodified culture. How might we ease the indignities of illness? What are ways of thinking about the world and acting within it that privilege kindness and caring, despite the runaway sludge of corporate total quality management, and its sewage tributaries, absentee ownership, amorality, objectification?

This is Frank's question, too. In what follows, I will explore some of Frank's ideas, and engage in some strategic critique and renaming. My intention is to expand the conversation that Frank offers to interactionists.

Invoking Max Weber, Frank proposes that as social scientists our vocation is to identify that which leads to "disenchantment," that which leads to "remoralization," and to know the difference between them. To address this writ large question, Frank organizes his thinking through two metaphors (what he calls tropes): The Ride and The Story.

The Ride is the *form* that leads to "disenchantment." The ride is a place (event, experience, site) where the individual has no influence; the ride replaces the reality of the person with an image; signs have primacy, truth-value; the ride tells people who they are and what they feel; and the ride proposes everything is going to be okay. But once you are on the ride, you are out of control.

Carnival rides come to my mind—shoot-the-shoots, the bungee jump, the Ferris wheel, especially the roller coaster. Frank's metaphor arises from and derives its strength from these carnival rides because there is probably not a one among us who has not consciously chosen—or consciously not chosen—to ride. We feel in our guts what he means by "the ride"; it is viscerally situated in our body's experiences.

Frank intends his metaphor of The Ride to encompass the multiple ways and institutions through which contemporary society alienates, dehumanizes, tricks, and steals agency from actors. The dominating cultural project that objectifies humans is *like* a ride. Developing his thesis primarily through cultural-texts (movies, books, plays), Frank helps us to understand (feel) the ride as an abstract yet "real" presence in our mundane lives. Nearly everywhere we go—to the movies, the theater, the mall, McDonald's, the hospital—we find ourselves on a ride, being told who we are and what we should feel, asking us to assent to the categories and definitions of the ride, our lives reduced to The Ride's "menu."

The medical ride often totally alienates one from one's Self, because commodified medicine incarnates a person as a blip on a monitor, numbers on a chart, specimens in a tube, computerized printouts; research data; money. It is the quintessential ride; the exemplar of how bad a world of rides can be, not only for those who get on the ride, but also for those who are refused entry—the uninsured, underinsured, the non-savvy, the too old, the too poor, the too rural. These and others are left standing outside the gates, invisible to the gatekeepers, the accountants.

As an alternative to the ride, Frank proposes the metaphor of The Story, through which medicine (and by analogy, the social world in general) can be "remoralized." Although I would truly rather live in a "remoralized" world—that is, I share Frank's ethics and values—I find his use of The Story as his metaphoric vehicle confusing and rhetorically problematic.

When arguing at the metaphoric level and constructing binaries (even binaries that fit into a single gestalt), as Frank has done, the rhetor does best by staging *comparable* metaphors (for example, whimsically, roller coaster versus bumper car). The Ride and The Story are not comparable metaphors. They are not even "apples and oranges"; they are more like "apples" and "camels." The Story metaphorically and commonsensically encompasses The Ride, that is, the "camel" can consume the "apples."

The Ride is a story, grown more dominant in postmodern times. Some "rides" are stories in the mundane sense—you can leave the theater, turn off the television, exit the mall, toss your McBurgers. Although other rides hide their stories, they can be "storied." One cannot easily leave the intensive care unit, for example, but one can talk about it; tell a story about the ride. One could even tell a story about confronting the ride. Thus, the bifurcation of "ride" and "story" (passenger/driver) is rhetorically confusing.

What makes more sense to me is to frame both The Ride and The Story under the overarching trope of *narrative*. This framing, I believe, has multiple advantages:

1. It avoids the rhetorical confusion discussed above.
2. It fits well with the kind of poststructural theorizing that engages Frank.
3. It provides an opportunity to analyze how one can be a character, author, coauthor, or simultaneously author and character in different stories, and what the consequences of one's position in a story are for one's sense of control.
4. Most important, it provides a frame for deploying other metaphors, other stories yet to be writ.

What stories might empower people caught in rides not of their own choosing? What stories can we as social scientists circulate that might help "remoralize" the social world?

One such story dear to the readers of this book is the "interaction story." Following Frank's reading of interactionism, the interaction story holds that although a person claims a Self, that Self is known and shaped through interaction—

meaningful conversations—with others. Should that interaction be disrupted, the Self is subject to disintegration. In this story, the person is a coauthor. A patient struggles to get medical staff out of the ride-story and into the interaction story—to engage with the patient in meaningful conversation, to be coauthor of the patient's story.

I take a break from writing and call my friend at her assisted living home. I read her what I have written so far. She tells me she's been to see a chiropractor.

"The medical doctors see me as body parts reduced to electronic body parts; the osteopaths see me as connected body parts reduced to graphs. The chiropractor's been the first one to treat me as a whole person, not as body parts or images of body parts. For the first time," she says, "I feel better, and I feel the possibility of leaving the home."

I find myself elevated by her lifted spirits, even as I know that because my friend has the wherewithal to find medical practices that will validate her Self, her individual search does nothing to alter the received conditions of standard medicine, or change the struggle of other ill people to command an authorial place in their own stories. I am reminded of a 1950s article by Alice Rossi about the difference between "liberal" solutions and "radical" solutions. The liberal solution "fixes" the individual; the radical one alters the system.

Frank wants a radical story, as do I. He places much of the responsibility for the writing of that story on the individual suffering person, who is (1) to link their suffering to that of others, and (2) to name the social structures that create and sustain that suffering. I think this is a lot to ask of many a sick person.

Even as medical practices now often include asking patients to decide what procedures they want, the doctor determines what procedures are on the menu, much as a parent determines the dinner menu for children. But, unlike children who can use their sense of taste to choose, choosing a procedure requires knowledge and expertise. These rest in the doctor, and thus the first-author, if you will, of the content and structure of the "interactional story" is the expert, the controller of the patient's possible story, plotlines limited by the sludge heap of HMOs, insurance, bottom lines—the "trash-fiction" of commodified medicine.

So, let me propose we help the remoralization project by circulating another story, a radical story which draws upon the sociological imagination, the knowledge and skills of the sociologist: the_____ (fill in the blank—survivor, PWA, recovering, and so on) *collective story.* The collective story tells the experience of a sociologically constructed category of people in the context of larger cultural and historical forces. The "problem" is not the person, but the system. People similarly situated *who may or may not be aware of their affinities* are coauthors with *sociologists* in the writing of the collective story. Its construction is an act of *symbolic interaction.* The intention of the collective story is to help construct a consciousness of kind in the minds of protagonists, a concrete recognition of sociological bondedness with others, because such consciousness can break down isolation among people, empower them, provide authoritative resources for critique, and lead them to collective action; it can alter the system.

Deploying the collective story does not require individual sufferers to take on the social world while waiting for their chemo, nor does it make sociologists moral arbiters or charismatic saviors. Rather, it gives us something of value to do about medical practices: the deployment of a critical discourse, a new collective story grounded in the sociological imagination.

I call my friend to read her the final version of this paper, and to get permission to include her thoughts.

"Years ago in Sedona," she tells me, "I bought myself a magic wand."

"Yes," I said. "You gave me one too, a long time ago when I was sick. I still have it. It's plastic with glitter-stars that slowly float through the ooze when you turn the wand upside down. My grandson loves to play with it."

"Mine, too," she says.

We are silent for a moment or two.

Then, she says, "Listening to your paper made me aware of my mythologies—you know Cinderella and the Wizard of Oz. You wave your magic wand and everything's okay. That's been my ride and my story . . . Looking for a miracle."

Note

I thank Ernest Lockridge, Nancy Johnson, and Betty Frankle Kirschner for their insights into writing, rhetoric, and illness.

Narrative Heat

H. L. GOODALL JR.

The aging detective checked into his ocean-view room in the old town of St. Pete Beach. It was mid-afternoon on a Wednesday of the last week of the first month of an already overblown new millennium.

Back home in central North Carolina—normally a place of mild if rainy winters—there had been record cold and snowstorms. When rendered narratively on day-long and then night-long forecasts and announcements of yet more school and business closings, these new millennium stories only served to increase the general public perception—one part made of old fears, the other part borne from increasingly mediated needs—that the snow was a sign. But a sign of *what?* In these times even the weatherman is supposed to be a fortune-teller.

The detective had come down to Florida for a little peace from the cold and hype, hoping for sunshine and light. He was hoping also to see old friends and maybe make some new ones. The occasion that warranted this trip was none other than the SSSI Couch-Stone Symposium, which, this year of all years, was dedicated to "Ethnography for the Twenty-First Century." So it was that the detective, an ethnographer by any other name, came to the Dolphin Beach

Resort Hotel on St. Petersburg Beach, much as any believer journeys toward any symbolic Mecca. He came to St. Pete on a quest that would consist of sacred (if academic) rituals—reading/listening to papers, watching/participating in performances, meetings and greetings in hallways and bars, eating at local restaurants. Given the symposium title, and the list of participants, it was likely also to be a rite of passage for ethnography. He came here because, in the company of other like-minded ethnographers, he wanted to celebrate what they, together, had made—indeed, what they were, together, making. Within the calendar heart of this cold twenty-first century winter, he came in search of narrative heat.

Heat, according to any engineer or physicist, is best understood to be a by-product of the release of energy. I'm sure that is technically correct, but understanding heat that way makes me glad I'm not an engineer or physicist. For me, er—for the detective—heat is about releasing energies too, but is less a physical experience than an emotional one. I *feel* the heat, I *warm* to stories of it. Together, our shared words and actions create and constitute it. As symbolic creatures, we experience and come to know the release of energies in meaningful ways that escape the straight lines and narrow arrows of the higher math.

There is a unique heat to personal sadness, too. I am feeling this heat from Ron Pelias, as he speaks plainly, yet poetically, about his painful experiences as a father who has become disconnected from his son, and tries to understand how it is to be the son to an increasingly distant father, who is, after all, *he*. This is the kind of rare performance that quiets an audience to the very core of our common genetic code. It makes me think, and painfully remember, my own final dissociation from my father, and fear the same damned thing happening between me and my own fine son despite my best efforts, and his best efforts, in the other direction. But it also inspires me as only the truth of poetry can, to not forget what is most passionate and misunderstood about life itself, and that is our own power to endure it, to absorb hurt and love as a single meaningful pattern, the purpose and creative energy in that. As Lesa Lockford summed it wonderfully to that assembled audience and to the poet/performer himself, "there can be a stillness" in such a performance, in such rare poetry, that acts as the moral equivalent of action. In her swirling turns of compassionate yet critical phrases from this moment forward in her carefully crafted response, I am feeling another form of narrative heat alive within this room. Can it both honor and help rekindle that poetic fire? Can the melodic spells cast by her words alter the personal dynamics of warmth through the work of nuance and subtlety? I am certain that they did. I could *feel* the fire.

I am out to dinner at a local seafood establishment with my pals Bob Krizek and Maria Cristina González. We order a big plate of raw oysters and glasses of beer. We talk about our lives, our hopes, our dreams. We laugh a lot. What is it about such talk that brings out the laughter among our species? Is it the heat that comes from shared camaraderie? The heat that creates a desire for deeper, better relationships? The heat that we are generating in energetic talk, all those human emotions burning off at velocity speed in laughter?

It occurs to me that these moments are part of what makes a conference interesting. Particles, or maybe waves, that contribute to its overall energy.

Thursday I wake up early and try the in-room coffee, which is predictably weak and oddly sour. This will never do. I find my way to the "C" level of the hotel, where the meetings are scheduled to take place, looking for the free continental breakfast and some decent java. On the way up the stairs I see Elissa Foster, who's at the registration desk but wears a big Australian smile anyway. I like Elissa; she's got that youthful enthusiasm for the scholarly life, but with her own unique attitude. A very winning combination. She greets me and says, happily, "Guess what came in this morning?"

"What?" I say.

"Your . . . new . . . book!" she says, handing me a copy out of a brown box beneath the desk. I didn't expect this, so I am surprised and delighted. *Writing the New Ethnography* is the book I always wanted to write about my learning how to become an ethnographer, a writer, and a member of the academy. I keep one copy with me, just to walk around with, like a proud daddy.

Thursday is filled with interesting presentations, and I, a good conference-goer, attend as many of them as I can. Although I enjoy all of what I see and hear, one session in particular stands out. It is dedicated to "Audio Documentary and the Study of Contemporary Culture."

The panel is introduced by Mark Neumann, looking these days exactly as hip as he has every right to be, just with a little less hair on top. I've just seen his new book on the Grand Canyon, with its gorgeous bronze-tintype style cover and a picture of him looking all tired and poetic in black tennis shoes on the back cover. Unlike most back cover author-art, nothing about that picture is a lie. With him on the session are Daniel Makagon, a current doctoral student at the University of South Florida, and Jim Carrier, an independent radio producer best known for his work in *Esquire, Harper's, The Atlantic,* and on the "This American Life" series on National Public Radio (NPR). Mark briefly states that these audio ethnographies more or less speak for themselves, and gets right down to business by dimming the lights and turning up the volume on the sound system.

Mark's audio ethnography is about people who visit, and pay tribute, to Jim Morrison's grave in Paris. Like Mark's work on the Grand Canyon, it is all about finding out why people go there, what they think it means, who they are when they are in its presence. This piece is an intriguing, artful juxtaposition and mix of disembodied voices, live concerts in which Morrison admonished and taunted crowds, random musings from world travelers about the meaning of Morrison's words in their lives, and it ends, appropriately, with the Doors' number-one hit, "Light My Fire."

Daniel's tape is titled "Bass/Super(sonic) Structure," and is an account of street youth who place huge amplifiers and bass speakers in their vehicles to enjoy music. Because his informants provide a wide range of reasons for making/using these sounds, we got a feel for a part of contemporary urban culture that, at least in my experiences, has been largely overlooked or at least underexplored. Throughout he poses recurring questions about the relationship of music to noise, about the ethics of invading others' public spaces, and about the "tick, tick, followed by the BOOM" of this American street life.

Jim's work is a piece he did on NPR called "Saints of the Last Days," which is about Mormon culture, power, God, visions, sex, love, and polygamy. It is a funny, sad, and ultimately disturbing account that, because of its artistry, invites the listener into an alternative world that coexists with our own. If this were a video I'd be distracted too much by the faces these Mormons have, but because all I get is the sound of their voices, I seem to hear more clearly what they are saying. That's what gets to me—*hearing* these voices. They speak with great passion, but, ironically, because of the twisted tale they tell, energy leaves our room when their words enter it.

I hear great things about a couple of panels that I missed. One thing I don't want to miss is the keynote by Mary and Kenneth Gergen on "representation as relationship."

I stand at the back of the room in what is a packed house and watch these two noted scholars work from a performance script. The experience, for me, is oddly like watching "Scenes From a Marriage" meets an imaginary prime-time

Fox network academic sitcom, kind of in the style of "Third Rock From the Sun." I hear several colleagues talk about how wonderful a teaching tool this "relational performance" could be, particularly the part where the Gergens stop in midscript and ask the audience, "What would you say to alter where this conversation/argument/fight is going?" Pretty cool. I also hear a couple of my peers discuss, at a theoretical level, the odd juxtaposition of two pros framing their performance as an "amateur" production. Kenneth Gergen addresses this by saying something profound about "not privileging the professional voice" and goes on to something else that I kind of lose track of while musing around the room.

There is a lot of mixed energy at work in that room. Some of it is creative and supportive and enthusiastic; some of it feels colder or maybe just distanced. And there is the usual academic hierarchical interplay of guilt and jealousy there, too. It becomes very warm in that room—the kind of warmth that requires release.

Dancing isn't optional if you hang out with Eric Eisenberg. Probably this explains at least part of the reason why a lot of us seek him out at conferences. After long days of conferencing, he offers us what we need, a source of balance and renewal in our lives. And what he offers us, what we need—this source of mysterious renewal and at least partly ineffable balance—is simply an invitation *to dance*.

Listen to the music, fool. Get into its life rhythms. Move with it. *Dance.* Don't tell me you don't know how to, or can't. Those are words that doom you to life undanced, and it can become a major source of your life's regrets. I know this to be true because I used to say those words too, pre-Eric. But I learned that the point is not to demonstrate talent so much as to dance *together*. To make a place for meaningful shared activity in this all too singular and occasionally meaningless life. To dance is existential. To dance is *to be*.

I don't remember the name of the bar. It was some crab joint, down by the gulf; somebody said she knew it well. Maybe she did, and then maybe she knew the music too. I didn't know the music at all. Some combination of techno-punk and disco, it seemed. But I'm a blues guy, so anything that doesn't come from the Delta or Chicago, or at least have roots there, is exotic and mostly foreign to me. So there we were, Eric & Company, including Maggie and Jen, Patricia and Maria Cristina, Linda, Linda, Lisa and Lexa, Margey and Nigel, and a couple more people whose names I never caught.

One of the extreme pleasures of dancing with women, a pleasure borne of heat that moves beyond coordinating rhythms on the edges of skin, is what they whisper to you as they slide by. "This is the best *fore*play," my dancing partner says, her face just red enough to pass any test for available evidence of the fact. And one of the pleasures of all this coordinated—and not so coordinated—action on the dance floor is the chance to observe, as Dr. Eisenberg puts it, the "difference between full professors and assistant professors dancing." The full among us are somehow more unwound, given to wilder, perhaps more open expressions of self within this context of academic others. Or maybe it's the tequila. Or the music. All of the above, or none of the above.

Whatever. The more I dance the less I care about theorizing. I feel rhythm as heat; heat as intensity; intensity as possibility; possibility as the sum of all that is right now.

Friday I avoid the in-room coffee and go straight to the Book Room for the real stuff. I also stop to peruse the various books and journals displayed on the tables. I have a hard time moving away from books, don't you? I want to touch them, hold them, open them, and read. Probably this goes back to my childhood, where reading was a way out of where I was, as well as a way toward something finer.

I'm in the middle of such musing when Larry Frey walks in, himself searching for sustenance made out of coffee and sweet rolls. Larry is a guy I've admired for a long time but I don't know him well. I figure it's about time I did. We strike up a conversation—from the professional to the personal and back again—and we discover that, as kids, we both went to the same school in London! As alums of the American School London, we share a kind of unusual heritage. I also discover that he is working on a new ethnography about American ex-patriots, and that his parents are among them. So much energy is generated when storied lives collide!

The first session I attend is on "new ethnographies." Herb Simons humorously deconstructs his adolescent experiences working as a busboy in the Catskills. I don't know if what he is doing is ethnography or comedy, or if maybe this, too, is a new genre, but it is a delightful rendering of the awkward in the ordinary. His talk is followed by Bob Krizek's beautifully crafted account of "barbershop talk," where a barbershop is framed as a "third place" in our culture. I wonder whether this conference might also be considered a "third place," even though what we are ostensibly doing here is "working." But we are removed from our homes and from our places of employment, and our talk together combines a sense of community with a sense of shared histories and futures, a blending of the personal and the professional.

That afternoon I go to Carolyn Ellis's "ethnographic aesthetics" panel and hear one of the best presentations of the conference. A young guy I'd never met named Greg Snyder from the New School for Social Research performs an account of tracking down graffiti artists in the city that is beyond cool. His rich evocation of the new (then) language of the streets, his ability to make sense of the art and the elusive artists, and his overall hip-hop style of oral presentation wins the crowd. His presentation seems charged by the raw energies of American urban street life, a sort of deeply ordered chaos.

After that I move from room to room, conference hopping. There are people whose papers/performances I want to see. Which, of course, means there are other presentations I will have to miss. But I do see Annette Markham's edgy "on-line scholarship" talk, which mostly—apparently inspired by the Gergens's energy the night before—consists of hard, unanswered questions about life on-line, the location of the body in cyberspace, and its perceived effects on the researcher and subject. I also see Rob Drew's "Emcees of Karaoke" presentation, sans his rendition of Prince's "Little Red Corvette." Gil Rodman does a rock-'n'-roll-inspired review/extension of this panel, in his own Elvis Forever way.

We enter a large darkened chamber and I choose a seat on the aisle near the stage. This performance, called "Dis/enchantment by Academe: Performing the Multiplicity of Our Personal/Professional Lives," is organized by Patricia Geist and Linda Welker, and features Margy Brookes, Nigel Brookes, Maggie Miller, Jennifer Ott, and, of course, Patricia and Linda themselves. Patricia has just guest-edited a special issue of *Communication Theory* on the same topic, and the energies that had been released in and around that volume continue to ripple through the academy. This night promises *more*. I want to hear and see it.

The next hour is pure magic. We are witnesses to representations and reflections of our own lives, from the lack of time we have for everything from reading to lovemaking to the constant damnable weirdness that we encounter (and contribute to) in the everyday making of our stubborn academic hierarchies, patriarchies, and bureaucracies. At one point Maggie Miller gives poignant voice to a sobering rendition of a Dylan song, accompanying herself on a mandolin. At another, Margey finds that what is in Nigel's pants are a series of floppy discs and a whole lotta academic *ennui*. In a constant refrain, Margey chants a fairy poem from "A Midsummer Night's Dream" in full Elizabethan voice that becomes a transition from one academic absurdity to another. Toward the end of this excellent, smart, funny, and all-too-true account of our lives we are asked to write down a source of disenchantment, and of enchantment, with the academy. Then, one by one, all members of the audience participate in a sage-ing ceremony wherein we ritualistically burn our disenchantment in a collective fiery cauldron. The performance ends with a celebratory dance that marks the energy of our common renewal.

Sometimes, in such magic times, you just want to keep the party, the energy, the heat, *going*.

Saturday I wake up with a bad case of cottonmouth and a throbbing headache of Ulyssian proportions. Damn those Sirens! Damn me for forgetting to pack the aspirin. Worse yet, there is a bright sun shining in my window, making everything with an edge on it have a sharper, harder edge on it. In other words, I hurt just *seeing*.

I struggle down a faintly pulsating hallway and ask a young woman who works in an office where the nearest bottle of aspirin is located. She says, gently, "There is an Eckerd's across the street."

She might as well have said it was on the other side of the moon.

Water might help. I seem to recall something about water being important to human life, particularly human life that has been damaged by a lack of it. I move slowly, somewhat tentatively, down the hallway and find the Book Room. There are pitchers of the clear liquid available and I drain several of them. Carolyn Ellis walks in bright-eyed and chipper. She asks me how I am, as if it isn't fairly obvious. "I'm not good," I admit. "Would you happen to have any aspirin?"

She smiles and pulls out a plastic bag filled with various antidotes to body poisoning caused by any number of cultural overloads. "Do you prefer something in ibuprofen, or will Excedrin do?"

I want to tell her just to pour whatever is in that bag down my throat and we'll hope for the best. But I was reared to be polite, so I just say, "Excedrin will be fine, thank you."

I remember something about lying down in a darkened room hastening the effects of aspirin, so I return to my room and comply with the dictates of memory. Twenty minutes later, I am healed! Hurrah!

Aspirin is a wonderful thing.

Due to being bad the night before and suffering the morning after, I miss most of the morning's presentations, but I do happen in on the last three-quarters of Arthur Frank's masterful keynote, "Illness and the Interactionist Vocation."

One of the fascinating features of his talk is the framing device he invented for the study of culture, which he terms "the ride versus the story." The "ride" refers to any RPM ("reality producing machine") that alters our consciousness in the direction of a nonreflexive state. So, for example, entering MacDonald's or Disney World, or watching television, or reading popular genre fiction, and so on, is to go for a "ride." So much of our contemporary culture is based on "the ride" that many people move from ride to ride without much contemplation. In part this is because RPMs are the perfect delivery system for hypercapitalism, wherein the purchase of "an experience" is the ultimate form of consumer choice.

The "story" is what happens when we pause long enough to become reflective, or reflexive, about our experiences and ourselves. We intervene in the ride by asking critical questions, empowering ourselves and others to do something other than participate in RPMs, and otherwise engage the spirit.

Professor Frank is a truly engaging speaker. Virtually without notes, he captivates the audience for over an hour, and then entertains questions. His is a moving and informative performance, a source of power and light, of narrative heat, for us all.

Our spirituality panel was at 4 P.M. in the Cypress Room.

I witness Cristina González's dramatic performance of "Freeing the Great Mother Archetype from Inherited Mexican-Catholic Historical/Cultural Women's Tales," a title that, while accurate, does not come close to representing the power of this performance/story.

On her knees, she holds a rosary, and begins recounting a scene from her childhood: seeing the movie "Song of Bernadette" when she was seven. She talks about how she wanted to see the image of the Great Mother on her wall, just as Bernadette had seen it, and so, every day, she went to her room and prayed to the wall, asking to see Mary. But she never saw her. Given that she was raised Catholic, she thought that this meant something was wrong with her.

She then displays a large color photo of the Virgin Mary with a dagger stuck in her heart, and explains to us that this is one of five central images of Mary she used in her second Ph.D. dissertation ("Yes, I'm crazy," she laughs). This one depicts a beatific face, one that has supposedly accepted the death of her only son (thus the dagger through her heart). She then recounts the legend of La Llorona, a spirit who can be heard in the wicked whistling of wind through bare trees, or that inhabits the thickness of fog, or that makes its ineffable self felt in other mysterious ways. Again, Cristina's experience of this spirit is revealed to be very deep in her soul, as both a source of power and of darkness. She then recounts an event from later in her life, during the mid-1980s, that begins with the line "I still remember what I was wearing when he took me to the abortion clinic." In a compelling voice, she reveals the pain that came when the man she loved did not want to share their baby. Lying down on the stage floor, she awakens to her own screaming. The nurses told her to shut up "because a woman who chooses gives up the right to scream."

From this moment on, Cristina then begins to understand the Virgin Mary's face, as well as the dagger in her heart. She can now identify with her, both her suffering and her grace. In this way, in her own life, she frees the Great Mother image from its Mexican-Catholic heritage and renews her lifelong unity of spirit with that image. Finally, she sees what Bernadette saw.

There is an energy that emanates from such deep passion, from sharing the truth of one's own experience. In its presence, we tend to fall silent. The spirit that has passed among us is beyond words and, like the stillness brought about by Ron's performance, makes a space for us to contemplate the big questions, the hard questions.

Carolyn and Art throw a big party that final night of the conference, complete with good food and a band called the Quivering Rhythm Hounds. There's an image for you. More dancing, singing, laughing, storying, and so on. Everyone is happy again and the music is fine.

This is the way to end a conference, I think. One big musical celebration. One part of it is a celebration of our selves, another is a celebration of our work, and of the triumphant future of ethnography at the dawn of this new century.

So much available energy and passion!

I'm sure everyone found time to personally thank Art Bochner and Carolyn Ellis for their role in organizing and bringing off this conference, this celebration. I know I did. In fact, I hear a lot of thanking going on, as if this occasion has been a huge exchange of gifts, which, in a major way, it has been. Stories are gifts.

What is missing, what was still to come for each of us, is the felt need for a ritual of reentry, some way of transitioning ourselves back into the native realities we have temporarily transcended. Without it we tend to feel lost and disoriented for a long time. Coming down from the experience of an ecstatic community like this one is hard to do, and perhaps because we have learned this, most of us just want to stay here. Preferably *forever*.

But we know we can't. Part of what it means to be a human being is the awful knowledge that all of this beauty and light, all of everything on this earth that we become, in fact, is only temporary. We are travelers en route to someplace else, somewhere else maybe, somehow. I don't pretend to know for sure. But what I do know is that we are here to learn and to share and to help each other, and how we make and use language together seems to have a big role in the major parts of that. So our time together in temporary communities is sacred time. Divine time.

To have a soul is to accept the urgency, the invitation, to celebrate this life.

To *fully* celebrate it.

It is our shared destiny and sacred responsibility to make fine music together. It is in our human purpose, our genetic charter, to surrender ourselves, fully, narratively, bodily, to this mystery. And through such total surrender, through these celebratory acts, these gifts of communication, to become one with the mystery, with the power of love, and with the ineffable meaning of life.

In these ways we strive always for a higher consciousness. We strive to become ever more mindful of this earth, this cosmos, and each other. We are, after all, every one of us, made of the same magical stuff as the stars.

Call it ethnography if you want to.

Late afternoon the next day and I am once again within the skin of my narrator, the aging detective. I am alone in a cheap hotel in downtown Atlanta on Super Bowl Sunday, with snow on the ground and no available ticket to the big show.

No planes are flying to my hometown and I am stuck here.

My luggage is somewhere in the United States.

I still have the comfort a small bottle of Jack Daniels can provide, which I usually take with a little ice. Unfortunately it is so cold here that the ice machine in the hallway is frozen.

But I have my Florida memories and the necessary narrative heat.

I am all smiles. Hey, who needs an ice machine, anyway?

When Does a Conference End?

CAROLYN ELLIS AND ARTHUR P. BOCHNER

Sunday, January 30, 2000

"**I** GUESS WE should have planned a closing," Carolyn says sadly to Art as they pass in the hallway after the last session of the symposium ends around noon on Sunday.

"Maybe, but what is there to say after so many presentations and conversations in the sessions, in the hallways, and in the bars?" Art asks.

"It's just, well, it's just that it all ended so abruptly. I usually feel a little let down when a conference is over. Especially this one. But you're probably right. Besides, as we anticipated, people are already in their leave-taking mode, including us," Carolyn agrees, looking down at the stack of bills and books she is carrying and at the conference programs and banners threatening to slide out of Art's hands.

"That's the truth," Art says. "You take care of the conference bills and I'll make sure the books from the exhibit are packed and the registration tables cleared off upstairs."

"Okay, will you take our suitcases to the van as well? I have one more task I must do." Art nods.

As we rush off in separate directions, we note that everyone else is rushing as well. For our visitors, in addition to suitcases to pack and bills to pay, there are airport limos to schedule, planes to catch, papers to be graded, and children to be nurtured. People nervously call on their cell phones to get updates on the winter storm in the Northeast and find out whether their plane will take off. Already the outside world leaks into the Dolphin, disturbing the serenity of the sunny beach resort on the west coast of Florida. Separately, Art and Carolyn fantasize that perhaps no one will be able to leave and the talk will continue.

Carolyn hurries to the hotel room of Karen Scott-Hoy. Expecting Carolyn, Karen has displayed around the room the five large (two-by-three-foot) original paintings she has brought to the conference for her presentation. The handmade metal box for safely transporting the paintings lies open on the floor, ready to be filled. One painting, titled *Autoethnography*, sits by itself against the bed. Like a magnet, the image pulls Carolyn's eyes into it. Drawn into the bright colors, she feels caught up in the swirls of paint connecting the two women: one, light-skinned, partially clothed, whose back is mostly visible in a mirror; the second, darker skinned, wearing native Vanuatu island clothing, only half of her included in the painting. Why is the background of the right side of the painting white, while the left side is richly colored? And what is that black rectangular object the light-skinned woman hides in her hand behind her back?

Carolyn and Karen discuss how the painting concerns revealing and concealing: The researcher can see parts of herself that we, the viewers, cannot; yet, we, the viewers, can see parts of her that she cannot; and the darker-skinned woman has yet another view. Nevertheless, there is always something—the black, rectangular object—hidden. We talk about perspective: We look at the woman looking over her shoulder into the mirror, which reflects back to her and to us yet another view. We talk about the blending of different worlds in ethnographic research: The background of the painting portrays two rooms; the white, ordered side represents the world of the researcher; the thatched, colorful, and flowing background, the world of participants. We talk about reaching across boundaries to make connections, and how our worlds can never quite be the other's or the other's ours.

Carolyn senses that she has only begun to understand and penetrate the painting. She is mesmerized by it. She can't wait to explore it further and use it to guide her writing on *Doing Autoethnography: An Ethnographic Novel,* a book she hopes to complete soon. For her, the painting portrays and legitimizes autoethnography in a way words cannot. She feels spiritually connected to the painting, and to Karen. A sense of vulnerability sweeps over her, and she holds back her tears. She wants to own the painting and is not sure that is a good feeling to have.

"Do you ever sell your paintings?" Carolyn asks, wondering if she sounds like a crass capitalist.

"Sometimes," Karen says. "I find it hard to put a price on them."

"If you ever decide to sell *Autoethnography,* I'd like to buy it," Carolyn adds cautiously, sensing a hesitation from Karen to part with it. Only later will she find out that Karen's reluctance came partially from her desire to ask Carolyn to be an external reviewer on her dissertation and not knowing if this transaction would be appropriate under those circumstances.

Karen goes with her heartfelt response. "I saw how lovingly you caressed the painting when we took the picture of you holding it after my session. I think you should have it. I've thought of giving it to you, for all you've done." She walks toward the painting, and picks it up.

"Oh, no," Carolyn protests quickly, "please let me pay for it. I insist."

After more discussion, Karen quotes a price that feels to both of them that she still is giving the painting as a gift; in response, Carolyn offers to pay some of Karen's hotel bill, which allows her to feel she is giving a part of the conference in return.

Carolyn carries the painting out to her van, gently places it in a secure position behind the driver's seat, and retrieves and signs copies of *Final Negotiations* and *of Investigating Subjectivity.* She walks back into the lobby of the Dolphin. Standing at the bottom of the spiral staircase, she feels as if this is her home and she must now bid each of her visitors farewell. During a lull, she spots Art on the other side of the staircase. He, too, is saying his good-byes. Without his knowing, she watches him through the slatted steps. He hugs and is hugged, time after time. Good feeling permeates the air, a sense of contentment akin to the gentle support of a warm summer breeze, a sign that something memorable, sustainable, and worthwhile happened here. The connections are palpable.

Carolyn turns back to her "guests," scanning the crowd to make sure that nobody leaves unnoticed. When she sees Karen walking by, she hurries over to give her the signed books. Karen smiles appreciatively, runs her hand gently first over one cover, then the other, opens each book, quickly reads the inscriptions, and hugs Carolyn. Ken Gergen comes through the lobby and hands Art a copy of Mary's book, *Toward a New Psychology of Gender,* edited with Sara Davis. Ian Prattis joins in, giving Art some chapters from a new book he is working on, and then walks over to hand Carolyn a signed copy of *Anthropology at the Edge.* Several graduate students walk through carrying Buddy Goodall's new book, *Writing the New Ethnography,* its unmistakable red cover on display. Virginia Olesen shares stories of her gardening exploits with Carolyn and of her computer bugs with Art.

Rose Jensen collects money for membership in SSSI. People grab Mitch Allen for one more attempt to sell their book proposal. Helena Lopata searches for a lunch partner, hoping to squeeze out one more good conversation before she goes home. People exchange gifts, more stories, more hugs, and e-mail addresses.

Finally, reluctantly, Carolyn and Art get into the gray van and depart. We are unusually quiet. Wanting, like Helena, one more experience before going home to Tampa, we stop for lunch in Gulfport, an artsy town close by. When Art spots a frame shop there, we take *Autoethnography* in for framing. "It's a good omen," Carolyn says, "even though I'll have to drive the forty miles back from Tampa to pick it up."

During lunch, Art brings up the idea of publishing an edited volume from the symposium. "We could feature the artwork and performative pieces in the book as well as personal narrative," he says, speaking in an excited manner.

"It will be a lot of work," Carolyn responds, clearly not sharing Art's excitement at the moment. "Remember *Composing Ethnography*?"

"How could I forget? But we could write a dynamic book of evocative stories and essays from the great presentations we heard."

"Yes, but how would we decide which of the presentations would fit together best as a book?"

"It would be difficult, but not impossible," reassures Art. "Let's see, we could have a section on aesthetics, one on performance, one on—"

"Hold it a minute. What about our students? How would we choose among their papers?"

"We probably shouldn't use any of our current students' papers," Art suggests, "so as not to show favoritism."

"I don't know. It all sounds like a hassle to me. I'm really exhausted from organizing the conference." Carolyn sighs and takes a long drink of her coffee. "And edited collections always take more time and effort than we think they will."

"You're probably right," Art responds, holding his head up with his hand, suddenly realizing how tired he is as well.

As we dig into our crab cakes without talking, Carolyn suddenly says, "The book would have to give readers a sense of the experience and feeling of the conference."

"But how would we do that within the traditional form of an edited collection?" Art asks cautiously, careful not to dampen Carolyn's sudden enthusiasm.

"We could play with form, perhaps connect sections with discussions that occurred in informal sessions. We could start with how we went about putting the conference together. Even include how we feel right now that it has ended," Carolyn suggests.

"My only concern," she continues, "is about how difficult it will be to write critiques to people who have become our friends."

"But that can be part of what we do in the book," Art challenges, now sitting on the edge of his seat, eyes glowing. "We can try to show empirically and ethnographically the process writers have to go through to produce evocative narratives. We'll emphasize the process of writing, critiquing, and rewriting. It's a way to extend the conference, perhaps even take it to a wider audience."

As Carolyn perks up even more, Art continues, knowing that he has hooked her with the last comment. "Okay, what do we have to do first?"

"First, we have to sell the idea to Mitch Allen at AltaMira Press."

"Mitch is always very supportive. We can do that," Art responds, and begins jotting notes on his napkin.

We continue to bat around ideas about what shape a book based on the symposium might take as we devour the last crumbs of our crab cakes, then share a piece of key lime pie. As we drive home, we feel the spirit of *Autoethnography* watching over us, beckoning us to look deeper into our lives and the lives of those around us, enticing us to extend ourselves more caringly to those in the painting and those looking at the painting, to turn around and look directly into the mirror, and to examine the black box more closely and with care. Appreciative of our lives, we watch another glorious Florida sunset disappear behind us, fulfilled by all we have experienced the past four days and by our rising expectation that the conference is not over.

Name Index

Abu-Lughod, L., 52, 54
Achebe, C., 300, 306
Althusser, L., 12
Anderson, Y., 214, 228
Angrosino, M. V., 14, 32, 172–74, 178,
    184, 327–35, 341, 342
Artuad, A., 18
Austin, D. A., 341–42

Bakhtin, M. M., 12, 216
Ball, M. S., 276, 281
Banks, A., 328, 335
Banks, S. P., 328, 335
Barone, T., 211, 218–20, 228, 278, 281,
    293
Barry, D., 364–65
Bascia, N., 256
Baudrillard, J., 367, 370
Bauman, R., 19, 32
Bava, S., 167–68, 189

Beasley, M., 7
Becker, G., 366, 370
Behar, R., 52, 54
Benjamin, J., 235–36, 256
Berger, L., 64, 73
Bernstein, R., 223, 229

Bird, C., 299, 306
Blair, C., 148
Blumenfeld-Jones, D., 228–29
Boal, A., 19, 32

Bochner, A. P., 1–10, 14, 32, 57, 74, 76,
    86–88, 91,107, 113, 115–19,
    125, 128–29, 147–48, 150–64,
    166–67, 169, 172, 173, 177,
    183–85, 189, 210, 215, 217–19,
    221, 228–29, 276–78, 293, 328,
    335, 340–42, 344, 356, 386,
    388–92
Bochner, M., 295
Bolen, J. S., 130, 143, 148, 256
Bordo, S., 362, 370
Bowman, M., 83, 86
Brossard, N. 204
Brecht, B., 53–54
Brent, T. D., 306
Brett, P., 19, 32
Brookes, M., 383
Brookes, N. M., 383
Bruner, J., 107, 113
Buber, M., 11, 32
Burke, K., 125, 148, 153
Butler, J., 21

Cahill, S. E., 6, 8
Camera, S., 306
Campbell, J., 124, 148

Camus, A., 124
Capo, K. E., 52, 54
Carrier, J., 380–81
Case, S., 19, 32
Celowski, D., 32

Chambers, R., 275, 293
Chaplin, E., 281, 294
Charmaz, K., 213, 229
Chernoff, J. M., 299, 306
Church, K., 168, 214–16, 229, 234–57
Church, L., 256
Clements, M., 47, 51, 53, 55
Clifford, J., 172–74, 184
Clough, P. T., 228–29
Coffy, A., 212–13, 229
Coles, R., 340, 342
Conaguay, T., 91
Conquergood, D., 19, 32, 52, 55, 57, 65,
    73, 77, 79, 86
Copeland, G. A., 148
Crawford, L., 52, 55

D'Andrade, R., 32
Davies, B., 14, 32,
Davis, A. Y., 53, 55
Davis, K., 362, 370
Davis, S., 390
Deemer, D., 224–25, 228, 231
Dent, B., 191–208
Denzin, N. K., 5, 13, 32, 53, 55, 57–60,
    68, 73, 76, 81, 86, 107, 113, 172,
    174, 178, 183, 185, 228–29, 276
    278–79, 294, 339–40, 342
DeVault, M., 223, 229
Doan, R. E., 107–8
Dolan, J., 51, 55, 113–14
Douglas, C., 138–39, 141–42, 148
Drew, R., 383
Dumont, J., 306
Du Pont, P., 363–65, 370, 371

Edson, M., 358, 361, 371
Eisenberg, E., 381
Eisner, E., 278, 281, 293
Ellis, C., 1–10, 14, 32, 51, 53, 55, 57, 64,
    67, 73–74, 76, 86–88, 92–94, 107,
    113–16, 117–20, 147, 165–66,
    168–69, 172, 174, 177, 183–85,
    188–90, 200–208, 210, 215,
    217–21, 228–29, 235, 256,

    276–78, 283, 293–95, 328, 335,
    341–42, 344–56, 382, 386, 388–92
Emerson, R. M., 171–72, 175, 185
Ernaux, A., 255, 257
Ezzy, D., 256–57

Farrell, K., 367, 371
Fergus, K., 74
Fine, M., 340, 342

Finney, M., 9
Fiorito, J., 59, 73
Fitch, M., 63, 74
Flaherty, M. G., 51, 55, 67, 73
Flemons, D., 87–94, 115–21, 165–69,
    187–90, 344–56
Forlenza, Y., 8
Foster, E. L., 379
Foster, S. L., 19, 32
Fox, K. V., 15–16, 32, 113–14
Frank, A. W., 4, 5, 59, 74, 117, 119–21,
    183, 185, 219, 221–22, 229, 255,
    257, 344, 357–69, 384–85
Frazer, J., 126–27, 148
Freeman, M., 215, 230
Frentz, T. S., 124, 148
Fretz, R. I., 171–72, 175, 185
Freud, S., 23, 122
Frey, L., 9
Friedan, B., 122
Friedwald, W., 53, 55
Friese, S., 241, 257
Fyfe, G., 281, 294

Gale, J., 87, 89–90, 93, 166, 189
Galeano, E., 367, 371
Gamber, W., 242, 257
Garratt, D., 223, 225, 228, 230
Geertz, C., 172–73, 185
Geist, P., 9, 383
Gergen, K. J., 5, 9, 11–32, 228, 230, 344,
    380–81, 390
Gergen, M. M., 5, 9, 11–32, 216–17, 228,
    230, 343, 380–81
Gimbutas, M. A., 127, 148

Goffman, E., 366, 371
Goldberg, R., 19, 32
González, C., 117–118, 121, 166–67,
    385–86
Goodall, H. L. Jr., 152, 377–87, 390
Gottlieb, A., 306
Graham, P., 306
Graves, R., 127–28, 137, 143, 148
Gray, R. E., 57–75, 79–85, 214,
    230, 256
Green, S., 87–94, 115–21, 165–69,
    187–90
Greenberg, M., 74

Hacking, I., 151–52
Hale, T., 298–99, 307
Hall, S., 259, 273
Hamilton, E., 126, 137, 148
Hamm, C., 51, 55
Hampaté Ba, A., 299, 306
Hampson, A., 74
Harding, M. E., 145, 148
Harper, D., 281, 294
Harvey, J. H., 107, 114
Heidegger, M., 77, 86
Hertz, R., 214–15, 230
Hiles, M., 124, 149
Hiles, N., 124, 149
Hodkinson, M., 223, 225, 229
Holiday, B., 47–48, 52–53, 55
Homiak, J., 306
hooks, b., 54–55, 130, 134, 148
Hopkins, M. F., 77, 86
Horney, K., 116
Hornsby-Minor, E., 3
Hudgins, A., 331, 335

Ingraham, C., 252, 257
Ivonoffski, V., 57–75, 79–85

Jabes, E., 22, 32
Jackson, D., 214, 216, 230, 340
Jackson, J. E., 171–72, 185
Jackson, M., 53, 55, 57, 65, 74, 342
Jaggar, A., 64

Jenks, E. B., 170–86
Jensen, R., 391

Johnson, N., 376
Jones, J., 44, 51–52, 55
Jones, S. H., 44–56, 78–82, 121
Jung, C. G., 138

Kenney, S., 91
Kiesinger, C. E., 95–114
King, J., 116–17, 169
Kirschner, B. F., 376
Kleege, G., 183–85
Kleinau, M. L., 82, 86
Kleinman, A., 358, 371
Krieger, S., 215, 230
Krizek, B., 382
Kundera, M., 49–50, 55
Kvake, S., 24, 33

Labrecque, M., 74
Langellier, K. M., 52, 83, 86
Lather, P., 228, 230
Law, J., 281, 293
LeCompte, M. D., 172–74, 185
Lecoq, J., 62
Lerner, G., 126–27, 140, 148, 228, 230
Levinas, E., 367, 371
Lincoln, Y. S., 13, 32, 172, 174, 183, 185,
    230, 339, 342
Lockford, L., 76–86, 169, 378
Lockridge, E., 308–26, 376
Lopata, H., 391
Lorde, A., 367, 371
Loseke, D. R., 6, 8
Lyman, P., 240, 257

Maguire, M., 84, 86
Makagon, D., 379–80
Manoa, P., 277–78, 294
Marcus, G. E., 57, 172–73, 185
Markham, A., 168
Martindale, W., 238, 256
Marx, K., 23
Mays de Perez, K. A., 172–74, 178, 184

McCall, M. M., 57, 74
McConatha, J. T., 306
McHughes, J. L., 82, 86
McLeod, J., 218, 230
McLuhan, M., 12, 33
Mienczakowski, J., 57–58, 62, 74–75
Miller, E., 110, 114
Miller, M., 383
Miller, N. K., 235–36, 255, 257
Mishler, E., 107, 114
Mitchell, R., 213
Mohtar, L. F., 84, 86
Monet, 262
Moore, J., 47, 51–53, 55
Morgan, S., 58, 62, 75
Morrison, B., 215, 230
Muller, W., 103, 109, 114
Mykhalovskiy, E., 214–18, 230, 256
Napier, D., 306
Narayan, K., 306
Narayan, U., 239, 256, 257
Nelson, W., 125, 148
Neumann, M., 379–80
Newman, F., 19, 33
Nietzsche, F. W., 121–22, 258
Nothstine, W. L., 148
O'Brien, F., 11, 33, 294
Olesen, V., 390
Orbuch, T., 107, 114
Paglia, C., 52, 55
Parry, A., 107–9, 113–14
Pelias, R. J., 35–43, 57–58, 62, 75, 78–82,
    86, 378
Perls, F., 345
Phelan, P., 49, 55
Phillips, C., 74
Picart, C. J. S., 118, 190, 258–73
Pobryn, E., 52, 56
Pratt, M. L., 186
Punch, M., 340, 342

Qualls-Corbett, N., 127, 135, 148

Rawlins, W. K., 174, 182, 186
Reed-Danahay, D. E., 51, 56, 276, 294

Rhinehart, R., 215, 231
Rich, A., 235, 257
Richardson, L., 16, 33, 69, 75, 87, 91–93,
    120, 166–67, 172, 174–75,
    183–84, 186, 188, 211–12, 228,
    308–26, 328, 335, 346, 356,
    372–76
Richter, D., 59, 75
Ritzer, G., 360, 365, 371
Robillard, A., 359–60, 362–63, 365–66,
    370–71
Rodman, G., 383
Ronai, C., 14–15, 32–33, 113–14, 343
Ropers-Huilman, B., 222, 231
Rose, D., 12, 33
Rosenberg, S., 256
Rossi, A., 375
Rouch, J., 328
Rushing, J. H., 122–49, 150–64

Sacks, O., 107, 114
Saldana, J., 58, 75
Sanjek, R., 171, 175, 186
Sawka, C., 74
Sayer, H. M., 56
Schechner, R., 19, 33
Schensul, J. J., 172–74, 185
Schwandt, T., 223, 228, 231, 277, 279, 294
Scott, B., 238
Scott-Hoy, K., 274–94
Sexton, L., 158
Sharf, B. F., 277, 293
Shaw, L. L., 171–72, 175
Shotter, J., 13, 33
Silvennoinen, M., 221
Simons, H., 382
Sinding, C., 57–75, 79–85
Singer, M., 172–73, 185
Skinner, B. F., 23
Smith, A. D., 52
Smith, B., 214, 219, 231
Smith, G. W., 276, 281, 293
Smith, J., 223, 224–25, 228, 231
Smith, P., 306
Sparkes, A. C., 209–32

Spence, D. P., 340, 343
Stanley, L., 64, 75, 216, 231
Steier, F., 90
Stein, E., 341, 343
Stewart, G., 370
Stoller, P., 297–307, 341, 343
Stoppard, T., 26
Streisand, B., 52, 56

Taft, K., 370–71
Taussig, M., 14, 33
Taylor, C., 365–66, 371
Tedlock, B., 52, 172, 186, 328, 335, 339, 343
Tillmann-Healy, L., 88–90, 107, 113–14, 158, 159, 219–20, 232, 336–43
Tompkins, J., 124–25, 148, 150
Trinh, T. M., 57, 75, 258, 273
Tsang, T., 217–20, 232
Turner, V., 19, 33
Tyler, S., 24, 33
Tylor, E., 327, 335

Ulanov, A., 133, 148
Uttermohlen, T. L., 182, 186

Van Maanen, J., 51, 56, 60, 75, 281, 294

Walker, B. G., 126, 148
Walkerdine, V., 240, 257
Walstrom, M., 57, 75
Warner, M., 341, 343
Warwick, K., 362–63, 365, 371
Weber, A. L., 107, 114
Weber, M., 357–58, 368, 371, 373
Weeks, M. R., 172, 185
Welker, L., 9, 383
White, J., 52, 56
White, M., 108, 114
Williams, B., 32
Wilson, V., 220, 232
Wise, S., 64, 75
Wolcott, H., 281, 294
Wolf, M., 173–74, 186, 328, 335
Woodman, M., 148–49
Wylie, P., 122

Yerby, J., 118
Young-Eisendrath, P., 133–34, 136, 141, 148

Subject Index

abortion, 100–101, 113n1
academia: censorship and, 158; disenchant-
    ment in, 357, 383; patriarchy, 128;
    publishing game, 58, 169; ritual,
    378; women in, 128, 287; writing,
    156–57
activism, 6, 13, 22, 76, 81, 85–86, 340
act of knowing, 77
aesthetics, *18,* 219, 258, 276, 382–83, 391
alienation of self, 373
ambiguities, 125
ambivalence, 245
American individualism, 319
analytic tension, 119
androcentric tradition, 24–25. *See also*
    patriarchy
art and science, 2–4, 344–56
art as mode of inquiry, 5–6, 18, 258–79.
    See also painting
At the Will of the Body, 4
audience: engagement, 19, 22, 29–31, 53,
    68–69; implied, 218; participation,
    29–31, 51–52, 68–69, 83–84, 166;
    targeting, 168
authentic selves, 81, 119
authenticity, 16, 53, 170
author's voice, 173
authorship and authority, 172–73
autoethnography, 14, 283, 390; costs of,
    167–68; credibility and, 170–85,
    182–84; dialogical process, 115;
    myth and, 122–48; as performance,
35–43; therapy and, 88–94, 106–7,
    120; torch songs and, 44, 51–54.
    See also vulnerability
autoethnography vs. life stories, 121

being in the world, 77
binaries/dualities, 19, 239, 259
blurring of boundaries, 115, 118, 389
boundary confusion, 235

call to action, 76
cancer research, 57–75, 80; *Handle with
    Care?,* 58–61, 63–65, 67–68,
    70–71, 79, 83; *No Big Deal?,* 58–66,
    71–72
catharsis, 43, 52, 79, 332
child abuse, 15–16, 97–100, 105–6, 109,
    113n1,153
Christian ideology, 240
coconstructed narrative, 5, 308–26
coding, 118, 120
coding vs. construction, 121
cognitive filtering mechanisms, 57
coherency, 125, 321
collaboration, 53, 60–62
collective understanding, 67, 77
collective voices, 80
commodified culture, 367, 372
communal sharing, 3, 386
communicative interaction, 170
community activists, 61
community involvement, 60, 69

compassion and empathy, 81, 210. *See also* emotion(s)/emotional sociology
Composing Ethnography, 1–3, 76, 88
composite characters, 156, 161
confessionalism, 215
conflicting points of view, 150
constructing/deconstructing, 19, 239, 259, 317, 374
constructive dialogue, 246
contextualizing lived experience, 107, 331
contradictions in experience, 183
creating space, 93–94
critiquing. *See* research process
cultural/cultural studies, 19, 77–79, 153, 328, 338; collision of cultures, 79; culture and being, 77–78; culture of silence, 84; differences, 308–12, 322; displacement, 276; domination, 19; identity, 263, 265–67, 275; pressures, 138; representations, 19, 173

deconstruction/reconstruction, 24, 77, 259
demoralized medicine, 358
demystifying, 150
destructive behavior, 99, 111
dialectics, 235, 255
dialogic relationships, 29, 345, 366
dialogue, 27, 115, 119, 210–11, 300, 321; constructive, 246–48; ethics in, 340; reconstructed, 339
dialogue vs. monologue, 27, 321
diaspora experience, 259. *See also* gender dysphoria; hybridity
disenchantment, 357–61, 373. *See also* academia
displacement of self, 360–67
disrupted self/disrupted lives, 366–68, 372
dissemination of research, 69–71, 211
duality(ies). *See* binary(ies)/duality(ies)

eating disorders, 89–90, 113n1
embodied research, 65, 318
embodiment, 5, 52, 65
embodying correction, 249–52
embracing differences, 353–54

emotion(s)/emotional sociology: caring, 197, 199, 242, 372; distancing, 68, 332; engagement, 64; evasion, 332; experience, 319, 329; exposure, 214–15; expressiveness, 14; recall, 210; truth, 248, 318; voice, 5
emotionality, 14, 53, 76, 201, 318–19, 323, 353
empathy, 278. *See also* emotion(s)/emotional sociology
empowerment, 95, 107, 340
erotic engagement, 134
erotic mentoring, 130. *See also* patriarchy
ethical concerns/moral choices, 156, 161, 210, 340; engagement, 341; imperative, 223; relationships, 84
ethnodrama, 35–43, 58
ethnography/ethnographic alternatives, 2, 6, 77, 305, 339; empowerment and, 95; freedoms, limitations, and constraints, 90, 167, 300; narrative, 339; representation as relationship, 12–33; traditional, 3, 17–18, 118–19, 327–31
evocative form, 51, 60, 184, 210, 392
explanatory principles, 248
externalization, 108

fallacy of dichotomies, 217
fallibility of language, 350
family: abuse patterns, 109; dynamics, 112; myths, 104; relationships, 35–43, 95–114, 194, 206, 227, 234–57, 319; as systems, 110–11; therapy, 88–89, 166
The Fatal Flaw, 212, 217, 221
feminine issues, 46, 146, 273n1
feminine vs. femininity, 244
femininity, 202–3, 240
feminist bias, 250–51
feminist critique, 123, 250
The Feminine Mystique, 122
fiction: as convention, 332; truth in, 300, *305, 326, 328, 334. See also* art and science

field notes, 171–79
Fields of Play, 188
focus groups, 58
forbidden narratives, 214
forms of action, 13
fragmentation, 15–16, 52
framing, 15, 108, 156, 161–62, 168, 235,
    384. *See also* reframing life stories
freedom vs. constraint, 90

gender dysphoria, 204
gender issues, 20–22, 153, 272, 341; gay
    and lesbian identity, 206, 336–31;
    gendered responses, 59, 66, 345. *See
    also* patriarchy; sexuality
grounded theory, 6

habits and roles, 78
habitual space, 78–79
Handbook of Qualitative Research, 183
healing, 103–4, 117, 188–90, 319
hermeneutics, 258
hierarchical relationships, 13
historically positioned, 339
history, 240, 299
hope, 94
hybridity, 258–59
hyperbole, 320–21

identification vs. separation, 235, 255
identity issues, 276; hybrid identity, 259;
    identity transformation, 191–200,
    239. *See also* self
illness narratives, 59, 64, 370n5
illumination, 305
imagination, 46, 69, 124
Immortality, 49
inner vs. outer events, 53, 274
insider vs. outsider, 245, 259
Institute for Interpretive Human Studies, 7
institutional depression, 128, 160, 162, 351
institutionalized conversation, 362–63
interaction: interactive interviewing, *156*;
    interactive process, 64; of reader,
    220; stories, 374–75

interdisciplinary collaboration, 3, 9
interpretation of experience, 53, 281
interpretive: communities, 211;
    differences, 225, 353; ethnogra-
    phy, 172
interviewing, 58, 155–56, 170
invention and intervention, 90
"isness" in stories, 90–91, 190

Jewish experience, 313, 318

knowledge claims, 320

layered voices, 83
legitimation, 150, 255
liminal spaces, 258–59
literature. *See* fiction
lived experience, 26, 57, 240
logocentrism, 18–19, 349

macro vs. micro, 321–22
media coverage, 70
medicine as commodity. *See* commodified
    culture
memoir, 78, 115
memory, 46–50, 176, 280
messy research, 85
messy texts, 57, 59, 219
metaconversation, 322–26
metaphor. *See* tropes
methodological issues. *See* research
    process
moral: description, 154; dilemmas,
    125; responsibility, 221–22;
    sensibilities, 76, 81, 210. *See
    also* ethical concerns/moral
    choices
multiculturalism, 263, 265–67, 273n1
multi-layered texts, 221
multiple interweaving, 79, 157
multiple perspectives, 94, 220, 325, 389.
    See also perspective(s)
multiple voices, 19, 258, 325
mundane charisma, 358, 368–69
music and literature, 49

myth: Brainchild, 130, 142–45, 163; cultural history and, 155, 376; gender
issues and, 122–49; life story and,
125; Maiden Lover, 130–35;
Mistress, 130, 139–42; Muse, 130,
135–39; reality and, 124; Virgin,
130, 145–47

narrative, 339; coherence, 125; reframing,
95–113; self and, 212; therapeutic
value and, 107; truth, 256, 340. See
also personal narrative
natural script dialogue, 58
norm of anonymous reviewing, 158
norms of behavior, 153
novelization, 83–84

objectifying vs. personifying, 108
objective vs. subjective, 274. See also
subjectivity
ocular presence, 239
openness in research, 224, 340
open texts, 190, 220
oral culture, 277, 298

painting, 282–83; relationship between
artist and audience, 286; relationship between artist and work, 283
participant-observation, 170, 327
participatory research, 64, 170
patriarchy, 356; Guinevere, 154; patriarchal
culture, 240; patriarchal mentorship, 128–48
paying the price, 200, 202, 204–5, 367
performance: as autoethnography,
44, 76, 278–79; performing
theory, 5, 23–31; and politics,
19–22, 54; as relationship,
18–22
personal narrative, 15; cultural, 177; personal vs. public, 216, 238; and politics, 322; and professionalism, 382
perspectivalism, 258
perspective(s), 18, 59, 65, 91–92, 346, 352
poetic representation, 14, 201

politics: political activism, 82, 340; political
consequences, 210, 321; of privi-
lege, 84, 163;
representation, 13, 54, 256, 258, 321
polyphonic, 235–57; definition, 256
polyvocality, 14, 82–84
postmodern, 25–26, 67, 119, 345, 372
poststructuralist theory, 319
private vs. public, 239, 247, 254, 265, 324.
See also personal narrative
privileging voice, 60, 84, 163
process of performance, 77
projection, 163

qualitative inquiry, 14, 93, 344. See also
research process
quest, 256

rational ideology, 5
rationalization of experience, 281
reader response/reader engagement, 221
realist ethnography, 6
realist mentality, 356
reductive process, 347
reflexivity, 13, 19, 76, 102–3, 156, 160,
184, 201, 275; reflexive voice,
155, 339
reframing life stories, 95, 107, 115,
220–21, 161
reinterpretation, 15, 152
relational alternative, 28–31, 323; in performance, 381; relationship forms,
12–18
relational space, 241
relational systems, 110
relationship building, 80–81, 207
relationship to data, 179
remoralization, 358, 367–68, 374
representational fidelity, 300
representation vs. interrogation, 73
research-based drama/performance texts,
57–75
research process: evaluation, 210–12,
223–26, 340; as experience, 223;
funding, 71–72; participants, 61,

136, 289–92; recursive process, 79; reductive process, 397
restitution narrative, 255
Rewriting the Soul: Multiple Personality and the Sciences of Memory, 151
rhetoric, 155, 157, 173
risk taking, 112, 167, 169, 214
role(s): conflict, 179–82, 285–88, 293; distancing, 68–69; expectations, 79, 170, 251–52, 254; role taking and authenticity, 170; of silence, 65, 249, 263, 265, 278, 299; women's, 235–40, 252, 254, 285

scholarly attitude, 158
scientific paradigm, 210, 345–50
script development, 57–66, 72
self: loss of, 130, 141, 146; and other, 53, 159, 173–74, 217, 339, 366; as relational, 216; sense of, 87, 239, 365–66, 372; and society, 216; as subject, 156
self-discovery, 300
self-indulgence, 209–28. *See also* solipsism
semantic analysis, 13
semantic contagion, 151–52
separation and identification, 235
sex reassignment, 204
sexual harassment, 131, 136, 139, 152–53
sexual identity vs. gender identity, 204
sexuality: autonomy, 244; orientation, 203, 206, 336–43; sexual transformation, 192–200, 204, 208
social change, 340
social construction, 27, 216, 254; of meaning, 69, 81, 107; of reality, 353
social expectations, 80
socialization, 150, 223
social knowledge, 299
social positioning, 51, 218, 240
Society for the Study of Symbolic Interaction, 7
sociological introspection, 176, 202, 210. *See also*, reflexivity
solipsism, 259. *See also* self-indulgence

somatic understanding, 85
speech impediment, 92–94
standpoint. *See* perspective(s)
stigma, 92–94, 165, 239
stigma by association, 239
story(ies): cancer, 57–75, 79, 358–67; collective, 375–76; corrective, 187–88, 249–53; as form of interaction, 367; healing, 187; identity and, 91–93; intersecting (tales), 239; reconstruction, 91; theory, 118, 125; as therapy, 91–94; transformation, 90, 104
story and ride, 360–68
storytelling, 51–52, 64, 79, 88; art of, 277–78; collective, 220–21
subjectivity, 15, 44, 52, 328

taping field notes, 174–75
terministic screen, 153
thematic analysis, 58, 88
thematic order, 333
theoretical concerns, 172, 346
theoretical rapprochement, 352
theorizing, 238–40, 346–47
theory by implication, 27, 397
therapy, 88, 93, 116–17. *See also* autoethnography; family; healing; narrative; story(ies); writing
thick description, 172–73, 333–34
time and space, 83
traditional academic writing, 13, 17–18, 23–24, 27, 147, 213–17
traditional research categories, 219
transformation of self, 146, 183
transforming understanding, 90
tropes: narrative as, 374; ride as, 360–65, 373–75; story as, 360, 367, 373–75

universality, 27, 218–19, 272

validity, 153, 423
value-centered, 5
value free/value neutral, 59, 327
verisimilitude, 60
visual representation, 276–77

voice, 16, 18, 158; censorship and, 367; of
  the Center, 84
vulnerability, 68, 167–69, 210

The Way We Were, 45–46, 50–51
Western thought, 132
witnessing, 221–22
worldview, 275
The Wounded Storyteller, 4, 183
writing: alternative writing, 14–15, 26; as
  inquiry, 6, 168, 319; as process, 168,

392; process of writing, 91, 317; as
  relationship, 12–18; rewriting, 66,
  157, 320, 392; as therapy, 190,
  318–19, 325
*Writing Culture: The Poetics and Politics of
  Ethnography*, 172–73
*Writing Performance: Poeticizing the
  Researcher's Body*, 81
Writing the New Ethnography, 379

"yes and" vs. "yes but," 345

About the Contributors

MICHAEL V. ANGROSINO is professor of anthropology at the University of South Florida. He has published extensively on ethnographic methods, particularly in regard to his anthropological fieldwork in the Caribbean and in the United States. He is the author of *Opportunity House: Ethnographic Stories of Mental Retardation* and the editor of the forthcoming *Ethnography: Data Collection Techniques*. His prose fiction and poetry have appeared in the *Green Mountains Review* and *Anthropological and Humanism Quarterly*.

ARTHUR P. BOCHNER has been a student of close relationships for more than thirty years. As chair of the Department of Communication at the University of South Florida, he was instrumental in developing the school's graduate program in interpretive social science and its Institute for Interpretive Human Studies, which he codirects with Carolyn Ellis, his partner in love and work. Author of many publications, Art is currently working on a book on narrative inquiry in the social sciences, *Storytelling As Research: The Narrative Turn in Social Science*. Art's four dogs play a huge role in his life, constantly reminding him of the necessity of balancing work and play, the simpler pleasures of life, and the meaning of unconditional positive regard. Participating in competitive sports was a major form of escape during his childhood and Art still enjoys games of risk, hiking in the mountains, and white-water rafting.

MEL BOCHNER is an artist who lives and works in New York.

KATHRYN CHURCH is an independent scholar and the author of *Forbidden Narratives: Critical Autobiography As Social Science*. A sociologist by training, she has extensive experience in the mental health field through clinical work, community organizing, and policy development, as well as community-based research, education, and advocacy. Kathryn is a long-standing ally of the psychiatric survivor movement in Canada. She has written a dozen plain-language documents that have circulated internationally for use by survivor groups in education and advocacy. Her current research focuses on ways in which trade unions and community organizations use informal learning to cope with economic restructuring. She is active in the use of mixed-media materials, and most recently participated in the creation of a broadcast-quality film called *Working Like Crazy*, and curating an award-winning exhibit. Kathryn lives south of the Danforth in Toronto with her partner, Ross Gray. They have no dogs.

BEVERLEY DENT is a doctoral student in interdisciplinary studies at the University of Saskatchewan. She has bachelor and master's degrees in education, both from the University of Saskatchewan, and both earned while she was still Tom Dent. Beverley has taught courses at the high school and university levels. Since transitioning from male to female she has returned to the university and now studies primarily in the area of women's and gender studies. Her doctoral dissertation will be an autoethnographical study of gendered identity formation. Theresa Beverley's passion is for high heels, swirling ball gowns, and flirting with partners of any sex.

CAROLYN ELLIS loves to write stories, experiment with form, think about methods, and feel and consider emotional experience. She generally enjoys teaching and writing as a professor of communication and sociology at the University of South Florida, though she could do with fewer meetings. When she is not working, she can be found lifting weights, traveling or making plans to travel, engaging in and observing herself in intense relational conversations, or playing unselfconsciously with her partner Art Bochner and their four dogs. Especially happy to have written *Final Negotiations* and edited *Composing Ethnography* (with Art Bochner), she will be happier still when she finally completes *Doing Autoethnography: A Methodological Novel* and can go to the beach with a "real" novel.

DOUGLAS FLEMONS teaches at Nova Southeastern University in Fort Lauderdale, Florida. When he's not running with his wife, Shelley Green—

accompanied by Eric, their son, on his scooter and Jenna, their daughter, in a jog-ging stroller—or coaching Eric's in-line hockey team, Douglas can be found teaching, making dinner, reading, seeing clients, practicing tai chi, or, occasion-ally, sleeping. An avid, if rather slow, writer, he's the author of books on therapy, *Of One Mind* and *Completing Distinctions,* and writing, *Writing Between the Lines.* He's presently working on three or four children's books derived from the stories that he and the kids improvise at bedtime and that he and Eric tell in Eric's class-room, and is coediting with Shelley a book on sex therapy.

ARTHUR W. FRANK is professor of sociology at the University of Calgary. He is the author of *At the Will of the Body: Reflections on Illness* and *The Wounded Storyteller: Body, Illness, and Ethics.* His current research focuses on illness sur-vivorship as craft and as moral awareness.

KENNETH J. GERGEN is the Mustin Professor of Psychology at Swarthmore College. He is the author of various works on social knowledge, cultural theory, and historical change, including *The Saturated Self, Realities and Relationships,* and *An Invitation to Social Construction.* At Swarthmore Gergen helped to create the pro-gram in interpretation theory; he is also a cofounder of the Taos Institute, dedicated to creating generative dialogue between social constructionist theory and societal practice. Among his many quirks, his dog Mephisto accompanies him to the office and he suffers radical age regression when playing with his grandchildren.

MARY M. GERGEN is professor of psychology and women's studies at Penn State University, Delaware County, where she teaches a potpourri of courses to undergraduate students. Her special research interest, which is represented in her most recent books, *Feminist Reconstructions in Psychology: Narrative, Gender, and Performance* and *Toward A New Psychology of Women,* joins feminist and social constructionist theory. She is also a cofounder of the Taos Institute, a nonprofit organization dedicated to promoting social constructionist ideas within profes-sional practice circles and personal life. Her favorite intellectual pursuit is having dinner with Ken Gergen, who equals "Andre" as a conversational partner. In addition, she enjoys playing tennis, making Sunday dinner for kids and grand-kids, and going to Paris.

H. L. GOODALL JR. is professor and chair of the Department of Communication at the University of North Carolina, Greensboro. His use of the detective, rock 'n' roll, and spiritual metaphors ground his ethnographic work, which includes the trilogy *Casing a Promised Land: The Autobiography of an Organizational Detective As Cultural Ethnographer; Living in the Rock n Roll Mystery: Reading Context, Self, and Others as Clues*; and *Divine Signs: Connecting Spirit to Community*. His newest book is *Writing the New Ethnography*. At the time of the Couch-Stone Symposium, Greensboro was experiencing a rare cold spell and very deep snows, a fact that should help readers understand some of the heat-related physics of his piece.

ROSS E. GRAY has worked in the Canadian cancer care system since 1987, doing psychotherapy with people with cancer and conducting social science research. He is codirector of the Psychosocial and Behavioural Research Unit at the Toronto-Sunnybrook Regional Cancer Centre and assistant professor in the Department of Public Health Sciences at the University of Toronto. In addition to his experiments with acting and scriptwriting, Ross has recently published an autoethnographic book, *Legacy: A Conversation with Dad*, and is working on a mystery novel set in a Buddhist Temple. He is also coauthor of a forthcoming book in AltaMira's Ethnographic Alternatives series on performance ethnography, *Standing Ovation*.

SHELLEY GREEN teaches at Nova Southeastern University in Fort Lauderdale, Florida. She tries rather desperately to find time to be a professional in the midst of raising (with her husband and coconspirator, Douglas Flemons) Eric, seven years old, Jenna, three years old, and their lovely dog, Jessie. To retain her sanity and amuse Douglas, she delivers devastating impersonations; she also runs, reads incessantly, and takes her kids to the beach. To retain her job and entertain herself, she teaches and writes about qualitative research, sex, brief therapy, and supervision. She is currently coediting a book with Douglas on brief approaches to sex therapy, titled, of course, *Quickies*.

VRENIA IVONOFFSKI has directed more than twenty full-length plays and has been artistic director for Act II Studio, a theater program for older adults, at Ryerson Polytechnic University in Toronto since 1988. Vrenia emphasizes the group creation process and social action in her theater work. She is an anarchist, a feminist, a woman who loves her work. Vrenia gathers broken glass from the streets and fashions sculptures that she gives to friends and neighbors. She makes a mean chocolate soufflé.

ELAINE BASS JENKS is associate professor of communication studies at West Chester University. Her current research interests focus on interpersonal communication between and among the blind, the sighted, and the visually impaired.

STACY HOLMAN JONES is an assistant professor at the University of South Florida. She is the author of *Kaleidoscope Notes: Writing Women's Music and Organizational Culture*, published as part of AltaMira's Ethnographic Alternatives Series. She has recently completed her dissertation, "Torch Singing As Political Performance Practice," during which she listened, over and over, to Nina Simone's "Since I Fell for You" and Joni Mitchell's "Both Sides Now."

CHRISTINE E. KIESINGER is assistant professor and chair of the Department of Communication at Southwestern University, where she teaches courses in communication and close relationships. Deeply committed to narrative as a therapeutic tool and as an important form of inquiry and expression, Christine's writing aims to capture the texture of emotional experience in descriptive ways. In addition to her work at the university, Christine practices and teaches hatha yoga in her community.

LESA LOCKFORD is an assistant professor teaching courses in acting, voice, and performance studies in the Theater Department at Bowling Green State University. She is particularly interested in exploring how experience informs meaning making, understanding, and the politics of knowledge creation; consequently areas of professional interest include performance as a way of knowing, gender and sexuality, ethnography, autoethnography, and phenomenology. She is grateful to the editors for opportunity to add her voice to those contained within this volume.

ERNEST LOCKRIDGE is professor emeritus of English at Ohio State University. He is the author of scholarly articles, and three published novels. His second novel was a Book of the Month Club selection.

RONALD J. PELIAS teaches performance studies at Southern Illinois University. His latest book, *Writing Performance: Poeticizing the Researcher's Body*, is available from Southern Illinois University Press. He is currently working on a manuscript entitled *The Critic's Performance: Toward a Poetics of Response*.

CAROLINE JOAN ("KAY") S. PICART is assistant professor of English and humanities at Florida State University and of philosophy at St. Lawrence University (on leave of absence from 2000 to 2001). Among her books are: *Resentment and "the Feminine" in Nietzsche's Politico-Aesthetics*; *Thomas Mann and Friedrich Nietzsche: Eroticism, Death, Music and Laughter*; *The Rebirths of Frankenstein*; and *The Frankenstein Film Sourcebook* (coedited with Frank Smoot and Jayne Blodgett). She also has published scholarly articles on social and political philosophy, philosophy and sociology of science, aesthetics, and feminism and philosophy; and popular articles on Philippine art and issues of multiculturalism in the United States, the Philippines, and South Korea. Kay studied medicine and molecular embryology and graduated as the Wolfson Prize Winner in History and Philosophy of Science in 1991. She has had solo exhibitions as an artist in South Korea and various parts of the United States and has been doing ballroom competitions since 1998.

LAUREL RICHARDSON is professor emerita of sociology and visiting professor of cultural studies at Ohio State University. She writes about qualitative research, theory, language, and gender. Her book *Fields of Play: Constructing An Academic Life* was honored with the C. H. Cooley Award from the Society for the Study of Symbolic Interaction. Her current project considers how the process of naming and categorizing of nonverbal experiences relates to the construction of the self.

JANICE HOCKER RUSHING is professor of communication at the University of Arkansas, where she teaches courses in rhetorical criticism, popular culture, gender, and conflict management. She has published essays on film, mythology, and American values, and coauthored a book, *Projecting the Shadow: The Cyborg Hero in American Film*. She is working on a book on women and myth in academia. She is from Texas and Colorado, but she now lives in Fayetteville with her husband, frequent coauthor, and partner-in-everything, Tom Frentz, and Mollie, who insisted that she live with them and always sits on the manuscripts she is trying to revise.

CHRISTINA SINDING is a doctoral candidate in the Department of Public Health Sciences at the University of Toronto and she has also recently joined the Psychosocial and Behavioural Research Unit, Toronto-Sunnybrook Regional Cancer Center. She has worked in women's health for the past ten years in both institutional and community contexts, focusing on breast cancer support and advocacy. Initially horrified about the idea of acting in *Handle with Care?*, Christina has (mostly) delighted in the process. She and her partner live in idyllic Dundas (Ontario), roasting marshmallows every Saturday night in their backyard at the base of the Niagara escarpment.

KAREN SCOTT-HOY is currently based at The Centre for Research in Education, Equity, and Work at the University of South Australia. For more than two decades she has been involved with community development projects and education and training of adults. Combining her love of visual arts, performance, and writing, her research focuses on interpretive ethnography as an attempt to understand and portray her experience as a cross-cultural health worker and everyday life, in an accessible and inviting form, so as to inform, encourage and challenge others. Artist/author of several artistic/autoethnographic works, she lives in the beautiful wine region of the Barossa Valley with her optometrist husband, their four sons, a cantankerous cockatoo, two dogs, and a spoiled cat.

ANDREW C. SPARKES is professor of social theory and director of the qualitative research unit in the Department of Exercise and Sport Sciences, School of Sport and Health Sciences, University of Exeter, St Luke's Campus, United Kingdom. His research interests are eclectic and include: interrupted body projects, identity dilemmas, and the narrative reconstruction of self; organizational innovation and change; and the lives and careers of marginalized individuals and groups. These interests are framed by a desire to seek interpretive forms of understanding and an aspiration to represent lived experience using a variety of genres.

PAUL STOLLER teaches anthropology at West Chester University of Pennsylvania. He has also been a visiting professor at L'Ecole des Hautes Etudes en Sciences Sociales in Paris. The author of many publications, his latest books include *Sensuous Scholarship,* a collection of essays, and *Jaguar: A Story of Africans in America,* a novel. He has conducted ethnographic fieldwork among the Songhay people in West Africa and more recently among West African immigrants in New York City. He is currently doing field research on the sociocultural aspects of the African art trading in North America and is at work on a second novel.

LISA M. TILLMANN-HEALY is a graduate of Marquette University and the University of South Florida. She has authored and contributed to articles and book chapters on relationship narratives and dialectics, interactive interviewing, and the lived, emotional experiences of family dissolution and eating disorders. Her most recent project is a narrative ethnography called *Between Gay and Straight: Understanding Friendship across Sexual Orientation*. An assistant professor of communication at Rollins College, she lives in Orlando with her husband and best friend, Doug Healy.